Business Finance for Decision Makers

Business Finance for Decision Makers

SECOND EDITION

E J McLaney

Plymouth Business School
University of Plymouth

PITMAN
PUBLISHING

PITMAN PUBLISHING
128 Long Acre, London WC2E 9AN

A Division of Pearson Professional Limited

First published as *Business Finance: Theory and Practice* in 1986
Published as *Business Finance for Decision Makers* in 1991
Second edition 1994

© E J McLaney 1986, 1991, 1994

A CIP catalogue record for this book can be obtained from the British Library.

ISBN 0 273 60421 X

10 9 8 7 6 5 4 3

Typeset by Create Publishing Services Ltd, Bath
Printed and bound in Singapore

The Publishers' policy is to use paper manufactured from sustainable forests.

CONTENTS

and the cost of capital – conclusion • MM, MPT and CAPM • Summary • Further reading • Work-based assignment • Questions with answers • Questions for class use • Appendix I – proof of the MM cost of capital proposition (pre-tax) • Appendix II – proof of the MM cost of capital proposition (post-tax)

PREFACE

This book attempts to deal with financing and investment decision making with particular focus on the private sector of the UK economy. In it an attempt has been made to set out the theories which surround each area of financial decision making and to relate these to what appears to happen in practice. Where theory and practice diverge, the book tries to reconcile and explain the differences. It also attempts to assess the practical usefulness of some of the theories which do not seem widely to be applied in practice.

Though the focus of the book is on the UK private sector, the theories and practices examined are, for the main part, equally valid in the context of the private sector of all the world's countries which have private sectors. It is also the case that much of the content of the book is relevant to many parts of the public sector, both in the UK and overseas.

Most of the organisations to which the subject matter of this book relates will be limited companies or groups of companies, though some may be partnerships, cooperatives or other forms. For simplicity the word *firm* has been used as a general term for a business entity, referring to specific legal forms only where the issue under discussion relates specifically to a particular form.

Though the topics in the book are interrelated, the book has been divided into sections. Chapters 1 to 3 are concerned with setting the scene, Chapters 4 to 7 with investment decisions, Chapters 8 to 12 with financing decision areas, leaving Chapters 13 to 15 with hybrid matters.

The book attempts to make the subject as accessible as possible to readers coming to business finance for the first time. In doing this, unnecessarily technical language has been avoided as much as possible and the issues are described in a narrative form as well as in more formal statements. Detailed proofs of theoretical propositions have generally been placed in appendices to the relevant chapters. Readers should not take this to mean that these proofs are particularly difficult to follow. The objective was to make the book as readable as possible and it was felt that sometimes formal proofs can disturb the flow if they are put in the main body of the text.

Nothing in this book requires any great mathematical ability on the part of the reader. However, some basic understanding of correlation, statistical probabilities and of basic differential calculus would be helpful. Any reader who feels that it might be necessary to brush up these topics could refer to Harper (1982 and 1991). These references and each of the others given in the chapters are listed alphabetically at the end of the book.

The book contains three types of end-of-chapter questions/tasks. Firstly, there are work-based assignments. These are intended to help the reader to see the practical aspects of the material covered in the chapter and to make the subject more relevant. There are questions which test the reader's understanding of the contents of each chapter, to which answers are provided in Appendix 3. Lastly, there are further questions which also test the reader's understanding, but here the answers are provided in a separate *Lecturer's Guide*. Questions marked * are more complex than the others.

The book is mainly directed at post-graduate, post-experience students who are either following a university course, or who are seeking a qualification like the Certified Diploma in Accounting and Finance. It is also directed at those who are studying business finance as part of an undergraduate course, for example a degree or Higher National Diploma in business studies. It should also prove useful to those studying for the professional examinations of the accounting bodies.

I should like to thank the Chartered Association of Certified Accountants for their permission to use questions from past papers of the Certified Diploma in Accounting and Finance and professional examinations as end-of-chapter questions.

Edward J. McLaney
February 1994

PLAN OF THE BOOK

PART ONE – THE BUSINESS FINANCE ENVIRONMENT

Chapter 1 Introduction	Chapter 2 A framework for financial decision making	Chapter 3 Financial accounting statements and their interpretation

PART TWO – INVESTMENT DECISIONS

Chapter 4 Investment appraisal method	Chapter 5 Practical aspects of investment appraisal	Chapter 6 Risk in investment appraisal	Chapter 7 The pricing of securities and its relevance to real investment decisions

PART THREE – FINANCING DECISIONS

Chapter 8 Sources of long-term finance	Chapter 9 The secondary capital market (the Stock Exchange) and its efficiency	Chapter 10 Cost of capital estimations and the discount rate	Chapter 11 Gearing, the cost of capital and shareholders' wealth	Chapter 12 The dividend decision

PART FOUR – MIXED DECISIONS

Chapter 13 Management of working capital	Chapter 14 Corporate restructuring (including takeovers and divestments)	Chapter 15 Small firms

REFERENCES	APPENDICES	INDEX

PART 1

The business finance environment

Business finance is concerned with making decisions about which investments the firm should make and how best to finance those investments. This part of the book attempts to explain the context in which those decisions are made. This is important in its own right, not just as an introduction to later parts of the book. Chapter 1 explains the nature of business finance. It continues with some discussion of the legal framework in which most private sector firms operate. Chapter 2 considers the decision making process, with particular emphasis on the objectives, in the pursuit of which, firms invest. It also considers the problem faced by managers where people, affected by a decision, have conflicting objectives. Chapter 3 provides an overview of the source and nature of the information provided to financial decision makers by accounting reports. As is explained in Chapter 1, business finance and accounting are distinctly different areas. Accounting statements are, however, a very important source of information for financial decisions.

CHAPTER 1

Introduction

OBJECTIVES

In this chapter we shall deal with the following:
- the role of business finance
- its relationship with other disciplines, particularly with accounting
- the importance of the consideration of risk in financial decision making
- the importance of the limited company as the legal form in which most UK businesses exist
- the nature of the limited company
- what is meant by limited liability
- the formation of limited companies
- directors and their relationships with shareholders
- the duty of directors to account for their actions
- typical means of financing companies and the rights of suppliers of corporate finance
- the requirement for firms trading as limited companies to signal the fact to the world through the company name
- liquidation of companies

THE ROLE OF BUSINESS FINANCE

Business firms may fairly be regarded as investment agencies or intermediaries. That is to say that their role is to raise funds from members of the public and from other investors and to invest those funds. Usually funds will be obtained from the legal owners of the firm (the shareholders) and from long-term lenders, with some short-term finance being provided by banks (perhaps in the form of overdrafts), other financial institutions, and trade creditors. Firms typically invest in 'real' assets such as land, buildings, plant and trading stocks, though they may also invest in 'financial' assets including making loans to and buying shares in other firms. People are employed to manage the investments, i.e. to do all those things necessary to create and sell the goods and services in the provision of which the firm is engaged. Surpluses remaining after meeting the costs of operating the business – wages, raw material costs, etc. – accrue to the investors.

Central to the firm will be decisions involved with questions of the types and quantity of finance to raise and with the choice of investments to be made. Business finance is the study of how these financing and investment decisions should be made in theory and how they are made in practice.

A practical subject

Business finance is a relatively new subject. Until the 1950s it mostly consisted of narrative accounts of decisions that had been made and how, if identifiable, the decisions had been reached. More recently theories of business finance have emerged and been tested so that the subject now has a firmly based theoretical framework – a framework which stands up pretty well to testing with real life events. In other words, the accepted theories which attempt to explain and predict actual outcomes in business finance broadly succeed in their aim.

Business finance draws from many disciplines. Financing and investment decision making relates closely to certain aspects of economics, accounting, law, quantitative methods and the behavioural sciences. Despite the eclecticism of business finance in drawing what it finds most useful from other disciplines, it is nonetheless a subject in its own right, vital to the business firm.

Decisions on financing and investment go right to the heart of the business firm and its success or failure. This is because:

- Such decisions often involve financial amounts which are very significant to the firm concerned.
- Once made, such decisions are not easy to reverse, so the firm is typically committed in the long term to a particular type of finance or to a particular investment.

Though modern business finance practice relies heavily on sound theory, we must be very clear that business finance is an intensely practical subject which is concerned with real-world, practical, decision making.

RISK AND BUSINESS FINANCE

All decision making involves the future. We can only make decisions about the future; no matter how much we may regret it, we cannot alter the past. Financial decision making is no exception to this.

There is only one thing certain about the future, which is that we cannot be sure what is going to happen. Sometimes we may be able to predict with confidence that what actually occurs will be one of a limited range of possibilities. We may even feel able to ascribe statistical probabilities to the likelihood of occurrence of each possible outcome, but we can never be completely certain of the future. Risk is therefore an important factor in all financial decision making and one which must be considered explicitly in all cases.

In business finance, as in other aspects of life, risk and return tend to be related. Intuitively we expect returns to relate to risk in something like the way shown in Fig. 1.1. In investment, for example, investors require a minimum rate to induce them to invest at all but they require an increased rate of return, the addition of a risk premium, to compensate them for taking risk. We shall see in Chapter 7 that, when considering marketable stocks and shares, there does actually appear to be the linear relationship, which Fig. 1.1 suggests, between levels of risk perceived and the returns which investors expect to receive. Much of business finance is concerned with striking the appropriate balance between risk and return.

**Figure 1.1
Relationship
between
return and risk**

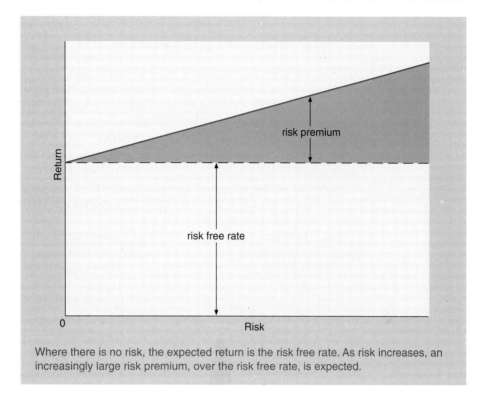

Where there is no risk, the expected return is the risk free rate. As risk increases, an increasingly large risk premium, over the risk free rate, is expected.

THE RELATIONSHIP BETWEEN BUSINESS FINANCE AND ACCOUNTING

Business finance and accounting are not the same thing. Accounting is concerned with financial record keeping, the production of periodic reports, statements and analyses, the dissemination of information to managers and to some extent to investors and the world outside the firm. It is also much involved with the quality, relevance and timeliness of its information output. Obviously financial decision makers will rely heavily on accounting reports and the accounting database generally. Knowledge of past events may well be a good pointer to the future so reliable information on the past is invaluable. However, the role of the financial manager is not to provide financial information but to make decisions involving finance.

In smaller firms, with narrow portfolios of management skills, the accountant and the financial manager may well be the same person. In the large firm the roles are most likely to be discharged by different people or groups of people. Not surprisingly many financial managers are accountants by training and background but some are not. With the increasing importance of business finance on the curricula of business schools and in higher education generally, the tendency is probably towards more specialist financial managers, with their own career structure.

THE ORGANISATION OF FIRMS

This book is primarily concerned with business finance as it affects firms in the private sector of the UK economy. Most of our discussion will centre on larger firms, i.e. firms which are quoted in the secondary capital market (e.g. the International Stock Exchange of the United Kingdom and the Republic of Ireland) and where there is fairly widespread ownership of the firm amongst individual members of the public and the investing institutions (insurance companies, pension funds, unit trusts, etc.). Towards the end of the book we shall take a look at the smaller, owner-managed firms to see how the issues, discussed up to that point in the context of large firms, apply to this important sector of the economy.

Irrespective of whether we are considering large or small firms, virtually all of them will be limited companies. There are businesses in the UK, indeed many of them, which are not limited companies. Most of these, however, are very small (one or two-person enterprises) or they are highly specialised professional service firms such as solicitors and accountants.

Since the limited company predominates in the UK private sector, we shall in this book discuss business finance in this context. Many of the principles which will emerge apply equally, however, irrespective of the precise legal status of the firm concerned.

In this chapter we shall consider briefly the legal and administrative environment in which limited companies operate. The objective here is by no means to provide a detailed legal examination of the limited company, it is simply to outline its more significant features. More particularly the aim is to explain, in broad terms, those aspects which impinge on business finance. A lack of a broad understanding of these aspects may make life difficult for us in later chapters.

WHAT IS A LIMITED COMPANY?

A limited company is an artificially created legal person. It is an entity which is legally separate from all other persons including those who own and manage it. It is quite possible for a limited company to take legal action, say for breach of contract, against any other legal persons, including those who own and manage it. Actions between limited companies and their owners or managers do occur from time to time.

Obviously an artificial person can only function through the intervention of human beings. Those who ultimately control the company are the owners who each hold one or more shares in the ownership or equity of it.

Limited liability

One of the results of the peculiar position of the company having its own separate legal identity is that the financial liability of the owners (shareholders) is limited to the amount which they have paid (or have pledged to pay) for their shares. If the company becomes insolvent (financial obligations exceed value of assets) its liability is, like that of any human legal person, limited only by the amount of its assets. It can be forced to pay over all of its assets to try to meet its liabilities, but no more. Since the company and the owners are legally separate, owners cannot be compelled to introduce further finance. The position of a shareholder in this regard does not depend upon whether the shares were acquired by taking up an issue from the company or as a result of buying the shares from an existing shareholder.

Transferability

As a separate legal entity, the company does not depend on the identity of its shareholders for its existence. Transfer of shares by buying and selling or by gift is therefore possible. Thus a part, even all, of the company's ownership or equity can change hands without it necessarily having any effect on the business activity of the company.

Since the company can continue irrespective of precisely who the shareholders happen to be at any given moment, the company can theoretically have a perpetual lifespan, unlike its human counterparts.

FORMATION OF A LIMITED COMPANY

Creating a new company is a very cheap and simple operation which can be carried out with little effort on the part of the promoters, for very little cost (from about £100).

Formation basically requires the promoters to make an application to the Registrar of Companies (Department of Trade and Industry). The application must be accompanied by several documents, the most important of which is a proposed set of rules or constitution for the company defining how it will be administered. These rules are contained in two documents known as the Memorandum of Association and Articles of Association.

All of the documentation becomes public once the company has been formally registered. A file is opened at Companies House in Cardiff on which are placed the various documents; the file is constantly available for examination by any member of the public who wishes to see it.

SHAREHOLDERS AND DIRECTORS

The shareholders (or members as they are sometimes known) are the owners of the company; profits and gains accrue to them, losses are borne by them up to a maximum of the amount of their investment in the company. The shareholders, at any particular time, may not be the original shareholders, i.e. those who first owned the shares. Transfers by sale or gift (including legacy on death) cause shares to change hands.

For a variety of sound practical reasons the day-to-day management of the company is delegated by the shareholders to directors, who may or may not themselves own some shares in the company. Shareholders elect directors in much the same way as citizens elect Members of Parliament in a parliamentary democracy. They also fail to re-elect them if the directors' performance is judged by shareholders to be unsatisfactory. Usually one-third of the directors retire from office each year, frequently offering themselves for re-election. Typically each shareholder has one vote for each share owned. Where a company has a large number of shareholders, a particular individual holding a large number of shares, even though not a majority of them, can wield tremendous power. The board of directors is the firm's top level of management, so to control its composition is substantially to control the company.

ACCOUNTABILITY OF DIRECTORS

The law imposes a duty on directors to account annually, both to the shareholders, and to some extent to the world at large, on the performance of the company's trading and on its financial position.

Each year directors are required to prepare (or to have prepared) a report for the shareholders. The minimum contents of the report are prescribed by law, though in practice this minimum is often exceeded. Principally the report consists of a profit and loss account, a balance sheet and a cash flow statement. These accounting statements are subject to audit by an independent firm of accountants whose role is to express an opinion on the truth and fairness of the view shown by them. The auditor's expression of opinion is attached to the annual report.

A copy of the report must be sent to each shareholder. A copy must also be sent to the Registrar of Companies for insertion on the company's file in Cardiff to be available for inspection by anyone wishing to do so. In practice large companies also send copies of the report to financial analysts and journalists. They will usually comply with a request from any private individual for a copy.

The annual report is a major, but not the only, source of information to interested parties, including existing and prospective shareholders, on the progress of the company. Companies whose shares are quoted on the Stock Exchange are required by its rules to publish summarised accounting statements for the half years. In practice most large companies, from time to time, issue information over and above that which is contained in the annual and half-yearly reports.

The nature of the accounting statements which appear in the annual report, and how those statements can be interpreted, are discussed in Chapter 3.

RECOGNITION OF COMPANIES

Limited companies are required to use the appellation *Limited (Ltd)* or *Public Limited Company (plc)* after their name in all formal documentation to warn those dealing with the company that its members' liability is limited.

Limited is used by private limited companies. These are basically the smaller, family-type companies which have certain rights on the restriction of transfer of their shares. Public companies are typically the larger companies with more widespread share ownership.

LONG-TERM FINANCING OF COMPANIES

Much of the semi-permanent finance of companies, in some cases all of it, is provided by shareholders. Many companies have different classes of shares. Most companies also borrow money on a long-term basis. (Many borrow finance on a short-term basis as well.) In later chapters we shall examine in some detail how and why companies issue more than one class of share and borrow money; here we shall confine ourselves to a brief overview of long-term corporate finance.

Ordinary shares

These are issued by the company to investors who are prepared to expose themselves to risk in order also to expose themselves to the expectation of high investment returns, which both intuition and the evidence, which we shall come across later in the book, tell us is associated with risk. Ordinary shareholders are usually rewarded by the company in the form of cash dividends. The fund available for payment of dividends is what remains after all expenses, including interest on long-term loans and preference dividends, have been met. Dividends may be further restricted at the discretion of the directors. Dividends are therefore uncertain; prior claims may exhaust the available funds or the directors may decide to plough back profits at the expense of ordinary share dividends.

In principle, where funds are retained rather than distributed they remain the property of the ordinary shareholders, who are the ultimate owners or equity holders. In that sense retained profits are as much part of the ordinary shareholder's return as are the dividends, since profits retained should have a direct effect on the value of the shares.

If the company were to be liquidated (wound up) each equity holder would receive an appropriate share of the funds left after all other legitimate claimants had been satisfied in full.

Where shares are traded between investors, there is no reason why shares should be priced according to their original issue price or according to their face value (nominal or par value). Perceptions of the value of a share in any particular company will change with varying economic circumstances, so that share prices will shift over time.

Historically, in the UK, increases in the market value of equities have tended to represent a larger element than have dividends in returns to shareholders, i.e. dividends have tended to be less important to shareholders than have capital gains.

It should be particularly noted that a shareholder selling shares in a particular company for some particular price has no direct effect on that company. The company will simply pay future dividends and give future voting rights to the new shareholder.

It is the ordinary shareholders who have the voting power within the company. Thus it is the equity holders who control the company.

Each ordinary share confers equal rights on its owner in terms of dividend entitlement, repayment on liquidation and voting power. Two shares carry exactly twice as much of these rights as does one share. The law forbids the directors from discriminating between the rights of different shareholders other than on the basis of the number of shares owned (assuming that the shares owned are of the same class). Miss X owning 100 shares in Z plc should have equal rights in respect of her shareholding to those of Mr Y who owns a similar number of shares in the same company. The Stock Exchange and other non-statutory agencies also seek to promote this equality.

Preference shares

These represent part of the risk-bearing ownership of the company though they usually confer on their holders a right to receive the first slice of any dividend which is paid. There is an upper limit on the preference share dividend per share, which is usually defined as a percentage of the nominal value of the share. Preference share dividends are usually paid in full, provided sufficient profit (and cash) exists. Preference shares give more sure returns than equities, though they by no means provide certain returns. Preference shares do not usually confer voting rights nor do they usually give the same preference in repayment in a liquidation as they do in payment of dividends, though in some companies they do.

Preference shares of many companies are traded in the capital market. As with equities, prices of preference shares will vary with investors' perceptions of future prospects. Generally preference share prices are less volatile than those of equities as dividends tend to be fairly stable and usually have an upper limit.

For most companies, preference shares do not represent a major source of finance.

Loan stocks

Most companies borrow funds on a long-term, occasionally on a perpetual, basis. Lenders enter into a contractual relationship with the company with the rate of interest, its date of payment, the redemption date and amount all being terms of the contract. Many long-term lenders require rather more by way of security for their loan than the rights conferred on any lender under the law of contract. Typically they insist that the principal and sometimes the interest are secured on some specific asset of the borrowing company, frequently land. Such security might confer on lenders a right to seize the asset and sell it to satisfy their claims where repayment of principal or interest payment is overdue. Loan stocks (debentures) are, in the case of many companies, traded in the capital market. It is thus possible for someone owed £100 by company X to sell this debt to another investor who, from the date of the sale, will become entitled to receive interest, and repayment of the principal in due course. Such payment amounts and dates are contractual obligations, so there is less doubt surrounding them than applies to dividends from shares, more particularly where the loan is secured. For this reason the market values of loan stocks tend to fluctuate even less than those of preference shares.

The relationship between the fixed return elements (preference shares and loan stocks) in the long-term financial structure and the equity is usually referred to as *capital gearing* (leverage in the USA).

Broadly speaking, companies have a fair amount of power to issue and redeem ordinary shares, preference shares and loan stocks. Where redemption of shares is to be undertaken, the directors have a duty to take certain steps to safeguard the position of creditors which might be threatened by significant amounts of assets being transferred to shareholders.

LIQUIDATION

A limited company, because it has separate existence from its shareholders does not die when they do. The only way in which the company's demise can be brought about is by following the statutorily defined steps to liquidate the company. Liquidation involves appointing a liquidator to realise the company's assets, to pay the claimants and formally to lay the company to rest.

The initiative to liquidate the company usually comes either from:

- the shareholders, perhaps because the purpose for which the company was formed has been served; or
- the company's creditors (including loan creditors), where the company is failing to pay its debts. In these circumstances the objective is to stop the company from trading and to ensure that non-cash assets are realised, the proceeds being used to meet (perhaps only partially) the claims of the creditors. This type of liquidation is sometimes referred to colloquially as *bankruptcy.*

Order of paying claimants

Irrespective of which type of liquidation is involved, the liquidator, having realised all of the non-cash assets, must take great care as to the order in which the claimants are paid. Broadly speaking the order is:

(1) *Secured creditors.* Where the security is on a specified asset or group of assets, the proceeds of disposal of the asset are to be applied to meeting the specific claim. If the proceeds are insufficient, the creditor must stand with the unsecured creditors for the shortfall. If the proceeds exceed the amount of the claim, the excess goes into the fund available to unsecured creditors.

(2) *Unsecured creditors.* This would usually include most trade creditors. It would also include any unsecured loan creditors.

In fact, ranking even before the secured creditors come a set of claimants who have preferential rights. These include the Inland Revenue for the company's Corporation Tax liability (if any) and the employees for their wages or salary arrears.

Only after the creditors have been paid in full will the balance of the funds be paid out to the shareholders. If the preference shares carry no right to priority of payment, each share (ordinary and preference) will be entitled to an equal portion of the residue of funds. Where preference shares bestow the right to payment before ordinary shareholders, each ordinary share will command an equal slice of the funds remaining after the creditors and preference shareholders have had their entitlement.

The order of payment of creditors will be of little consequence except where there are insufficient funds to meet all claims. Where this is the case, each class of claim must be met in full before the next class may participate.

SUMMARY   Business finance is the study of how investment and financing decisions should be made in theory and how they are made in practice. It is a relatively new discipline which has drawn liberally from disciplines with which it shares common borders.

Risk is a feature of all decision making and so it is one which must be considered explicitly with finance decisions.

Business finance is a separate discipline from accounting but is obviously closely related, financial managers often having backgrounds in accountancy and leaning heavily on accounting reports to aid their decision making.

In the UK, most business firms of greater than very small size are limited companies.

Limited companies are artificially created legal personalities possessing many of the rights and obligations possessed by their human counterparts. They are owned and controlled by human beings whose liability to potential claimants of the company is limited to the amount paid for the shares i.e. they cannot be legally required to put their personal assets at the disposal of claimants. The owners of the company hold shares in the company. Shares are equally sized slices of the ownership of the company which may be transferred from one owner to the next, for value or by gift. The number of shares which a shareholder owns dictates the entitlement to dividends, voting power, and the share of any surplus if the company is liquidated. Companies are cheap and easy to create.

Companies are ultimately controlled by the shareholders but are managed on a day-to-day basis by directors elected by the shareholders. The directors are accountable for their actions to shareholders, and to some extent to the world at large. They formally account through the annual report and accounts.

Companies typically involve themselves in capital gearing, i.e. they usually raise part of their long-term finance from preference shares and part from long-term lenders, as well as some from ordinary (or equity) shares.

Long-term lenders have contractual rights as to payment of interest and repayment of capital. Shareholders, both ordinary and preference, as owners of the company have no such rights and are therefore the ultimate risk takers. Since preference shares usually entitle their owners to a dividend before ordinary shareholders become so entitled, the preference shareholders are somewhat less at risk than ordinary shareholders. Preference shareholders do not usually have the right to vote which the ordinary shareholders have.

Companies are able to issue and to redeem shares and loan stocks as they see fit and without excessive legal restriction.

Limited companies must warn those who deal with them that this is their status by use of the legend Limited (Ltd) or plc after their name.

Some positive action by shareholders or creditors must be undertaken in order to bring the life of a company to a close or to liquidate the company. Where there are insufficient funds to meet all claims against the company, care must be taken by the liquidator to pay claimants in the legally prescribed order.

**FURTHER
READING**   The role of business finance is discussed by Brealey & Myers (1991) and by Puxty & Dodds (1991). Numerous books deal with the provisions of UK company law. Cole, Shears & Tiley (1990) include a very readable chapter outlining the more important aspects. For a more detailed coverage, see Keenan (1990).

WORK-BASED ASSIGNMENT	(a) In your organisation, are financial management decisions dealt with by the accounting department personnel or is there a separate department concerned with financing and investment decisions?
	(b) If there is a separate department, what is the career background of its senior staff?
	(c) Are they qualified accountants?

QUESTIONS WITH ANSWERS (see Appendix 3)	**1** What do you think explains the popularity of the limited liability company as the legal form of so many UK firms?
	2 Does a limited company have limited liability? How does its position in this regard differ from that of a human person?

CHAPTER 2

A framework for financial decision making

In this chapter we shall deal with the following:
- the steps in financial decision making
- the various objectives which, it has been suggested, might be followed by firms
- some UK evidence on objectives which UK firms actually follow
- some theoretical rules for financial decision making; the separation theorem

FINANCIAL DECISION MAKING

Like any other decision-making area, financial decisions involve choices between two or more possible courses of action. If there is only one possible course of action, no decision is needed. Often continuing with a situation which has existed until the time of the decision is one option open to the decision maker. All decision making should involve the following considerations.

Defining objectives

The decision maker should know what the course of action which is the subject of the decision is intended to achieve, or at least towards what it is intended to work. A person leaving home in the morning needs to make a decision on which way to turn into the road. In order to do this it is necessary to know what the immediate objective is. If the objective is going to work, it might require a decision to turn to the right; if it is a visit to the local shop, the decision might be to turn left. If our decision maker does not know the desired destination, it is impossible to make a sensible decision on which way to turn. Likely objectives of the business firm will be considered later in this chapter.

Identifying possible courses of action

The available courses of action should be recognised. In doing this, consideration should be given to any restrictions on freedom of action imposed by law or other forces not within the control of the decision maker.

Good decision making requires that the horizon should constantly be surveyed for opportunities which will better enable the objectives to be achieved. In the business finance context, this includes spotting new investment opportunities and the means to finance the firm. Such opportunities will not often make themselves obvious and firms need constantly to be searching for them. A firm failing to do so will almost certainly be heading into decline, and opportunities will be lost to its more innovative competitors.

Assembling data relevant to the decision

Each possible course of action must be reviewed and the relevant data identified. Not all data on a particular course of action are necessarily relevant. Suppose that a person wishes to buy a car, the only objective being to get the one with the best trade-off between reliability and cost. Only data related to reliability and cost of the possible cars available will be of any interest to that particular person. Other information such as colour, design or country of manufacture is irrelevant. That is not to say that a car buyer's objectives should be restricted to considerations of cost and reliability, simply that if they are in a particular case, then other factors become irrelevant.

Even some data which bear directly on running cost, such as Road Tax, should be ignored if they are common to all cars. As decisions involve selecting from options, it is on the basis of differences that the decision can sensibly be made. If the decision were between buying or not buying a car, then Road Tax would become relevant as it is one of the costs of car ownership. It will not be incurred if the car is not bought.

It is important therefore to recognise what information is relevant to the decision and what is not. Gathering the information can be costly and time-consuming; thus restricting it to the relevant may well lead to considerable savings in the costs of making the decision. Also, the presence of irrelevant information can cause decision makers not to be able to see the wood for the trees, leading to suboptimal decisions.

Assessing the data and reaching a decision

This involves comparing the options by using the relevant data in such a way as to identify those courses of action which will best work towards the achievement of the objectives.

Much of this book will be concerned with the ways in which assessment of data relating to financial decisions should be carried out.

Implementing the decision

It is pointless taking time and trouble to make good decisions if no attempt is to be made to ensure that action follows the decision. This action is not restricted to what is necessary to set the selected option into motion, but includes controlling it through its life. Steps should be taken to ensure, or to try to ensure, that what was planned actually happens.

Monitoring the effects of decisions

While perhaps not strictly central to the decision-making process, good decision making requires that the effects of previous decisions are closely monitored. There are broadly two reasons for this:

(a) It is valuable to assess the reliability of forecasts on which the decision was based. If forecasts prove to be poor, then decision makers must ask themselves if reliability could be improved by using different techniques and bases. It is obviously too late to improve the decision already made and acted upon, but this practice could improve the quality of future decisions.

(b) If a decision is proving to be a bad one for any reason, including unforeseeable changes in the commercial environment, monitoring should reveal this so that some modification might be considered which could improve matters. This is not to say that the original decision can be reversed. Unfortunately we cannot alter the past, but we can often take steps to limit the bad effects of a poor decision. For example, suppose that a firm makes a decision to buy a machine to manufacture plastic ducks as wall decorations, for which it sees a profitable market for five years. One year after buying the machine and launching the product it is obvious that there is little demand for plastic ducks. At that point it is not possible to decide not to enter into the project a year earlier, but it is possible and may very well be desirable to abandon production immediately so as not to throw good money after bad.

In practice most of the monitoring of financial decisions is through the accounting routines, particularly the budgetary control routines.

OBJECTIVES OF THE FIRM

What business firms are seeking to achieve and therefore what investment and financing decisions should seek to promote is a question central to business finance and one which has attracted considerable discussion as the subject has developed. We shall now review some of the more obvious and popular suggestions and try to assess how well each of them stands up to scrutiny.

(a) *Maximisation of profit.* This suggestion arises from the fact that the shareholders are the owners of the firm and as such both the exercisers of ultimate control and the beneficiaries of profits. It is therefore argued that the shareholders will cause managers to pursue policies which would be expected to result in the maximum possible profit. This analysis is acceptable up to a point, but maximising profit could easily be suboptimal to the shareholders. Profit may be able to be increased by expanding the scale of operations of the firm. If the increase merely results from the raising of additional external finance it might mean that profit per share could actually decrease, leaving the shareholders worse off.

Firms which make pharmaceutical products typically spend vast amounts of money on developing and testing new products. It is in the nature of the industry that the time taken to bring a new drug to the market can easily be ten years. A particular firm which stopped spending money on research and development would enhance current profit because costs would be cut, and revenues, arising from development costs in past years, would continue for the time being. Thus current profits would be buoyant but the firm would have a bleak future since there would be no new drugs to replace the old ones.

It is probably open to most firms to increase their profits without additional invest-ment, if they are prepared to take additional risks. For example, cost cutting on the control of the quality of the firm's output could lead to increased profits, at least in the short term. In the longer term substandard products being sold could lead to the loss of future sales and profits.

Clearly, increasing profitability through greater efficiency is a desirable goal from the shareholders' point of view. However *maximisation of profit* is far too broad a definition of what is likely to be beneficial to shareholders.

(b) *Maximisation of the return on capital employed.* This is probably an improve-ment on profit maximisation since it relates profit to the size of the firm; however, as with profit maximisation, no account is taken of risk and long-term stability.

(c) *Survival.* Undoubtedly most firms would see survival as a necessary but insuf-ficient objective to pursue. Investors would be unlikely to be attracted to become shareholders in a firm which had no other long-term ambition than merely to survive. In times of economic recession and other hardship many firms will see survival as their short-term objective, but in the longer term they would almost certainly set their sights somewhat higher.

(d) *Long-term stability.* This is similar to survival and is similarly unrealistic in its lack of ambition as a long-term target.

(e) *Growth.* Growth of profits and/or assets does seem a more realistic goal and appears to reflect attitudes articulated by managers. Growth implies that short-term profit will not be pursued at the cost of long-term stability or survival. Growth is not really a precise enough statement of an objective. This is because growth (as we have seen) can be achieved merely by raising new finance. It is doubtful if any firms have it as their objective to issue as many new shares as possible.

(f) *Satisficing.* Many see objectives which relate only to the welfare of shareholders as unrealistic in the 1990s. They see the business as a coalition of suppliers of capital, suppliers of managerial skills, suppliers of labour, suppliers of goods and services, and customers. None of the participants in the coalition is viewed as having pre-eminence over any of the others. This coalition is not seen as a self-contained entity but viewed in a wider societal context. Cyert & March (1963) were among the first to articulate this view.

The objectives, it is argued, should reflect this coalition so that the firm should seek to give all participants a *satisfactory* return for their inputs, rather than seek to maximise the return to any one of them.

(g) *Maximisation of shareholders' wealth.* This is probably a more credible goal than either those concerned with return/growth or risk/stability/survival as single objectives, since wealth maximisation takes account of both return and risk simul-taneously. Rational investors will value firm A more highly than firm B if the returns expected from each firm are equal but those from firm B are considered more risky (less likely that expectations will be fulfilled). Wealth maximisation also balances short- and long-term benefits in a way that profit-maximising goals cannot.

A wealth maximisation objective should cause financial managers to take decisions which balance returns and risk in such a way as to maximise the benefits, through dividends and enhancement of share price, to the shareholders.

Despite its credibility, wealth maximisation seems in conflict with the perhaps still more credible *satisficing*. Wealth maximising seems to imply the pursuit of the interests of only one member of the coalition, perhaps at the expense of the others. To the extent that this implication is justified, the shareholder wealth maximisation criterion does give a basis for financial decisions which must then be balanced against those derived from objectives more directed towards the other members of the coalition.

It could, however, be argued that satisficing and shareholder wealth maximisation are not necessarily as much in conflict as they might, at first sight, appear to be. That is to say that wealth maximisation might best be promoted by other members of the coalition receiving satisfactory returns. Consider one of the members of the coalition, say the employees. What would be the effect on share prices and dividend prospects if employees do not receive satisfactory treatment? Unsatisfactory treatment seems likely to lead to high rates of staff turnover, lack of commitment by staff, the possibility of strikes, etc. – in short, an unprofitable and uncertain future. Clearly this is not likely to be viewed with enthusiasm by the investing public. This in turn would be expected to lead to a low share price. Conversely, a satisfied workforce seems likely to be perceived favourably by investors. It seems reasonable to believe that a broadly similar conclusion will be reached if other members of the coalition are considered in the same light.

Maximisation of shareholders' wealth may not be a perfect summary of the typical firm's financial objective(s). It does however provide a reasonable working basis for financial decision making which probably leads firms following it to make decisions which promote their goals. What must be true is that firms cannot continually make decisions which reduce their shareholders' wealth since this would imply that the worth of the firm would constantly be diminishing. Each firm has only a finite amount of wealth, so sooner or later it would be forced out of business by the results of such decisions.

Evidence on objectives

A number of studies has been conducted in the UK, most of which have involved questioning senior managers of large firms by interview or postal questionnaire.

Pike & Ooi (1988) conducted a postal questionnaire at two points in time, 1980 and 1986. The 1980 questionnaire was sent to 208 large UK firms. The 1986 questionnaire was sent to the firms that had responded in 1980, provided that they had not disappeared as a result of amalgamations, takeovers, etc. In both surveys the usable response rate exceeded 70 per cent. In both surveys senior finance executives were asked, *inter alia*, to indicate on a five-point scale the importance to their firms of five financial objectives, two of which were short term and three of which were long term.

The mean rankings for the objectives were as shown in Table 2.1. Note that a ranking of 5 implies that the objective is very important and a ranking of 1 implies an unimportant objective.

Table 2.1 The importance of financial objectives (1980–1986)

Objective	1980	1986
Short-term (1 to 3 years):		
Profitability (e.g. percentage rate of return on investment)	4.28	4.61
Profits or earnings (i.e. a profit target)	4.01	4.41
Long-term (over 3 years):		
Growth in sales	3.18	2.97
Growth in earnings per share	2.83	4.38
Growth in shareholders' wealth	3.07	4.06

Source: Pike & Ooi (1988)

These results indicate a number of goals, important to the firm, being simultaneously pursued. They also imply an increasing importance of four of them (sales growth being the exception) over time. It appears that shorter-term objectives were more important to the respondents than were the longer-term ones. However, by 1986, EPS (earnings per share) and shareholders' wealth growth had become nearly as important as the shorter-term goals.

The Pike & Ooi results show some consistency with evidence from other surveys conducted both in the UK and in the USA over recent years.

It should be noted that profit or earnings are properly defined as the net increase in a firm's wealth as a result of its commercial activities. Thus goals which emphasise an importance being placed on profits or EPS are not necessarily in conflict with a shareholder wealth objective. It is only where the longer-term benefit is being jeopardised in favour of short-term profitability that there is conflict. Thus when Pike & Ooi's respondents identified short-term profitability as a goal they were presumably not identifying it at the expense of longer-term goals. In fact the importance placed on EPS and shareholders' wealth growth by the same respondents emphasises this point.

Conflicts of interests: shareholders versus managers

Whoever may control the firm in theory, in practice it is controlled on a day-to-day basis by the managers. It has been suggested that most firms pursue policies which are likely to maximise the welfare of its managers, at the same time giving the other participants in the firm sufficient rewards to stop them from becoming too dissatisfied and causing discomfort to the managers. The ways in which managers might seek to maximise their welfare include:

- paying themselves good levels of salary and 'perks', but not too much to alert shareholders to whom, by law, directors' salaries must be disclosed,
- providing themselves with larger empires, through merger and internal expansion, thus increasing their opportunities for promotion and social status,

- reducing risk through diversification which, as we shall see in Chapter 7, may not benefit the shareholders, but may well improve the managers' security.

There is no reason to believe that professional managers are all rogues, feathering their own nests at the expense of all other participants in the firm. However, human nature being as it is, it would be unusual people who would make a decision without considering its possible effect on themselves. This, no doubt, can cause decisions to be made which are suboptimal from the shareholders' viewpoint. Unfortunately the costs of undertaking some sort of management audit to monitor managers' decisions are likely to be considerable, making it unreasonable to attempt. There is however a strong sanction against the management which continually makes suboptimal decisions and that is the possibility of takeover. A firm whose share price reflects under-utilisation of assets is likely to become a prime target for a takeover which might well leave the delinquent managers without jobs. Buoyant share prices make firms unattractive as takeover targets, so that managers have a vested interest in promoting buoyancy, if not maximisation, of share prices.

The existence of this sanction may not be sufficient to cause management to be completely selfless in its conduct of the firm's affairs. We shall, however, assume that any tendency towards nest-feathering by managers is not of any great significance in practice.

One area where the takeover sanction may not be effective is where managers take too short term a view. Though the best interests of the shareholders may be served by an emphasis on long-term profitability, the best interests of managers could be served by so-called *short-termism*. Managers may see their careers as lasting perhaps just two or three years with a particular firm before they move on to other employment. Their reputations may therefore depend on what happens while they are still with the firm rather than on the ultimate effect of their actions. Perhaps more importantly, management remuneration may well be based on immediate profit flows. Both of these factors could promote a tendency to concentrate on the short term. To what extent, if any, this produces a real conflict of interests between managers and shareholders is not clear.

For the remainder of this book we shall assume that shareholder wealth maximisation is the major financial goal of the firm. However, we should continually bear in mind that, in reality, decisions reached on the basis of this objective might be in conflict with a firm's non-financial goals. If this is the case, the final decision may need to be a compromise.

FINANCING, INVESTMENT AND SEPARATION

If we accept that firms should seek to maximise the wealth of the shareholders in making their financial decisions, we can now turn our attention to how, in theory at least, managers should approach their decision making so as to promote this objective. Let us do this by consideration of an example.

EXAMPLE   **Project X – to invest or to spend**

Industries Ltd is a firm owned by a number of independently minded shareholders. Three of these, Eager, Patient and Steady, each owns 20 000 of the firm's total of 200 000 ordinary shares. At present Industries only has one asset, namely £100 000 in cash. The firm's management is undecided whether to pay this cash to the shareholders as a dividend, which would amount to £10 000 (one-tenth of £100 000) in the case of each of the above trio, or to invest it in Project X. This investment project requires an initial cash investment of the whole of the £100 000 payable now, and will produce a cash receipt of £120 000 in a year's time, then come to a close. If the project is undertaken the whole of the cash proceeds will be paid as a dividend next year (£12 000 each for Eager, Patient and Steady). For the time being let us assume that there is no alternative investment project available to the firm, nor are there any shareholdings in other firms available to investors, also that it is not possible to borrow or lend money.

Suspecting that there might be disagreement between shareholders on Project X, the management decided to call a shareholders' meeting to sound out opinion. During the discussion at the meeting the following three comments were made.

(a) Eager said that she thought Industries should not make the investment but should pay the dividend immediately because, whilst she does not necessarily want to spend the money now, it would be nice to have it available should some need arise. She does not consider the additional £2000 of dividend will compensate her for delaying.

(b) Patient said that he would prefer Project X to be undertaken because he would not, in any case, spend his dividend before next year and would prefer to have £12 000 than £10 000 when he does come to spend it.

(c) Steady said that she would be in favour of Project X but that, since she needs the cash in six months' time to pay for a new extension to her house, she would reluctantly have to vote for the immediate dividend.

Similarly, diverse views were expressed by the firm's other shareholders.

Clearly, management has a problem. If it is trying to maximise the wealth of the shareholders then perhaps a decision to undertake Project X would be the correct one. This would not be acceptable to at least two shareholders; Eager would rather have her money now and Steady must have it in six months at the latest. Clearly £12 000 is more wealth than £10 000, but if it is not to be available to spend when it is wanted or needed, the £10 000 may be preferred. It seems impossible to maximise the satisfaction that each shareholder gets from the firm; satisfying some dissatisfies others because timing of spending matters to people, but not to each person in the same way.

Borrowing and lending

If we introduce a bit more realism into the example by assuming that both Industries Ltd and its shareholders can borrow and lend money, management's dilemma disappears. To illustrate this, let us assume that the interest rate is 15 per cent p.a. and see how the introduction of borrowing and lending affects the position of the trio if Project X is undertaken.

(a) Eager, who wants her money now, could borrow from the bank such an amount that would, with interest, grow to £12 000 by next year. The borrowings could then be discharged using the dividend to be received in a year's time.

The borrowed amount would be £10 435, i.e. £12 000 × 100/(100 + 15) (check £10 435 + (15 per cent × £10 435) = £12 000). Thus she could immediately have £435 more to spend than were Project X to be rejected by the firm. Of course she would still owe the bank £12 000 by the end of the year, but she would use her dividend to pay this.

(b) Patient, who prefers to wait the year, will receive and spend his £12 000 in a year's time. If Project X were to be rejected, the best that he could do would be to lend the £10 000 dividend to the bank which, with interest at 15 per cent, would grow to £11 500 over the year.

(c) Steady, who needs her money in six months' time could at that time borrow such an amount which will grow with interest to £12 000 by the end of the year. Since she does not need the money during the first six months she will only need to borrow for the second half of the year. The borrowed amount would be £11 163, i.e. £12 000 × 100/(100 + 7½). If Project X were rejected by the firm and Steady lent her £10 000 to the bank for six months, it would grow to only £10 750, i.e. £10 000 + (£10 000 × ½ × 15 per cent).

It seems clear that all three investors will have more to spend if Project X is undertaken than if it is not, irrespective of when they wish to spend. It also seems likely that this is true for each of the firm's other shareholders. The shareholders will be unanimous that Project X should go ahead.

Project Y

Now let us suppose that Project X is not available but that the choice lies between paying the dividend now or undertaking Project Y. This project also requires an immediate cash investment of £100 000, but will only produce £110 000 next year when it will cease.

Let us consider how accepting Project Y will affect Eager, who wants her money now. Again she could borrow against next year's dividend (£11 000); the amount which she could borrow will be £9565 (i.e. 11 000 × 100/(100 + 15)). On the other hand, if Project Y is rejected she would have £10 000 to spend. Clearly she would prefer rejection of the project. We could easily illustrate, using the same logic as that which we applied to Project X, that Patient and Steady would agree with her, as indeed would all of the other shareholders. Project X and Project Y suggest what is obviously true, namely that where the firm undertakes projects whose rates of return are greater than the interest rate at which shareholders can borrow or lend, their wealth will be increased. Projects which yield a lower rate than the shareholders' interest rate will have the effect of reducing the wealth of the shareholders. Project X produces a return of 20 per cent p.a. (i.e. (£120 000 – £100 000)/£100 000), Project

Y makes a 10 per cent return; the interest rate is 15 per cent. It is obvious that a project yielding 15 per cent would not alter the wealth of shareholders.

Opportunity cost of finance

The borrowing/lending interest rate represents the *opportunity cost* to the shareholder of making investments in the projects. The existence of the facility to borrow or to lend means that those who have the cash but do not want to spend have the opportunity to lend at the interest rate as an alternative to investing. Any investments in projects must therefore compete with that opportunity and, to be desirable, produce returns in excess of the interest rate.

Borrowing by the firm

Suppose that Industries' management decided to undertake Project X, but for some reason or another, it also decided to pay an immediate dividend of £50 000, making up the shortfall of the cash needed for the investment by borrowing, at 15 per cent p.a., for the duration of the project. This would mean that the £50 000 borrowed with interest, a total of £57 500, will have to be repaid from the £120 000 proceeds from the investment, leaving £62 500 of the £120 000 proceeds from Project X to be paid as a dividend next year.

For Eager this would mean a dividend of £5000 now and another one of £6250 next year. What effect will this have on her present wealth? She can borrow the amount which will, with interest, grow to £6250; this will be £5435 (i.e. £6250 × 100/(100 + 15)) which together with the £5000 dividend will give her £10 435, an increase in wealth of £435. Note that this is identical to the increase in her current wealth that we found when we assessed Project X assuming that it was to be financed entirely by the shareholders. Not surprisingly it could equally well be shown that this would also be true for the other shareholders and no matter what proportion of the £100 000 the firm borrows, Project X will remain equally attractive.

Therefore, it seems not to matter where the cash comes from; if the investment will increase shareholders' wealth under one financing scheme, it will increase it by the same amount under some other scheme.

The theoretical implications of Projects X and Y

This example illustrates three important propositions of business finance.

(a) *Firms should invest in projects which have higher rates of return than the prevailing interest rate.* By doing this the wealth of the shareholders will be increased. By investing in as many such projects as are available, shareholders' wealth will be maximised.

(b) *Personal consumption/investment preferences of individual shareholders are irrelevant in making corporate investment decisions.* Irrespective of when and how much individuals wish to spend, there will be more available to them (their wealth will be maximised) provided that the investment policy outlined in (a) above is followed. This is because individual shareholders can use borrowing or lending to adjust the dividends from the firm to match their personal tastes. Put another way, the pattern of dividends does not affect the wealth of the shareholders.

(c) *The financing method does not affect the shareholders' wealth.* Provided that the investment policy outlined in (a) above is followed, it does not matter whether the investment is financed by the shareholders or by borrowing.

These propositions amount to what is known as the separation theorem, which was first identified by Irving Fisher in the 1930s and was formally set out by Hirshleifer (1958).

These propositions may seem like not-too-subtle glimpses of the obvious, yet when they were first formally propounded they met with quite a lot of scepticism, not entirely because of the lack of reality of some of the assumptions which we have made.

The assumptions
Our consideration of Projects X and Y, and indeed of the separation theorem generally, is based on four major assumptions:

(a)   that investments only last for one year;
(b)   that returns from investments are known with certainty, e.g. there is no doubt that if Project X is undertaken, £120 000 will flow in next year;
(c)   all individuals prefer more wealth to less;
(d)   borrowing and lending rates are equal as between one another, and as between individuals and firms.

Clearly some of these are unrealistic, particularly (a) and (b). Whether this seriously weakens the separation theorem and its implications is probably impossible to assess directly. Even if the theorem does not strictly hold true in practice, it does give some insights into the relationship between shareholders and managers in the context of real investment decisions. The theorem certainly provides a foundation for several major financial theories which we shall encounter later in the book.

The formal derivation of the separation theorem by Hirshleifer is reviewed in the Appendix to this chapter.

THEORY AND PRACTICE

We have discussed what business finance is about and what financial decisions are intended to achieve. We have also considered some theoretical propositions of how we should make financing and investment decisions. In the remainder of this book we shall explore in more detail how in theory such decisions should be made, how in practice they appear to be made and we shall try to reconcile the differences between theory and practice where they occur.

SUMMARY   Good financial decision making requires the adherence to a sequence of steps, the first one of which is to define the firm's objectives.

Many suggestions have been made in the literature as to what are and should be the objectives of firms. Maximisation of shareholder wealth is generally assumed to be the single objective which most adequately summarises firms' financial goals.

The separation theorem provides some theoretical guidelines for financial decision makers. These may be summarised as:

- firms should take on all investment projects which offer returns of a higher rate than the prevailing interest rate; and
- firms should make their investment decisions without regard to how the investment is to be financed and what preferences individual shareholders may have as regards the timing of their spending.

These guidelines are theoretical and much of the remainder of the book will be devoted to consideration of how valid they are in practice.

FURTHER READING   The subject of corporate objectives has been widely dealt with in the literature. Cyert & March (1963), to which reference was made in the chapter, discuss it at length. Most finance texts devote some space to it as do most business economics texts. The article by Pike & Ooi (1988) to which reference was made in the chapter is worth reading, as is the original article by Hirshleifer (1958) referred to in the chapter and reviewed in the Appendix. Lumby (1991) clearly explains the separation theorem and its formal derivation.

WORK-BASED ASSIGNMENT   Is there a formal statement of objectives by your organisation?
If yes, does the organisation seem to use it as a basis of its decision making?
If there is no formal statement of objectives, what do the objectives *appear* to be?

QUESTIONS WITH ANSWERS (see Appendix 3)

1 A firm has £1m at its disposal. The financial managers feel that this could either be invested in new production facilities or paid to shareholders as a dividend. What does the separation theorem suggest that the firm should do?

2 On what assumptions does the separation theorem depend and how realistic do you feel them to be?

APPENDIX – FORMAL DERIVATION OF THE SEPARATION THEOREM

The nature of investment

Investment is essentially outlaying cash in order to give rise to future cash receipts. Usually most or all of the outlay occurs before the inflows. Thus investment has a time dimension.

Let us now consider the position of an investor who has an amount of wealth, which may either be spent (consumed) or invested in productive assets (plant, machinery, trading stocks, etc). At this stage let us restrict ourselves to considering only investment horizons of one period (say a year). Thus the individual may invest part or all of the current wealth for one year and consume the proceeds of the investment next year, or consume it all immediately.

In Fig. 2.1 $0W_0$ represents the total amount of wealth available for present consumption and/or investment by an individual. The curved line W_0W_1 represents the investments available to our investor. All of the present wealth ($0W_0$) may be invested, thus yielding $0W_1$ after a year, or all of the present wealth ($0W_0$) could be consumed, leaving no wealth at the end of the year. A third (and perhaps more likely) possibility is that the investor would choose to consume part of the present wealth and invest part – after all there is a need to eat, both now and next year. If our investor decided to invest C_0W_0 of the present wealth (and consume $0C_0$), this investment would result in $0C_1$ at the year end.

Note incidentally that the investment opportunities become less and less attractive as the amount invested by the individual increases, i.e. the line W_0W_1, becomes less steep as it rises – meaning that increasing amounts of present wealth will need to be invested to yield an extra £1 of wealth after a year. An investment XW_0 will yield wealth of $0Y$ after a year, but a similar-size investment C_0X will only increase next year's wealth by YC_1.

Line W_0W_1 does not represent a single investment opportunity but a large number of them – in fact all of the opportunities available to the investor at the time. The shaded space between the two sets of unbroken parallel lines in Fig. 2.1 represents just one of that large number of hypothetical investments available. This particular one involves an investment now (reduction in current consumption) of amount £a, which will yield (increase future consumption by) £b in a year's time. Since the line W_0W_1 flattens towards the horizontal as it goes from right to left, the better investment prospects (greater return per £1 invested) lie to the right, the less good ones to the left. The investment opportunity lying closest to W_0 is the best one and opportunities decrease in desirability as the curve moves from right to left. This reflects reality in that investors, particularly those who invest in real assets, find that as they take on more and more investments the yield from each subsequent one becomes less. This is because they will tend to undertake the most advantageous investments first, leaving the less desirable ones.

Investment and utility

The investor whose wealth and investment opportunities are shown in Fig. 2.1 will want to know how much to invest, but will probably not want to invest all of the present wealth because this leaves nothing with which to buy food, shelter or indeed any luxuries which may be desired. On the other hand it would be an unusual person who decided to spend all of the money now and face starvation next year. How much would be invested and how much would be spent, which is clearly a question of personal taste, could be represented by the utility curves shown in Fig. 2.2. These curves depict this individual's attitude to the trade-off between consumption now and consumption after one year.

Each point on any particular curve represents some combination of present and future consumption which will render this individual similar amounts of satisfaction or utility. The

Figure 2.1
The productive
investment
opportunities
available to an
individual whose
wealth totals W_0

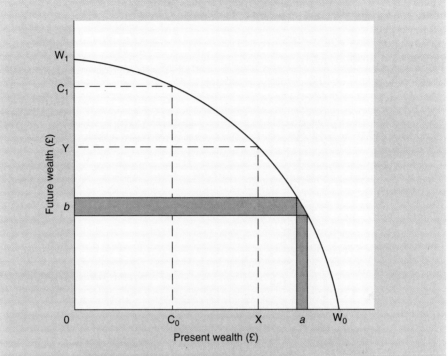

This could all be invested, in which case it would yield wealth totalling W_1 after one time period. These investment opportunities consist of a number of individual opportunities, like the shaded one. Here an investment of amount a made immediately would generate amount b after one time period.

higher the curve, the greater the satisfaction. (Readers who are unfamiliar with the notion of utility and utility curves should refer to page 149.)

The curves in Fig. 2.2 indicate that the investor is very reluctant to forgo consumption completely, either now or next year. The fact that the curves are moving towards the vertical at the top left and towards the horizontal at the bottom right shows this. For example, at the lower levels of present consumption (i.e. reduction in present wealth, where the curves are steepest) any further lowering of consumption will only be undertaken if large increases in future consumption will follow. This tendency increases as the level of present consumption is reduced until we should reach a point where no amount of future consumption would justify further reductions in present consumption. The converse applies at low levels of future consumption. The curves depicted in Fig. 2.2 do, of course, represent the present/future consumption preferences of an individual. Other individuals might well have different attitudes. It is not likely, though, that their attitudes would be fundamentally different since they too would need to eat, both now and next year. The consumption/investment utility curves of all rational individuals would therefore be broadly similar to those shown in Fig. 2.2.

If we combine Figs 2.1 and 2.2, the result of which is shown in Fig. 2.3, we can see that point P is the best combination of investment/consumption for our particular investor as it gives the highest level of utility. No other point along the production curve would enable this person to achieve as high a level of satisfaction as will the investment/consumption decision implied by point P. Therefore the amount invested should be BW_0 (which will yield 0A after

**Figure 2.2
Utility of present/
future
consumption
for some individual**

Each point along any particular curve represents a combination of present and future wealth which a particular individual would find equally satisfactory. The higher the line the greater the satisfaction which the combinations would give.

**Figure 2.3
Utility of
consumption/
investment
for some individual**

This person would invest along curve W_0W_1 to the point where maximum utility would be achieved. This would be at point P.

a year) and 0B should be consumed now, giving 0A to consume next year. Suppose that our individual in fact only invested to point Z, which is a feasible possibility. While this would give some consumption, both now and next year, it does not give what this person would regard as the most satisfying combination of present and future consumption. We know this because Z coincides with a lower utility curve. Given our individual's preferences (represented by the shape of the utility curve) and the state of the world as far as investment is concerned (represented by the investment line $W_0 W_1$), P is clearly the most satisfying level of investment for our individual.

This is not necessarily the same as would be chosen by other individuals because they are unlikely to have the same views on the trade-off between present and future consumption. So there would be *no unanimity* as to the desirable level of investment – it would vary from person to person.

The borrowing/lending opportunity

At this point let us introduce a further factor into the analysis and so make it more realistic. That factor is the opportunity available to individuals for borrowing and lending via banks and other financial institutions (the financial market).

Figure 2.4 shows another possibility which could be used alone or in conjunction with the production opportunities. If the investor were to lend all of the wealth (W_0) now, it would, with interest at rate i, become $W_0 + i W_0$ after a year. Thus the slope of the borrowing/lending line is $(W_0 + i W_0)/W_0 = 1 + i$.

Figure 2.4

The borrowing/ lending opportunity available to an individual with an amount of wealth W_0

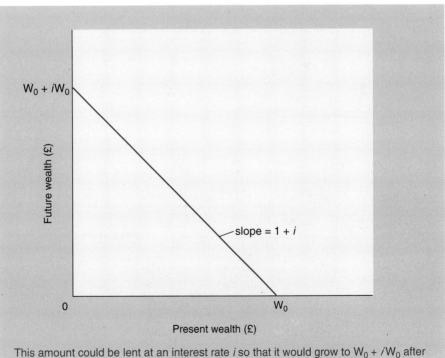

This amount could be lent at an interest rate i so that it would grow to $W_0 + i W_0$ after one time period. Alternatively, an amount W_0 borrowed at an interest rate would lead to $W_0 + i W_0$ being owed after one time period

The existence of borrowing/lending opportunities enables levels of investment to be undertaken in excess of the amount of wealth left after a desired level of consumption has been undertaken. This is achieved by borrowing the required amount now and repaying it (with interest) next year. Similarly not all of the present wealth left after consuming the desired amount need be invested in production; some of it can be lent, to be received back (again with interest) next year. This broadening of the possibilities may well enable the investor to achieve higher levels of satisfaction (utility).

Figure 2.5 combines Figs 2.3 and 2.4, i.e. it introduces the borrowing/lending line into the investment/consumption configuration. Figure 2.5 does look rather complicated, but it is basically only what we have already met.

Figure 2.5 Utility of consumption/ investment of some individual with the borrowing/ lending opportunity

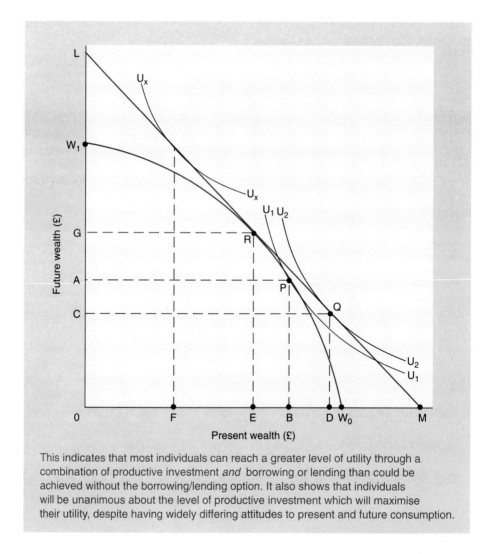

This indicates that most individuals can reach a greater level of utility through a combination of productive investment *and* borrowing or lending than could be achieved without the borrowing/lending option. It also shows that individuals will be unanimous about the level of productive investment which will maximise their utility, despite having widely differing attitudes to present and future consumption.

Without the borrowing/lending opportunity, point P represented the optimum consumption/investment combination for our investor, achieving utility curve U_1U_1. With the introduction of borrowing/lending, a higher level of satisfaction can be achieved, moving up to utility curve U_2U_2. Our individual can now invest amount EW_0 and consume amount 0D. This can be done by borrowing the shortfall (ED). Obviously this amount will have to be repaid (with interest) next year, but nonetheless consumption of 0D now and 0C next year represents a more attractive (higher utility) prospect than consuming 0B now and 0A next year. Thus the introduction of borrowing/lending has increased utility. Note that GC (the amount which must be repaid next year out of 0G to leave the individual with 0C) is equal to ED (the amount borrowed now) plus interest on ED, i.e. ED $(1 + i)$. This is evident from Fig. 2.5 if we bear in mind that the slope of the borrowing/lending line is $(1 + i)$.

The separation theorem

An examination of Fig. 2.5 reveals an important point. Irrespective of the individual's time preferences (shape of utility curve), all investors faced with the productive investment opportunities depicted in Fig. 2.5 would invest up to point R and then achieve their personal highest level of utility by use of the borrowing/lending opportunity. Those investors whose highest utility curve would be tangential to the borrowing/lending line above R would invest up to R and lend that part of the remainder of their wealth which they wish not to consume. In Fig. 2.5 U_xU_x is a utility curve of a different investor from the one whose preferences are represented by U_1U_1, U_2U_2, etc. This second individual would choose to invest up to point R on the productive investment curve and then lend amount FE, leaving 0F for consumption.

An individual whose highest utility curve coincides with point R will obviously wish to invest up to that point but will not need to use the borrowing/lending opportunity.

Irrespective of the personal preferences of various investors they all agree that it is best to invest up to point R, i.e. the point where the slope of the production curve W_0W_1 is equal to that of the borrowing/lending line.

This unanimity between investors as to the optimum level of productive investment is quite interesting in the context of individuals. In the context of firms where managers should try to make investments which most benefit all their shareholders, the unanimity becomes of major importance.

The assumptions on which the above is based and its implications were each discussed in the main body of the chapter.

CHAPTER 3

Financial accounting statements and their interpretation

OBJECTIVES

In this chapter we shall deal with the following:

- the financial accounting statements published by companies
- the accounting conventions which underpin those statements
- interpretation of the statements
- the use of accounting ratios
- accounting ratios in detail

INTRODUCTION

All UK firms which trade as limited companies are required to publish three financial statements each year. These are:

- the profit and loss account (or income statement)
- the balance sheet (or position statement)
- the cash flow statement.

These statements provide a very valuable source of information for financial managers who work within the firm and investors, potential investors and their advisers. It is likely that managers will have access to information other than that which is made public. The nature of the additional information and the way in which it is derived, however, is probably very similar to that which is published. In this chapter we shall consider the nature of the three accounting statements, the rules which are followed in preparing them and the way they may be interpreted, so that the user is able to draw conclusions about the firm which go beyond the obvious.

It should be said that the approach to accounting which is taken in the UK is, in principle, very much the same as is taken throughout the world.

The intention of this chapter is not to provide a detailed course in accounting, but to give a broad overview of the subject. This should be useful in later chapters because reference will be made to the value of accounting information and the use of accounting ratios. If you feel that you would like to look at the subject in greater detail you could take up one or more of the suggestions for further reading which are given at the end of this chapter.

THE ACCOUNTING STATEMENTS

We shall now take a look at the accounting statements. These will be explained in the broadest way. Some of the points which will be made about the statements will be qualified in the next section when we consider the rules which underpin the statements.

Firms which trade as companies are required to produce the accounting statements annually. Most firms actually produce these statements much more frequently for their own internal, managerial purposes. The statements are often used for internal purposes as aids to financial planning in that the data which they contain will be based on plans and forecasts. The published accounts are, of course, based on past events.

The profit and loss account

This is a statement which sets out a summary of the trading events which will have affected the wealth of the firm over a particular period, the amount by which each type of event has affected the wealth and the resulting net effect on wealth. The statement also goes on to show how any net increase in the firm's wealth over the period has been deployed by the firm.

Wealth in this context is not restricted to cash. It is all the things which have economic value to the firm, net of such obligations which the firm may have to outsiders in respect of any part of its wealth. Things which have economic value to the firm (assets) include, for example, an office building owned by the firm and some money owed to the firm by a customer who has bought some of the firm's output of goods or services on credit. Outside obligations in respect of the firm's wealth might include an amount owed to a loan stockholder.

We shall now look at an example of a profit and loss account. Jackson plc is an imaginary manufacturing firm. The nature of the firm's marketing strategy is that goods are made to order so there is never any stock of finished goods. The form of accounting statements varies from one firm to the next. The layout which is shown here is broadly in line with that which UK law requires for the annual published accounts. Individual firms can and do use layouts of their own choice for accounts which are to be used for their own, internal purposes.

Jackson plc

Profit and Loss account for the year ended 31 December 1994

	£000	£000	£000
Sales			837
Cost of sales (including depreciation £28 000 and raw materials stock usage £253 000 Raw material purchases totalled £255 000)			478
Gross profit			359
Distribution costs			
Salaries and wages	37		
Motor expenses	43		
Depreciation of motor vehicles	16		
Sundry distribution expenses	15	111	
Administrative expenses			
Salaries and wages	58		
Motor expenses	22		
Depreciation of motor vehicles	19		
Sundry administrative expenses	14	113	224
Operating profit for the year			135
Interest payable			30
Profit on ordinary activities before taxation			105
Tax on ordinary activities			27
Profit on ordinary activities after taxation			78
Retained profit brought forward from last year			151
			229
Proposed dividend on ordinary shares			20
Retained profit carried forward to next year			209

(Note that this statement does not strictly follow the layout which is required by law for published limited company accounts.)

The statement shows that the firm generated wealth (earned revenues) of £837 000 by making sales to external customers. This led directly to the wealth being reduced (expenses incurred) in respect of meeting the cost of making the sales, also in distributing the goods sold and meeting the administrative costs of running the firm. This left the firm with a net increase in wealth, as a result of operating for the year, of £135 000. The interest which the firm was under a contractual obligation to pay accounted for a further £30 000.

The last part of the statement looks at how the firm deployed the wealth which it had generated. This includes after-tax profits of the current year. It also includes any profits from previous years which had not been specifically allocated. £27 000 will be paid to the Inland Revenue for Corporation Tax on the firm's profit for the year and £20 000 will be paid to the shareholders. You should be clear that the £209 000 of unappropriated profit at the end of the year is that part of the firm's end-of-year wealth which has arisen from past profits. This is unlikely to be in the form of cash.

As has already been pointed out, wealth does not just mean cash. In practice the £209 000 is probably in various forms – plant, stocks, etc.

The balance sheet

This is a statement of the manner in which the firm holds its wealth, how much of its wealth it has in each category, how much of the wealth which the firm controls is committed to outsiders and the net wealth of the firm. This net wealth obviously belongs to the shareholders. Unlike the profit and loss account which summarises the effects of various trading events on the wealth of the firm over a period, the balance sheet shows the firm's position at a specified point in time.

The balance sheet of Jackson plc, at the end of the year covered by the profit and loss account which we just considered, is as follows:

Jackson plc

Balance Sheet as at 31 December 1994

	£000 cost	£000 depre- ciation	£000
Fixed assets			
Freehold land	550	–	550
Plant and machinery	253	226	27
Motor vehicles	102	56	46
	905	282	623
Current assets			
Stock	43		
Trade debtors	116		
Prepaid expenses	12		
Cash	25	196	
Creditors: amounts falling due within one year			
Trade creditors	45		
Accrued expenses	18		
Taxation	27		
Dividend proposed	20	110	
Net current assets			86
Total assets less current liabilities			709
Creditors: amounts falling due after more than one year			
10% secured loan stock			300
			409
Ordinary share capital – 200 000 shares of £1 each			200
Profit and loss account			209
			409

(Note that this statement does not strictly follow the layout which is required by law.)

This balance sheet tells us that the wealth of the firm is £819 000. This is made up of fixed assets of £623 000 and current assets of £196 000. The firm has obligations to transfer part of this wealth to groups outside. £110 000 is in respect of obligations which must be met within one year, and £300 000 in respect of longer-term obligations.

The distinction between fixed and current assets is concerned with the intended use of those assets. Fixed assets are those which are intended to be used within the business to help to generate wealth, not to be sold at a profit. Current assets are those which are acquired by the firm with the intention of turning them over in the normal course of trading. A particular fixed asset might be sold at a profit but this would not mean that it should have been treated as a current asset, provided that the primary reason for buying it was for using rather than selling it. Fixed assets can be seen as the tools of the firm.

Depreciation recognises that certain fixed assets are not worth as much at the end of their life with the firm as they were at the beginning and, therefore, that some part of the firm's wealth will be lost. This is why depreciation appears in the profit and loss account as an expense and why the balance sheet value of depreciating fixed assets is reduced below cost. The total amount of depreciation of a particular asset is calculated by taking its cost and deducting its estimated disposal value at the end of its life with the firm. This total must then be apportioned between accounting periods in some reasonable manner. In practice in the UK this is typically accomplished by sharing the total equally between the number of accounting periods of the life of the fixed asset concerned.

It is considered useful to readers of balance sheets to deduct current (short-term) liabilities from current assets and to show the net figure of net current assets or working capital. This is because, in normal circumstances, it is out of the assets included under current assets that the current liabilities will be met. Relating current liabilities to current assets in this way highlights the extent to which the firm will find it easy to meet its short-term obligations. This is a particularly important matter since a failure of a firm to meet its short-term obligations can easily lead to financial collapse.

The bottom section of the balance sheet shows how the shareholders have contributed to the current wealth of the firm. This was by a combination of specifically putting assets, normally cash, into the firm to acquire shares, and by allowing wealth generated within the firm to remain there rather than being paid to themselves as dividends. These ploughed-back profits, shown under the heading 'profit and loss account' are known as reserves. Reserves represent part of the wealth of the shareholders just as much as dividends do.

The cash flow statement

This is simply an analysis of the cash received and paid out by the firm during a period. It is arranged in such a way that it will enable readers to derive helpful insights to the sources and uses of cash over the period. It may seem strange that one particular asset – cash – is highlighted in this way when others, e.g. stock, are not. What is so special about cash? The answer to this question is that cash tends to be at the heart of most aspects of business. A firm's ability to prosper and survive is likely to depend on its ability to generate cash. This typically is not true for other types of asset.

The cash flow statement of Jackson plc is as follows:

Jackson plc

Cash flow statement for the year ended 31 December 1994

	£000	£000
Net cash inflow from operating activities		177
Returns on investments and servicing of finance		
Dividends paid		(15)
Taxation		
Corporation tax paid		(18)
Investing activities		
Payments to acquire tangible fixed assets		(33)
Net cash inflow before financing		111
Financing		–
Increase in cash and cash equivalents		111

This statement shows that the firm generated a net cash inflow of £177 000 from its trading activities. That is to say that during the year the receipts of cash from sales exceeded payments of cash to pay wages and salaries, suppliers of goods and services, etc., by £177 000. You should be clear that this is not the same as profit. Profit is the net increase in wealth generally as a result of trading – not just cash.

The remainder of the statement shows where any other cash has come from (none in the case of Jackson plc in 1994) and gone to. In this case cash has been spent on paying the dividend which was declared in 1993, but not paid until 1994; the tax which arose from the 1993 profit but was paid in 1994; and some cash was spent acquiring additional fixed assets.

Had any cash been raised through an issue of shares or loan stocks, or had any cash been paid to redeem shares or loan stocks, the effect of these would have appeared under the 'financing' heading in the statement.

DEFINITIONS AND CONVENTIONS OF ACCOUNTING

Accounting is a language which is used to store and communicate economic information about organisations. It has a set of rules, which have emerged through practice rather than as a result of an exercise to decide what is the best approach. It is particularly important that anyone trying to read accounting statements and draw conclusions from them is clear on the rules of accounting. Severe misunderstandings could arise from reading accounting statements by someone not familiar with the rules.

Accounting definition of an asset

An asset has a particular meaning in accounting, which is rather more restrictive than the general one which we use in more everyday speech. To be included in a balance sheet as an asset of a particular firm, the item would need to have the following attributes:

- It is likely to produce future economic benefits to that firm
- it has arisen from some past transaction or event involving that firm
- the right of access to it by others can be restricted by that firm

The benefit of having a loyal workforce has the characteristics of an asset, to the extent of it being capable of producing probable future economic benefits, e.g. through savings in recruitment costs as a result of low labour turnover. It would not be included on the firm's balance sheet, however, because it has almost certainly not arisen as a result of any particular transaction or event. It is also the case that the firm would probably find it impossible to deny rival firms access to members of the staff to try to employ them.

Money measurement convention

Accounting defines things in terms of money and can do no other. Thus information which cannot be expressed in monetary terms cannot be included in accounting statements. This can be seen as a deficiency of accounting.

Historic cost convention

Assets are shown in the balance sheet at a value which is based on their cost to the firm when they were first acquired, not their current market value or any other basis of valuation. This means that attempts to use the balance sheet to place a value on a firm are likely to lead to misleading results. Some firms break this convention and show certain assets, particularly those relating to land and buildings, at an estimate of their current market value. Certain items of value may be omitted from the balance sheet because they do not have a cost which can be measured in money terms. Also a particular asset may have a low market value but be worth much to the firm itself. This could arise where the asset is highly specialised or specific to the firm and have little or no use to any other firm.

Adherence to the historic cost convention means that the reader of accounting statements is unable to assess the opportunity cost of using a particular asset for some purpose. For example, when the historic cost of some stock sold is included in a profit and loss account, as an expense, the reader is not able to make a judgement about how much more the wealth of the firm would have been increased had the stock been deployed in some other way.

Prudence convention

Accounting should err on the side of caution. For example, if an item of stock in trade has a sales value which is below cost, this should be reflected by reducing its value in the balance sheet to the lower figure, with the same reflection of the loss of wealth being shown in the profit and loss account. Following the same philosophy, a gain in the value of an asset is not taken into account until it is realised as a result of a disposal of the asset concerned to some person or organisation outside the firm. In this way the prudence convention tends to underpin both the historic cost and the realisation conventions.

It has been argued that adherence to the prudence convention tends to lead to a fairly consistent bias in accounting information, which could mislead a reader of accounting statements.

Going concern convention

In the absence of evidence to the contrary, it is assumed that the firm will continue indefinitely. This means, for example, that it will be assumed that a fixed asset will be capable of being used by the firm for the whole of its useful life, rather than it being assumed that the firm will be forced to dispose of the asset as a result of the firm collapsing financially. Thus a firm can base its depreciation policy on the cost, expected life and disposal proceeds of the particular asset, rather than on the current value of the asset at intermediate periods over its life. As a result the fact that many fixed assets have a current market value below their balance sheet value does not cause the prudence convention to be invoked.

Stable monetary unit

Accounting tends to assume that the value of the currency remains constant in terms of its ability to buy goods and services. In other words, accounting statements are prepared as if there were no inflation. The fact that inflation is a constant feature of almost every economy in the world means that this is likely to be a major cause of accounting statements giving impressions which could be misleading. Attempts have been made to agree an approach to allowing for the distortions of inflation in accounts. So far no major economy in the world has developed an approach which is consistently and widely used by its firms in their accounts.

Realisation

This convention is concerned with the point in time at which a revenue, i.e. an increase in wealth arising from trading, is recognised in the accounts. For example if a customer orders goods in one month, receives them in the next and pays for them in the third month, when should the firm supplying the goods treat the revenue (sale) as having taken place? This is not an academic question where the firm is preparing accounts for each month and comparing one month's performance with another, or where the three months do not all fall within the same accounting year.

The realisation convention says that the revenue should be recognised at the point where:

- the amount (value) of the revenue is capable of being measured with substantial accuracy
- the necessary work to undertake the sale has substantially been completed
- it is reasonably certain that the cash will be received.

This point is usually taken to be the point at which the customer takes delivery, and accepts, the goods or service. Thus recognition of the revenue and receipt of the cash do not occur at the same point, except in the case of cash sales. Outside of the retail trade cash sales are rare. Thus for most firms cash receipts from sales tend to lag behind recognition of sales.

Matching

Expenses (trading events leading to reductions in wealth) are matched to the particular revenues, which they helped to generate in the same accounting period. For example, where the sale of some goods is recognised as a revenue in a particular accounting period, the cost of those goods to the supplying firm should be treated as an expense in the same period.

The objective which this convention pursues is to assess the net effect on wealth which a particular revenue or set of revenues generates.

Accruals

Profit or loss is concerned with net increases or decreases in wealth, not with increases or decreases in cash. Thus when deriving the amount of the expenses which are to be matched to particular revenues, the fact that cash may not yet have been paid is not relevant. For example, the cost of stock sold for inclusion in the profit and loss account will be the same, irrespective of whether payment for the stock concerned has yet been made.

PROBLEMS WITH USING ACCOUNTING INFORMATION FOR DECISION MAKING

There are significant problems in using accounting information to help to make decisions. These fall under two headings: income measurement and balance sheet values.

Income measurement

A major problem here is concerned with the costs which are matched against revenues. The costs are normally not expressed in the same terms as the revenues where there are changing prices (historic cost and stable monetary unit conventions). Since the costs tend to be incurred before the revenues are recognised, there is a tendency for costs to be understated causing profit to be overstated. Also the fact that historic costs are used rather than opportunity costs means that only a partial impression of the effect of a particular transaction's effects on wealth is given. Again the distortion is consistently likely to overstate profit, i.e. to imply that more wealth has been created than is justified by the facts.

Balance sheet values

Adherence to the historic cost, prudence, going concern and stable monetary conventions, coupled with the use of a fairly restricted accounting definition of an asset, tends to cause accounts to understate the amount of wealth which is invested in the firm. This tends to be the case both asset by asset and taking the firm overall. Many assets have a greater value than is represented by the balance sheet. Some things which are of economic value to the firm may not even be included in the balance sheet at all. Many firms have goodwill, i.e. an ability to earn abnormally high profits due to some factor, like a loyal workforce or a loyal clientele. This asset is rarely included in the balance sheet since to do so would contravene one or other of the accounting rules. Yet a distorted impression of the wealth committed to the firm is given if most assets are either understated or are excluded.

It is perhaps worth noting that accounting's deficiencies for decision-making purposes stem from the fact that financial accounting did not really evolve to meet the needs which decision makers currently try to satisfy. Rather it developed to provide an historical financial record of the firm. On the one hand this was a record of where funds had come from – shareholders, creditors, etc. – and how much each had contributed. On the other hand there was a record of how these funds had been deployed. So when shareholders subscribed for shares of £1 million and the firm used the cash to buy a building, this appeared on the balance sheet as share capital £1 million and freehold land £1 million. The fact that five years later the land has a market value of £10 million is not relevant, because the balance sheet simply records the transaction. For one reason or another accountants have never really sat down with a clean sheet of paper and tried to design a system which would be more useful to decision makers. From time to time they have grafted on additional features, like the profit and loss account, but these features were always underpinned by the same approach as had been taken to the balance sheet.

Despite the deficiencies of accounting statements, they remain a very major, if not the only, source of information for many decision makers. Provided that accounting information is used with care, it should be useful, despite its limitations.

There is no reason of principle why a particular firm should not prepare accounts for its internal purposes in such a way as to correct for the distorting factors. Undoubtedly some firms do this, but probably most do not.

RATIO ANALYSIS

As well as gaining information about, and insights into, a firm's trading and position by reading the published accounts, it is also useful to calculate ratios relating particular figures to one another. It can even be useful to relate certain accounting figures to non-accounting measures, like the number of employees. One reason for calculating ratios is to attempt to summarise quite complex accounting information into a relatively small number of key indicators. An associated reason for calculating ratios is to make figures more easily comparable. For example, if firm A made a profit last year of £1 million and firm B made a profit of £2 million, what does this tell us? Clearly it tells us that firm B made the larger profit, but does it tell us that firm B was better managed or more efficient? The answer is that it does not give us any impression of relative efficiency. Firm B may be much larger than firm A. If we were to relate each firm's profit to its size a more valid comparison of efficiency can be made. The amount which the shareholders have invested (share capital plus reserves, which equals total assets less total liabilities) is a commonly used indicator of size, so we could use that.

Comparison between firms is not the only one which we may wish to make. We may want to compare the firm's current performance with its past performance to try to identify trends, etc. We may wish to assess the firm's performance against that which was planned.

Calculating ratios from a set of accounts is a relatively easy task. A suitably primed computer will do it almost instantaneously. The hard part of interpretation of accounts lies in using skill and experience to draw valid and useful conclusions from the ratios.

Traditionally ratios are classified into five groups and we shall look at a selection of ratios under those same headings. As we proceed to consider each ratio we shall calculate each one for Jackson plc for 1994. When this is completed, to give us some basis of comparison, we shall also look at the same ratios for the firm in 1993.

Profitability ratios

These ratios are concerned with the effectiveness of the firm in generating profit.

A very popular means of assessing a firm is to assess the amount of wealth generated for the amount of wealth invested.

Return on net assets (return on capital employed)

$$\frac{\text{Net profit before long-term interest and tax}}{\text{Total assets less creditors falling due within one year}} \times 100\%$$

The ratio for Jackson plc for 1994 is $\dfrac{135}{709} \times 100 = 19.0\%$

This ratio looks at the return on the fixed and current assets less current liabilities. The logical profit figure to use in calculating this ratio is the operating profit. This is because we are considering the effectiveness of the assets financed both by the shareholders and by the long-term creditors and, therefore, we should logically use the profit which is shared between these two groups.

Provided that short-term profit is not being generated at the expense of the long term, this ratio should probably be as high as possible. In Chapter 2 we saw that it might be open to most firms to increase current accounting earnings and, with it, the return on assets ratio, through taking actions which could adversely affect long-term profitability, or at the expense of taking on higher levels of risk.

Since this ratio goes to the heart of what most private sector firms are trying to achieve it is sometimes known as the primary ratio.

Return on equity (return on shareholders' funds)

$$\frac{\text{Net profit after long-term interest and tax}}{\text{Share capital and reserves}} \times 100\%$$

The ratio for Jackson plc for 1994 is $\dfrac{78}{409} \times 100 = 19.1\%$

This is quite a similar ratio to the previous one, but considers matters more specifically from the shareholders' viewpoint. For this reason the profit figure is that which is earned by the shareholders after all charges have been met.

Gross profit margin

$$\frac{\text{Gross profit}}{\text{Sales}} \times 100\%$$

The ratio for Jackson plc for 1994 is $\dfrac{359}{837} \times 100 = 42.9\%$

This shows what percentage of the sales revenue remains after the expense of making the stock available to the customers is taken into account. There is a range of pricing and output strategies which a firm can employ. At one end of the range is the strategy of charging very low prices for the output, so that customers are attracted, leading to a high sales revenue (turnover). At the other end is the strategy of offering the firm's output at a fairly high price, leading to a relatively low sales turnover. In principle neither strategy is preferable to the other. Where in the range the firm seeks to operate is a matter of managerial judgement. In making this judgement management will need to take account of the nature of the market and of the firm's own cost structure.

Net profit margin

$$\frac{\text{Net profit before long-term interest and tax}}{\text{Sales}} \times 100\%$$

The ratio for Jackson plc for 1994 is $\dfrac{135}{837} \times 100 = 16.1\%$

This ratio shows what is left of sales revenue after all of the expenses of running the firm for the period have been met. Once again it should be as large as possible, provided that the firm is not earning high profit margins at the expense of some other aspect. Again a 'short-termist' attitude to profit could lead to an apparently impressive net profit margin, but one which may not be sustainable into the future.

Activity ratios

These ratios are used to try to assess the effectiveness of a firm in using its assets.

Net asset turnover

$$\frac{\text{Sales}}{\text{Total assets less current liabilities}} \times 100\%$$

The ratio for Jackson plc for 1994 is $\dfrac{837}{709} = 1.18$ times

This ratio enables a judgement to be made on the extent to which the firm has generated sales. As in the return on capital employed ratio, the net assets figure is used as a measure of the size of the firm. This ratio is a measure of the effectiveness with which the firm is using its assets to generate sales. The size of this ratio will be a reflection of the firm's strategy on margins and turnover, discussed above in the context of the gross profit margin ratio. A high ratio is not necessarily beneficial if margins are so small that the net profit generated is unsatisfactory.

It is worth noting the direct relationship between return on net assets, net profit margin and net asset turnover. If you look back at the definition of each of these ratios you will see that:

$$\text{Return on net assets} = \text{net profit margin} \times \text{net asset turnover}$$

It can be quite helpful to look at sales relative to various elements of the net assets. For example, if there is a relatively small net asset turnover ratio, further analysis can be undertaken to assess fixed asset turnover, current asset turnover, etc. This may enable an analyst to make a judgement about the reason for the low net asset turnover figure. This in turn may reveal that the firm has an abnormal balance between the various elements of net assets, e.g. relatively high fixed assets.

Stockholding period

$$\frac{\text{Stock held}}{\text{Stock used}} \times 365 \text{ days}$$

Jackson is a manufacturing firm, which makes things to order and, therefore, has no stock of finished goods. Let us assume that all the stock at the year end is of raw materials (rather than work-in-progress).

The ratio for Jackson plc for 1994 is $\dfrac{43}{253} \times 365 = 62.0$ days

This ratio indicates the average number of days which stock remains in the firm before it is taken into production. Good stock management would cause this figure to be as low as possible, consistent with there being sufficient stock available to meet the firm's needs.

The stock turnover ratio is the reciprocal of this, i.e. $\dfrac{\text{Stock used}}{\text{Stock held}}$

The management of stock and the other working capital elements is discussed in some detail in Chapter 13 of this book.

Debtor collection period (Days debtors)

$$\frac{\text{Trade debtors}}{\text{Credit sales}} \times 365 \text{ days}$$

The ratio for Jackson plc for 1994 is $\dfrac{116}{837} \times 365 = 50.6$ days

(Assuming that all of the firm's sales are on credit.)

This ratio tells us how long, on average, after the sale on credit, trade debtors meet their obligation to pay. A well managed debtor policy will lead to debtors taking as short a time as possible to pay, yet not damage good customer relations.

Creditor payment period (Days creditors)

$$\frac{\text{Trade creditors}}{\text{Credit purchases}} \times 365 \text{ days}$$

The ratio for Jackson plc for 1994 is $\dfrac{45}{255} \times 365 = 64.4$ days

(Assuming that all of the firm's purchases are on credit and that the trade creditors only relate to purchases of raw materials stock.)

This ratio tells us how long, on average, after a purchase on credit the firm meets its obligation to pay for its purchases. A well managed creditor policy will lead to the firm taking as much 'free' credit as is possible, but at the same time preserving the goodwill of suppliers.

Liquidity ratios

These ratios are used to assess how well the firm is managing its working capital.

Current ratio

$$\frac{\text{Current assets}}{\text{Creditors falling due within one year}}$$

The ratio for Jackson plc for 1994 is $\dfrac{196}{110} = 1.78 : 1$

Note that this ratio is usually expressed by stating the amount of current assets per £1 of current liabilities.

This provides some measure of how the balance has been struck between the two aspects of working capital. Usually firms seek to have ratios higher than 1:1, i.e. they try to avoid having current assets financed entirely from current liabilities. In this way they hope to give the short-term creditors confidence that there are sufficient liquid assets comfortably to cover their claims.

Rule-of-thumb figures for this ratio tend to be bandied about in the literature and in financial management folklore, a popular figure being 2:1. In fact actual figures tend to vary widely but there seem to be characteristic figures for different industries. The high street supermarket chains typically seem to have ratios close to 1:1, whereas manufacturing firms have very much higher levels. The difference is almost certainly explained by the make-up of the current assets. In supermarkets they consist of cash and fast-moving stock-in-trade; supermarkets do not sell on credit (therefore they have no trade debtors) and typically stock does not gather dust on the shelves. Thus all their current assets are in a fairly liquid state, being either cash or, in the normal course of events, items naturally turning into cash within a week or two. Manufacturers, by contrast, typically sell on credit and – since they do need to hold stocks of raw materials, finished goods and some amount of work in progress (WIP) – much of their current assets are perhaps several months away from turning into cash.

According to Table 8.1 (page 200), which shows the aggregate balance sheet of a large number of UK firms, the average current ratio is 1.4:1.

Quick assets (liquid or acid test) ratio

$$\frac{\text{Liquid assets}}{\text{Creditors falling due within one year}}$$

The ratio for Jackson plc for 1994 is $\dfrac{153}{110} = 1.39:1$

This ratio addresses itself fairly directly to the question: if short-term creditors were to demand payment of their claims more or less immediately, would there be sufficient in the way of liquid assets to meet them? What is included in *liquid assets* is a matter of judgement. For our supermarket, these would probably include all current assets since none of them is likely to be too far away from turning into cash. For a manufacturer they would probably exclude stocks and possibly some debtors.

We can probably say that, irrespective of the nature of business involved, this ratio should be about 1:1. The difference between the type of business is in effect adjusted in the definition of liquid assets. Defining liquid assets as current assets less stock, Table 8.1 shows the average quick assets ratio as 0.9:1.

We might ask ourselves whether it is likely that all the short-term creditors would demand their money at once. The answer is probably no, provided that they remained confident that payment would be forthcoming at the normal time. Those advancing credit without cast-iron security, which would be the position of the typical provider of short-term credit, do so for their own commercial advantage (e.g. in order to sell their wares) and they do so because they have reasonable confidence that they will be paid. Signs, including a weak acid test ratio, that the firm may not be able to pay, are likely to erode that confidence, triggering off demands for immediate payment.

No credit period

$$\frac{\text{Liquid assets}}{\text{Average daily cash running costs}}$$

The ratio for Jackson plc for 1994 is $\dfrac{25}{(478+111+113+30-63)/365} = 13.6$ days

The numerator of this is cash. The denominator is the average expenses, excluding depreciation (£63 000 for the year). Depreciation is excluded because it is not an expense which gives rise to a cash flow.

This is a more dynamic measure of liquidity than is the quick asset ratio. It asks for how many days the firm could continue to operate without any further injection of cash. In this way it relates the firm's liquid assets to its need for those liquid assets to enable it to maintain normal operations.

This ratio should be as large as possible, consistent with not having too much unproductive cash at the bank. There is some discussion of the advantages and disadvantages of holding cash in Chapter 13.

Capital gearing ratios

Capital gearing is concerned with the relative sizes of the funds provided by shareholders, on the one hand, and by loan creditors on the other. This is an important issue in business finance, about which there are various theories and a body of empirical evidence. This is discussed in some detail in Chapter 11.

For reasons which are raised in Chapter 11 loan financing tends to be cheaper than equity financing. On the other hand loan financing exposes the shareholders to greater risk than does equity financing. Ratios in this area tend to be concerned with assessing the level of capital gearing.

Debt to equity ratio

$$\frac{\text{Borrowings (long- and short-term)}}{\text{Total equity (shares plus reserves)}} \times 100\%$$

The ratio for Jackson plc for 1994 is $\dfrac{300}{409} = 0.73 : 1$

It is not possible to say whether a particular figure represents a high figure. 'High' is probably defined as significantly larger than is typically found in the industry in which the firm operates.

Times interest covered

$$\frac{\text{Profit before interest and tax}}{\text{Interest charges}} \times 100\%$$

The ratio for Jackson plc for 1994 is $\dfrac{135}{30} = 4.5$ times

This ratio looks at how many times the interest could be met from the profits. It is, therefore, some measure of how easily the firm is able to cover its interest payment obligations out of its profits.

Investors' ratios

These ratios are concerned with looking at the firm from the point of view of a shareholder, perhaps owning shares in a Stock Exchange traded firm. These ratios are of the type which appear in the financial pages of newspapers. Two of those which we shall be considering are partly based on the current market price of the shares. We shall work on the basis that Jackson plc's ordinary shares had a market value of £5.10 on 31 December 1994.

Earnings per share

$$\frac{\text{Profit after interest and tax}}{\text{Number of ordinary shares}}$$

The ratio for Jackson plc for 1994 is $\dfrac{78}{200} = £0.39$ (or 39p) per share

This is the profit attributable to each share. It is not the dividend paid per share, unless all of the profit is paid as a dividend, which would be very unusual. We should bear in mind that the profit, or at least the wealth represented by that profit belongs to the shareholders whether it is paid to them or not. In Chapter 12 we shall consider whether shareholders prefer to receive dividends or to 'plough back' their profits.

Price/earnings ratio

$$\frac{\text{Current market price per share}}{\text{Earnings per share}}$$

The ratio for Jackson plc at 31 December 1994 is $\dfrac{5.10}{0.39} = 13.1$

This ratio can be seen as the number of years that it would take, at the current share price and rate of earnings, for the earnings from the share to cover the price of the share. This has been a very popular means of assessing shares.

A share with a high PE ratio is one which has a high price compared with its recent earnings. This implies that investors are confident in future earnings of the firm. It will, of course, be on the basis of expectations of future profits that investors will assess the value of shares.

Dividend yield

$$\frac{\text{Dividend per share (grossed-up for tax)}}{\text{Current market price per share}} \times 100\%$$

The ratio for Jackson plc at 31 December 1994 is $\dfrac{(20/200) \times (100/75)}{5.10} \times 100 = 2.6\%$

This ratio seeks to assess the cash return on investment earned by the shareholders. To this extent it enables a comparison to be made with other investment opportunities available. It is necessary to 'gross up' the dividend received because it is received as if Income tax at 25 per cent had been deducted before payment. Since rates of return on investment are usually quoted in gross (pre-tax) terms, it makes for a more valid comparison.

Whether a high or a low figure is to be preferred for dividend yield depends greatly on the needs and investment objectives of the shareholders.

Dividend cover

$$\frac{\text{Earnings per share}}{\text{Dividend per share}}$$

The ratio for Jackson plc for 1994 is $\dfrac{78/200}{20/200} = 3.9$ times

This ratio indicates how comfortably the firm can meet the dividend out of current profits. The higher the ratio, the more confident shareholders can be that the dividend will be maintained at, at least, the current level, even if there were to be a downturn in profits.

We can now go on to assess Jackson plc through its accounting ratios. To give us a basis for comparison we shall assess the 1994 results against those for 1993. The profit and loss account and balance sheet of the firm, for the earlier year, are given in the appendix to this chapter. The following is a table of the 1994 ratios with their 1993 counterparts:

Jackson plc

Accounting ratios for the years ended 31 December:

	1993	1994
Profitability ratios		
Return on net assets (%)	14.9	19.0
Return on equity (%)	13.1	19.1
Gross profit margin (%)	43.8	42.9
Net profit margin (%)	13.8	16.1
Activity ratios		
Net asset turnover (times)	1.08	1.18
Stock holding period (days)	78.8	62.0
Debtor collection period (days)	64.0	50.6
Creditor payment period (days)	83.9	64.4
Liquidity ratios		
Current	1.0:1	1.78:1
Quick assets	0.76:1	1.39:1
No credit period (days)	(54.0)	13.6
Gearing ratios		
Debt to equity	1.1:1	0.73:1
Times interest covered (times)	2.9	4.5
Investors' ratios		
Earnings per share (£)	0.23	0.39
Price/earnings	15.2	13.1
Dividend yield (%)	2.8	2.6
Dividend cover (times)	3.1	3.9

Comment on the ratios

In 1994 there was a significantly higher ratio for return on net assets, which would normally be seen as desirable. This has been achieved mainly through an increased net asset turnover which more than overcame the small decrease in the gross profit margin. Thus the firm was more effective at making sales in 1994 than it was in 1993. Net profit margin rose because of the strong increase in turnover, despite an increase in the actual amounts spent on overheads.

Liquidity increased dramatically from a level which was probably an unhealthy one to one which would probably be considered fairly strong. This was partly achieved through the reduction in the amount of time for which the firm was holding stock and the time taken to collect trade debts. Creditors were more promptly paid in 1994 than they were in 1993. This represents a reduction over the year in the extent to which the firm took advantage of the availability of this theoretically cost-free form of finance. This may have been done deliberately with a view to improving relations with suppliers.

Partly as a result of the elimination of the overdraft, and partly as a result of relatively high ploughed-back profit expanding reserves, the gearing ratio dropped significantly.

The increased profit with no increase in the number of shares issued led directly to an increase in earnings per share. The price/earnings ratio diminished despite a much better profit performance by the firm in 1994. This can be explained by the fact that the share price will be driven by investors' expectations of the future of the firm. Thus the price in 1993 reflected the future, rather than the 1993 profits, which were used in the calculation of the ratio. The increased profit led to an increase in the dividend cover despite the increased dividend in 1994.

Generally we have a picture of a firm which has significantly improved in most aspects of its performance and position over the year. It was more profitable which led to strong cash flows (see the cash flow statement) and, therefore, to much better liquidity and lower capital gearing.

Apart from the problems of ratio analysis which we shall consider shortly, it must be recognised that this analysis is very limited in its scope. We have only considered two years' figures. It would probably be much more instructive to have looked at ratios stretching over a number of years. We have only used another period for the same firm as our basis of comparison. It would be at least as useful to compare this firm's performance with that of other companies in the industry, perhaps the industry averages for the various ratios. We know that the debtor collection period was shorter for Jackson plc in 1994 than it had been in 1993, but this is not to say that this represented a satisfactory performance compared with the industry average, or compared with that which the firm had budgeted the debtor collection period to be.

Other ratios

There is an almost limitless number of ratios which can be calculated from one set of financial accounts. Those which we have considered only represent a sample, though these are what seem to be the more popular ratios used in practice. Certain ratios may be particularly appropriate in certain types of business. Obviously a stockholding period ratio is appropriate to a firm which deals in stock in some way. To a firm offering a service, it would be inappropriate.

Ratios need not be derived exclusively from accounting reports. The sales per employee ratio is widely used. Cost per tonne/mile (i.e. the cost of transporting a tonne of cargo for one mile) is widely used in the transport industry. Sales revenue per square metre of selling area is fairly widely used in the retail trade.

Caution in interpretation of ratios

It must be obvious from what we have seen so far that ratio analysis is not a very exact science. The choice of the ratios which are calculated, the precise definition of these ratios and the conclusions which are drawn are very much matters of judgement and conjecture. Ratios tend to raise questions rather than to answer them. Ratios can highlight areas where this year's performance was different from that of last year, or where one firm's performance was different from that of other firms in the industry.

They will not tell you whether this year's performance was better than that of other years, or whether Firm A is better than the rest.

It follows that it is not appropriate to be dogmatic in interpreting ratios. For example the debtor collection period for Jackson plc was shorter for 1994 than it was for 1993. This cannot automatically be interpreted as an improvement, however. It might be that a lot of pressure has been put on debtors to pay promptly and that this has led to some loss of customer goodwill, which will, in due course, have an adverse effect on the firm's profitability.

Problems with accounting figures

Earlier in the chapter, we considered the nature of accounting information and problems with using it. In the context of accounting ratios, there are probably two particularly significant weaknesses. Firstly there is a tendency for the profit and loss account to overstate profit, relative to a more true assessment of the amount of wealth created. Secondly there is a tendency for balance sheet figures to understate the amount of wealth which is tied up in the firm. This is a particular problem when we are dealing with ratios which are calculated using one figure from the profit and loss account and one from the balance sheet. A good example of this is the return on net assets ratio. For example would it be wise to conclude that Jackson plc's return on net assets of 19.1 per cent for 1994 represents a better return than bank deposit account interest of, say 15 per cent, even ignoring the disparity in the level of risk?

Another problem with using balance sheet figures is that they represent the position at a single, defined, point in time. This point in time, the firm's accounting year end, may not be typical of the firm throughout the rest of the year. This may be true by design. For example the management of a particular firm may choose a particular year end date because stocks tend to be unusually low at that time. It is quite common for firms to need to carry out a physical count of the stock at the accounting year end. Obviously this task will be made easier if stock levels are low. This problem with balance sheet figures may lead to inappropriate interpretation of ratios where balance sheet figures are involved.

Where a particular ratio relates a balance sheet figure to one from the profit and loss account there is a further problem. The balance sheet represents the position at a particular point in time, but the profit and loss account summarises a series of transactions over the period. If the balance sheet figure is not typical of the period, this can lead to distorted ratios. For example, we calculated the return on net assets for Jackson plc by relating the profit before interest and tax to net assets at the *end* of the year. Yet it is clear that at other times in the year the net assets were not the same as the year-end figure (see the 1993 balance sheet, in the Appendix to this chapter). In other words the net assets which were invested to generate the £135 000 were probably less than £709 000 for almost all the year.

An obvious solution to this problem is to average the opening and closing net assets figures and use this in the calculation of the ratio. This would give a ratio for 1994 of 19.9 per cent (i.e. [135/((651 + 709) / 2) × 100 per cent]), compared with the original figure calculated of 19.1 per cent. As we have already seen, it is not necessarily the case that the balance sheet figures are representative of the rest of the year. Here simply averaging the start-of-year and end-of-year figures may not do much to remove the distortion. This will not pose a problem to those who have access to the underlying figures because they can deduce a more representative average figure. Outsiders can do no more than average the figures which are available.

Though a combination of the law and the rules laid down by the accounting profession seek to promote the extent to which accounts are prepared on a consistent basis, from one firm to another, there are still areas where one firm may legitimately deal with the same transaction or event differently from another. This creates yet another problem for the analyst when trying to use accounting information to make inter-firm comparisons.

Other limitations of accounting ratios

Accounting ratios are derived by dividing one figure by another. As with all such indicators, information is lost. A significant reason for using ratios is to enable comparison to be made between factors which are not of the same scale. Sometimes, however, it is important to be aware of scale. For example the size of a firm could double from one year to the next, yet ratios alone would not reveal this fact.

It can be instructive just to look at the accounting statements, trying to take a critical and enquiring approach. For example if we look back at Jackson plc's balance sheet for 1994, several points are worthy of note, none of which would be picked up from using the standard accounting ratios.

The first of these relates to fixed assets, specifically to plant and machinery. The depreciation provision, i.e. that part of the cost which has already been treated as an expense, is almost as large as the cost figure (£226 000 compared with £253 000). This implies that the plant is coming close to the end of the life which was predicted for it by the firm. This, in turn, has several implications:

- The firm is operating with old plant. This may mean it is not using the most sophisticated methods available to it. This may or may not be an important factor. Nevertheless it is something which someone trying to make an assessment of the firm might find useful to know in building up the picture.
- Perhaps, more significantly, it seems likely that there will be a need to replace various items of plant in the fairly near future. This will probably lead to a major outflow of cash. This raises the question of where the cash will come from. Has the firm got the levels of cash required or will it need to borrow or to raise new share capital?
- In a period of inflation old fixed assets implies a low annual depreciation expense charged in the profit and loss account. Thus profits may be overstated relative to that which would result if newer plant were to be used.

The next point relates to the reserves. It would be perfectly legal for the shareholders to be paid a dividend of £209 000 as at 31 December 1994, perhaps selling some of the non-cash assets to raise the necessary funds. This massive outflow of assets could have disastrous effects on the firm in terms of its ability to continue to trade. Though this large dividend is not a likely outcome, the possibility is there and it should be recognised.

A third point is that, according to the balance sheet, there is a reasonable amount of scope for further secured borrowing. The loan stock is probably secured on the freehold land. The freehold land is probably understated on the balance sheet in terms of its market value. This could mean that the firm would be able to double the amount of its secured borrowings. Since it is very much easier for a firm to borrow where it can offer the security of an asset like land, this might be a significant point. Perhaps the firm does not want to raise further loan capital. Perhaps there are separate reasons why the firm would find it difficult to borrow. On the other hand, the point about unused security might be an important one.

Similar points could be identified by a careful scrutiny of the financial statements, without even bothering to calculate any ratios.

USING ACCOUNTING RATIOS TO PREDICT FINANCIAL FAILURE

One objective of ratio analysis is to try to make a judgement about a particular firm's ability to survive and to prosper. Analysts have shown much interest in ratios which may be able to indicate firms which are in danger of getting into financial difficulties. The reason for this is that several groups who have relationships with the firm stand to suffer significantly should the firm collapse. Creditors may find that they will not receive the money they are owed, employees will probably lose their jobs, suppliers will probably lose a customer, shareholders will probably lose some or all of their investment. If these parties were able to identify 'at risk' firms, they could take steps to try to put the firm back on a sounder footing, or they could take damage limitation actions like getting their money repaid quickly, changing their jobs, finding new customers or selling their shares.

Originally interest focused on identifying individual ratios which might represent good indicators of likely financial collapse. Researchers, therefore, sought to be able to make statements that if the value for a particular ratio (like the acid test ratio) fell below a particular threshold figure, the firm was then significantly at risk. They sought to do this by identifying particular ratios which might be good discriminators between potential failures and survivors.

The researchers then found a group of firms which had actually collapsed. They matched this with a second group of firms, one of which was as like one of the collapsed group as possible in size, industry, etc. This provided them with two groups of firms, as far as possible identical, except that all the members of one group had collapsed and none of the second group had. Using past data on all the firms, attempts were made to examine whether the particular ratios selected were significantly different between the two groups. Where this proved to be the case for a specific ratio, it was possible to say that a figure of above a particular figure implied that the firm was safe, whereas a figure below this benchmark implied that it was at risk.

Although researchers achieved some success at identifying ratios which were reasonably good discriminators, thoughts turned to the possibility that combining several quite good discriminator ratios might produce a Z-score (so called) which would be a very good discriminator. The most notable UK researcher in this field, Taffler, derived the following model:

$$Z = C_0 + C_1 \frac{\text{Profit before tax}}{\text{Current liabilities}} + C_2 \frac{\text{Current assets}}{\text{Total liabilities}} + C_3 \frac{\text{Current liabilities}}{\text{Total assets}} + C_4 \frac{\text{Liquid current assets}}{\text{Daily cash operating expenses}}$$

where C_0 to C_4 are constants.

According to Taffler (1991) a positive Z-score means that the firm is sound, at least in the medium term. A negative Z-score implies a relatively high risk of failure. As might be expected, the higher or lower the Z-score, the more powerful is the indication of the potential survival or failure of the firm.

The recommended reading at the end of this chapter provides some discussion on the benefits and problems of using Z-scores.

SUMMARY

Decision makers, including financial decision makers, make much use of accounting statements. Decision makers outside the firm use the annual published accounts of the firm in which they have an interest. People who work for the firm are likely to have access to other, perhaps more detailed or more frequently produced, accounting information. Accounting is based on a number of rules. It is important that anyone attempting to use accounting information is familiar with those rules.

Though the basic accounting statements, the balance sheet, the profit and loss account and the cash flow statement, are useful to the decision maker, greater insights can be gained if accounting ratios are calculated. These enable events to be summarised in key indicators.

Accounting ratios are usually classified as:

- profitability ratios
- activity ratios
- liquidity ratios
- capital gearing ratios
- investors' ratios.

The ratios which fall into each of these classes look at things from a particular perspective or are concerned with a particular facet of the firm's performance and position.

The imperfections of accounting itself, added to the particular problems of using any ratios, mean that caution must be exercised in drawing conclusions from accounting ratios. Despite this, accounting ratios are widely used and valuable tools of financial analysis.

FURTHER READING

Most books on accounting provide an introduction to accounting and to accounting ratios. Many business finance books include a chapter on accounting ratios. Parker (1988) provides a readable and informative introduction to accounting ratios. Weston and Copeland (1988) includes a chapter on accounting ratios. Taffler (1991) describes the author's research into the use of 'Z-scores' in the identification of firms which are potential financial failures.

(a) Obtain the published accounts of your organisation for the past two or three years and carry out a ratio analysis.

(b) Does your organisation use any accounting ratios in its day-to-day management?

1 The following financial statements for Blackstone plc are a slightly simplified set of published accounts. Blackstone plc is an engineering firm which developed a new range of products in 19X9; these now account for 60 per cent of turnover.

Blackstone plc

Profit and Loss account for the year ended 31 March

	19X1	19X0
	£000	£000
Turnover	11 205	7 003
Cost of sales	(5 809)	(3 748)
Gross profit	5 396	3 255
Operating expenses	(3 087)	(2 205)
Operating profit	2 309	1 050
Interest payable	(456)	(216)
Profit before taxation	1 853	834
Taxation	(390)	(210)
Profit after taxation	1 463	624
Dividends	(400)	(300)
Retained profit for the year	1 063	324
Retained profit brought forward	685	361
Retained profit carried forward	1 748	685

Balance Sheet as at 31 March

	19X1		19X0	
	£000	£000	£000	£000
Fixed assets				
Intangible assets	700		–	
Tangible assets	7535		4300	
		8235		4300
Current assets				
Stocks	2410		1209	
Trade debtors	1372		807	
Other debtors	201		134	
Cash	4		28	
	3987		2178	

Balance Sheet as at 31 March

Creditors: Amounts falling due within one year				
Trade creditors	1306		607	
Other creditors	201		124	
Taxation	390		210	
Dividends	400		300	
Overdraft	1625		–	
	3922		1241	
Net current assets		65		937
Creditors: Amounts falling due after more than one year				
Bank loan (repayable 19X5)		(3800)		(1800)
		4500		3437
Share capital		1800		1800
Capital reserve		952		952
Retained profits		1748		685
		4500		3437

Calculate the following financial statistics for Blackstone plc, using year-end figures where possible, for *both* 19X0 and 19X1.
(a) Return on capital employed.
(b) Return on shareholders' funds.
(c) Gross profit margin.
(d) Net profit margin.
(e) Gearing ratio.
(f) Current ratio.
(g) Liquid ratio.
(h) Days debtors.
(i) Stock turnover.

Comment on the performance of Blackstone plc, using the published financial statements and the information above, from the viewpoint of:
(a) an individual who owns 10 per cent of the issued share capital;
(b) the bank which has granted Blackstone plc its overdraft facility.

(Certified Diploma – adapted)

2 Quardis Ltd is an importer of high-quality laser printers which can be used with a range of microcomputers. The balance sheet of Quardis Ltd as at 31 May 19X0 is as follows:

	£000	£000	£000
Fixed assets			
Freehold premises at cost		460	
Less: Accumulated depreciation		30	430
Fixtures and fittings at cost		35	
Less: Accumulated depreciation		10	25
			455
Current assets			
Stock		24	
Debtors		34	
Cash at bank		2	
		60	
Creditors: Amounts falling due within one year			
Trade creditors	22		
Taxation	14		
Dividends	10	46	14
			469
Creditors: Amounts falling due beyond one year			
Loan – Highland Bank			125
			344
Capital and reserves			
£1 ordinary shares			200
Retained profit			144
			344

The following forecast information is available for the year ended 31 May 19X1.

(i) Sales are expected to be £280 000 for the year. 60 per cent of sales are on credit and it is expected that, at the year end, three months' credit sales will be outstanding. Sales revenues accrue evenly over the year.

(ii) Purchases of stock during the year will be £186 000 and will accrue evenly over the year. All purchases are on credit and at the year end it is expected that two months' purchases will remain unpaid.

(iii) Fixtures and fittings costing £25 000 will be purchased and paid for during the year. Depreciation is charged at 10 per cent on the cost of fixtures and fittings held at the year end.

(iv) Depreciation is charged on freehold premises at 2 per cent on cost.

(v) On 1 June 19X0 £ 30 000 of the loan from the Highland Bank is to be repaid. Interest on this loan is at the rate of 13 per cent per annum and all interest accrued to 31 May 19X1 will be paid on that day.

(vi) Stock-in-trade at the year end is expected to be 25 per cent higher than at the beginning of the year.

(vii) Wages for the year will be £34 000. At the year end it is estimated that £4000 of this total will remain unpaid.

(viii) Other overhead expenses for the year (excluding those mentioned above) are expected to be £21 000. At the year end it is expected that £3000 of this total will still be unpaid.

(ix) A dividend of 5p per share is expected to be announced at the year end. The dividend outstanding at the beginning of the year will be paid during the year.

(x) Corporation tax is payable at the rate of 35 per cent. Corporation tax outstanding at the beginning of the year will be paid during the year.

All workings should be shown to the nearest £000.

Required:

(a) Prepare a forecast profit and loss account for the year ended 31 May 19X1.

(b) Prepare a forecast balance sheet as at 31 May 19X1.

(c) Comment on the significant features revealed by these statements.

(Certified Diploma)

3 The following information has been extracted from the published accounts of two companies during 19X2.

	Company	
	Gamma	Delta
(A) Profit before Interest and Tax as % Sales Turnover	16.0	5.9
(B) Profit before Interest and Tax as % Capital Employed	11.6	14.5
(C) Equity as % Capital Employed	54.0	32.3
(D) Profit after Tax as % Equity	5.0	10.8
(E) Earnings per £1 ordinary share (pence)	60.0	12.5

You are required to:

(a) Calculate the following for Company Gamma given that the Capital Employed of Company Gamma used as the basis for the statistics given above was £18 000 000:

(i) profit before interest and tax,

(ii) sales turnover,

(iii) profit after interest and tax,

(iv) total shareholders' funds,

(v) number of issued ordinary shares, and

(vi) retained profits and other reserves.

(b) Explain and examine the relationship between ratios (A) and (B) above.

(c) Explain and examine the relationship between ratios (B) and (D) above.

(d) Does the higher Earnings per Share of Company Gamma indicate that it is 4.8 times more efficient than Company Delta? Give your reasons.

(e) Consider if the relationship shown in ratio (B) above is a good indicator of effective company management.

QUESTIONS FOR CLASS USE

1 Conday and Co. Ltd have been in operation for three years and produce antique reproduction furniture for the export market. The most recent set of accounts for the company are set out below:

Balance Sheet as at 30 November 19X0

	£000	£000	£000
Fixed assets			
Freehold land and buildings at cost			228
Plant and machinery at cost		942	
Less: Accumulated depreciation		180	762
			990
Current assets			
Stocks		600	
Trade debtors		820	
		1420	
Less Creditors: amounts falling due within one year			
Trade creditors	665		
Taxation	95		
Bank overdraft	385	1145	275
			1265
Less Creditors: amounts falling due in more than one year			
12% Debentures (See Note 1)			200
			1065
Capital and reserves			
Ordinary shares of £1 each			700
Retained profits			365
			1065

Profit and Loss account for the year ended 30 November 19X0

	£000	£000
Sales		2600
Less: Cost of sales		1620
Gross profit		980
Less: Selling and distribution expenses		
(See Note 2)	408	
Administration expenses	174	
Finance expenses	78	660
Net profit before taxation		320
Corporation tax		95
Net profit after taxation		225
Proposed dividend		160
Retained profit for the year		65

Notes:
1 The debentures are secured on the freehold land and buildings.
2 Selling and distribution expenses include £170 000 in respect of bad debts.

An investor has been approached by the company to invest £200 000 by purchasing ordinary shares in the company at £6.40 each. The company wishes to use the funds to finance a programme of further expansion.

Required:
(a) Analyse the financial position and performance of the company and comment on any features you consider to be significant.
(b) State, with reasons, whether or not the investor should invest in the company on the terms outlined.

(Certified Diploma)

2 Rose Limited operates a small chain of retail shops which sell high quality teas and coffees. Approximately half of sales are on credit. Abbreviated and unaudited accounts are given below.

Rose Limited

Profit and Loss Accounts for the years ended 31 March

	19X0		19X9	
	£000	*£000*	*£000*	*£000*
Sales		12 080		7800
Cost of sales		6 282		4370
Gross profit		5 798		3430
Labour costs	2658		2106	
Depreciation	625		450	
Other operating costs	1003		92	
		4 286		2648
Net profit before interest		1 512		782
Interest payable		66		–
Net profit before tax		1 446		782
Tax payable		259		158
Net profit after tax		1 187		624
Dividend payable		300		250
Retained profit for year		887		374
Retained profit brought forward		872		498
Retained profit carried forward		1 759		872

Balance Sheets as at 31 March

	19X0		19X9	
	£000	*£000*	*£000*	*£000*
Fixed assets		2728		1536
Current assets:				
Stocks	1583		925	
Debtors	996		488	
Cash	26		312	
	2605		1725	
Creditors: amounts due within one year				
Trade creditors	1118		660	
Other creditors	417		321	
Tax	259		158	
Dividends	300		250	
Overdraft	180		–	
	2274		1389	
Net current assets		331		336
Creditors: amounts due after more than one year				
Secured loan (19X5)		(300)		–
		2759		1872

Balance Sheets as at 31 March

Share capital		
(50p shares, fully paid)	750	750
Share premium	250	250
Retained profit	1759	872
	2759	1872

Calculate the following financial statistics for Rose Limited for both 19X0 and 19X9, using end of year figures where possible.
(i)   Return on capital employed.
(ii)   Return on shareholders' funds.
(iii) Dividend per share.
(iv) Earnings per share.
(v)   Net profit margin.
(vi) Gross profit margin.
(vii) Current ratio.
(viii)Liquid ratio.
(ix) Days debtors.
(x)   Days creditors.
(xi) Stock turnover.

Comment on the performance of Rose Limited from the viewpoint of:

(a) a shareholder with a 5 per cent holding who believes that Rose Limited will announce a rights issue in the near future;

(b) the bank which has given Rose Limited its current overdraft facility.

(Certified Diploma – adapted)

3 The following financial statements for Papers plc are a slightly simplified set of published accounts. Papers plc was formed to launch a new daily regional newspaper in late 19X7.

Papers plc

Profit and Loss Account for the year ended 30 September 19X9

	Notes	19X9 £000	19X8 £000
Turnover		44 056	27 756
Cost of sales		(35 426)	(27 313)
Gross profit		8 630	443
Operating expenses	1	(8 613)	(9 314)
Operating profit/(loss)		17	(8 871)
Investment income		16	340
Interest payable		(1 596)	(935)
Loss before taxation		(1 563)	(9 466)
Taxation		–	–
Loss for the financial year		(1 563)	(9 466)
Accumulated deficit, brought forward		(12 886)	(3 420)
Accumulated deficit, carried forward		(14 449)	(12 886)

Balance Sheet as at 30 September 19X9

	Notes	19X9 £000	19X8 £000
Fixed assets			
Intangible assets	2	18 700	18 700
Tangible assets		7 608	7 186
		26 308	25 886
Current assets			
Stocks		374	161
Debtors		8 287	5 387
Cash at bank and in hand		4	38
		8 665	5 586
Creditors: Amounts falling due within one year			
Trade creditors		(5 498)	(3 809)
Other creditors and accruals		(2 968)	(2 360)
Bank overdraft		(3 139)	(443)
		(11 605)	(6 612)
Net current liabilities		(2 940)	(1 026)
Total assets less current liabilities		23 368	24 860

Balance Sheet as at 30 September 19X9

		19X9	19X8
Creditors: Amounts falling due			
after more than one year		£000	£000
Bank loans – repayable 19X3		(10 923)	(10 856)
Net assets		12 445	14 004
Capital and reserves			
Called-up share capital	3	131	131
Share premium account	3	8 063	8 059
Revaluation reserve		18 700	18 700
Profit and loss account		(14 449)	(12 886)
Total capital employed		12 445	14 004

Notes to the accounts:
1. *The operating expenses* include the launch costs of a new weekend magazine first published in September 19X9 totalling £1.12m.
2. *The intangible fixed assets* represents the professional valuation of the newspaper title owned by Papers plc on the basis of the amount that is estimated the title could realise if disposed of on its own without any other assets or liabilities.
3. *Called-up share capital.* During 19X9 4000 ordinary shares of 1p were issued at a premium of £4000, in consideration for cash.

Calculate the following financial statistics for Papers plc, using the end of year figures where possible, for 19X9 and 19X8.
(a) Return on capital employed.
(b) Return on shareholders' funds.
(c) Net profit margin.
(d) Gross profit margin.
(e) Gearing ratio.
(f) Current ratio.
(g) Liquid ratio.
(h) Days debtors.
(i) Days creditors.

Comment on the performance of Papers plc, using the published financial statements from the viewpoint of:

(a) a bank which has made a substantial medium-term loan to Papers;
(b) a financial institution which owns 2 per cent of the issued share capital of Papers.

(Certified Diploma)

APPENDIX

Jackson plc

Profit and Loss account for the year ended 31 December 19X3

	£000	£000	£000
Sales			701
Cost of sales (including depreciation £22 000 and raw materials stock usage £190 000. Raw material purchases totalled £187 000)			394
Gross profit			307
Distribution costs			
Salaries and wages	35		
Motor expenses	41		
Depreciation of motor vehicles	16		
Sundry distribution expenses	14	106	
Administrative expenses			
Salaries and wages	53		
Motor expenses	21		
Depreciation of motor vehicles	18		
Sundry administrative expenses	12	104	210
Operating profit for the year			97
Interest payable			33
Profit on ordinary activities before taxation			64
Tax on ordinary activities			18
Profit on ordinary activities after taxation			46
Retained profit brought forward from last year			120
			166
Proposed dividend on ordinary shares			15
Retained profit carried forward to next year			151

(Note that this statement does not strictly follow the layout which is required by law.)

Jackson plc

Balance Sheet as at 31 December 19X3

	£000 cost	£000 depre-ciation	£000
Fixed assets			
Freehold land	550	–	550
Plant and machinery	232	198	34
Motor vehicles	90	21	69
	872	219	653
Current assets			
Stock	41		
Trade debtors	123		
Prepaid expenses	10	174	
Creditors: amounts falling due within one year			
Bank overdraft	86		
Trade creditors	43		
Accrued expenses	14		
Taxation	18		
Dividend proposed	15	176	
Net current liabilities			(2)
Total assets less current liabilities			651
Creditors: amounts falling due after more than one year			
10% secured loan stock			300
			351
Ordinary share capital – 200 000 shares of £1 each			200
Profit and loss account			151
			351

(Note that this statement does not strictly follow the layout which is required by law.)

The market price of the ordinary £1 shares was £3.49 at 31 December 19X3.

PART 2

Investment decisions

Investment decisions are at the very heart of the management of all firms, except the very tiniest. Errors in these decisions can, and do, prove fatal for many firms. Chapter 4 starts with an explanation of the nature and importance of investment decisions. It continues with some fairly detailed explanations of the major investment appraisal methods used in practice. It concludes with some discussion of the extent of the use of the methods in practice. Chapter 5 is concerned with some of the practical aspects of making investment decisions. These include taxation, inflation and the problem of dealing with shortages of investment finance. Chapters 6 and 7 are concerned with various approaches to trying to make investment decisions where, as is always the case in reality, the outcome of an investment is not known with certainty. Chapter 7 is particularly concerned with attempting to assess the likely effect of the risk of a particular investment on the firm's owners.

CHAPTER 4

Investment appraisal methods

OBJECTIVES

In this chapter we shall deal with the following:

● the importance of the investment decision
● the derivation of the concept of net present value
● an explanation of the meaning of net present value
● a consideration of the other approaches used to assess investment projects
● a consideration of some recent research bearing on the investment appraisal techniques used by firms in the UK and USA

INTRODUCTION

Firms operate by raising finance from various sources which is then invested in assets, usually real assets. Investment involves outflows (payments) of cash causing inflows of cash. It is in the nature of things that cash flows (out and in) do not all occur at the same time, i.e. there is some time lag, perhaps a considerable one, between them. The typical investment project opportunity with which a firm may be faced involves a relatively large outflow of cash initially, giving rise to a subsequent stream of cash inflows.

The firm's balance sheet gives, at any particular point in time and subject to the limitations of such accounting statements, the types of investment which it still has running. Balance sheets group assets by type (fixed assets, current assets, etc.) rather than by investment project. Thus it is not possible from the standard balance sheet to discern which part of the fixed and current assets relate to any particular project. Nonetheless, a glance at a firm's balance sheet would give us some idea of the scale of investment and to some extent an idea of its nature.

Selecting which investment opportunities to pursue and which to avoid is a vital matter to firms because:

(a) individual projects frequently involve relatively large commitments of finance; and
(b) they involve this commitment for long, often very long, periods of time.

Clearly the investment decision is central to the firm. Costly and far-reaching mistakes can and probably will be made unless firms take great care in making their investment decisions. Bad decisions usually cause major financial loss and any particular firm can only make a limited number of misjudgements before collapse occurs.

In this chapter we shall consider how such decisions should best be made, after which we shall go on to consider how they appear to be made in practice.

Note that for the time being we shall continue to assume that all cash flows can be predicted with certainty and that the borrowing and lending rates of interest are equal to one another and equal between all individuals and firms.

NET PRESENT VALUE

A basis for decision making

Given the crucial importance of firms' investment decisions, managers need a logical and practical assessment procedure by which to appraise the investment opportunities which come to their notice. This procedure must promote the shareholders' wealth maximisation objective, though in the final decision other objectives may well be taken into account.

We discovered in Chapter 2 that if we assume that interest rates are equal, both as between borrowing and lending and as between firms and individuals, an investment project undertaken by the firm which will increase the spending power of all shareholders, or of any particular one of them, at one point in time, will also increase it at any other point in time. (We may remember that in the example in Chapter 2, all three of our shareholders were advantaged by acceptance of Project X, despite having different attitudes to the timing of their spending.)

It seems therefore that it does not matter whether our assessment procedure focuses on the effect on present wealth or on wealth in a year's time, or indeed at any other time. If undertaking a particular project will increase present wealth, it will also increase future wealth; that project which will most increase present wealth will most increase future wealth. Thus, both for accept/reject decisions and for ranking projects in order of desirability, it does not matter in respect of which point in time the effect on wealth is assessed, provided that consistency is maintained.

Since we are always at 'the present' when making the decision, to consider a project's effect on present wealth is probably most logical. This tends to be the approach taken in practice.

The time value of money

Suppose that a firm is offered an opportunity which involves investing £10m which will give rise to a cash receipt of £12m. Should the firm make the investment? Obviously if the cash expenditure and the cash receipt are to occur at the same time (most unlikely in real life) this represents a good investment since it will work towards the firm's assumed objective of maximising its value. It will increase the value of the firm by £2m.

Now suppose that the opportunity means investing £10m now which will give rise to a £12m cash inflow after one year. Here the decision is not so straightforward because we cannot directly compare £1 now with £1 after a year (or any other period of time). Each £1 of present expenditure is not equal in value to each £1 receipt in the future. This is for three reasons:

(a) *Interest forgone*. If the £10m is tied up in the investment for a year, the firm cannot invest it elsewhere so there is an interest *opportunity cost*.

(b) *Inflation*. Due to the loss of purchasing power of money if there is inflation in the economy (which has been the case in each post-war year in the UK), £1 will not buy as much in the way of goods and services next year as it would this year.

(c) *Risk*. The £1 paid out today is certain but the £1 anticipated receipt next year is not certain. However confident we may be of the receipt, we can never be sure of it. In many business contexts the degree of uncertainty about future receipts is profound.

At present we shall concentrate on only the first of these three, namely interest forgone, leaving issues involving inflation and risk to be dealt with in later chapters. At this point it must be clearly emphasised that even if there were no inflation and that the investment were regarded as risk free, the point would remain that £1 today is not equivalent to £1 tomorrow simply because of the opportunity cost of interest forgone.

Given that money has a 'time value' (£1 today is not equivalent to £1 after some period of time), how are we to make a comparison between the £10m now and the £12m in a year's time, and so reach a decision?

Net present value

One approach which we could take would be to add the interest forgone to the £10m, i.e. to assess the amount to which the £10m would have grown after one year, with interest, and then to compare it with the £12m. Suppose that the current rate of interest is 10 per cent, then the value of the £10m after one year would be £11m (£1m interest). In other words, if the firm were to pursue the alternative opportunity of putting the money into an interest-yielding bank deposit account, it would have £11m by the end of the year, whereas the firm will get £12m if it makes the investment under consideration. This is a totally logical and correct approach to take and the conclusion that the investment should be made because it will lead to a *net future value* of £1m (i.e. £12m – £11m) is a correct one (i.e. the firm will be £1m better off at the end of the year than had it pursued the alternative of putting the money in a bank deposit account for the year).

Another approach is to ask ourselves, if it is possible to borrow money at 10 per cent, how much could be borrowed immediately against the £12m such that the £12m would exactly repay the borrowing plus interest thereon. Put another way, if the firm could compare the £10m outflow with the present equivalent of £12m, an alternative basis for the decision could be achieved. The present value of the £12m is not necessarily a theoretical notion since it would be possible for the firm to borrow and have the present value of £12m immediately if it wanted to do so. Indeed, it could even do so to raise the finance with which to make the £10m investment (assuming that the present value of the £12m is greater than £10m).

The next question is what is the present value of £12m receivable after one year with an interest rate of 10 per cent p.a.?

If we let the amount which could be borrowed (the present value of £12m in a year's time) be B, then,

$$£12\dot{m} = B + \left(B \times \frac{10}{100} \right)$$

(i.e. the borrowing plus the interest thereon for one year)

$$\text{i.e. } £12m = B\left(1 + \frac{10}{100} \right) = B \times 1.10$$

$$B = £12m/1.10$$
$$= £10.9m$$

If we now compare the present value of the future receipt with the initial investment, we have an investment whose *net present value* (NPV) is £0.9m (i.e. £10.9m – £10m). Since this is positive, the investment should be undertaken assuming that there is not a mutually exclusive alternative with a higher positive NPV.

What the £0.9m NPV tells us is that the firm can invest £10m immediately to gain a benefit whose present value is £10.9m, i.e. a £0.9m increase in the value of the firm.

More generally we can say that the NPV of an investment opportunity lasting for one year is

$$\text{NPV} = C_0 + \frac{C_1}{1+i}$$

where

C_0 is the cash flow immediately (time 0) (usually negative, i.e. an outflow of cash);
C_1 is the cash flow after one year;
i is the interest rate.

In practice we tend to use the NPV approach to investment decision making (i.e. we *discount* future cash flows) rather than the net future value approach (*compounding* present cash flows), though in essence neither is superior to the other.

The reasons for favouring NPV are:

(a) When comparing investment opportunities (choosing between one and the other), if net future value is to be used a decision must be made on when in the future the value should be assessed (i.e. how many years compounding). If the opportunities are of unequal length (e.g. one lasts three years, the other five years) this can cause difficulties.
(b) If the opportunity is to be assessed by looking at its effect on the value of the firm it seems more logical to look at the present effect rather than the future effect.

Investment opportunities lasting for more than one year

In reality, few investment opportunities last for only one year. Suppose that an investment opportunity involves an immediate cash outflow C_0 which will give rise to inflows C_1 and C_2 after one and two years respectively. We already know that the present value of C_1 (effect on the value of the firm) is $C_1/(1 + i)$. By the same logic that we used to derive this, we could borrow an amount, say A, which would exactly be repaid with interest compounded annually out of C_2. Then

$$C_2 = A + Ai + (A + Ai)i$$

(i.e. the original borrowing plus interest on that amount for the first year plus interest on these two during the second year).

This expression expands to:

$$C_2 = A + Ai + Ai + Ai^2$$

Taking A outside brackets,

$$C_2 = A(1 + 2i + i^2)$$
$$C_2 = A(1 + i)^2$$
$$A = C_2/(1 + i)^2$$

Following this logic, it can be shown that the present value of any amount of cash receivable after n years (C_n) would be $C_n/(1 + i)^n$.

Thus the NPV of any investment opportunity is given by:

$$\text{NPV} = \sum_{n=0}^{t} C_n/(1 + i)^n$$

where t is the life of the opportunity in years, i.e. the NPV of an opportunity is the sum, taking account of plus and minus signs, of each of the annual cash flows discounted according to how far into the future each one will occur.

EXAMPLE

Seagull plc has identified that it could make operating cost savings in production by buying an automatic press. There are two suitable such presses on the market, the Zenith and the Super. The relevant data relating to each of these are as follows:

	Zenith £	Super £
Cost (payable immediately)	£20 000	£25 000
Annual savings:		
Year 1	4 000	8 000
2	6 000	6 000
3	6 000	5 000
4	7 000	6 000
5	6 000	8 000

The annual savings are, in effect, opportunity cash inflows in that they represent savings from the cash outflows which would occur if the investment were not undertaken.

Which, if either, of these machines should be bought if the borrowing/lending cost is 12 per cent p.a.?

SOLUTION The NPV of each machine is as follows:

		Zenith £	Super £
Present value of cash flows:			
Year	0	(20 000)	(25 000)
	1	$\dfrac{4000}{1+0.12} = 3\ 572$	$\dfrac{8000}{1+0.12} = 7\ 143$
	2	$\dfrac{6000}{(1+0.12)^2} = 4\ 783$	$\dfrac{6000}{(1+0.12)^2} = 4\ 783$
	3	$\dfrac{6000}{(1+0.12)^3} = 4\ 271$	$\dfrac{5000}{(1+0.12)^3} = 3\ 559$
	4	$\dfrac{7000}{(1+0.12)^4} = 4\ 449$	$\dfrac{6000}{(1+0.12)^4} = 3\ 813$
	5	$\dfrac{6000}{(1+0.12)^5} = 3\ 404$	$\dfrac{8000}{(1+0.12)^5} = 4\ 539$
		£479	£(1 163)

(This process of converting future cash flows to their present value is known as *discounting*.)

The firm should therefore buy the Zenith as this would have a positive effect on its wealth, whereas the Super would have a negative effect. The firm would not be prepared to buy the Super even if it were the only such machine on the market, as to do so would be to the firm's detriment. The value of the firm would, theoretically, fall as a result of buying the Super. Only if it were possible to negotiate a price lower than £23 837 (i.e. the sum of the discounted savings) would the value of the annual savings justify the cost of that machine, given the financing cost. Similarly up to £20 479 could be paid for a Zenith and it would continue to be a profitable investment.

It is important to recognise that the size of the initial investment is not of any direct relevance to the decision (except to the extent that it is used in the calculation of the NPV); only the NPV is important. Thus if the Super had a positive NPV of £480 it would be selected in preference to the Zenith. The only occasion where we would need to consider the size of the NPV in relation to the amount of investment is when there is some shortage of investment finance and projects need to compete for it. This is an aspect which we shall consider in Chapter 5.

The use of tables and annuity factors

Tables are readily available which will give the discount factor $1/(1 + i)^n$ for a range of values of i and n. Such a table appears in Appendix 1 to this book. Note that it is not necessary to use the table for discounting; the calculation can easily be done from first principles.

Sometimes an investment involves a series of identical annual cash flows. In these circumstances there is a short cut to the present value of those cash flows.

EXAMPLE

A firm is faced with an investment opportunity which involves an initial investment of £35 000 which is expected to generate annual inflows of £10 000 at the end of each of the next five years. What is the NPV of this opportunity?

SOLUTION

If we discounted the cash inflows using the table of discount factors in Appendix 1, the calculation would be as follows:

(10 000 x 0.909) + (10 000 x 0.826) + (10 000 x 0.751) + (10 000 x 0.683) + (10 000 x 0.621)

This could be rewritten as:

10 000 (0.909 + 0.826 + 0.751 + 0.683 + 0.621)

where the figures in brackets are the discount factors at 10 per cent for a series of annual cash flows of £1 for five years. In cases like this the calculation is made easier for us in that tables giving the sum of discount factors, for specified periods of years and discount rates, is readily available. There is one shown in Appendix 2 to this book. Such tables are usually known as *annuity* tables. Even if such a table is not available, you can easily deduce the appropriate annuity factor. It is:

$$\sum_{n=1}^{t} \frac{1}{(1+i)^n}$$

If we look up the annuity factor for five years and 10 per cent, we find that the factor is 3.791. (This only differs from the sum of the five discount factors through rounding.) Thus the NPV of the investment opportunity is:

$$- £35\ 000 + (£10\ 000 \times 3.791) = + £2910$$

It is probably fair to say that situations where there is a steady stream of cash flows are, in real life, relatively rare.

How a positive NPV leads to an increase in shareholder wealth

It has been said, quite reasonably, that the essence of good investment is to buy assets for less than they are worth. Clearly, doing this will enhance the value of the firm. When assessing an investment opportunity like the Zenith, it comes down to the question of how much the estimated future benefits of owning the Zenith are worth to Seagull plc. The future benefits obviously are the potential operating cost savings (£4000 in year 1, £6000 in year 2, etc.).

In order to know whether the value of these future benefits exceeds the cost of the asset (£20 000), it is necessary to place some value on them. The only logical way to value them is to discount each one according to how far into the future the benefit will occur, and to sum the discounted values. Thus NPV is an entirely logical approach to investment decision making, assuming that enhancing the value of the shareholders' wealth is the objective being pursued.

Discounting – a slightly different view

Staying with the example, a superficial assessment of the Zenith might be that it should be bought because it cost £20 000 but would yield total savings of £29 000 (the sum of the annual savings), i.e. a benefit of £9000. A second look reveals however that this cannot be a correct assessment as no rational investor regards all of the £s in the question as equivalent to one another. We should all prefer £1 today to £1 next year and we should prefer it still more to £1 in five years' time, even if we assume no erosion of value through inflation. This is because if we have the £1 today we could, if we wished, lend it so that after a year we should have not only the £1 but the interest on it as well.

Simply adding the annual savings and comparing the total with the initial outlay would be illogical. It would be like saying that a certain item is more expensive to buy in France than in the UK because it costs 50 in France and only 5 in the UK, without mentioning that the 50 is francs whereas the 5 is pounds (£s). To make a sensible price comparison we should need to convert the francs to pounds (£s) or vice versa.

Similarly, it is necessary to undertake a conversion exercise to make the various cash flows associated with the Zenith comparable. In fact we usually convert the future cash flows to their present value and then make the comparison. The conversion exercise is, of course, achieved by discounting, by multiplying each of the cash flows by $1/(1 + i)^n$. NPV can thus be viewed as a *time adjusted* measure of financial benefit.

Conclusions on NPV

We have seen that NPV is a totally logical way of assessing investment opportunities. It is logical and potentially useful, because it possesses the following attributes.

- It is directly related to the objective of maximisation of shareholders' wealth (value of the firm).
- It takes full account of the timing of the investment outlay and of the benefits, i.e. the time value of money is properly reflected. Put another way, we can say that NPV properly takes the cost of financing the investment into account.
- All relevant, measurable financial information concerning the decision is taken into account.
- It is practical and easy to use (once the anticipated cash flows have been identified) and it gives clear and unambiguous signals to the decision maker. It should be emphasised that identifying future cash flows is usually very difficult to do in reality.

INTERNAL RATE OF RETURN

This approach seeks to identify the rate of return that an investment project yields on the basis of the amount of the original investment remaining outstanding during any period, compounding interest annually. Identifying this internal rate of return (IRR), at least by hand, can be laborious.

EXAMPLE

What is the IRR of a project where an initial investment of £120 is followed a year later by a cash inflow of £138 with no further inflows?

SOLUTION

Obviously it is:

$$\frac{138 - 120}{120}(\times100) = 15\%$$

What though if the project were £120 initial outlay, followed by inflows of £69 at the end of each of the following two years?

Despite the total inflows still being £138, the IRR is not 15 per cent because it now runs over two years. Nor is it 7.5 per cent (i.e. 15 divided by 2) because much of the £120 is repaid in year 1 and so is not outstanding for both years. In fact the first £69 represents a payment of the *interest* on the investment during the first year plus a repayment of part of the *capital*. By the same token the second £69 represents interest on the remaining capital outstanding after the end of year 1, plus a second instalment of capital such that this second instalment will exactly repay the £120 initial outlay.

A moment's reflection should lead us to conclude that the IRR is closely related to the NPV discount rate. In fact the IRR of a project is the discount rate which if applied to the project yields a zero NPV. For this example it is the solution for i to the following expression:

$$-120 + \frac{69}{(1+i)} + \frac{69}{(1+i)^2} = 0$$

which could be solved using the standard solution to a quadratic equation, not a difficult matter. (The answer incidentally is $i = 0.099$, or 9.9 per cent.)

When we look at, say, the Zenith from our earlier example the equation from which we must solve for i is:

$$-20\,000 + \frac{4000}{(1+i)} + \frac{6000}{(1+i)^2} + \frac{6000}{(1+i)^3} + \frac{7000}{(1+i)^4} + \frac{6000}{(1+i)^5} = 0$$

Solving for *i* here is not so easy and in fact some iterative (trial and error) approach becomes the only practical one. One such method (involving differential calculus), *Newton's approximation*, could be used. In practice however, we usually solve for *i* by trying various values of *i* until we find one which satisfies or almost satisfies the equation. On page 74, we calculated that the Zenith has an NPV of +£479 when discounted at 12 per cent. This tells us that it must have an IRR of above 12 per cent, because the higher the discount rate, the lower the present value of each cash flow. How much above 12 per cent lies the Zenith's IRR we do not know, so some higher discount rate needs to be tried, say 14 per cent.

Referring to the 14 per cent column of the NPV table in Appendix 1 we can deduce the following:

Time	Cash flow £	Discount factor	Present value £
Year 0	(20 000)	1 000	(20 000)
1	4 000	0 877	3 508
2	6 000	0 769	4 614
3	6 000	0 675	4 050
4	7 000	0 592	4 144
5	6 000	0 519	3 114
			NPV £(570)

As the NPV when the cash flows are discounted at 14 per cent is negative, we know that the discount rate which gives this project a zero NPV lies below 14 per cent and apparently close to the mid-point between 14 and 12 per cent. We can prove this by discounting at 13 per cent.

Time	Cash flow £	Discount factor	Present value £
Year 0	(20 000)	1 000	(20 000)
1	4 000	0 885	3 540
2	6 000	0 783	4 698
3	6 000	0 693	4 158
4	7 000	0 613	4 291
5	6 000	0 543	3 258
			NPV £(55)

Given the scale of the investment, an NPV of –£55 is not significantly far from zero, so we can conclude that for practical purposes the IRR is 13 per cent.

Where IRR is used to assess projects, the decision rule is that only those with an IRR above a predetermined hurdle rate would be accepted; where projects are competing, the project with the higher IRR is selected.

The IRR approach so closely resembles the NPV method that at first glance it appears that they are completely interchangeable. This might lead us to assume that they will always come to similar conclusions on any particular decision. This is not true, as can be seen by the following comparison of methods.

(a) IRR is *not* directly related to the value of the firm maximisation criterion. If the hurdle rate used in conjunction with IRR is the cost of finance then in most cases the two methods will give identical results. Certainly this will tend to be the case on straightforward accept/reject decisions (i.e. those where the decision is either to invest or not to invest). With competing projects the two methods sometimes give conflicting signals. This can happen where two mutually exclusive projects involve a different scale of investment.

EXAMPLE

Two mutually exclusive projects have the following features.

Time	Cash flows	
	Project A	Project B
	£	£
Year 0	(10 000)	(6 000)
1	6 000	3 650
2	6 000	3 650
NPV @ 10 %	413	334
IRR(approximately)	13%	14%

If the cost of finance to support the project is 10 per cent p.a., which of these two projects should the firm pursue (assuming no shortage of finance)?

SOLUTION

There is obviously a conflict here. Both NPV and IRR are based on discounting cash flows, both have IRRs in excess of 10 per cent, yet there are different signals coming from the NPVs and the IRRs. Figure 4.1 shows a graph of NPV against discount rate for these two projects. Not surprisingly, as the discount rate is increased the NPV falls. The points where the curves cross the horizontal axis are the respective IRRs for each of the two projects.

It is possible to read off, for each project, the NPV for any particular discount rate. For example, at an 8 per cent discount rate the NPV for Project A is about £700 and for Project B about £500. At discount rates up to about 11.3 per cent Project A has the higher NPV. Beyond 11.3 per cent, Project B has the higher NPV.

Going back to the question as to which project should be selected, the correct answer (from a wealth maximisation viewpoint) is Project A. Although Project B would be more attractive if the cost of finance were over 11.3 per cent, the fact of the matter is that in this example it is 10 per cent and, since we are pursuing wealth maximisation, Project A is the one which should be selected. The conflict arises because of an incorrect implicit assumption of the IRR model. The discount rate used with NPV should be the *opportunity* cost of finance. That is, it is the cost of funds raised to support the project or, if funds are available already, it is the rate which they could alternatively earn. According to the basic principles of NPV, referred to earlier in this chapter, this is the borrowing/lending rate. IRR, on the other hand, makes the assumption that the opportunity cost of finance is equal to the IRR, so that funds generated by the project could either be used to repay finance raised at the IRR or

Figure 4.1
Graph of the
NPV against the
discount rate for
two projects
(A and B)

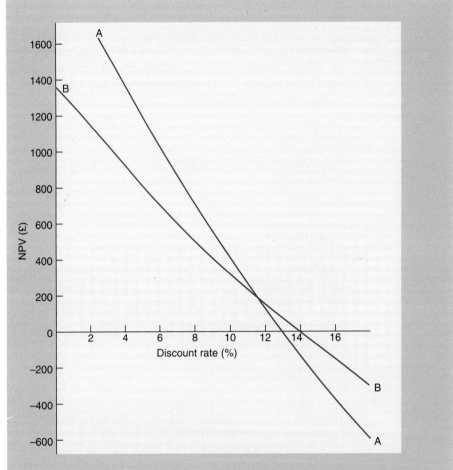

As the discount rate increases, NPV decreases. The discount rate at zero NPV is the IRR. The rate at which NPV decreases differs from one project to another. Whereas project A has the higher NPV where the discount rate is below about 11.3%, Project B has the higher NPV where the discount rate is higher than 11.3%. This leads to a conflict between the signals given by NPV and IRR, where the discount rate is less than 11.3%.

they could be re-invested at that rate. Clearly this is illogical; why should it be the case in our present example that if Project A is undertaken the opportunity cost of finance is 13 per cent, whereas if Project B is pursued it suddenly becomes 14 per cent? The choice by a particular firm of specific projects would not alter the economic environment so that either the cost of finance or the investment alternatives change with the firm's decision.

What IRR fails to recognise in the above example is that if finance is available at 10 per cent the firm's wealth would be more greatly increased by earning 13 per cent on a £10 000 investment than 14 per cent on a £6000 one. IRR fails to recognise this because it does not consider value, it is only concerned with percentage returns.

(b) Like NPV, IRR takes full account both of the cash flows and of the time value of money.

(c) All relevant information about the decision is taken into account by IRR, but it also takes into account the irrelevant, or perhaps more strictly the incorrect, namely the wrong assumption (which we discussed in (a) above) made by IRR.

(d) IRR can be an unwieldy method to use unless, as will usually be the case nowadays, a computer and a suitable software package is available. The trial and error process, which is the only practical way to arrive at IRRs, can be very time-consuming, especially where long projects are involved, if it is done by hand. Computers also try and err, but they can do it so much more quickly than humans that deriving IRRs is not usually a great practical difficulty.

(e) IRR cannot cope with differing required rates of return (hurdle rates). IRR provides an average rate of return for a particular investment project. This rate is normally compared with a required rate of return to make a judgement on the invest-ment. If financing costs are expected to alter over the life of the project, this compar-ison might cause difficulties. The reasons why the required rate may differ from one year to another include the possibility that market interest rates might alter over time. If the IRR for a particular project is consistently above or below all of the different annual required rates of return, there is no difficulty in making the decision. Where, however, the IRR lies above the required rate in some years but below it in others, the decision maker has a virtually insoluble problem. This situation poses no problem for NPV because it is perfectly proper to use different discount rates for each year's cash flows.

(f) The IRR model does not always produce clear and unambiguous results. As we have seen, the IRR for a particular project is the solution to an equation containing only one unknown factor. This unknown factor is, however, raised to as many powers as there are time periods in the project. Any project therefore which goes beyond one time period (in practice one year) will usually have as many IRRs as there are time periods. In practice this is not very often a problem because all but one of the roots (IRRs) will either be unreal (e.g. the square root of a negative number) or negative themselves and, therefore, of no economic significance. Sometimes, though, all of the roots can be unreal so that there is no IRR for some projects. Sometimes a project can have more than one real root (IRR).

These problems of multiple and no IRRs can arise with projects which have *uncon-ventional* cash flows. Projects A and B in the previous example have conventional cash flows in that chronologically a negative cash flow is followed by positive ones, i.e. there is only one change of sign in the cumulative cash flow total (from negative to positive between years 1 and 2 in both projects).

However, now consider the following two projects:

	Cash flows	
	Project C	*Project D*
Time	£	£
Year 0	(10 000)	10 000
1	33 000	(16 000)
2	(24 000)	12 000

Both of these are unconventional in that they each have two changes of sign. Project C changes from negative to positive between years 0 and 1 and from positive to negative between years 1 and 2. Project D does precisely the opposite.

The graphs of NPV against discount rate for each of these unconventional projects are shown in Figs 4.2 and 4.3. Project C has two IRRs (8 per cent and 122 per cent), both of which are equally correct. Which of these should be taken as being the appropriate one for investment decisions? There is no answer to this question and so here IRR gives an ambiguous result. NPV can be used though: with any cost of finance between 8 per cent and 122 per cent the project is favourable; if the firm's cost of finance is below 8 per cent or above 122 per cent the project should be rejected.

**Figure 4.2
Graph of the
NPV against the
discount rate for
Project C**

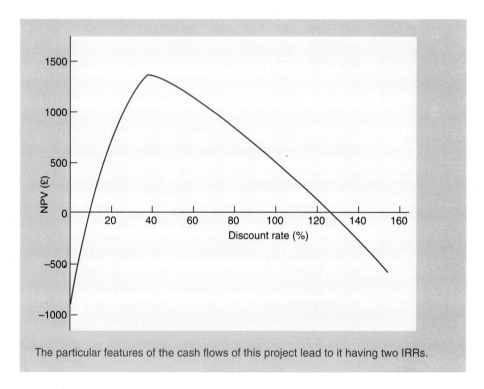

The particular features of the cash flows of this project lead to it having two IRRs.

Trying to find the IRR of Project D by trial and error would be a frustrating experience because there simply is not one, not at least a real one. The graph shows there to be no intercept between the horizontal axis and the curve. Once again IRR is incapable of assessing the project despite the fact that it has a large NPV at all discount rates.

**Figure 4.3
Graph of the
NPV against the
discount rate for
Project D**

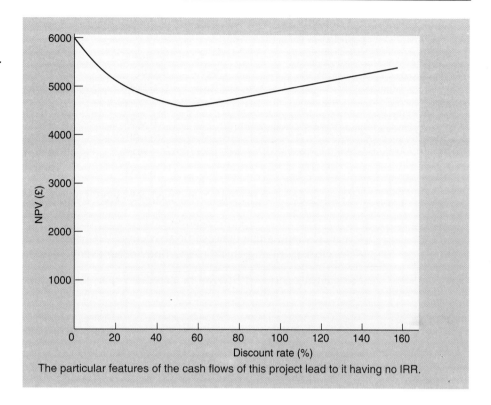

The particular features of the cash flows of this project lead to it having no IRR.

It would be wrong to imagine that projects with unconventional cash flow profiles do not really happen in practice. Probably they form a minority of the total of all projects, but nonetheless they do exist. For example, many projects involving mineral extraction would show something like the cash flow characteristics of Project C. Such projects frequently involve large commitments of cash in order to restore the land to its original contours after the mine or quarry has been fully exploited.

Generally, on IRR, we can conclude that if the opportunity cost of finance is used as the hurdle rate, it will usually give the same signals as the NPV model. Sometimes, though, IRR will give false, ambiguous or incoherent signals, which if heeded could lead to suboptimal decisions being made. It seems that IRR is a mathematical result rather than a reliable decision-making technique. Usually, by coincidence, it will give the right signal but not always. There are means of modifying IRR to overcome some of these problems, but is there any point in our doing so? NPV always gives logical and clear signals and so we might as well use it as the primary assessment method all the time.

PAYBACK PERIOD

This technique asks the simple question, how long will it take for the investment to pay for itself out of the cash inflows which it is expected to generate?

Continuing to assess the investment opportunity in the example from page 73, the cash flows for which were:

	Zenith £	Super £
Year 0	(20 000)	(25 000)
1	4 000	8 000
2	6 000	6 000
3	6 000	5 000
4	7 000	6 000
5	6 000	8 000

we should find that the anticipated paybacks would be:

Zenith	Super
4 years (assuming that the cash flows occur at year ends), or 3⅔ years (assuming that the cash flows occur evenly over the year)	4 years

The payback period (PBP) for the Zenith is represented in Fig. 4.4.

**Figure 4.4
Payback period for
the Zenith machine**

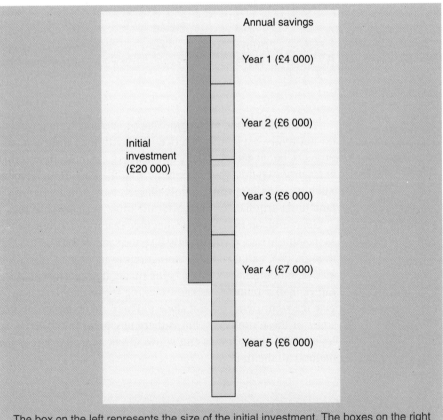

The box on the left represents the size of the initial investment. The boxes on the right represent the size of each year's net cash inflows from the project. We can see that the total of the inflows will equal the initial investment at some point between the beginning and end of the fourth year.

The decision rule for PBP is that projects will only be selected if they pay for themselves within a predetermined period. Competing projects would be assessed by selecting the one with the shorter PBP (provided it was within the predetermined maximum). Thus PBP favours the Zenith over the Super (if cash flows are assumed to occur evenly).

Let us now consider PBP's attributes against those of NPV.

(a) PBP is badly flawed to the extent that it does *not* relate to the wealth maximisation criterion. It promotes the acceptance of shorter-term projects and thus promotes liquidity rather than increased value.

(b) PBP takes account of the timing of the cash flows only in the most perfunctory way. The method divides the life of the project into two portions, the payback period and the period beyond it. PBP does not therefore really treat cash flows differently depending on when they arise. It merely puts any particular cash flow into one of two categories, the relevant category and the irrelevant one. We can see this incompleteness of consideration of the timing of cash flows by reference to the example. With the Super, the payback period would be identical (four years) if there were no savings in each of the first three years but a £25 000 saving in year 4. Clearly these two situations would not be regarded as equally desirable by any rational investor, yet PBP is incapable of distinguishing between them. Some firms use a refinement to the PBP method which to some extent overcomes this weakness. These firms look at the discounted figures when assessing the payback period. Taking the discounted figures for the Zenith from page 74 we can see that the discounted payback period is $4^{2925}/_{3404}$ years (about 4.86 years), assuming that the cash flows occur evenly over the year; otherwise it is 5 years. The Super does not have a discounted payback period, i.e. its discounted inflows never sum to its initial investment.

(c) Not all relevant information is considered by PBP. The method completely ignores anything which occurs beyond the payback period. For example, PBP is incapable of discriminating between the anticipated cash flows for the Super and those of some other project with identical outflows and inflows until year 4 and then annual savings of £20 000 each year for the next ten years.

(d) PBP is very easy to use and it will almost always give very clear results. How those results are interpreted is not so straightforward though. How does the firm decide what is the minimum acceptable payback period? Inevitably this is a pretty arbitrary decision, which means that the PBP method itself will tend to lead to arbitrariness of decision making, unless the project with the shortest PBP is always selected. Even then it would promote quick returns rather than wealth maximisation.

Advocates of PBP argue that it will tend to identify the less risky projects, i.e. those for which the investment is at risk for least time. Even so, PBP takes a very limited view of risk. It only concerns itself with the risk that the project will end prematurely. It ignores such risks as sales being less than anticipated or costs being greater than planned.

We may generally conclude that PBP is not a very good method for selecting investment projects and its use is likely to lead to suboptimal decisions. It can, however, give insights into projects which NPV fails to provide, particularly on the question of liquidity. Thus PBP can be seen as a useful complement to NPV.

ACCOUNTING (UNADJUSTED) RATE OF RETURN

This method compares the average annual profit increase, after taking the cost of making the initial investment into account, with the amount of the initial investment. The outcome is usually expressed as a percentage.

For the two opportunities in the example, the accounting rates of return (ARR) would be:

Zenith

$$\frac{[(4000 + 6000 + 6000 + 7000 + 6000) - 20\,000]}{5} \text{ divided by } 20\,000 = 9.0\%$$

(The £20 000 is deducted from the total annual savings to take account of the cost of the depreciation of the machine over the five years.)

Super

$$\frac{[(8000 + 6000 + 5000 + 6000 + 8000) - 25\,000]}{5} \text{ divided by } 25\,000 = 6.4\%$$

The decision rule would be that projects would only be accepted where they are expected to yield an ARR higher than some predetermined rate. With competing projects the one with the higher ARR (the Zenith in this case) would be selected. It should be noted particularly that ARR deals with accounting flows, *not* with cash flows. This is to say that ARR looks at the effect on future reported profits which a particular project will cause.

Though in the example it has been assumed that cash flows and accounting flows arising from the purchase of either of the presses (Zenith or Super) are the same for the years concerned, this will not always be the case for all projects to be assessed, as is explained shortly.

ARR is also known as *Return on investment* (ROI).

Comparing ARR with NPV

(a) ARR does not relate directly to value maximisation but pursues maximisation of a rate of return measured by accounting profits.

(b) ARR almost completely ignores the timing of the cash flows and hence the financing cost. The above ARRs for the Zenith and the Super would be identical irrespective of when within the five years they fell, provided that they had the same totals. With the Zenith, for example, the alternative cash flows shown below would give the same ARR as the original ones.

	Original	Alternative
	£	£
Year 0	(20 000)	(20 000)
1	4 000	25 000
2	6 000	1 000
3	6 000	1 000
4	7 000	1 000
5	6 000	1 000

Any rational investor would prefer the alternative, yet ARR cannot distinguish between them. The method makes no attempt to adjust the cash flows to reflect their timing.

(c) Typically all relevant information on the cash flows (except their timing) is used in arriving at the ARR of an investment prospect. However, ARR often picks up some irrelevant data as well. This is because accounting profit is calculated on a basis which, for example, apportions a share of overheads to a particular project, even where the overheads do not vary according to whether or not the project is undertaken. In practice, it can be very misleading to use accounting information to make decisions about the future in the way that the ARR approach does. This is not to say that measuring accounting profit is not a useful activity, simply that it is not a useful approach to assessing future real investment opportunities.

(d) ARR is simple and easy to use, easier than NPV.

Like PBP, ARR seems likely to lead to poor decisions. Also like PBP, there is the question of how the firm arrives at a minimum ARR which it is prepared to accept. This cannot logically be the cost of finance because ARR does not represent a return on investment. One of its features is the fact that it does not reflect repayments of the original investment. Take for example the 'alternative' cash flows for the Zenith given above. Here all of the original investment would be repaid in the first year and it is thus a very attractive investment with a very high rate of return. Yet despite this, if the devotee of ARR decided to use the cost of borrowing (say 12 per cent) as the hurdle rate, the project would be rejected because its ARR is only 9 per cent! Perhaps more logically, the net profit to net assets rate taken from recent profit and loss accounts and balance sheets would be used as this is the approach that ARR uses (hence its name). This would still be an arbitrary approach though, for why should past accounting returns on assets be felt to be a useful basis for decisions relating to the future? In any case maximisation of accounting rates of return will not, except by coincidence, promote value maximisation.

Table 4.1 summarises the relative merits of investment appraisal techniques.

Table 4.1 Summary of the relative merits of the four investment appraisal techniques

	NPV	IRR	PBP	ARR
Directly related to the wealth maximisation objective	Yes	No	No	No
Fully accounts for timing of cash flows and the time value of money	Yes	Yes	No	No
Takes account of all relevant information (other than timing)	Yes	Yes	No	Yes
Practical, easy to use and provides clear signals	Yes	Usually	Yes	Yes

INVESTMENT APPRAISAL METHODS USED IN PRACTICE

Having considered the attributes and the theoretical strengths and weaknesses of the methods found in practice, it seems appropriate to consider the extent to which these methods are actually used by firms.

The past 30 years have seen a large volume of research into the methods of investment appraisal actually used by firms. The more relevant of these for UK firms were conducted by Pike (1982 and 1992), by Pike and Wolfe (1988) (P&W), by McIntyre & Coulthurst (1985) (M&C) and by Drury, Braund, Osborne and Tayles (1993) (DBOT).

Pike and P&W concentrated on very large firms, in fact 100 of the largest 300 UK firms. M&C looked at a sample of 141 firms which fell within the Companies Act 1985 definition of a 'medium-sized' company. These are firms which satisfy two of the three criteria; annual turnover between £1.4m and £5.75m, gross assets between £0.7m and £2.8m and total number of employees between 50 and 250 people. Compared with largest UK firms, the firms in the M&C study would be rather small ones, whatever the formal legal designation of their size. The DBOT survey was of 260 UK manufacturing firms of various sizes.

The results of these studies may be summarised as shown in Table 4.2.

Table 4.2 Investment appraisal methods used in practice in the UK

	Large firms				Smaller firms	Manufacturing firms (various sizes)
	1975 %	1981 %	1986 %	1992 %	1985 %	1993 %
Net present value	32	39	68	74	36	91
Internal rate of return	44	57	75	81	28	80
Payback period	73	81	92	94	82	86
Accounting rate of return	51	49	56	50	37	77
Other methods					4	
Totals	200	226	291	299	187	334

Appraisal methods and corporate objectives

These results suggest a number of factors which we shall go on to consider. An important point which we should bear in mind as we do this is that the choice of investment appraisal methods can quite logically be seen as evidence of the financial objective which firms are following. This is because, when making investment decisions, firms are frequently making judgements which will have the most profound effect on their future welfare and success.

We have already seen in this chapter that NPV's major theoretical justification stems from an assumption that firms pursue the objective of shareholder wealth maximisation. If this is the objective which firms pursue in fact, we should expect to find strong adherence to NPV as the primary appraisal technique in practice.

It would probably be wrong, however, to conclude that, since NPV is not used by all firms, shareholder wealth maximisation is not the primary objective. Indeed, Pike and Ooi (1988) found that there was no significant association between the importance to a particular firm of shareholder wealth maximisation and the use of NPV. It may be that there is a lack of sophistication among some financial decision makers which causes them not to relate a particular objective to the appraisal method which will, in theory, promote it. The fact that NPV is much less popular with the smaller firms, where less sophistication would be expected, may provide evidence for this point. On the other hand the disparity in the use of NPV between the larger and the smaller firms may be explained by a difference between the objectives followed by the typical large firm as compared with the typical smaller one.

Multiple appraisal methods

The fact that the totals in Table 4.2 are all greater than 100 per cent reveals that there is a large element of the use of more than one method. This does not necessarily mean that more than one method is consistently being used by a particular firm in respect of each decision. It seems that firms vary their approach according to the nature of the capital investment decision concerned. For example, Pike found that, although 74 per cent of his 1986 respondents used NPV, only a bit less than one-half of those firms used it for all decisions and about one-sixth of that 74 per cent rarely used it. It seems likely, however, that many firms use more than one method concurrently to assess a particular investment project. The extent of the use of multiple methods seems to be greater among the large firms than among the smaller ones. Its incidence also seems to be increasing over time. M&C found that almost half of their sample used only one method, and that only 13 per cent of that group used a discounting technique (NPV or IRR); 74 per cent of the single-method firms relied entirely on the payback method.

The fact that the use of multiple appraisal methods is so widespread may provide evidence that firms pursue multiple financial objectives. On the other hand, as was suggested above, a lack of managerial sophistication may be the reason for this phenomenon.

Discounting techniques

Both NPV and IRR have shown strong growth in popularity over time with the large firms. Though the Pike and P&W studies show increasing popularity for all four methods, it is the discounting methods, particularly NPV, which have made the greatest progress. It seems likely that all, or all but a few, of the large firms now use a discounting method in respect of most investment decisions. By contrast only 44 per cent of the smaller firms surveyed by M&C used a discounting method.

The increasing popularity of the discounting techniques with the large firms is comforting to the theorists who have long argued the merits of NPV and, to a lesser extent, IRR. Why IRR remains the more popular of the discounting methods, despite its theoretical weaknesses, is not clear. It is felt by some observers that financial decision makers respond more readily to a percentage result than to an NPV expressed in £s.

It is also felt by some that decision makers prefer to leave the question of the 'hurdle rate' (minimum acceptable IRR) until after the analysis, something which NPV will not allow since the NPV cannot be deduced without selecting a discount rate. Since most discounted cash flow analysis will now be done using a computer 'spreadsheet' or similar device, this point does not seem totally valid. This is because it is very easy to enter the predicted cash flows for a particular project and then to try various discount rates to see their effect on the NPV figure.

The suggestion has also been made that some firms may prefer to keep the minimum acceptable IRR as information confidential to senior management and by leaving it out of the quantitative analysis it need not become accessible to less senior staff who may be involved in deducing the IRR for particular projects.

From the popularity of NPV and the fact that, in most circumstances, IRR will give exactly the same decision as NPV, there is some evidence that firms do, in fact, pursue shareholder wealth maximisation as a primary objective.

Payback period

The continued popularity of PBP has confounded academics interested in the subject of investment decision making for decades. As we have seen, it has serious theoretical flaws; perhaps most significantly it ignores the shareholder wealth maximisation objective. Despite these flaws it is very widely used by both large and smaller UK firms. For 50 firms (74 per cent) of the 68 firms in the M&C study of smaller firms which used only one method of investment appraisal, PBP was that method. It is also very popular with the large firms.

There has been much conjecture among academics as to why PBP remains so popular. Some have suggested that it provides evidence that firms do not pursue shareholder wealth maximisation or at least that they couple it with 'short-termism', a point which was discussed in Chapter 2. Pike (1985) conducted some research, the results of which suggested that firms whose objectives emphasise shareholders' interests place less reliance on PBP. Others (e.g. Boardman, Reinhart & Celec (1982)) have suggested that PBP may fit into a strategic framework involving matching returns from investments with the need to repay a term loan of some description. Another possible reason for its continued popularity may lie with its simplicity and therefore usefulness as a means of one manager arguing the case for a particular project when confronted by opposition to that project from other managers who do not have a financial background. Perhaps it is used in conjunction with a discounting method or is only used for relatively minor decisions. Another possibility is that PBP is used as an initial 'screening' device through which all project proposals must pass before the detailed analysis is conducted.

This point is somewhat undermined, however, by the fact that both PBP and the discounting methods use the same basic inputs (predicted cash flows). Having identified these inputs it is little additional effort to apply discount factors to them.

A further, and perhaps more likely reason, for PBP's continued popularity may lie in the fact that the discounting methods whose theoretical development mostly occurred during the 1960s have not yet fully established themselves. This may be particularly so with non-financial managers. The popularity of PBP may stem from a lack of managerial sophistication. This point is supported by the fact that PBP is overwhelmingly the most popular approach taken by the smaller firms, according to M&C. It would be expected that there would be a narrower range of financial management skills in the smaller firms than in the larger ones.

Accounting rate of return

Despite its almost complete lack of theoretical justification ARR continues to be widely used. As with PBP, this fact could call into question whether firms do actually seek a shareholder wealth maximisation objective. The widespread use of ARR may indicate that firms are in fact pursuing some accounting return objective, possibly in conjunction with some wealth-enhancing one (also discussed in Chapter 2). However, as with PBP, use of ARR may imply a lack of managerial sophistication. Most managements are fairly used to accounting statements, profit and loss accounts, etc. It may be that they prefer to think in accounting terms rather than in discounted cash flow terms, despite the fact that accounting measures are inappropriate for assessing individual investment opportunities, certainly where shareholder wealth maximisation is the goal.

The United States experience

Survey research evidence undertaken in the USA shows that the same broad usage of the investment appraisal methods applies there as in the UK (Moore & Reichert, 1983; Scapens, Sale & Tikkas, 1982; Levy & Sarnat, 1988). There seems to be a greater incidence of the use of discounting methods than in the UK but, in contrast with the UK, NPV is more popular than IRR with US firms. Interestingly PBP seems to be as popular in the USA as it is in the UK.

SUMMARY   Firms may in one sense be regarded as investment agencies. As such, one of their most important decision-making areas is in choosing between possible investment projects in real assets. In practice firms tend to use one or more of these methods:

(a) net present value;

(b) payback period;

(c) accounting rate of return; and

(d) internal rate of return.

Of these NPV is much the most conceptually correct, mainly because it is the only one of the four which is directly related to the generally accepted criterion of wealth maximisation. In fact IRR will in most cases give similar results but it can in some circumstances be problematical. Recent research in the UK and USA shows that the conceptual arguments in favour of NPV, and to a lesser extent of IRR, seem not yet to be fully reflected in practice. The reasons for this are difficult to discern, though the increasing popularity of the discounting method suggests that it might be a lack of sophistication in firms' assessment procedures.

FURTHER READING

There are literally dozens of good texts covering topics discussed within this chapter, including those by Brealey & Myers (1991), Davis & Pointon (1991), Drury (1992) and Lumby (1991), all of which clearly and thoroughly deal with the basic principles of the investment appraisal techniques. The reports by Pike & Wolfe (1988), Drury, Braund, Osborne and Tayles (1993), and the article by McIntyre & Coulthurst (1985) all provide very readable and interesting accounts of the research evidence on investment appraisal methods used in the UK which was cited in this chapter. Mills (1988) gives a useful summary of the results of a number of surveys of appraisal methods used in both the UK and the USA.

WORK-BASED ASSIGNMENT

(a) Which investment appraisal method is used by your organisation?

(b) If more than one method is used, are the results from each method used equally weighted in the decision, or is one particular method seen as more important?

QUESTIONS WITH ANSWERS (see Appendix 3)

1 Turners Ltd is considering the purchase of a new machine which is expected to save labour on an existing project. The estimated data for the two machines available on the market are as follows:

	Machine A £000	Machine B £000
Initial cost (year 0)	120	120
Residual value of machines (year 5)	20	30
Annual labour cost savings:		
Year 1	40	20
2	40	30
3	40	50
4	20	70
5	20	20

Which machine will be selected under the following criteria:

(a) NPV, assuming a cost of finance of 10 per cent p.a.?

(b) IRR?

(c) ARR?

(d) PBP?

Ignore taxation throughout.

2 Silicon Limited over the past four years has spent £3 million on developing a new silicon chip. It is now faced with three mutually exclusive choices:

(1) It can manufacture the chip itself in which case the plant will cost £5 million. This will be spent at the end of December 19X7. Additional working capital of £2.1 million will be required when production commences at the start of 19X8. Sales and selling prices are expected to be as follows:

	19X8	19X9	19X0	19X1	19X2
Number sold (000s)	100	100	100	80	80
Sales price (£ per unit)	120	120	120	100	90

Silicon usually depreciates plant of this type over five years using the straight line method and assumes a zero scrap value. Variable costs are expected to be £65 per unit and fixed costs, including depreciation, £3 million per year.

(2) Sell the know-how to a major international firm for a single payment of £3.1 million, receivable at the end of December 19X7.

(3) Sell the know-how for a royalty of £10 per unit. Anticipated sales of chips would be as shown above.

If choices (2) or (3) are taken, then the company will not manufacture the chips itself. Silicon estimates that its weighted average cost of capital is 12 per cent. You should assume that sales revenue and costs occur at the end of the year in which they arise. Ignore taxation.

Required:

(a) Calculate the cash flows relevant to a decision whether or not to manufacture the chips. You can ignore choices (2) and (3) for this part of the answer.

(b) Calculate the net present value of each option.

(c) What other factors should be taken into account before a decision is made? What would your decision be?

(Certified Diploma)

3 The accountant of your company has recently been taken ill through overwork. In his absence his assistant has prepared some calculations of the profitability of a project which are to be discussed soon at the board meeting of your company. His workings, which are set out below, include some errors of principle. You can assume that the statement below includes no arithmetic errors.

	19X7 £000	19X8 £000	19X9 £000	19X0 £000	19X1 £000	19X2 £000
Sales revenue		450	470	470	470	470
Less costs:						
Materials		126	132	132	132	132
Labour		90	94	94	94	94
Overheads		45	47	47	47	47
Depreciation		120	120	120	120	120
Working capital	180					
Interest on working capital		27	27	27	27	27
Write off of development costs		30	30	30		
Total costs	180	438	450	450	420	420
Profit/(loss)	(180)	12	20	20	50	50

Total profit/(loss)   (£28 000)= Return on investment (4.7%)
Cost of equipment   £600 000

You ascertain the following additional information:

The cost of equipment contains £100 000 being the book value of an old machine. If it was not used for this project it would be scrapped with a zero net realisable value. New equipment costing £500 000 will be purchased on 31 December 19X7. You should assume that all other cash flows occur at the end of the year to which they relate.

The development costs of £90 000 have already been spent.

Overheads have been costed at 50 per cent of direct labour which is the company's normal practice. An independent assessment has suggested that incremental overheads are likely to amount to £30 000 per year.

The company's weighted average cost of capital is 12 per cent.

Ignore taxation in your answer.

Required:

(a) Prepare a corrected statement of the incremental cash flows arising from the project. Where you have altered the assistant's figures you should attach a brief note explaining your alterations.
(b) Calculate:
    (i) the project's payback period,
    (ii) the project's net present value.
(c) Write a memo to the board advising on the acceptance or rejection of the project.

(Certified Diploma)

4 The directors of Mylo Ltd are currently considering two mutually exclusive investment projects. Both projects are concerned with the purchase of new plant. The following data is available for each project.

	Project	
	1	*2*
	£	£
Cost (immediate outlay)	100 000	60 000
Expected annual net profit (loss)		
Year 1	29 000	18 000
2	(1 000)	(2 000)
3	2 000	4 000
Estimated residual value	7 000	6 000

The company has an estimated cost of capital of 10% and employs the straight-line method of depreciation for all fixed assets when calculating net profit. Neither project would increase the working capital of the company. The company has sufficient funds to meet all capital expenditure requirements.

Required:

(a) Calculate for each project:
   (i)   the net present value;
   (ii) the approximate internal rate of return;
   (iii) the payback period.

(b) State which, if any, of the two investment projects the directors of Mylo Ltd should accept, and why.
(c) State, in general terms, which method of investment appraisal you consider to be most appropriate for evaluating investment projects and why.

(Certified Diploma – amended)

QUESTIONS FOR CLASS USE

1 Newton Electronics Ltd has incurred expenditure of £5 million over the past three years researching and developing a miniature hearing aid. The hearing aid is now fully developed and the directors of the company are considering which of three mutually exclusive options should be taken to exploit the potential of the new product. The options are as follows:

(i) The company could manufacture the hearing aid itself. This would be a new departure for the company which has so far concentrated on research and development projects only. However, the company has manufacturing space available which it currently rents to another business for £100 000 per annum. The company would have to purchase plant and equipment costing £9 million and invest £3 million in working capital immediately for production to begin.

A market research report, for which the company paid £50 000, indicates that the new product has an expected life of five years. Sales of the product during this period are predicted as follows:

Predicted sales for the year ended 30 November

	19X3	19X4	19X5	19X6	19X7
No of units (000s)	800	1400	1800	1200	500

The selling price per unit will be £30 in the first year but will fall to £22 in the following three years. In the final year of the product's life the selling price will fall to £20. Variable production costs are predicted to be £14 per unit and fixed production costs (including depreciation) will be £2.4 million per annum. Marketing costs will be £2 million per annum.

The company intends to depreciate the plant and equipment using the straight-line method and based on an estimated residual value at the end of the five years of £1 million.

The company has a cost of capital of 10%.

(ii) Newton Electronics Ltd could agree to another company manufacturing and marketing the product under licence. A multinational company, Faraday Electricals plc, has offered to undertake the manufacture and marketing of the product and, in return, will make a royalty payment to Newton Electronics Ltd of £5 per unit. It has been estimated that the annual number of sales of the hearing aid will be 10% higher if the multinational company, rather than Newton Electronics Ltd, manufactures and markets the product.

(iii) Newton Electronics Ltd could sell the patent rights to Faraday Electricals plc for £24 million, payable in two equal instalments. The first instalment would be payable immediately and the second instalment would be payable at the end of two years. This option would give Faraday Electricals the exclusive right to manufacture and market the new product.

Required:

Ignoring taxation,

(a) Calculate the net present value of each of the options available to Newton Electronics Ltd.
(b) Identify and discuss any other factors which Newton Electronics Ltd should consider before arriving at a decision.
(c) What do you consider to be the most suitable option and why?

(Certified Diploma)

2 C. George (Controls) Ltd manufactures a thermostat that can be used in a range of kitchen appliances. The manufacturing process is, at present, semi-automated. The equipment used cost £540 000 and has a written-down value of £300 000. Demand for the product has been fairly stable and output has been maintained at 50 000 units per annum in recent years. ·

The following data, based on the current level of output, has been prepared in respect of the product:

	Per unit	
	£	£
Selling price		12.40
Less:		
Labour	3.30	
Materials	3.65	
Overheads – variable	1.58	
– fixed	1.60	
		10.13
Profit		2.27

Although the existing equipment is expected to last for a further four years before it is sold for an estimated £40 000, the company has recently been considering purchasing new equipment which would completely automate much of the production process. The new equipment would cost £670 000 and would have an expected life of four years at the end of which it would be sold for an estimated £70 000. If the new equipment is purchased the old equipment could be sold for £150 000 immediately.

The assistant to the company accountant has prepared a report to help assess the viability of the proposed change which includes the following data:

	Per unit	
	£	£
Selling price		12.40
Less:		
Labour	1.20	
Materials	3.20	
Overheads – variable	1.40	
– fixed	3.30	
		9.10
Profit		3.30

Depreciation charges will increase by £85 000 per annum as a result of purchasing the new machinery; however; other fixed costs are not expected to change.

In the report the assistant wrote:

'The figures shown above which relate to the proposed change are based on the current level of output and take account of a depreciation charge of £150 000 per annum in respect of the new equipment. The effect of purchasing the new equipment will be to increase the net profit to sales ratio from 18.3% to 26.6%. In addition, the purchase of the new equipment will enable us to reduce our stock level immediately by £130 000.

'In view of these facts I recommend purchase of the new equipment.'

The company has a cost of capital of 12%.

Ignore taxation.

Required:

(a) Prepare a statement of the incremental cash flows arising from the purchase of the new equipment.

(b) Calculate the net present value of the proposed purchase of new equipment.

(c) State, with reasons, whether the company should purchase the new equipment.

(d) Explain why cash flow forecasts are used rather than profit forecasts to assess the viability of proposed capital expenditure projects.

(Certified Diploma)

3 Consolidated Oilfields plc is interested in exploring for oil near the west coast of Australia. The Australian government is prepared to grant an exploration licence to the company for a five-year period for a fee of £300 000 per annum. The option to acquire the rights must be taken immediately otherwise another oil company will be granted the rights. However, Consolidated Oilfields is not in a position to commence operations immediately and exploration of the oilfield will not start until the beginning of the second year. In order to carry out the exploration work the company will require equipment costing £10 400 000 which will be made by a specialist engineering company. Half of the equipment cost will be payable immediately and half will be paid when the equipment has been built and tested to the satisfaction of Consolidated Oilfields. It is estimated that the second instalment will be paid at the end of the first year. The company commissioned a geological survey of the area and the results suggest that the oilfield will produce relatively small amounts of high quality crude oil. The survey cost £250 000 and is now due for payment.

The assistant to the project accountant has produced the following projected profit and loss accounts for the project for years 2–5 when the oilfield is operational.

Projected Profit and Loss accounts

	Year							
	2		3		4		5	
	£000	£000	£000	£000	£000	£000	£000	£000
Sales		7400		8300		9800		5800
Less expenses								
Wages and salaries	550		580		620		520	
Materials and consumables	340		360		410		370	
Licence fee	600		300		300		300	
Overheads	220		220		220		220	
Depreciation	2100		2100		2100		2100	
Survey cost written off	250		–		–		–	
Interest charges	650		650		650		650	
		4710		4210		4300		4160
Profit		2690		4090		5500		1640

The following additional information is available:
(i) The licence fee charge appearing in the accounts in Year 2 includes a write off for all the annual fee payable in Year 1. The licence fee is paid to the Australian government at the end of each year.
(ii) The overheads contain an annual charge of £120 000 which represents an

apportionment of head office costs. This is based on a standard calculation to ensure that all projects bear a fair share of the central administrative costs of the business. The remainder of the overheads relate directly to the project.

(iii) The survey costs written off relate to the geological survey already undertaken and due for payment immediately.

(iv) The new equipment costing £10 400 000 will be sold at the end of the licence period for £2 000 000.

(v) The project will require a specialised cutting tool for a brief period at the end of Year 2 which is currently being used by the company in another project. The manager of the other project has estimated that he will have to hire machinery at a cost of £150 000 for the period the cutting tool is on loan.

(vi) The project will require an investment of £650 000 working capital from the end of the first year to the end of the licence period.

The company has a cost of capital of 10%.

Ignore taxation.

Required:

(a) Prepare calculations which will help the company to evaluate further the profitability of the proposed project.

(b) State, with reasons, whether you would recommend that the project be undertaken.

(Certified Diploma)

CHAPTER 5

Practical aspects of investment appraisal

OBJECTIVES

In this chapter we shall deal with the following:

- the importance of cash flows rather than accounting flows for investment decision making
- the relationship between cash flows and accounting flows
- the importance of assessing the timing as well as the magnitude of cash flows
- the necessity of identifying only those cash flows which differ according to the decision and to identify all of them even where they are not very obvious
- the treatment of inflation in the investment decision
- how the basic NPV rule must be adapted to deal with situations where there are shortages of investment finance
- replacement decisions
- the importance of establishing routines to try to identify possible projects

INTRODUCTION

In the last chapter we established that the most theoretically correct approach to assessing investment opportunities is on the basis of their net present values. This involves identifying the cash flows and their timing and then discounting by an appropriate factor.

In this chapter we shall examine how the firm should go about identifying the cash flows and assessing them, particularly in the NPV context. We shall also consider some other practical problems, including how the company should deal with a situation of having insufficient finance to support all of the projects which appear desirable. While we shall mainly be concerned with the more practical aspects of using NPV, many of the points relate equally well to the other techniques for assessing investment projects, particularly to IRR.

CASH FLOWS OR ACCOUNTING FLOWS?

When assessing a particular business investment opportunity, should the firm identify and discount cash payments and receipts or should it discount profits arising from the project? This is an important question as the cash flows from a particular project in a particular time period will rarely equal the accounting profit for the project during the same period.

If we go back to the principles on which the concept of NPV is based (discussed in Chapter 4), we see that discounting takes account of the opportunity cost of making the investment. It is not until cash needs to be expended in the project that the opportunity for it to produce interest will be lost. Only when cash flows back from the project, can the firm use it to pay dividends, repay borrowings, to lend it or to reinvest it in another project.

Over the life of a project the accounting profits will equal the net cash flows (undiscounted) in total; it is the timing which will be different. Why should this be the case?

The roles of financial accounting and investment appraisal

In the context of income measurement, financial accounting sets out to assess the profit (increase in wealth) for a period, perhaps a year. In doing so it needs to treat each period as a self-contained unit. This is despite the fact that most of the firm's investment projects will not be self-contained within that same period. Fixed assets, perhaps acquired in a previous period, may be used in the period and continue to be owned and used by the firm into future periods. Stock in trade acquired in the previous period may be sold in the current one. Sales made (on credit) in the current period may be paid for by customers in the following period. Financial accounting tends to ignore the timing of payments and receipts of cash but to concentrate on benefits gained and detriments suffered during the period. Costs, less anticipated disposal proceeds, of fixed assets are spread in some equitable way (depreciated) over their lives so that each period gets a share of the cost, irrespective of whether or not any cash is actually paid out to suppliers of fixed assets in the particular accounting period under consideration. Sales are usually recognised and credit taken for them by the selling firm when the goods change hands even though the cash receipt may lag some weeks behind. The detriment suffered by using up stock in trade in making sales is recognised when the sale is made – and not when the stock is purchased or when it is paid for.

These points are not weaknesses of financial accounting. Its role is to seek to measure income (profit) over time periods so that interested parties can obtain a periodic assessment of the firm's progress. As projects will not usually be self-contained within time periods as short as a year, it is necessary for financial accounting to take some consistent approach as to how to deal with the problem; the approach taken seems a very logical one.

Investment appraisal has a somewhat different objective from that of financial accounting, however. This is to assess a project over its entire life, not to assess it for a particular portion of that life. This difference of purpose is represented graphically in Fig. 5.1. This shows a firm with six investment projects (A to F), each of which starts and ends at a different time. Financial accounting seeks to assess the profit for a period such as p in Fig. 5.1. During this period one project ends (Project E), one starts (Project B), whilst the other four run throughout period p. Investment appraisal seeks to assess, in advance of its commencement, whether any particular project is a viable one. Profit measurement tends to be cross-sectional, investment appraisal longitudinal.

Figure 5.1
Six investment projects of a firm. All of these projects operate during at least two accounting periods.

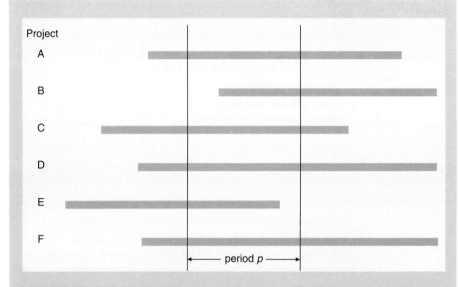

The problem of financial accounting is to try to make an assessment of the amount of wealth generated by all of the firm's projects during a particular period when not all of each project's cash flows are self-contained within that period.

Converting accounting flows to cash flows

We know from Chapter 4 that when using the NPV approach it is cash flows, not accounting profits, which should be discounted, yet frequently when projects are being assessed in advance of possible implementation they are expressed in terms of anticipated profit. As regards the operating items, i.e. those concerned with sales and material, labour and overhead costs, the differences between the accounting flows and the cash flows will be concerned principally with timing differences. The adjustment to convert accounting flows to cash flows can be done by taking account of the working capital requirement of the project.

EXAMPLE

A project to manufacture widgets, if undertaken, will start on 1 January with the purchase of (and payment for) a widget-making machine. Materials for use in the manufacture of widgets will be bought in January and paid for in February and these will be used in production in February. February's production will be sold in that month, on credit, and customers will pay in April. If the monthly purchase of raw materials is £10 000 and the monthly sales revenue from widgets £20 000, then once the project gets under way the working capital investment at any given moment will be:

	£
Debtors (two months at £20 000 p.m.)	40 000
Stocks (one month at £10 000 p.m.)	10 000
	50 000
Less: Creditors (one month at £10 000 p.m.)	10 000
	£40 000

(This assumes that the level of activity, the stock holding and the credit periods remain the same.) So to take account of the difference between operating accounting flows and cash flows we could treat the £40 000, which is the magnitude of the difference between accounting and cash flows, as an initial investment of the project. We should also need to treat it as a receipt of the project at its end. During the last few months of the project more cash would be received from sales than sales made; debtors will continue to pay after the end of the project for two months. Stocks will not be bought during the last month of production, though creditors for stocks bought the previous month will need to be paid during that last month.

Provided that this recognition of the timing difference which the £40 000 represents is correctly adjusted for, operating accounting flows can be used as a surrogate for the (more strictly correct) cash flows.

Failure to make this adjustment to accounting flows will tend to cause a bias in the appraisal usually giving a more favourable impression than justified by the facts. It will tend to give this more favourable impression as accounting flows do not reflect the fact that sales are usually made on credit so that the cash inflows may lag some time behind the sale. Whilst it is true that an opposite effect is caused by the fact that the firm is likely buying its raw materials on credit, this opposite effect is likely itself to be offset by the fact that the firm probably holds stocks of raw materials and perhaps finished goods as well.

In any case, for projects which are likely to be favourably considered by the firm, the sales revenues will tend to be larger than the operating costs. Also sales are usually made on credit whereas some significant operating costs (e.g. wages) are payable more or less immediately.

With the initial capital expenditure, its level and more particularly the timing difference between recognition of the expenditure in accounting flows and cash flows make it vital to adjust the accounting flows to get the cash flows.

EXAMPLE

A project involving an initial outlay of £20 000 is expected to generate annual profits of £6000 (after deducting depreciation) each year for four years. Depreciation is calculated on an even (straight line) basis, assuming that disposal proceeds of the original investment will be £4000 receivable at the end of year 4. If it is assumed that there are no significant time differences between accounting recognition and cash payment or receipt in respect of operating revenues and costs then the cash flows may be taken to be:

		£	
Year	0	(20 000)	
	1	10 000	(i.e. predepreciation profit £6000 + £4000)
	2	10 000	
	3	10 000	
	4	14 000	

and it is these figures which should be discounted, using an appropriate rate, to arrive at the NPV. The figures are arrived at by adding back the annual depreciation figure of £4000 (i.e. [£20 000 – £4000]/4) and treating the initial cost as an outflow in year 0 (immediately) and the disposal proceeds as an additional inflow in year 4.

Discounting cash flows rather than profits does not really mean that depreciation is ignored. It is in effect taken into account by treating the initial investment as an outflow of cash and the disposal proceeds as an inflow, thus effectively charging the difference between these amounts to the project.

DO CASH FLOWS REALLY OCCUR AT YEAR ENDS?

In the examples which we have considered so far all of the cash flows have occurred exact numbers of years after the start of the project. This obviously is not very representative of real life.

Most investments undertaken by firms are in land, buildings, plant, machinery, trading stocks, etc. The returns from these are in the form of sales revenues against which have to be set costs of labour, materials and overheads. Clearly these cash flows are not likely to occur at year ends. They tend to be spread throughout the year, perhaps fairly evenly or perhaps more concentrated at some parts of the year than at others, reflecting a seasonal aspect of certain trades.

Strictly the precise timing of the cash flows should be identified and they should be discounted accordingly. The discount factor $1/(1 + i)^n$ would be the same; however, the n would not necessarily be a whole number.

In practice, whilst the precise timing of cash flows could be recognised, it seems not usual to do so. The simplifying assumption that cash flows occurring within a year occur at the year end is thought to be popular in practice. Making this assumption tends to introduce an element of bias in that it usually treats cash flows as occurring a few months later than they actually do. This tends to have the effect of systematically understating NPVs. It is probably best in practice to identify the forecast cash flows month by month and to discount them according to when they actually are expected to occur.

WHICH CASH FLOWS?

As we saw in Chapter 2, only those cash flows relevant to the decision should be brought into the appraisal. Cash flows will be relevant only where they will be different, depending upon the decision under review. Items which will occur in any case should be ignored.

For example, where a decision involving a choice as to whether or not to make a new product would not have an effect on the fixed overheads of the firm, the fixed overheads should be disregarded when making the decision. They will be unaffected by the decision and so must be ignored when making it.

Similarly, past costs are irrelevant as they will inevitably be the same whatever happens in the future. For example, where a machine costing £50 000 one year ago is under review as to whether or not it should be replaced, the decision should not take the £50 000 into account. All that should be considered are the future benefits which could be derived from the machine, in terms of either proceeds of disposal or cash flow benefits of its retention. The present decision is not whether or not to buy the machine a year ago; that decision was made over twelve months ago and was either a good decision or a bad one. In either case it is not something which can now be altered.

Opportunity cash flows

It is not only cash flows which are expected to occur physically which should correctly be taken into account. Opportunity cash flows are as important as physical cash flows. In the above example, if the machine has a current market value of £10 000 then one of the cash flows associated with retaining the machine will be a £10 000 outflow at whatever time it would be disposed of if the alternative action (disposal) were followed. Obviously if the machine is retained this cash flow will not actually occur, nonetheless it should be taken into account because retention of the machine deprives the firm of the opportunity to dispose of it. The £10 000 represents a difference arising from the decision. Some opportunity cash flows may be fairly remote from the project under review and so can quite easily be overlooked unless care is taken. An example of such opportunity cash flows are losses of sales (and variable costs) of one of the firm's existing activities as a result of introducing a new one. For example, a chain store contemplating opening a new branch should not just assess the cash flows of that branch. It should also consider cash flow changes which might occur in other branches in the locality as a result. Sales might be lost at existing branches if a new one is opened.

Forecasting cash flows

We are, of course, dealing here with forecasts of future cash flows. Forecasting the cash flows associated with particular courses of action is likely to be difficult and subject to error. The techniques and problems of forecasting go beyond the scope of this book. These techniques include such approaches as the use of statistical data on past events (generated inside and outside the firm), market research projects and soliciting the opinions of experts.

Financing costs

One type of cash flow which should not be included in the appraisal is the cost of finance (interest) to support the project. Discounting deals with the financing cost in a complete and logical manner in that future cash flows are reduced (discounted) to take account of the time that finance will be tied up and the relevant interest rate.

TAXATION

Cash flows associated with taxation must be brought into the assessment of the project. Most projects will cause differences in Corporation Tax. This may be because of capital expenditure attracting relief (capital allowances), profits from the project attracting additional tax, or losses attracting tax relief. As tax is not assessed by the Inland Revenue project by project but for the company as a whole, then the tax cash flows which must be considered are differences between the tax cash flows that would exist without the project under review and those which will occur if it is undertaken.

The taxable profit

Basically companies are taxed on the basis of the profit shown by a profit and loss account (income statement) drawn up following the generally accepted accounting rules and conventions. This profit figure is, however, subject to some adjustment. There are certain items of expense and revenue which though legitimately appearing in the profit and loss account have been singled out by statute as being illegitimate for tax purposes.

Most of these items are fairly unusual in occurrence or relatively insignificant in effect, though there is one which is neither of these. This is depreciation, the accounting device for spreading capital costs of long-term (fixed) assets over their useful lives. Depreciation must be added back to the profit revealed by the profit and loss account, to be replaced by capital allowances.

Capital allowances

These are allowances which are set against the taxable profit in order to relieve expenditure on fixed assets. There are several categories of asset into which statute has placed the various types of business fixed asset. Each of these has its own rules and basis for granting the allowance. In practice two of these, dealing with plant and machinery and with industrial buildings, are by far the most important to the typical firm.

(a) *Plant and machinery*. This includes a wide range of assets, from industrial machinery to the reference books of a lawyer, including motor vehicles. For expenditure on plant and machinery, companies are allowed to deduct 25 per cent of the cost of the asset from the (otherwise taxable) profit of the period during which the asset was acquired. In each subsequent year of ownership of the asset, 25 per cent of the balance brought forward may be deducted.

EXAMPLE

In 1993 Carriers Ltd buys a delivery lorry for £12 000. The capital allowances would be claimable as follows:

Year	Balance		Capital allowance
	£	£	
1993	12 000	3000	(25% of £12 000)
1994	9 000	2250	(25% of (£12 000 – £3000))
1995	6 750	1688	etc.
1996	5 062	1266	
	etc.		

This pattern will continue until the asset is sold or scrapped.

When the asset is disposed of, in broad effect, any unrelieved expenditure is relieved, and any excess of relief is 'clawed back' by the taxman.

For example if Carriers Ltd (above) disposed of the lorry for £6000 in 1996, tax would be charged on £938 (i.e. £6000 – £5062). On the other hand, were the disposal proceeds to be £4000, additional relief of £1062 (i.e. £5062 – £4000) would be given to the company.

The broad effect of capital allowances is to give tax relief on the difference between the acquisition cost of the asset and its disposal proceeds (if this is a lower figure), spread over the life of the asset.

(b) *Industrial buildings*. These are buildings used directly or indirectly in manufacturing, the transport industry and other restricted purposes. Not included in the definition are shops and offices.

Relief is granted by allowing companies to deduct 4 per cent of the cost of the building from the taxable profit in each year of its ownership and use. On disposal the proceeds will cause a claw-back of excess allowances or an additional allowance, if the difference between cost and the disposal proceeds has not already been fully relieved.

Other types of asset which attract capital allowances are:

- Hotels
- Agricultural buildings and works
- Patents
- Scientific research
- Mines, oil wells, etc.
- Know-how
- Expenditure on dredging
- Cemeteries and crematoria.

Having considered the basis on which company profits are taxed in the UK, it will be useful to proceed to an example.

EXAMPLE The profit and loss account of Amalgamated Retailers plc, for the year ended 31 March 1993, showed a net profit of £1 440 000. In arriving at this figure depreciation was charged as follows:

	£
Shop premises	120 000
Shop equipment and fittings	85 000

During the year the company purchased new computerised cash registers for all its branches at a total cost of £500 000 and spent £350 000 on acquiring the freeholds of several new shops, all of which commenced trading during the year. The tax written down values of the company's fixed assets at 1 April 1992 were as follows:

	£
Shop premises	280 000
Shop equipment	210 000

The company always claims all possible allowances and reliefs at the earliest opportunity.

The taxable profit of the company would be as follows:

		£
Net profit (from the profit and loss)		1 440 000
Add: Depreciation:		
Premises	120 000	
Equipment	85 000	205 000
		1 545 000
Less: Capital allowances		
(see below)		177 500
Taxable profit		£1 367 500

Capital allowances – shop equipment

	£
Written down value at 1.4.92	210 000
Add: Additions	500 000
	710 000
Less: Allowance @ 25%	177 500
Written down value at 31.3.93	£532 500

No capital allowances would be given on the acquisition of the freeholds as they do not fall within the definition of any of the classes of asset for which capital allowances are given.

Rates of tax and dates of payment

The taxable profit is taxed at 33 per cent where the annual figure exceeds £1 250 000 (as above) and 25 per cent where it is less than £250 000. Between these levels of profit the rate is on a sliding scale, so that profits of just over £250 000 will be taxed at just over 25 per cent and profits of just under £1 250 000 at nearly 33 per cent. Companies whose taxable profit fluctuates from year to year will pay at different rates from year to year, unless their profits are always over £1 250 000 or under £250 000.

Thus the liability of Amalgamated Retailers in the above example will be:

$$33\% \times £1\ 367\ 500 = \underline{£451\ 275}$$

Tax will be payable on 1 January 1994, nine months after the end of the company's accounting year.

Where the company has paid any dividends to its members during the accounting period concerned, part of the total liability is paid shortly after the dividend payout date.

As is evident from the above, the tax cash flows frequently lag well behind the cash flow events giving rise to them. It is important to recognise this time lag, particularly as the cash flows concerned are likely to be large.

INFLATION

Throughout almost the whole of the twentieth century the UK has experienced erosion of the purchasing power of the pound. Much has been written on the causes of and possible cures for it, neither of which is within the scope of this book. The effects of inflation, the problem which it causes to capital investment decision makers and how they might cope with the problem are our concern here, however.

Even with relatively low levels of inflation (say, less than 5 per cent), over long periods prices will be greatly affected. An item costing £100 today would cost £127.6 after five years if its price increased by 5 per cent each year. In the UK our recent history tends to cause us to regard even a 5 per cent rate of inflation as pretty modest.

The principal problem facing the decision maker is whether to forecast future cash flows associated with an investment project in real terms or in money terms. Real terms here means in terms of today's (the date of the decision) price levels; money terms refers to actual price levels which are forecast to obtain at the date of the future cash flow.

Seeking to forecast in real terms is probably going to be easier because it does not require any estimation of rates of inflation. Forecasting in money terms is not simply taking the real terms forecasts and adjusting for the rate of inflation because different types of cash flows will be differently affected by inflation. We tend to view inflation as operating at one rate across all commodities; this is incorrect. Inflation acts differentially. An index such as the Retail Price Index (RPI) by which inflation is quite often assessed is simply a weighted average of the inflation rates of commodities bought by a 'typical' household. Within that, some commodities may have static or even declining prices though the average may still be increasing.

Assessing projects in money terms requires forecasts of future price levels for each element of the decision. In many instances, however, it probably will not materially affect the issue if prices of all elements are assumed to grow equally. In other cases this simplifying assumption may cause unreasonable distortions.

The other element of the decision which inflation will affect is the discount rate. Interest and finance costs generally reflect expectations in the general level of inflation rates. Suppliers of finance require compensation for being prepared to delay consumption. They tend to require additional compensation where they not only delay consumption by lending, but reduce the amount which they can ultimately consume as a result of commodity price rises during the period of the loan. The relationship is

$$1 + i_m = (1 + i_r)(1 + h)$$

where i_m is the money rate of interest (the actual rate of interest payable by borrowers), i_r is the real rate of interest (the rate that would be payable if the inflation rate were zero) and h the expected rate of inflation in the economy generally. Where no inflation is expected i_m will equal i_r.

Consistency of approach

For practical purposes it probably does not matter whether money cash flows or real ones are used in the NPV analysis, provided each is used in conjunction with the appropriate discount rate.

Where the cash flows are estimated in money terms (i.e. incorporating the forecast effects of inflation), then the discount rate should also reflect inflation expectations. Therefore the discount rate should be based on the money interest rate.

If the cash flows are to be assessed in real terms, then the discount rate should be based on the real interest rate.

It is important that there is consistency of approach. To use real cash flows in conjunction with a money discount rate would be to understate the NPV of the project, which could quite easily lead to desirable projects being rejected. A survey conducted in the UK during the 1970s by Carsberg & Hope (1976) suggested that this rejection of desirable projects, resulting from wrongly dealing with inflation, was indeed a problem.

Drury, Braund, Osborne and Tayles (1993), in their survey of 260 UK manufacturing firms, found that only 27 per cent of those firms dealt correctly with inflation, 13 per cent of the firms surveyed made an error which was probably not very significant, but this left 60 per cent of firms dealing with inflation in such a manner as to give a significantly misleading result.

Dealing with cash flows and discount rate in real terms does not completely avoid forecasting the rate of inflation. Real rates of interest are not directly identifiable in the way that money rates are. Money rates on government stocks, for example, are quoted daily in several national newspapers. Money rates can be converted into real rates by adjusting for expectation of future inflation rates which are incorporated in them. In order to identify inflation rate expectations we probably could not improve on taking some average or consensus view from the various economic forecasts which are published regularly by a number of commercial and academic institutions.

The central point regarding inflation in investment decisions is that it cannot be ignored, not as long as inflation runs at significant rates. Not only must it be confronted but consistency of approach must apply. Money cash flows must be discounted at money discount rates and real cash flows at real discount rates.

AN EXAMPLE OF AN INVESTMENT APPRAISAL

Having considered the practical aspects of applying the NPV rule in principle, we shall now go on to see how it would be applied to a practical example.

EXAMPLE

Kitchen Appliances plc is assessing an investment project which involves the production and marketing of a sophisticated household food mixer, the Rapido. Annual sales are expected to run at 10 000 Rapidos for five years.

The development department has produced the following estimate of annual profit from the project:

	£000
Sales	1000
Raw materials	300
Labour	300
Depreciation	120
Rent	30
Overheads	100
Interest	50
	900
Annual net profit	100

The following additional information is relevant:

(a) The production will require the purchase of a new machine at a cost of £600 000, payable on delivery. The machine will be depreciated on a straight line basis over the five years. It is not expected to have any second-hand value at the end of that time.

(b) Production of Rapidos will take place in a building presently used for storage. Apportioning the rent of the entire site occupied by the firm on the basis of area, the building has a rental cost of £30 000. If production goes ahead the firm can rent a small warehouse, which will be adequate for storage purposes, for £5000 p.a. payable annually in arrears.

If Rapido production is not undertaken there are plans to sublet the building to a neighbouring firm at a rent of £20 000 p.a. payable annually in arrears and to rent the small warehouse for £5000 p.a.

(c) £18 000 has been spent on developing the Rapido and £5000 on a market survey to assess demand.

(d) The overheads of £100 000 p.a. represent an apportionment of the entire firm's overheads on the basis of labour hours. The operating overheads of the firm will be increased by £45 000 p.a. as a result of Rapido manufacture. This includes £15 000 p.a. salary to a manager who is due to retire immediately on a firm's pension of £5000 p.a. If Rapido manufacture goes ahead he will not retire for another five years. Staying on for the additional period will not affect the pension which the manager concerned will ultimately receive. Pensions are paid by the firm and the amounts charged to non-operating overheads.

The remaining £30 000 represents salaries payable to two managers who will be taken on for the duration of the project, should it go ahead.

(e) If Rapidos come onto the market there is expected to be a reduction in antici-pated demand for the existing food mixer, the Whizzo, which the firm manufactures. The reduction in sales of Whizzos would be expected to be:

	Units
Year 1	10 000
2	10 000
3	5 000
4	5 000
5	5 000

Whizzos sell at £40 each with variable costs of £20 each. Lower Whizzo sales would not be expected to affect overhead costs, which are fixed.

(f) The firm's Corporation Tax rate is 35 per cent with payment date falling one year after the event giving rise to it.

(g) The expenditure on the new machine would attract capital allowances at the rate of 25 per cent p.a. with any unrelieved expenditure being allowed on disposal.

(h) All of the data given are expressed in current terms. Inflation is expected to run at about 5 per cent p.a. over the next decade. All of the relevant cash flows are expected to increase at this annual rate.

(i) The firm's after tax financing cost is (and is expected to remain at) 12 per cent p.a. in money terms.

(j) Working capital of £50 000 will be required from the start of the project and will be returned at the end of year 5.

(All of the above cash flows have been expressed in real terms, i.e. in terms of prices at the date of the start of the project.)

On the basis of NPV should the project be undertaken or not?

SOLUTION

Kitchen Appliances plc

Assessment of Rapido project

Since the cash flows are all expressed in real, rather than money, terms, it is probably easier to leave them in real terms and apply a real discount rate to them. We shall, therefore, take this approach. Note that the alternative of adjusting the cash flows to money terms and applying a money discount rate, will give an identical NPV.

In the assessment of the project our guiding principles must be:

● to identify the cash flows relevant to the decision (i.e. differences between the cash flows which will occur if the project is undertaken and those which will take place without the project)

- to identify the timing of those relevant cash flows
- to discover the NPV of the project by applying the adjustment for the time value of money to the relevant cash flows according to when it is anticipated that they will occur

Annual operating cash flows (in real terms)

	£000
Sales	1000
Raw materials	300
Labour	300
Rent	20
Overheads	40
Contributions lost from Whizzo sales	200
	860
Annual net operating cash flow	140 (240 for years 3, 4 and 5)

Notes

(a) *Depreciation*. This is irrelevant as it does not represent a cash flow.

(b) *Rent*. The appropriate figure here is the difference, which is the rent from the subtenant should the project not go ahead. Irrespective of the decision, both the rent of the entire site (of which £30 000 is part) and the £5000 rent of the outside warehouse will be paid; thus they are irrelevant to the decision.

(c) *Overheads*. The retiring manager's salary makes a difference of £10 000 p.a. dependent on the decision. Irrespective of the decision the manager will be paid £5000 p.a. so it is the £10 000 which is relevant. The other £30 000 is also relevant. The apportionment of overheads is not relevant as this is not the amount of the difference in overheads associated with rejection or acceptance of the project.

(d) *Interest*. This will be taken into account by discounting.

(e) *Contributions from lost Whizzo sales*. These amount to £200 000 (i.e. 10 000 x £(40 – 20)) for years 1 and 2 and £100 000 (i.e. 5000 x £(40 – 20)) for years 3, 4 and 5.

As lost Whizzo sales do not affect overheads, only sales revenue lost (£40 per unit) and variable costs saved (£20 per unit) are relevant to the decision.

This aspect must be accounted for, as accepting the project will affect Whizzo sales.

Corporation Tax cash flows

The relevant operating cash flows will also be the basis of the differential tax charges.

Capital allowances on the initial investment will be as follows:

	Balance £000	Allowance claimed £000	Tax savings (at 33%) £000
Year 1 Acquisition	600		
Writing down allowance (25%)	150	150	50
	450		
2 WDA (25%)	113	113	37
	337		
3 WDA (25%)	85	85	28
	252		
4 WDA (25%)	63	63	21
	189		
5 Balancing allowance (nil proceeds)	189	189	62

The tax payable will be as follows:

	Operating cash flow surplus £000	Tax payable (at 33%) £000
Year 1	140	46
2	140	46
3	240	79
4	240	79
5	240	79

Notes

(a) Each of these payments will lag one year (strictly, nine months) behind the year to which it relates.

(b) The tax payable amounts represent the difference between the tax which would be payable if the project is accepted and that which would be payable if it is rejected. It is not necessary for us to know what the tax payable would be in total; we only need know the difference.

Since we are working in real terms, we must adjust these tax savings and payments to put them into real terms.

Tax savings on capital allowances

Using a real discount rate requires that we also use real cash flows. The cash flows arising from the capital allowances are the actual amounts which will be saved in the year concerned, i.e. they are expressed in money terms. This is because, even during a period of inflation, the cash flows arising from capital allowances remain pegged to the original cost of the asset concerned.

Using a real discount rate implies that all cash flows increase by the rate of inflation. The cash flows arising from the capital allowances do not increase at all. We must, therefore, discount the capital allowance cash flows by the rate of inflation to convert them to real terms.

Year of payment	Tax saving in money terms £000	Discount factor $1/(1 + i)^n$	Tax saving in real terms £000
2	50	$1/(1.00 + 0.05)^2$	45
3	37	$1/(1.00 + 0.05)^3$	32
4	28	$1/(1.00 + 0.05)^4$	23
5	21	$1/(1.00 + 0.05)^5$	16
6	62	$1/(1.00 + 0.05)^6$	46

Note that the first of these inflation discount factors is raised to the power of 2 because the cash flow effect of the first capital allowance will occur two years (strictly one year, nine months) after the date of the start of the project.

Tax payable on operating cash flows

There is a similar need to convert the amount which we have calculated to real terms. Here the difference between the figures calculated and their equivalents in real terms is less significant than it was with the capital allowances. This is because the tax on the operating cash flows is pegged to operating cash flows of just one year (strictly nine months) earlier. All we need do is discount each of the operating profit tax cash flows by the rate of inflation over one year, i.e. $1/(1.00 + 0.05)^1$.

Year of Payment	Tax payable £000	Tax payable in real terms £000
2	46	44
3	46	44
4	79	75
5	79	75
6	79	75

The discount rate

Since all of the cash flows are expressed in real terms, the simplest approach is to discount them using a real discount rate. As the discount rate is given in money terms, we must adjust for the expected inflation rate to discover the real discount rate.

The real discount rate $= \left(\dfrac{1 + \text{money discount rate}}{1 + \text{rate of inflation}} \right) - 1$

(see page 110)

$= \left(\dfrac{1 + 0.12}{1 + 0.05} \right) - 1 = 7\%$ (approx.)

Notes

(a) We must use a rate which takes account of the fact that interest costs are tax deductible (as the 12 per cent does) because we shall be discounting after the tax cash flows.

(b) Quite how the discount rate is established (in this case, where the 12 per cent came from) is a matter which we shall consider in some detail later.

Discounting

	Initial investment £000	Working capital £000	Operating cash flows £000	Tax cash flows Operating £000	CAs £000	Net cash flows £000	Discount factor	Discounted cash flows £000
Year 0	(600)	(50)				(650)	1.000	(650)
1			140			140	0.935	131
2			140	(44)	45	141	0.873	123
3			240	(44)	32	228	0.816	186
4			240	(75)	28	193	0.763	147
5		50	240	(75)	21	186	0.713	133
6				(75)	62	(13)	0.666	(9)
							Net present value	61

As the NPV is positive and significant, from a financial viewpoint, the production of the Rapido should be undertaken.

Notes

(a) The costs of developing the product and of the market survey will not vary with the present decision and must therefore be ignored. They exist irrespective of the decision.

(b) Treating the working capital commitment in the way shown takes account, in a broadly correct way, of the timing difference between operating cash flows and accounting flows.

(c) All the calculations in this example have been rounded to the nearest £1000. Whilst this is not strictly correct, the accuracy to which cash flows, timings and discount rates can be predicted is such that this rounding is not out of place. It could be argued that doing other than this in such calculations would give the result an air of precision not justified by the levels of possible (probable?) inaccuracy of the input data.

(d) This example (except to the extent of the rounding mentioned in point (c) above) has completely ignored the question of risk.

How reliable are the predictions of labour costs? What if the bottom fell out of the domestic food mixer market? Would the increased level of activity which this project engenders prove too much for the competence of the firm's management?

These and many other matters are present with this project and similar ones with any other project. These risks should be formally assessed and their effect built into the decision-making process. How this may be done will be addressed in the next two chapters.

(e) The net cash flows figures in the example could be used as the basis of an IRR or a PBP assessment of the project without modification. IRR and PBP would simply use them differently.

CAPITAL RATIONING

In Chapter 4 we saw that firms will maximise the wealth of their shareholders by undertaking all investment opportunities which have a positive NPV when discounted at the borrowing/lending interest rate.

In some circumstances the firm may be unable or unwilling to undertake all such opportunities because it cannot or does not wish to raise finance to the level required. Where it cannot raise the finance because sources of supply are limited, the situation is known as *hard capital rationing*. Where the constraint is self-imposed because, for example, the firm feels that it does not have a sufficient volume of management talent to expand beyond a certain point, it is referred to as *soft capital rationing*. Research evidence (Pike and Ooi (1988)) suggests that in real life hard capital rationing is relatively rare, finance seeming to be available for viable projects. Most instances of capital rationing seem to be of the soft variety. One way or another, capital rationing means that there are more calls on finance than there is finance available.

Irrespective of whether there are hard or soft constraints, capital rationing requires that the basic NPV rule cannot be applied without modification. The modification depends on whether the constraint is to operate for one year only or is to persist over several years.

Single-period capital rationing

Where there is single-period capital rationing, projects should be ranked according to the NPV per £ of scarce initial investment capital.

EXAMPLE

A firm is unable or unprepared to invest more than £500 000 in the current year, but has the following projects available to it:

Project	Initial investment	NVP
	£	£
A	100 000	15 000
B	150 000	29 000
C	140 000	31 000
D	210 000	22 000
E	180 000	36 000

SOLUTION

The NPV per £ of investment and thus the ranking of the projects is as follows:

Project	NPV/£ of investment	Ranking
A	0.15	4
B	0.19	3
C	0.22	1
D	0.10	5
E	0.20	2

The firm should therefore take on the projects in the order shown until the capital is exhausted. This would mean taking on projects as follows:

Project	£
C	140 000
E	180 000
B	150 000
A (30/100 thereof)	30 000
	500 000

This solution assumes that it is possible to take on 30/100 of Project A and that the cash flows of that project will simply be reduced to 30 per cent of their original figures, giving an NPV of 30 per cent of the original NPV. In reality this assumption may well be without foundation. If this is the case the decision maker would have to look at the various combinations of the projects which have total initial investment outlays of £500 000; that combination with the highest total NPV would be selected. Some trial and error is likely to be involved with finding this combination. Obviously use of the *NPV per £ investment* approach (usually known as the *profitability index*), will cause NPV to be maximised for the level of investment finance involved.

Multiple-period capital rationing

Where the constraint operates for more than one time period, a more sophisticated approach needs to be adopted. Linear programming (LP) is such an approach.

EXAMPLE   Listed below are the cash flow characteristics of four investment projects. Investment finance is rationed at years 0 and 1 to £100 000 at each time. Projects cannot be delayed nor can they be brought forward. The cost of finance is 10 per cent.

Project	Year 0	Year 1	Year 2	Year 3	NPV (at 10%)
	£000	£000	£000	£000	£000
W	(70)	(20)	60	60	6.44
X	–	(90)	60	50	5.30
Y	(80)	10	60	30	1.18
Z	–	(50)	30	30	1.86

(Note that the NPVs are as at year 0 (now) even for projects X and Z which, even if selected, will not commence until year 1. Also note that project W requires cash outflows both in year 0 and in year 1.)

SOLUTION   We should seek to undertake such a combination of the four projects as would give the highest possible total NPV, subject to the capital constraints at years 0 and 1. Letting w, x, y and z be the proportions of the four projects which it is desirable to undertake, we are seeking to maximise the function:

$$NPV = 6.44w + 5.30x + 1.18y + 1.86z$$

subject to $70w + 80y \leq 100$, i.e. the total outlays at year 0 on W and Y being £100 000 or less; and

$$90x + 50z + 20w - 10y \leq 100$$

i.e. the total outlays on projects X, W, and Z, less the inflow from project Y at year 1, must not exceed £100 000.

In fact further constraints will have to be applied, since each of the proportions must be positive or zero and cannot (presumably) exceed 1.

i.e.

$$1 \geq w \geq 0$$
$$1 \geq x \geq 0$$
$$1 \geq y \geq 0$$
$$1 \geq z \geq 0$$

There is no reason (not a mathematical one, at least) why the optimal solution should not completely exclude one of the projects. Note that the above formulation assumes that any uninvested funds cannot be carried forward from one year to be invested in the next, but it does assume that inflows from existing projects can be reinvested. It need not make these assumptions, however.

The optimal solution can be derived manually or by computer through the LP technique, finding the maximum value of the objective function subject to the various constraints. In addition to providing the proportion of each project which should be undertaken to achieve the maximum NPV, the LP output will also show, directly or indirectly, the following:

- the value of the maximum NPV
- how much it is worth paying for additional investment funds in order to increase the NPV
- how much funds would be needed in each year before that year's shortage of investment funds ceased to be a constraint.

LP will give results which assume that the projects can be partially undertaken. As with the profitability index approach to single-period constraints, this will not be practical to apply in many real life situations because many business investments cannot be made in part. Real life instances of firms going into partnership on large projects (e.g. the financing of the tunnel under the English Channel) can be found. These may provide examples of firms undertaking only part of a project, because capital is rationed.

An alternative technique, integer programming, can be applied which derives the optimal combination of complete projects.

Most texts on operations research and quantitative methods in business explain how to arrive at a solution to the above example through linear programming.

Replacement decisions

A particular type of investment decision in which the decision maker may be involved is deciding when to replace an existing asset with an identical one.

EXAMPLE

A firm owns a fleet of identical motor vehicles. The firm wishes to replace these vehicles after either three or four years. Each one costs £10 000 to replace with a new vehicle. If the firm replaces the vehicles after three years it can trade in the old vehicle for £5000. If it retains the vehicle for a further year the trade-in price falls to £4000. Assuming that the firm regards a 15% discount rate as appropriate, which trade-in policy will be cheaper for the firm?

Assuming that the running costs of the vehicles, ignoring depreciation, are identical each year, the relevant cost of owning one vehicle, expressed in present value terms, as at the date of buying a new vehicle, is:

	Replace after 3 years £	Replace after 4 years £
Cost of the vehicle	(10 000)	(10 000)
Present value of the disposal proceeds:		
£5000 x [1/(1.00 + 0.15)^3]	3 288	
£4000 x [1/(1.00 + 0.15)^4]		2 287
Net present cost of owning the vehicle	£6 712	£7 713

For a wealth-maximising firm it would appear that the three-year replacement cycle offers the better option. These two figures cannot, however, be directly compared because one of them is the net present capital cost of owning a vehicle for three years, which is naturally cheaper than the other which is the net present capital cost of owning the vehicle for four years.

One solution to this problem is to look at the position over 12 years. This is because whichever of the two replacement periods (after three years or after four years) is selected, after 12 years the firm would be on the point of replacing the vehicle and would have had continual use of a vehicle throughout this period. In other words we should be comparing two costs which have both led to a similar provision.

Time		Replace after 3 years £	Replace after 4 years £
0	Cost of a new vehicle	(10 000)	(10 000)
1		–	–
2		–	–
3	PV of the disposal proceeds: $£5000 \times [1/(1.00 + 0.15)^3]$	3 288	
	PV of the cost of a new vehicle $£10\,000 \times [1/(1.00 + 0.15)^3]$	(6 575)	
4	PV of the disposal proceeds: $£4000 \times [1/(1.00 + 0.15)^4]$		2 287
	PV of the cost of a new vehicle $£10\,000 \times [1/(1.00 + 0.15)^4]$		(5 718)
5		–	–
6	PV of the disposal proceeds: $£5000 \times [1/(1.00 + 0.15)^6]$	2 162	
	PV of the cost of a new vehicle $£10\,000 \times [1/(1.00 + 0.15)^6]$	(4 323)	
7		–	–
8	PV of the disposal proceeds: $£4000 \times [1/(1.00 + 0.15)^8]$		1 308
	PV of the cost of a new vehicle $£10\,000 \times [1/(1.00 + 0.15)^8]$		(3 269)
9	PV of the disposal proceeds: $£5000 \times [1/(1.00 + 0.15)^9]$	1 421	
	PV of the cost of a new vehicle $£10\,000 \times [1/(1.00 + 0.15)^9]$	(2 843)	
10		–	–
11		–	–
12	PV of the disposal proceeds: $£5000 \times [1/(1.00 + 0.15)^{12}]$	935	
	$£4000 \times [1/(1.00 + 0.15)^{12}]$		748
	Net present cost of owning the vehicles	£15 935	£14 644

Now that we are able to make a valid comparison we can see that it is less costly to replace the vehicles after four years.

In this case using this approach was not too laborious because the lowest common multiple (LCM) is only 12 years. Suppose, however, that we were considering replacement after either eight or nine years? Here the LCM is 72 years. If we were also considering a seven-year possibility, the LCM would be 504 years! Clearly we need a more practical approach.

An alternative approach is to imagine that we were able to rent a vehicle, either to be replaced with a new one after three years or after four years. In either case let us also imagine that the rent is of a fixed annual amount and that payment is made at the end of each year. If we could deduce the annual rent which would represent the equivalent cost, in NPV terms, to £6712 (three-year replacement) and £7713 (four-year replacement) (see above), we could make a valid comparison between the two replacement policies.

One way to do this is by trial and error. We could try to find an amount such that the NPV of three payments of that amount, one at the end of each of the next three years, equals £6712. Fortunately there is a quicker way, using the annuity table (Appendix 2 of this book). You may care to look back to page 74 for an explanation of the annuity table.

Looking at the annuity table for 15 per cent and 3 years we find an annuity factor of 2.283. This means that the present value of £1 receivable at the end of this year and of the next two years totals £2.283. Thus the amount payable at the end of this year and of the next two years, which has an NPV of £6712, totals £6712/2.283 = £2940.

The four-year annuity factor (from the table) is 2.855. Thus the equivalent annual cost of replacing the vehicle after four years is £7713/2.855 = £2702.

Again we find that the four-year replacement cycle is the less costly option. Note that the equivalent annual cost approach gives the same signal as the LCM approach because they follow exactly the same principles, even though the two approaches seem quite different.

The example we have used is a very basic one. In reality there would probably be a tax aspect, different running costs of the vehicle in each of the four years and the effects of inflation. All these can be incorporated without any great difficulty. There may well also be non-quantifiable factors like the effect on the image of the firm of having its staff driving relatively new vehicles.

ROUTINES FOR IDENTIFYING, ASSESSING, IMPLEMENTING AND REVIEWING INVESTMENT PROJECTS

In Chapter 2 we saw how the decision making process involves six steps; these are:

- Identifying the firm's objectives
- Identifying possible courses of action
- Assembling data relevant to the decision
- Assessing the data and reaching a decision
- Implementing the decision
- Monitoring the effects of decisions.

Accepting that wealth maximisation is the principal financial objective for all decisions, we can now look at the other four of these in the context of investment decisions.

Identifying possible investment opportunities

The assessment of possible investment projects is only one step in a process of the search for opportunities. This process should not be regarded as one which should be undertaken, say at five-yearly intervals, but as one which should be part of the routine of the firm. Good investment opportunities do not tend to beat a path to the firm's door; they must be sought out. Business tends to be highly competitive, so opportunities overlooked by one firm will probably be taken up by another. Any firm which regularly overlooks opportunities must sooner or later fall by the wayside.

Staff need to be encouraged to identify new products, new markets, new ways of supplying those markets and new approaches to production. Technical help should be available to help staff to develop ideas into formal investment proposals.

Assembling the relevant data for an investment proposal

Estimates of the relevant costs associated with the proposal must be made. This probably needs to be carried out by a financial manager. Care must be taken to gather all relevant costs and benefits. There is a danger that bias can influence some of the cost estimates, particularly where a particular manager has a strong commitment for or against the proposal. If an independent finance manager can carry out this task, it may help to promote freedom from bias.

Assessing the data and reaching a decision

The data must be fed into the decision making model which the firm is using. Assuming that the firm is a wealth maximiser this model should be NPV. Once again this process demands certain technical skill and freedom from bias, so it is best carried out by someone who has those attributes, like an independent financial manager.

Monitoring the effects of the decision

Reviews, sometimes known as post audits, need to be carried out to try to assess the effectiveness of the project. One of the reasons for this is to assess the quality of the decision making process, so that improvements in this process can be sought in respect of future decisions. Perhaps it is discovered that some factor which has caused the original decision to be a bad one was ignored when the original decision was taken. In this case steps can be taken to ensure that that factor has account taken of it in all future decisions of the same type.

The progress of the project must also be monitored to assess whether or not it is economic to continue with it. Periodically over the life of the project the question as to whether the project should be abandoned needs to be raised. The project will not be able to continue indefinitely – plant wears out, markets decline, etc. – so identifying the economically optimum moment for its abandonment is important. For the wealth maximising firm, this process logically involves an NPV analysis of the relevant costs and benefits of continuation relative to those associated with abandonment.

Some criticism has been made of researchers in capital investment appraisal implying that they have tended to concentrate on the minutiae of the quantitative assessment of projects, leaving largely untouched questions surrounding the search for possible projects.

The quantitative assessment is a purely technical process, even though a complicated one at times. The real test of management talent is not whether they are able to assess projects but whether they can identify good projects which will promote the achievement of the firm's objectives.

SUMMARY   When applying the NPV rule to investment decisions, it is cash flows rather than accounting flows which must be discounted. Often, accounting flows are used as a surrogate for cash flows; this is acceptable provided adjustments for working capital and depreciation are made. Accounting and investment appraisal have different objectives. All cash flows which vary with the decision, including opportunity cash flows, must be taken into account in the investment appraisal. In practice cash flows are often discounted as if they occurred at year ends, a simplifying assumption which should not necessarily be followed blindly.

Inflation must be considered; in doing so it is important to take a consistent view. Money cash flows must be discounted using a money discount rate, real cash flows using a real discount rate.

Where there is capital rationing a variation to the usual NPV rule must be followed. For single-period rationing, projects can be ranked on the basis of their NPV per £ of investment. Where the constraint is to last for more than one period some mathematical programming technique must be used in finding the optimal use of the capital.

Where the investment decision involves replacing one asset with a similar one on a continuing basis, special techniques can be used.

The quantitative assessment of projects is just the culmination of a process of identifying possible projects. The earlier stages of this process are aspects which require considerable management talent. Routine systems should be established to seek out possible investment opportunities. Failure to identify possible projects will sooner or later result in the demise of a firm.

FURTHER READING   Most texts on business finance and capital investment appraisal deal to a greater or lesser extent with the practical aspects. The following tend to deal with those aspects to a greater extent: Weston & Copeland (1988), Brealey and Myers (1991), Samuels, Wilkes & Brayshaw (1990). Harper (1982) gives clear coverage of linear programming.

WORK-BASED ASSIGNMENT   What is the process for identifying and assessing investment opportunities in your organisation?

QUESTIONS WITH ANSWERS (see Appendix 3)   1 You have just been handed a report on the economics of two proposals for providing a fixed link across the English Channel. One is for a railway tunnel and the other is for a bridge carrying both rail and road traffic. This report shows the following results.

	NPV	IRR	Initial capital
	£ billion	%	£ billion
(a) Tunnel	2.0	15	2.0
(b) Bridge	3.0	12	6.0

The cost of capital is estimated at 10 per cent in real terms after tax.

Required:

(a) Explain the term 'cost of capital'.

(b) In discussions concerning the cost of capital what do you understand by the words 'real terms after tax'.

(c) Explain why the Net Present Value is more favourable for the bridge project than the tunnel, while the Internal Rate of Return gives the tunnel project as the best choice.

(Certified Diploma)

2 United Conglomerates plc owns a large smelting company in a coastal location. Recently it has been considering closing down its operations because of substantial losses caused by a combination of high raw material costs, low selling prices for its output and poor plant operations. The last of these difficulties has led the plant to accumulate large raw material stocks. If the plant is closed immediately the raw materials will have to be sold at well below cost. However, if the plant is allowed to continue in operation substantial operating losses will arise.
The following figures are available:

(a) Close immediately:

	£ million		
	Year 0	Year 1	Year 2
Book value of fixed assets	14.0		
Sales proceeds of fixed assets	4.0		
Book value of working capital	8.0		
Recovery of working capital	2.5	2.5	1.0
Redundancy payments	3.4		
Sundry costs following closure (excluding depreciation)	0.3	0.1	

(b) Operate plant for two years with gradual run down:

	£ million			
	Year 0	Year 1	Year 2	Year 3
Sales proceeds of fixed assets			2.0	3.0
Recovery of working capital			2.5	3.0
Redundancy payments			1.1	2.0
Operating losses (excluding depreciation)		0.9	0.7	

You should assume that all cash flows occur at the end of each year. The company has large tax losses.

Required:

(a) Calculate the NPV for each alternative using a 10 per cent discount rate.
(b) Calculate the incremental NPV.
(c) What other considerations would you take into account before making a decision?
(d) If you were forced to make a decision on the available evidence, what would it be? State why.

(Certified Diploma)

3 Beacon Chemicals plc is considering the erection of a new plant to produce a chemical named X14. The new plant's capital cost is estimated at £100 000 and if its construction is approved now, the plant can be erected and commence production by the end of 19X6. £50 000 has already been spent on research and development work. Estimates of revenues and costs arising from the operation of the new plant appear below:

	19X7	19X8	19X9	19X0	19X1
Sales price (£ per unit)	100	120	120	100	80
Sales volume (units)	800	1000	1200	1000	800
Variable costs (£ per unit)	50	50	40	40	40
Fixed costs (£000s)	30	30	30	30	30

If the new plant is erected sales of some existing products will be lost and this will result in a loss of contribution of £15 000 per year over its life.

The accountant has informed you that the fixed costs include depreciation of £20 000 per annum on the new plant. They also include an allocation of £10 000 for fixed overheads. A separate study has indicated that if the new plant was built, incremental overheads, excluding depreciation, arising from its construction would be £8000 per year.

The plant would require additional working capital of £30 000.

For the purposes of your initial evaluation ignore taxation.

Required:

(a) Prepare a statement of the incremental revenues, costs and net cash flows arising from a decision to build the plant.
(b) Calculate the payback period to the nearest year.
(c) Compute the net present value of the project using an 8 per cent discount rate.
(d) Write a short report to the managing director recommending acceptance or otherwise of the project. Explain the reasons for your recommendation and state what further investigations may be necessary.
(e) Should companies take taxation into account when they evaluate investment proposals? Explain your answer.

(Certified Diploma)

4 R. Jones (Salford) Limited has just received a quotation for £4470 for installing cavity wall insulation in its office building during December 19X7. You ascertain the following information:
- Its fuel bill in 19X7 for heating the office is expected to be £10 000.
- The bank has recently offered a loan at 12 per cent per year.
- Fuel prices are expected to increase at 5 per cent per year.
- The scheme is expected to save 10 per cent of the fuel bill.
- In six years, the firm is planning to move to another area, so it has decided to base its initial evaluation on a six-year project life. Because of the uncertainties involved it also has decided to ignore any effect of the improvement on the sale value of the building.
- The firm requires a risk premium of 2 per cent above its cost of bank borrowing for investments of this type.

Assume that all cash flows arise at the end of the year in which they occur. Ignore taxation.

Required:

(a) Calculate for the project:
  (i) The payback period (to the nearest year).
  (ii) Its net present value.
  (iii) Its approximate internal rate of return.
(b) Comment on the advantages and disadvantages of each of the three methods which appear in part (a) of this question.
  State which method is likely to give the best answer.
(c) Explain briefly three methods by which the company could allow for risk and uncertainty in the project.

(Certified Diploma)

5* The Product Development Manager of Ward Public Limited Company has made a suggestion to produce and sell a range of personal computers. The machinery required to produce the personal computers would be purchased at a cost of £120 000.

His analysis, on an accounting basis, of the project's profitability is:

Note: * indicates a more complex question.

Operating Year	1	2	3	4
	(£000)	(£000)	(£000)	(£000)
Sales	200	300	400	300
Costs				
Materials used				
Opening stock	20	40	40	30
Purchases	100	120	150	90
	120	160	190	120
Closing stock	40	40	30	–
Cost of material used	80	120	160	120
Labour	40	60	60	40
Other production				
expenses	40	45	46	50
Depreciation	20	20	20	20
Administrative charge	27	38	37	37
Interest	11	11	11	11
	218	294	334	278
Gross profit	(18)	6	66	22
Tax	(9)	3	33	11
Net profit	(9)	3	33	11

The following points are made in the Product Development Manager's report to the Board:

(i) The machinery is highly specialised and is unlikely to have any residual value after meeting dismantling costs at the end of its life of at least 4 years.

(ii) Opening stock in year 1 will be purchased at the same time as the machine. All other changes in stock levels will occur at year ends.

(iii) 'Other production expenses' include apportioned fixed overhead equal to 25% of labour costs. Labour costs and the remaining 'other production expenses' are all incremental cash costs.

(iv) Depreciation is based on the usual 6-year life assumed for this type of machine.

(v) 'Administrative charge' is an apportionment of central fixed overheads.

(vi) If the proposal goes ahead it will enable an existing machine to be sold as its function will be performed more efficiently by the new plant in otherwise idle time with a saving of operating costs of £6000 per annum. The machine has a book value of £30 000 and could be sold now for £10 000. It would otherwise be sold in 4 years' time for £4000. Details of the machine and the incidental savings are not included in the above analysis except that the expected disposal proceeds of the machine have been deducted from the envisaged external incremental borrowings needed to finance the project and are reflected in a reduced interest charge to the project.

(vii) The accounting figures show that the average pre-tax book rate of return on initial capital outlay is nearly 16%, and this exceeds the 14% required by the Board on all capital projects.

The Marketing Director objects that the analysis excludes:
(a) the required advertising campaign which will cost £20 000 at the start of the project and £5000 per annum in each of the years 1 to 3;
(b) the effect on the sales of Ward's sophisticated calculators. Sales forecasts and unit prices will need revision as follows:

Sales Forecast – Calculators

		Original forecast		Revised forecast	
		Units	Sales price per unit	Units	Sales price per unit
		(000s)	£	*(000s)*	£
Year	1	5	80	5	75
	2	4	60	3	50
	3	2	40	–	–
	4	–	–	–	–

The production costs, per unit, of calculators are:

	Year 1	Year 2	Year 3
	£	£	£
Variable costs	60	45	30
Fixed cost–apportionment of general factory overheads	10	10	10
Total cost	70	55	40

The Financial Director suggests that the treatment of taxation in the analysis could be improved. He emphasises:

(1) The tax rate is 50% and the tax delay is 1 year.
(2) The machinery is eligible for 100% First Year Capital Allowances and Ward has sufficient total taxable profits for this to be utilised in full at the earliest opportunity.
(3) Proceeds from the sale of the existing machinery would be subject to tax.
(4) Expenditure on advertising is tax deductible.
(5) The 14% required return quoted in the Report is the after-tax discount rate applicable in a DCF appraisal.

Required:

Produce a Discounted Cash Flow appraisal of the proposed project and advise Ward on the acceptability of the proposal. Specify any assumptions made.

(ACCA – amended)

6* A new polishing machine is required. The polishing machine forms a part of the production process and most products manufactured require polishing at various stages in their production. A polishing facility is expected to be required for as long as the factory remains in operation and no closure can be anticipated.

Details of the two machines under consideration are:

Machine	A	B
Initial cost	£50 000	£90 000
Life – years	4	7
Salvage value at end of		
year 4 – machine A	£5 000	
year 7 – machine B		£7 000
Annual running costs	£10 000	£8 000

Both machines fulfil the same function and have equal capacities. The appropriate discount rate is 10%. Taxation may be ignored.

Required:

Determine which machine should be purchased. Specify any assumptions made.
To what amount would the initial cost of machine A be required to alter in order that the two machines were then of equal financial attractiveness?

(ACCA – part of question)

QUESTIONS FOR CLASS USE

1 Haverhill Engineers Limited manufactures components for the car industry. It is considering automating its line for producing crankshaft bearings. The automated equipment will cost £700 000. It will replace equipment with a scrap value of £50 000 and a book written-down value of £180 000.

At present the line has a capacity of 1.25 million units per annum but typically it has only been run at 80 per cent of capacity because of the lack of demand for its output. The new line has a capacity of 1.4 million units per annum. Its life is expected to be five years and its scrap value at that time £100 000.

The accountant has prepared the following cost estimates based on output of 1 000 000 units per annum.

	Old line (per unit)	New line (per unit)
	p	p
Materials	40	36
Labour	22	10
Variable overheads	14	14
Fixed overheads	44	20
	120	80
Selling price	150	150
Profit per unit	30	70

Fixed overheads include depreciation on the old machine of £40 000 per annum and £120 000 for the new machine. It is considered that for the company overall, fixed overheads are unlikely to change.

The introduction of the new machine will enable stocks to be reduced by £160 000.

The company uses 10 per cent as its cost of capital.

You should ignore taxation.

Required:

(a) Prepare a statement of the incremental cash flows arising from the project.
(b) Calculate the project's net present value.
(c) Calculate the project's approximate internal rate of return.
(d) Explain the terms net present value and internal rate of return. State which method you consider to be preferable, giving reasons for your choice.

(Certified Diploma)

2 Lansdown Engineers Limited is considering replacing its existing heating system. A firm of heating engineers has recommended two schemes, each of which will give a similar heating performance. Details of these and of the cost of the existing system appear below:

	Year	Existing system £000	System A £000	System B £000
Capital cost	0		70	150
Annual running cost	1–10	145	140	120
Scrap value	10	10	14	30

The existing heating system at present has a book value of £50 000 and a scrap value of £5000. To keep the existing system working an overhaul costing £20 000 would be required immediately. For your calculations you should ignore inflation and taxation. The company has a 12 per cent cost of capital.

Required:

(a) Calculate the net present cost of each of the two new schemes. You should consider each in isolation and ignore the existing system.
(b) Calculate the incremental cash flows of scheme B over the existing system.
(c) Calculate the internal rate of return on the cash flow calculated in section (b).
(d) On the basis of your calculations give briefly your recommendations with reasons.
(e) Should the items listed below be included in the relevant cash flows for appraising the profitability of capital projects?
   (i) Taxation and government grants.
   (ii) inflation.

(Certified Diploma)

3 Orwell Chemicals Ltd has recently received an offer to produce a new type of synthetic fibre for a large international company. The offer is to produce 14 000 tonnes of the new fibre each year for a three-year period at a price of £44 per tonne. The directors of Orwell Ltd are currently considering the offer and have collected the following information:

(i) New equipment costing £85 000 will be required immediately in order to commence production. The equipment required is highly specialised and can only be used by the company for production of the new fibre. At the end of the three-year period the equipment will be sold for an estimated £6000.

(ii) Eleven new workers will be required to help produce the fibre. The wage costs for the additional workforce are expected to be £200 000 in the first year and will rise at a compound rate of 10 per cent per annum. Recruitment and selection costs, to be paid at the outset, are expected to be £15 000. At the end of the three-year contract the workers will no longer be required and redundancy payments of £2000 per worker will be paid.

(iii) Overheads relating to the contract are estimated at £60 000 per annum. One-third of this figure is arrived at by the reallocation of existing overheads to the contract.

(iv) The production process requires the use of 6000 tonnes of chemical XT3 each year in order to produce the required amount of fibre. The company already has 3000 tonnes of this chemical in stock. The original cost of this stock was £16 per tonne; however, if the contract is not undertaken the chemical could not be used in any other of the company's production processes or resold in the market. The directors have agreed that, if the new fibre is not produced, the existing stock of XT3 will be disposed of immediately at a cost to the company of £2 per tonne. The replacement cost of the chemical is £20 per tonne.

(v) The production process also requires the use of 8000 tonnes of chemical ZF6 each year to produce the required amount of fibre. The company has 4000 tonnes of this chemical already in stock. The original cost of this stock is £22 per tonne and the replacement cost is £25 per tonne. This chemical is widely used in other production processes of the company.

The directors of Orwell Chemicals believe that successful execution of the contract may result in further contracts being offered by the same company. Orwell Chemicals has an estimated cost of capital of 12 per cent.

Ignore taxation.

Required:

(a) Prepare a statement showing those incremental cash flows which are relevant to a decision concerning whether or not to accept the offer.

(b) Calculate the net present value of the offer.

(c) State whether or not you believe the offer should be accepted.

(d) Outline the basic principles to be applied when identifying relevant costs and benefits relating to the offer.

(Certified Diploma)

4* Upstart is likely to experience capital rationing. A maximum of £4 million is likely to be available immediately and a further £1 million in one year's time. Details of the expected cash flows of the new projects are shown below. Projects are divisible and may not be postponed. Cash flows generated from the projects are available for further capital investment. The discount rate is 14 per cent per year.

Cash flow (£000)

Project	Year 0	1	2	3	4
S	(1900)	(800)	1800	1800	200
T	(2200)	800	800	800	800
U	(1500)	–	1200	600	500
V	(4400)	–	2000	2500	2500
W	(1500)	500	500	500	500
X	(2200)	(500)	1300	1200	1500

Required:

(a) Calculate the expected net present values of the projects and then formulate, but do not solve, the linear programming problem to select the optimal combination of projects.

(b) Explain what are meant by dual values and discuss how they might be useful to financial managers in a capital rationing situation.

(c) Discuss the problems of using linear programming in capital investment appraisal.

(ACCA – part of question)

5 The board of directors of Apcon plc is reviewing the company's operations. There is concern about the performance of the textile division, and the board is considering the divestment of the division. Apcon has received an informal offer of £6 million for the division.

Divisional profits are estimated after the allocation by head office of some central costs and a depreciation charge. The losses for the last two years for the textile division are shown below:

	£000	
	19X1	*19X2*
Turnover	13 500	12 900
Direct costs of production	9 500	9 600
Allocated central overhead	2 320	2 400
Finance charge	1 250	1 600
Depreciation charge	600	500
Loss before tax	(170)	(1200)
Imputed tax	–	–
Loss after tax	(170)	(1200)

Balance Sheet summaries of the textile division

£000

	19X1	*19X2*
Land and buildings	2100	2100
Plant and machinery (net)	3800	3650
Current assets:		
Stock	2300	2550
Debtors	1700	1900
Cash	40	20
Less: Current liabilities		
Trade creditors	(3200)	(3750)
Other creditors	(400)	(600)
	6340	5870
Finance provided by		
Apcon's central treasury	6340	5870

The division's accountant estimates that 65% of the allocated central overhead has actually been incurred on behalf of the division and would be saved if the division closed. The depreciation charge is currently believed to be at a realistic level relative to the division's investments, and is expected to remain at approximately this level. Depreciation for tax purposes is the same as the accounting depreciation charge. All finance is provided by Apcon's central treasury, and is charged at a composite rate representing Apcon's estimated weighted average cost of capital which is currently 14% per year in money terms, and 7% per year in real terms. The textile division is believed to be more risky than Apcon's average operations; this extra risk would justify adding 3% per year to both Apcon's money and real discount rate. Turnover of the textile division is expected to grow at 4% per year for the next five years. Direct costs are forecast to increase by 8% per year and central overhead by 10% per year. The central finance charge will remain approximately constant.

At the end of five years the textile division is estimated to have a net of tax disposal value at least equal to the 19X7 market value of land and buildings, plus £1 million. Land and buildings have an estimated current market value 80% above their book value, and plant and machinery 25% below their book value. Both are expected to increase in value by 8% per year. If divestment was to take place Apcon would be responsible for immediate redundancy payments, with an estimated after tax cost of £1.5 million. If divestment does not occur redundancy payments of £0.5 million (after tax) are expected in two years' time. Corporation tax is at the rate of 35% per year, payable in the year that it arises.

Assume that it is now December, 19X2.

Required:

(a) Evaluate whether, on financial grounds, Apcon should accept the offer of £6 million for the textile division. Your evaluation should include a discounted cash flow analysis. State clearly any assumptions that you make.
(b) Discuss possible reasons for a company undertaking divestment.

(ACCA)

CHAPTER 6

Risk in investment appraisal

OBJECTIVES

In this chapter we shall deal with the following:

- the importance of risk and of its formal consideration in the decision-making process
- the use of sensitivity analysis to try to assess the riskiness of a particular project
- the use of statistical probabilities to try to assess risk
- expected value and its deficiencies in the treatment of risk
- systematic and specific risk
- utility theory
- risk aversion
- the logic of the expected value/variance criterion for selecting risky investments in some circumstances
- the particular risks of making overseas investments
- evidence on dealing with risk by firms in practice

INTRODUCTION

Until this point in the book we have all but ignored questions of risk. We are now going to start to confront the issue and though this is the only chapter with the word 'risk' in its title, much of the remainder of the book is concerned with problems of making decisions about a future in which we just do not know what is going to happen. Some events we can predict fairly confidently (e.g. the population of the UK in five years' time, give or take a million). Other matters (e.g. how many of that population will buy our firm's product) are rather more difficult to predict. None of the input data for decisions is known with absolute certainty, so risk is a constant problem to decision makers.

Despite this awkward environment, decisions must still be made. Delaying decisions until the mist of doubt lifts will not be a very fruitful approach, since it never will lift. In the context of a particular decision, it might be that delay may remove some major uncertainties but it will never remove them all. For example, a firm manufacturing mining equipment might await an expected major policy statement by the government on the future of the UK coal mining industry before making a decision on a significant investment in its own manufacturing capacity.

Risk and uncertainty

Some observers have sought to distinguish between risk and uncertainty. Risk is seen as the phenomenon which arises from circumstances where we are able to identify the possible outcomes and even their likelihood of occurrence without being sure which will actually occur. The outcome of throwing a true die is an example of risk. We know that the outcome must be a number from 1 to 6 (inclusive) and we know that each number has an equal (1 in 6) chance of occurrence, but we are not sure which one will actually occur on any particular throw.

Uncertainty describes the position where we simply are not able to identify all, or perhaps not even any, of the possible outcomes, and we are still less able to assess their likelihood of occurrence. Probably most business decisions are characterised by uncertainty to some extent.

Since no one has yet suggested any way of dealing with uncertainty, it represents a particularly difficult area. Perhaps the best that decision makers can do is to try to identify as many as possible of the feasible outcomes of their decision and to attempt to assess each outcome's likelihood of occurrence.

The importance of taking account of risk

It is vital we take account of risk. This should be done in the most formal possible way, not as an afterthought. The level of risk fundamentally affects a decision. We should view very differently the opportunity to wager on a throw of a die and to wager on the spin of a coin. If on payment of £1 we could either guess which face of the die would land upward or which face of a coin would land upward, in either case the prize for a correct guess being £5, which would we choose? Most people would probably be happy to enter the coin spinning wager but few would be eager to go in for the die throwing. This is because the level of risk attaching to each wager would cause us to view them differently, even though they both only have two possible outcomes (lose £1 or gain £4). It is the likelihood of each possible occurrence which would cause us to distinguish between them.

We shall now go on to consider some ways in which risk in investment decisions can be dealt with.

SENSITIVITY ANALYSIS

All business investment decisions have to be made on the basis of predictions of the various inputs. One approach is to assess the decision on the basis of the 'best estimate' of each of the input factors. Assuming that this assessment is favourable, the risk of the project can be assessed by taking each input factor and asking by how much the estimate of that factor could prove to be incorrect before it would affect the decision. This approach is known as sensitivity analysis.

| EXAMPLE | Greene plc has the opportunity to invest in plant for the manufacture of a new product, the demand for which is estimated to be 5000 units a year for five years. The following data relate to the decision: |

- The machine is estimated to cost £50 000 (payable immediately) and to have no residual value.
- The selling price per unit is planned to be £10.
- Labour and material costs are estimated to be £4 and £3 per unit respectively.
- Overhead costs are not expected to be affected by the decision.
- The firm's cost of finance for such a project is estimated to be 10 per cent.
- The project is not expected to require any additional working capital.
- In the interests of simplicity taxation will be ignored.
- Assume, also in the interests of simplicity, that all cash flows occur at year ends.

Required:

(a) an assessment of the project (via NPV) on the basis of the above estimates; and
(b) a sensitivity analysis of the above estimates.

SOLUTION

The annual cash flows will be: 5000 x £[10 – (4 + 3)] = £15 000 each year. Thus the project's cash flows are estimated to be:

	£
Year 0	(50 000)
1	15 000
2	15 000
3	15 000
4	15 000
5	15 000

The annuity factor for five years at 10 per cent is 3.791 (see Appendix 2, page 397). The NPV is therefore:

$$-50\ 000 + (15\ 000 \times 3.791) = +£6865$$

Thus on the basis of the estimates the project is favourable (it has a positive NPV) and should be undertaken.

The estimates are not certain however, so we shall now go on to look at each of the input factors one by one to see how sensitive the decision is to each factor, i.e. to see by how much each one could vary from the original estimate before the project would become unfavourable (negative NPV). While we consider each factor we shall assume that the others will all be as originally estimated.

The factors whose estimates were used in calculating the NPV were as follows:

Original investment	I
Annual sales volume	V
Sales revenue/unit	S
Labour cost/unit	L
Material cost/unit	M
Cost of capital	r
Life of the project	n

We can represent the project as:

$$-I + [V \times (S - (L + M))] \, A_r^n = NPV$$

where A_r^n is the annuity factor for period n years
at discount rate r per cent.

To carry out the sensitivity analysis in respect of each of the input factors we shall equate the NPV to zero (the lowest NPV value for which the project could still be accepted) and put in the original estimates for all factors except the particular one under consideration. The value of the factor under consideration which satisfies the equation is the value at which that factor alone will cause the project to be marginal.

(1) Original investment:

$$-I + 5000 \, [10 - (4 + 3)] \ 3.791 = 0$$
$$I = £56 \, 865$$

Thus the initial investment could increase by £6865 before the project would become marginal.

(2) Annual sales volume:

$$-50 \, 000 + V \ [10 - (4 + 3)] \ 3.791 = 0$$

$$V = \frac{50 \, 000}{(10 - 7) \times 3.791}$$

$$= 4396 \text{ units}$$

(3) Sales revenue/unit:

$$-50 \, 000 + 5000 \, [S - (4 + 3)] \ 3.791 = 0$$

$$S = \frac{50 \, 000}{5000 \times 3.791} + 7$$

$$= £9.64$$

(4) Labour cost/unit:

$$-50 \, 000 + 5000 \, [10 - (L + 3)] \ 3.791 = 0$$

$$L = 7 - \frac{50 \, 000}{5000 \times 3.791}$$

$$= -\frac{10}{3.791} + 7$$

$$= £4.36$$

(5) Material cost/unit:

$$-50 \, 000 + 5000 \, [10 - (4 + M)] \ 3.791 = 0$$

$$M = 6 - \frac{50 \, 000}{5000 \times 3.791}$$

$$= £3.36$$

(6) Cost of capital:

$$-50\ 000 + 5000\ [10 - (4 + 3)]\ A_r^n = 0$$

$$A_r^n = \frac{50\ 000}{5000 \times 3}$$

$$= 3.333$$

It is now a question of looking at the annuity table to find the discount rate for which the annuity factor over five years is 3.333.

At 15 per cent the annuity factor is 3.352 and at 16 per cent it is 3.274. interpolating between these two we can say that the rate is

$$15\% + \left(\frac{3.352 - 3.333}{3.352 - 3.274}\right)\% = 15.24\%$$

(7) Life of the project:

Once again we shall look at the annuity table for 3.333 but this time we are looking in the 10 per cent column to find the year. At four years the factor is 3.170 and at five years it is 3.791. Once again we can interpolate between these. The life will be

$$4\ \text{years} + \left(\frac{3.333 - 3.170}{3.791 - 3.170}\right)\ \text{years} = 4.26\ \text{years}$$

(Note that linear interpolation to find the cost of finance and the life is not a strictly correct approach as the relationship between these factors and the annuity factor is not linear. It is however fairly close to linear over small ranges so the above figures are a reasonable approximation.)

We can now tabulate our results as follows:

Factor	Original estimate	Value to give zero NPV	Difference as percentage of original estimate for the particular factor %
Original investment	£50 000	£56 865	13.7
Annual sales volume	5000 units	4396 units	12.1
Sales revenue/unit	£10	£9.64	3.6
Labour cost/unit	£4	£4.36	9.0
Material cost/unit	£3	£3.36	12.0
Cost of capital	10%	15.24%	52.4
Life of the project	5 years	4.26 years	14.8

From this we can see at a glance how sensitive the NPV calculated on the basis of the original estimates is to changes in the variables in the decision. This gives us some basis on which to assess the riskiness of the project. If we can look at the table confident that all of the actual figures will fall within a reasonable safety margin, then we should regard the project as very much less risky than if this were not the case. If, on the other hand, we felt that all other factors seemed safe but that we were doubtful about, say, labour costs, the fact that only a 9 per cent rise would cause the project to become unfavourable might reduce our confidence in the investment.

Sensitivity analysis is a type of breakeven analysis where, in respect of each factor, we can assess the *breakeven point* and the *margin of safety*.

If the essentials of the project being assessed can be put into a computer which is usually a pretty straightforward matter, the decision maker can, fairly effortlessly, take the analysis rather further than we have just done. A series of assumptions can be made about the variables and the effect on the project's NPV of each combination of assumptions can be assessed.

Since it is most unlikely that all but one of the variables will turn out as estimated, the rather static approach taken in our example gives a very limited perspective on the project. Without the aid of a computer, however, doing much more than this would tend to be so laborious that it would be unreasonable to attempt. Commercial spreadsheet packages capable of undertaking sensitivity analysis are cheap and readily available for most computers, including the cheap microcomputers.

Irrespective of the depth to which sensitivity analysis is taken, it enables the decision maker to 'get inside' a project, see which are the crucial estimates and get a feel for its riskiness. It is clear that sensitivity analysis can be a very useful approach to gaining an impression of a project.

Knowledge of the more sensitive factors might enable us to reassess those factors or even take steps to reduce or eliminate their riskiness. In the above example we discovered that the project's success, in NPV terms, is very sensitive to the estimates both of sales volume and of sales revenue per unit. We may feel that undertaking additional market research would be a way either of reinforcing our confidence in the original estimates or of changing our view of the project.

The results from a sensitivity analysis might cause us to take more positive steps to deal with particularly sensitive factors. The analysis in the example shows the project's success to be fairly sensitive to material costs. It would be quite possible to place orders at fixed prices for the raw material or to take out insurance cover against the possibility of a material price increase.

Clearly these approaches to risk reduction are not without cost. Market research costs money. A supplier who is required to be committed to a fixed price contract would need that fixed price to take account of the risk that its own costs might increase. Insurance companies do not cover risks for nothing. We may feel, however, that these are prices worth paying to reduce the risk to a point where the project would become acceptable.

Despite its benefits to the decision maker, the technique does have its weaknesses:

(a) Sensitivity analysis does not provide us with any rule as to how to interpret the results. We could carry out more market research and possibly reinforce our confidence in the original estimate. If we could not, we have no formal basis on which to proceed to a decision.

(b) The sensitivities are not directly comparable from one factor to the next. In our example, it might seem that the life of the project (14.8 per cent sensitive) is less of a problem than the amount of the original investment (13.7 per cent sensitive). However, this is not true. The original investment is to be made immediately and for that reason alone is likely to be known with more certainty than the life reaching well into the future. Also, if it is found that the cost of making the original investment creeps to above £56 865, the project could be cancelled. Only when the project has been undertaken and large amounts of finance committed to it would we discover whether or not the estimate of the project's life was over-optimistic.

USE OF PROBABILITIES

Perhaps more useful than looking at the amount by which a particular factor may vary from its estimate before it renders a project unprofitable, is to look at how likely it is to do so. If the whole range of possible outcomes for each factor can be estimated together with each one's statistical probability of occurrence, a much fuller picture would be obtained. These could be combined to discover the range of possibilities and probabilities for the NPV of the project as a whole. Before we go on to look at how this could be done, it should be pointed out that reliably identifying possible outcomes and their probabilities is very difficult to achieve in practice.

In ascribing probabilities to various aspects, decision makers might use:

(a) *Objective probabilities*, based on past experience of the outcomes and their likelihood of occurrence. For example, if we know what the annual demand for a particular product has been over the years, we could assume that this would define the possible outcomes and their probabilities for next year. Suppose that during each of six of the past ten years the demand for the product had been 2 million units and it had been 3 million for each of the other four years, we could conclude that next year's demand will either be 2m or 3m with a 0.6 and 0.4 probability respectively. If we have reason to believe that the past is not a good guide to the future because, for example, the product has just been superseded by a more technologically advanced version, this approach could not be justified.

(b) *Subjective probabilities*, based on opinions, preferably of experts, on the possibilities and on their probability of occurrence.

However ascribed, the use of probabilities enables a fuller picture of the range of outcomes to be considered.

EXAMPLE

Using the data from the sensitivity analysis example (Greene plc) let us assume that all the factors are known with certainty (impossible in real life) except sales volume.

Extensive market research suggests that annual demand will be:

   (a) 4000 units (0.2 probable)
or (b) 4500 units (0.5 probable)
or (c) 5000 units (0.3 probable)

What are the possible outcomes?

SOLUTION	NPV at 4000 units p.a.	$= -50\,000 + 4000\,(10 - 7)\,3.791$
		$= -£4\,508$ (probability 0.2)
	NPV at 4500 units p.a.	$= -50\,000 + 4500\,(10 - 7)\,3.791$
		$= +£1\,179$ (probability 0.5)
	NPV at 5000 units p.a.	$= -50\,000 + 5000\,(10 - 7)\,3.791$
		$= +£6\,865$ (probability 0.3)

Thus we have a description of the range and probabilities of the outcomes.

This example vastly oversimplifies the situation both by assuming that there are only three possible outcomes for sales volume and by assuming that there is only one possible outcome for each of the other factors. Let us, however, take one more small step towards reality.

EXAMPLE

Still staying with the same data, let us assume not only that the sales volume has the same three possible outcomes, but that, independent of the sales volume, the cost of labour will either be:

(a) £3/unit (0.1 probable)
(b) £4/unit (0.7 probable)
(c) £5/unit (0.2 probable)

What are the possible outcomes and how likely is each one?

  (Note that the word 'independent' in the above context means that the actual outcome as regards sales volume implies nothing about which labour cost is most likely.)

SOLUTION

This situation is rather more complicated in that there are now nine possible outcomes. Each of the three possible sales volume outcomes could occur in conjunction with each of the three possible labour costs.

  The outcomes might usefully be represented in a diagram (see Fig. 6.1). For ease of reference the nine possible outcomes are labelled A to I inclusive. Outcome F, say, will occur if 4500 units p.a. are sold and the labour cost is £5/unit. As the probability of the first is 0.5 and of the second 0.2 then the joint probability is the product of these, which is 0.10.

  Note that the sum of the probabilities of all the nine possibilities is 1.00, i.e. one of them is certain to occur.

**Figure 6.1
Possible outcomes
of Greene plc's
investment
opportunity**

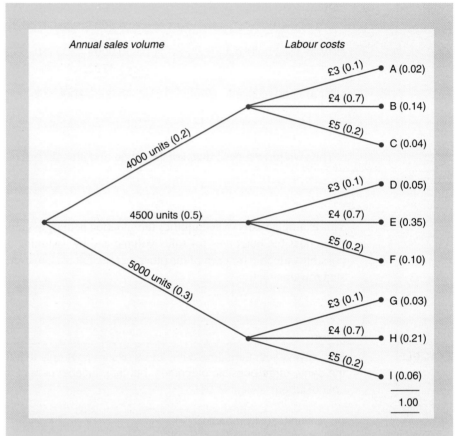

Annual sales volume   *Labour costs*

£3 (0.1)   A (0.02)
£4 (0.7)   B (0.14)
£5 (0.2)   C (0.04)

4000 units (0.2)

£3 (0.1)   D (0.05)
£4 (0.7)   E (0.35)
£5 (0.2)   F (0.10)

4500 units (0.5)

£3 (0.1)   G (0.03)
£4 (0.7)   H (0.21)
£5 (0.2)   I (0.06)

5000 units (0.3)

1.00

This shows the nine possible outcomes (A to I) which could result from this project.
Each one's likelihood of occurrence is found by multiplying the probability of the
relevant outcome for sales volume with its counterpart for labour cost.

The NPVs of each possibility are:

A: NPV $= -50\,000 + 4000\,[10 - (3 + 3)]\,3.791$
$\quad = +£10\,656$

B: NPV $= -50\,000 + 4000\,[10 - (4 + 3)]\,3.791$
$\quad = -£4508$

C: NPV $= -50\,000 + 4000\,[10 - (5 + 3)]\,3.791$
$\quad = -£19\,672$

D: NPV $= -50\,000 + 4500\,[10 - (3 + 3)]\,3.791$
$\quad = +£18\,238$

E: NPV $= -50\,000 + 4500\,[10 - (4 + 3)]\,3.791$
$\quad = +£1179$

F: NPV $= -50\,000 + 4500\,[10 - (5 + 3)]\,3.791$
$\quad = -£15\,881$

G: NPV $= -50\,000 + 5000\,[10 - (3 + 3)]\,3.791$

$\qquad = +\pounds25\,820$

H: NPV $= -50\,000 + 5000\,[10 - (4 + 3)]\,3.791$

$\qquad = +\pounds6865$

I: NPV $= -50\,000 + 5000\,[10 - (5 + 3)]\,3.791$

$\qquad = -\pounds12\,090$

Listing these in order of size, we get:

Possible outcome	NPV £	Probability
C	−19 672	0.04
F	−15 881	0.10
I	−12 090	0.06
B	−4 508	0.14
E	+1 179	0.35
H	+6 865	0.21
A	+10 656	0.02
D	+18 238	0.05
G	+25 820	0.03
		1.00

Note that, given the data from the question, one of the above nine must occur and only one can occur.

As we have seen, a very modest attempt at reality causes complications. We can well imagine the number of possible outcomes were we to explore a more realistic set of possibilities for each of the input factors, even with our simple example.

How useful to us is the array of nine outcomes and probabilities shown above? The NPV rule is to accept projects with positive NPVs and reject those with negative ones. Here we know that four of the nine possible outcomes will yield a negative NPV, yet the other five give positive ones. One of these nine possibilities will occur, but which one? One way forward on the problem of the vast array of possible outcomes and the problem of making the decision once we have them is through the notion of 'expected value'.

EXPECTED VALUE

As ever, when we are confronted by a mass of data, it can be useful if we can find some way of summarising it so that we can more readily absorb and use it.

One way of summarising is to calculate a weighted average or *expected* value. This involves multiplying each possible outcome by its probability of occurrence. Taking the array of outcomes from the example gives us the following result.

Possible outcome	NPV £	Probability (p)	NPV × p
C	−19 672	0.04	−787
F	−15 881	0.10	−1588
I	−12 090	0.06	−725
B	−4 508	0.14	−631
E	+1 179	0.35	+413
H	+6 865	0.21	+1442
A	+10 656	0.02	+213
D	+18 238	0.05	+912
G	+25 820	0.03	+775
		Expected value	+24

Incidentally, if the decision maker were not interested in the individual outcomes (A to I) there is a much more direct approach to arriving at the expected value. This is to calculate the expected value of the risky factors and then to calculate the NPV, incorporating these expected values.

$$\text{Expected sales volume} = (4000 \times 0.2) + (4500 \times 0.5) + (5000 \times 0.3)$$
$$= 4550 \text{ units}$$
$$\text{Expected labour cost} = (£3 \times 0.1) + (£4 \times 0.7) + (£5 \times 0.2)$$
$$= £4.1$$
$$\text{NPV} = -50\,000 + 4550\,[10 - (4.1 + 3)]\,3.791 = +£22$$

The difference between this figure and the original expected NPV (+£24) is entirely due to rounding errors in the original calculation.

We now have one single factor to which we could apply the NPV rule. (In this case the expected NPV is very close to zero and thus the project would be on the margin between acceptance and rejection if (E)NPV is the decision criterion.)

There are some obvious weaknesses in the (E)NPV approach.

(a) As with all averaging, information is lost. The figure of +£24 for the (E)NPV of the project in the example does not tell us that there is a 4 per cent chance of the project yielding a negative NPV of £19 672. It also fails to tell us that the single most likely outcome, outcome E, gives a positive NPV of £1179.

How could we distinguish between this project and one with a certain NPV of +£24? We need some measure of dispersion, such as range or standard deviation.

(b) The (E)NPV may well represent a value that could not possibly exist. In our example an NPV of +£24 is certain not to occur. The possible outcomes are A to I, one of which must occur, and +£24 is not amongst them. In this sense expected value is a misnomer as it could not possibly occur (not in this example at least), let alone be expected in the normal meaning of the word. Does this invalidate (E)NPV as a decision-making criterion?

We know that the probability of a fair coin landing heads up is 0.5. If we are offered a wager such that we should gain £1 if a coin lands heads up and nothing if it lands tails up, one such throw would have an expected value of £0.50 (despite the fact that the outcome could only be £1 or nothing). If the wager were repeated say 100 times we should be very surprised if the expected value (£50) and the actual outcome differed by much. In other words, where there is a large number of projects, the expected value and the actual outcome are likely to be close, provided that the projects are independent.

Firms typically hold *portfolios* of investment projects; they have a number, perhaps a large number, of projects in operation at any given time. They do this, amongst other reasons, to diversify risk, i.e. to seek actually to achieve the expected value of the sum of the projects. Managers know that the expected value of each project probably will not (probably cannot) actually occur but that 'swings and roundabouts' will cause the sum of the expected values to be the outcome. Greene plc (in the example) may well have many other projects and it expects that the unlikely event of outcome C occurring will be matched by an unexpectedly favourable outcome in another project. The firm would expect this in the same way as a coin landing heads up five times in a row is possible (a 1 in 32 chance) but should it occur, over a reasonably large number of throws chance will even out so that heads will face upwards in only about 50 per cent of the total number of throws.

Diversification

This holding of a portfolio of investment projects in order to seek risk reduction is known as 'diversification'.

EXAMPLE

A firm has two investment opportunities in each of which it can invest any amount up to £2m. The firm has £2m to invest. The characteristics of the two opportunities are as follows:

Project	Outcome (NPV as % of investment)	Probability
A	(i) +20%	0.5
	(ii) −10%	0.5
B	(i) +20%	0.5
	(ii) −10%	0.5

SOLUTION

If all of the £2m is invested in either project the outcome will either be +£0.4m or −£0.2m. However, if part, say half, is invested in each project then there are four possible outcomes for the firm:

A(i) and B(i):   Total NPV = (£1.0m x 20%) + (£1.0m x 20%)
$$= \underline{£0.4m}$$
Probability = 0.5 x 0.5 = <u>0.25</u>

A(i) and B(ii): Total NPV = (£1.0m x 20%) + (£1.0m x –10%)

= +£0.1m

Probability = 0.5 x 0.5 = 0.25

A(ii) and B(i): Total NPV = (£1.0m x –10%) + (£1.0m x 20%)

= +£0.1m

Probability = 0.5 x 0.5 = 0.25

A(ii) and B(ii): Total NPV = (£1.0m x –10%) + (£1.0m x –10%)

= –£0.2m

Probability = 0.5 x 0.5 = 0.25

As both projects have identical possible returns, diversification does not change the highest or lowest outcome (still +£0.4m or –£0.2m). Diversification does however introduce two new possibilities, both of which would combine a favourable outcome from one project with an unfavourable one from the other. These two possibilities, between them, are 0.5 probable.

The expected NPV of either or both of the projects with a total investment of £2.0m is:

(£2.0m x 20% x 0.5) + (£2.0m x –10% x 0.5) = +£0.1m

We can see that, as far as this example is concerned, diversification means that the expected value starts to become a likely outcome. Diversification has also reduced the chance of the best outcome occurring, the worst outcome is also less likely (in both cases down from 0.5 to 0.25 probability).

We shall see a little further on that most investors will readily accept a reduction of expectations of high returns in order to reduce the likelihood of low ones.

Systematic and specific risk

How likely in real life is it that a firm's investment projects are independent of one another in the way that spins of a fair coin are? Is it not quite likely that the very factors which will cause one project to turn out unfavourable will similarly affect each of the others? In the last example is it not true that outcome (ii) occurring with project A in real life, implies outcome (ii) occurring to project B as well, meaning that there would be no advantage from diversification?

The answer to these questions seems to be that whilst there are factors specific to each individual investment such that they will affect only its outcome, there are also underlying factors which will affect just about all projects.

Specific risk is the expression used to describe the part of the risk which relates to the particular project. This portion of the risk can be eliminated by diversification, in the way that the example suggests, because specific risk factors for separate projects are independent of each other.

Consider the perhaps unlikely example of a firm whose investments are diversified between making light bulbs and making chocolate. Project X might fail if a new means of making light bulbs is discovered by a rival, Project Y might fail if there is a world shortage of cocoa. These are specific risk factors for separate projects which are independent of each other. There is no reason to believe that the world market for cocoa could possibly affect light-bulb making.

That part of the risk which cannot be diversified away because it is caused by factors common to all activities is known as *systematic risk*. Such factors would include the general level of demand in the economy, interest rates, inflation rates, labour costs. Few, if any, activities are unaffected by these factors so diversification will not remove the risk. These factors seem likely to affect both light bulb and chocolate manufacture.

Clearly firms eager to eliminate specific risk by diversifying between industries must have more than half an eye on the fact that this is likely to have the effect of taking the firm into areas in which it has no expertise or experience.

The existence of systematic risk means that expected value is not the whole answer to dealing with risk. Not all of the risk is susceptible to elimination through diversification. Systematic factors mean that expected value may well not occur for the firm as a whole, even though forecast assessments of financial effect and probability of occurrence of the various possible outcomes may be impeccable.

Before going on to consider another reason why expected value may not be a complete way of dealing with risk, let us take a brief look at a useful way of expressing attitudes towards risk.

UTILITY THEORY

The notion of utility provides a means of expressing individual tastes and preferences. This is an important aspect of business finance and something to which we shall return on several occasions in this book. Utility is the level of satisfaction which an individual derives from some desirable factor, e.g. going away on holiday, having drinking water available, eating caviar or having wealth. Utility and differing levels of it are frequently represented graphically by *indifference curves*, each one showing a constant level of utility or satisfaction for differing combinations of related factors.

UU in Fig. 6.2 represents the utility curve of the attitude of some individual towards holidays and how much of his or her savings the person is prepared to devote to them. 0S represents the total of the person's savings, all of which could be spent on going away on holiday this year. Alternatively all or part of them could be retained for other purposes. The curve suggests that this particular individual is prepared to forgo some savings to go on holiday. In fact the person is prepared to give up a lot of savings in order to go for a short time (the curve is fairly close to being horizontal at the bottom right). As we move up the curve (bottom right to top left) less and less utility is derived from each extra day of holiday so that the individual is prepared to give up less and less savings to it. In fact this individual reaches a point towards the top of the curve where there is a reluctance to give up any more savings to get extra days of holiday (the curve becomes vertical). This suggests that once this person has had a certain amount of holiday there is an unwillingness to spend more money on extra days. It is important to recognise that the curve depicted applies only to this individual and reflects his or her personal tastes; any other individual may see things

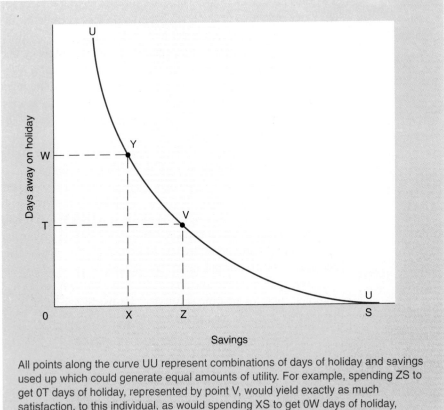

Figure 6.2
Utility of going
away on holiday
for some individual

All points along the curve UU represent combinations of days of holiday and savings used up which could generate equal amounts of utility. For example, spending ZS to get 0T days of holiday, represented by point V, would yield exactly as much satisfaction, to this individual, as would spending XS to get 0W days of holiday, represented by point Y.

very differently – perhaps even not liking being away from home very much and so being unwilling to devote any savings to it.

For the individual whose preferences are depicted in Fig. 6.2, all points along the curve UU represent combinations of days away on holiday and savings retained which will give equal satisfaction. Thus points V and Y on curve UU represent just two of the many combinations of days of holiday and savings retained which would be of equal satisfaction or utility to our individual. This person would view having 0T days of holidays and retaining 0Z of savings as equally satisfying to going on holiday for 0W days, leaving only 0X of savings. The person would be indifferent to which of these two combinations, or indeed of any other combinations lying along UU, were to be taken.

Figure 6.3 shows the same combinations of days of holiday and savings retained but at varying levels. Each of the curves U_1U_1, U_2U_2, U_3U_3 and U_4U_4 of themselves show combinations which yield equal satisfaction or utility but the higher the curve, the higher the level of utility. For example, any point along U_2U_2 is more satisfactory than any point along U_1U_1 for our individual. This is because, at any level of savings used, more days of holiday could be taken; or, at any number of days of holiday, the inroads into the person's savings would be less. For example, if PS of savings were devoted to paying for a holiday (leaving 0P to save or spend other than on holidays), 0Q days of holiday would be obtained if the state of the world implied curve U_1U_1, but the much larger 0R days if it implied curve U_4U_4. Different levels of utility imply different states of the world, e.g. U_4U_4 implies that holidays are cheaper and/or our individual can get the first few days of holiday without cost as compared with the U_1U_1 position. Thus the individual would prefer the range of possibilities portrayed by U_2U_2 over those shown on U_1U_1. To be on U_3U_3 would be even better and on U_4U_4 even better still. Thus whilst the individual is indifferent to where he or she is on any particular curve there is a clear preference to be on the highest possible curve (i.e. the one furthest to the top right) as this gives the maximum possible level of satisfaction or utility.

**Figure 6.3
Various levels of
utility of going
away on holiday
for some individual**

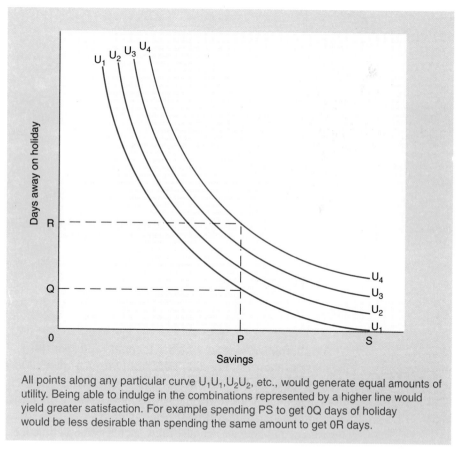

All points along any particular curve U_1U_1, U_2U_2, etc., would generate equal amounts of utility. Being able to indulge in the combinations represented by a higher line would yield greater satisfaction. For example spending PS to get 0Q days of holiday would be less desirable than spending the same amount to get 0R days.

Figure 6.3 represents just four of an infinite number of similarly shaped curves, parallel to the curves shown. Note that the shape of these curves is determined by our individual's preferences; which curve actually applies is decreed by the state of the world (e.g. price of holidays). This example concerning the trade-off between savings used and days away on holiday illustrates a phenomenon which seems to apply generally to human behaviour. The more individuals have of a particular factor which they might find desirable (e.g. going away on holiday) the less they are willing to pay for additional amounts of it. Thus the worth (in financial terms) of an additional day of holiday not only varies from individual to individual; it probably also depends on how much holiday the individual already has.

Figure 6.4
The utility function of some individual for going away on holiday

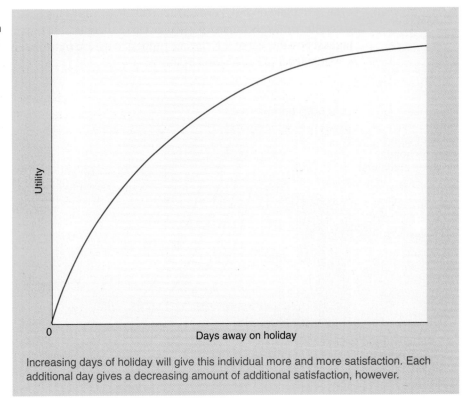

Increasing days of holiday will give this individual more and more satisfaction. Each additional day gives a decreasing amount of additional satisfaction, however.

An alternative way in which we could represent this individual's attitude to holidays is shown in Fig. 6.4. Here utility itself is plotted against days of holiday. We can see from Fig. 6.4 that our individual derives great utility from increases in days of holiday at the lower end but, as more days are obtained, the additional utility given by each extra day diminishes. Figure 6.4 raises the question of how utility is measured, and how we actually draw such a graph in practice. In fact utility is not a readily measurable factor and therefore graphs of it are difficult to construct. Utility is in the mind of the individual.

Utility theory has been criticised for the fact that utility is difficult to measure. Most observers agree, however, that the notions represented in the theory have an inexorable logic. For our present purposes it is sufficient that we accept these notions; we shall not need to concern ourselves further than that.

ATTITUDES TO RISK AND EXPECTED VALUE

Let us now go back to expected value and the other reason why it is not apparently as useful as it might be to decision makers in firms.

Like the attitude of our individual to holidays, depicted in Fig. 6.4, most people's attitude to wealth varies with the amount of it that they have. On the face of it, the expected value of a risky venture is what a rational person would pay for it. For example, the expected value of a wager on the spin of a fair coin which pays out £200 for a head and nothing for a tail is £100 (i.e. (£200 × 0.5) + (0 × 0.5)). We might expect that a rational person would be prepared to pay £100 to take part in the wager. In fact it would appear that only a minority of people would be prepared to risk losing £100 in order to stand a one in two chance of winning £100. This is because most of us are risk-averse.

Figure 6.5 shows the utility of wealth curve for a risk-averse individual. Utility, as we saw in the previous section, is a level of satisfaction. W on the horizontal axis represents the present level of wealth of an individual. To this individual, increasing

**Figure 6.5
A graph of the
utility of wealth
against wealth for
some risk-averse
individual**

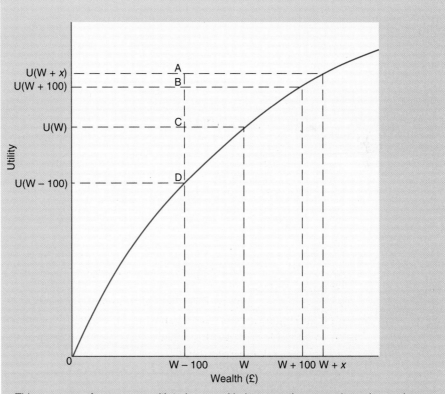

This person prefers more wealth to less wealth, because the curve shows increasing utility for increasing wealth. It also shows the individual to be risk-averse, because each successive increase of £1 of wealth yields a smaller increase in satisfaction. This person would lose more satisfaction from losing £1 than would be gained from gaining £1.

**Figure 6.6
Graphs of the
utility of wealth
against wealth for
individuals with
different attitudes
towards risk**

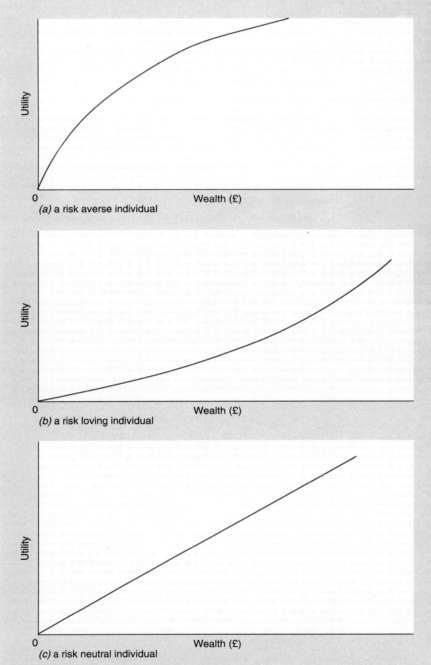

(a) a risk averse individual

(b) a risk loving individual

(c) a risk neutral individual

The risk-averse individual (graph (*a*)) would gain less satisfaction from having an additional £1, than the satisfaction which would be lost from having £1 less. The risk-loving individual (graph (*b*)) would gain more satisfaction from having an additional £1, than would be lost from having £1 less. To the risk-neutral individual (graph (*c*)), the gain in satisfaction from having an additional £1 is equal to the loss in satisfaction of having £1 less.

wealth by £100 would increase personal satisfaction (utility) by CB, but losing £100 would reduce that satisfaction by CD, a rather larger amount. This individual would only become indifferent to the wager if the potential gain were x, so that the increase in utility from the gain (should it arise) would equal the potential loss of utility from the loss of the money (i.e. CA = CD). The risk-averse person would need the prize for the coin landing heads to be in excess of £100 to make the wager attractive.

The precise shape of a utility curve (and thus how much the prize in the above wager needs to be) depends on the personal preferences of the individual concerned. The curve in Fig. 6.5 represents the preferences of just one hypothetical individual, though all risk-averse individuals will have a curve of roughly the same shape. Note that how much the prize in the wager would need to be, to tempt any particular individual, depends both on that person's utility curve and the level of wealth of that individual at the time when the wager is on offer.

Figure 6.6 shows the general shapes of the utility curves of (a) a risk-averse investor, (b) a risk-loving investor, and (c) a risk-neutral investor. A risk-neutral investor views equally entering a wager whose expected value is zero, and doing nothing.

There might well be some individuals in the world who are risk-lovers. Such an individual might, for example, be prepared to enter a coin-spinning wager standing to lose £100 but to gain only £90. Such might be the desire to be exposed to risk that he or she would be willing to take on wagers with negative expected value. Most of us are not.

There is quite a lot of evidence around us to support the assertion that most people are risk-averse. People's general desire to cover potential disasters by insurance is an example. Most house-owners, with no legal compulsion, choose to insure their property against destruction by fire. Clearly, taking account of the potential financial loss and the risk of fire, the premium must be more than the expected value of the loss, otherwise the fire insurance companies would consistently lose money. For example, if the potential damage from a fire for a particular house is £30 000 and the probability of a serious fire during a year is 1 in 1000 (i.e. 0.001 probability), the expected value of the loss is £30 (i.e. £30 000 × 0.1). Unless the house-owner is prepared to pay a premium higher than £30 p.a. the insurance company would not accept the risk, yet most house-owners seem to insure their houses at a premium, presumably more than the expected value of the potential loss. They are prepared to do this because the loss of utility caused by paying the premium is less than the anticipated loss of utility caused by the cost of a fire (if the house is uninsured) multiplied by its probability of occurrence. This arises from the fact that for risk-averse individuals utility of wealth curves are not straight lines, i.e. there is not a linear relationship between wealth and utility of wealth.

Figure 6.7 shows the range of possible outcomes for two investment projects A and B. Both have expected values of £15 000 (the outcomes of each are symmetrically arrayed around this value); in fact £15 000 is the single most likely outcome (the mode) in each case.

Both of these projects would be acceptable to the investor as they both have positive NPV, irrespective of where in the range the actual outcome falls. Since most of the human race seems to be risk-averse, project A would be most people's first choice if they had to choose between the projects. This is despite the fact that project B holds the possibility of an actual NPV as high as £30 000 whereas project A's maximum is only £21 000. The risk-averse investor's eyes would be drawn to the lower end of the scale where that person would note that project A gives a guaranteed minimum NPV of £9000 whereas project B's outcome could be as low as zero. To the risk-averse, the so called *downside risk* looms larger than the *upside risk*. By contrast a risk-lover would be more attracted to project B. A risk-neutral investor would be unable to distinguish between these two projects.

Figure 6.7
A graph of the probabilities of the NPV for two projects each having equal expected NPVs

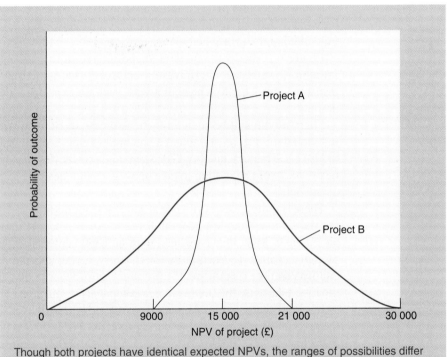

Though both projects have identical expected NPVs, the ranges of possibilities differ between them. A risk averse investor would prefer Project A. This is because the worst possible outcome is an NPV of £9000, which is quite a lot higher than the minimum outcome from Project B.

Expected value and firm's investment decisions

From what we have seen (above), in deciding on risky investment projects we cannot directly translate the wealth maximisation rule into one of expected wealth maximisation, i.e. we cannot simply take on all available projects with a positive expected NPV. The reason for this is that shareholders, despite probably all being risk-averse, may show different degrees of risk aversion (different shaped utility curves and levels of wealth). An investment whose risk/return profile might be acceptable to one shareholder may not be acceptable to another.

This potential lack of unanimity may seem familiar. It is, of course, analogous to the investment decision without the borrowing/lending facility (a matter which we discussed in Chapter 2), and it poses the same problem. How do managers make their investment decisions when shareholders take different attitudes to risk? As before, it is really the utility, or satisfaction of wealth, that shareholders want maximised, but shareholders will not necessarily all agree on what satisfies them most. Maximisation of the utility of wealth involves some consideration of the range of possible outcomes (as is evident from Fig. 6.5).

In the next section we shall look at a partial solution to management's problem.

THE EXPECTED VALUE/VARIANCE (OR MEAN/VARIANCE) CRITERION

A popular statistical measure of dispersion is the variance (or its square root, the standard deviation). The variance (σ^2) is defined as follows:

$$\sigma^2 = \sum_{i=1}^{n} p_i [x_i - E(x)]^2$$

where p_i is the probability of outcome x_i, $E(x)$ its expected value or mean, and there are n possible outcomes.

EXAMPLE

A project will yield one of three NPVs whose amount and probabilities of occurrence are as follows:

NPV £	Probability
−1000	0.2
+1000	0.5
+2000	0.3

What is the expected NPV of the project and its variance?

SOLUTION

(E)NPV $= (0.2 \times -1000) + (0.5 \times 1000) + (0.3 \times 2000)$

$\underline{= £900}$

$\sigma^2 = 0.2(-1000 - 900)^2 + 0.5(1000 - 900)^2 + 0.3(2000 - 900)^2$

$= (0.2 \times 3\ 610\ 000) + (0.5 \times 10\ 000) + (0.3 \times 1\ 210\ 000)$

$\sigma^2 = \underline{\underline{1\ 090\ 000}}$ (in £²)

The variance is a particularly useful device for our present purposes. It can be shown (Levy & Sarnat, 1988) that if we assume that the range of possible outcomes from a decision is distributed normally around the expected value, then knowledge of the expected value and the variance (or standard deviation) is all that risk-averse investors need, to enable them to select between two risky investments.

In other words, provided that the investor is risk-averse and that the dispersion of possible outcomes is normal, then selecting investments on the basis of their expected (or mean) value and variance will cause a maximisation of the investor's utility of wealth.

EXAMPLE

A risk-averse investor is faced with two competing investment projects, dispersions of both of whose possible outcomes are *normal* about their expected values. Which should the investor select?

Project	A	B
Expected value (£)	20 000	20 000
Variance (£)	10 000	12 000

SOLUTION

Project A would be selected since this offers an equal expected value to Project B but with less risk. By selecting Project A, maximisation of the utility of wealth of the risk-averse investor will be promoted.

The expected value/variance criterion (EVC) may be summarised as

(a) where the expected value of Project A is equal to or greater than that of Project B, A should be preferred to B if it has a lower variance; and

(b) where the variance of Project A is equal to or smaller than that of Project B, A should be preferred to B if it has a higher expected value.

What EVC does not tell us is how to choose between two investments where both the expected value and the variance of Project A are greater than those of Project B. We shall look at how this dilemma can be addressed in the next chapter.

Particular risks associated with making investments overseas

In principle, investing in a project based overseas is the same as investing in a similar one in the UK. There are several respects in which the overseas project is likely to be more risky. These include:

(a) *Lack of local knowledge.* There is the danger that the decision makers may have insufficient knowledge of the political and financial environment in which the investment is to be made. The obvious means of eliminating this risk is by using expert consultants to advise on factors which represent gaps in the knowledge of the managers making the decision.

(b) *Foreign exchange risk.* Where the investment is being made at one time and the rewards are expected to occur at another, there is the risk that the exchange rate, between the home currency and the currency in which the investment is to be made, may move in a manner adverse to the project. Where the shareholders predominantly spend their wealth in the home country, this is important. For example, a firm makes an investment overseas. At that point the project has a positive NPV. Shortly after converting the required amount of the home currency into the local currency and making the investment, the home currency strengthens against the local currency. This means that the benefits of the investment, when converted into the home currency, are now less, possibly by an amount large enough to render the project adverse, from an NPV perspective.

This is a very real and significant risk. Any overseas investor who entered a project in the UK just before 16 September 1992, the day that the UK left the European Monetary System and devalued by about 15 per cent, may well have made an adverse investment. This means that the wealth of the shareholders of that overseas company could be less as a result of making the investment.

There are ways of avoiding the exchange rate risk. They amount, in effect, to passing this risk on to someone else. One way is to use the foreign exchange market to sell the overseas currency, expected to be derived from the project, for the home currency (i.e. convert the overseas currency into the home currency) with delivery of both currencies to take place at a future time, but at the current exchange rate. This means that outflows and inflows of the project will be converted at the same exchange rate.

A disadvantage with forward sales of currency is that if the exchange rate moves in a manner favourable to the investment, the advantage will go to the other party to the forward transaction. This can be overcome through a currency options deal. Here the investing firm can buy the right to sell the overseas currency at a particular time in the future (a put option). The rate at which the sale will be made will be specified in the option contract. It could be the rate at which the investment finance was converted. If, at the time when the overseas currency needs to be converted, the exchange rate has moved in a manner adverse to the project, the investing firm can exercise its option. Otherwise, the firm will allow the option to lapse and simply use the normal (spot) currency market to carry out the conversion.

Both of these hedging strategies remove the exchange rate risk, but they cost money. Generally future exchange rates are not as favourable as are the spot rates. Similarly, currency options sellers need to be rewarded for providing their service.

(c) *Political risk.* Investing overseas exposes the investing firm to risks associated with the overseas country concerned. These include dangers of war, civil unrest, unexpected increases in taxes on the revenues from the project, restrictions on the extent to which the cash outflows can be remitted to the home country. These risks may be no more or even less than those to which the firm is exposed at home. The problem is that they are likely to be in addition to those which are faced at home. Clearly one way of avoiding political risk is to avoid investing in high political risk countries. There are commercial services which provide information on political risk, country by country. Another way of avoiding the risk is by passing it on to others through insurance. It is not uncommon for firms to insure their overseas investments.

SOME EVIDENCE ON RISK ANALYSIS IN PRACTICE

To gain some insight into the extent to which, and how, risk is taken into account, in practical investment decision making we shall rely on the researches of Ho and Pike (1991), whose findings are consistent with other, similar studies conducted recently. This evidence relates to a survey of 146 of the very largest firms in the UK, conducted in 1987.

The evidence seems to suggest:

(a) Formal consideration of risk is not a universal practice. Eighty-seven per cent of the firms questioned formally considered risk in relation to their capital investment decisions. Earlier research by Pike and Woolf (1988) suggests that it is unlikely that many of the firms surveyed formally assessed risk in respect of every investment decision. It might be reasonable to suppose that among the firms who do not formally assess risk all the time, there is a greater tendency to assess it in respect of larger investment decisions.

A reason suggested for the popularity of the use of the payback method of investment appraisal (see Chapter 4) is that it provides an assessment of the riskiness of the project. Though the validity of using this method of investment appraisal as a means of dealing with risk is theoretically somewhat dubious, its widespread use by firms of all sizes may imply that consideration of risk is also widespread. It is difficult to believe that many firms completely ignore the question of risk in investment decision making, even though it may be done on an informal basis in many cases.

(b) There is an increasing tendency formally to take account of risk. As we have seen, 87 per cent of the firms surveyed by Ho and Pike in 1987 formally accounted for risk. However, Pike (1982) found (with a similar survey sample) that in 1975 there were only 26 per cent of firms which formally accounted for risk, a figure which had grown to 38 per cent by 1981.

(c) Some of the firms which formally take account of risk use more than one approach to dealing with it.

(d) There are two main approaches to assessing the riskiness of projects:
    (1) sensitivity analysis, used by 85 per cent of Ho and Pike's respondents; and
    (2) use of probabilities, used by 51 per cent

(e) There are also two main approaches distinguishing between projects on the basis of their riskiness:
    (1) shortening the payback period for riskier projects (used by 75 per cent);
    (2) requiring higher rates of return (presumably discount rate or IRR hurdle rate) for riskier projects (used by 77 per cent).

Both of these methods seem fairly popular amongst those who tackle the problem of risk in a formal way.

Conclusions on practice in risk analysis

It is perhaps surprising how small a proportion of firms formally account for risk. If we bear in mind that the evidence relates to large firms, it seems likely that little consideration of it will occur in the smaller firms.

It is not clear why the risk-adjusted rate of return has become so popular (speaking relatively, of course). Perhaps it is intuition based partly on observation that high risk seems to engender high returns.

In the next chapter we shall go on to see that the practice of requiring higher rates (discount rates) for riskier projects can be seen as a rational way of taking account of risk and of selecting investments. We shall also see that there is a theoretically correct way for management to make decisions on risky investment projects with which all the firm's shareholders will agree.

SUMMARY

Risk is ever-present in decision making as decisions only concern the future and the future is not known with certainty. Risk must formally be considered in each decision taken.

One approach to dealing with risk is to assess the decision using the best estimate for each of the data inputs and then to carry out a sensitivity analysis to test how sensitive the particular decision would be to estimation errors in each input. This approach has several defects, not least of which is the fact that having discovered how sensitive the decision is, we do not really know quite what to do about it.

Identifying the possible outcomes and ascribing probabilities to each one can be enlightening, though possibly mind-boggling, due to the large number of outcomes which a project would have in the real world. A range of possible outcomes does not really provide us with the basis of a clear decision rule.

Expected value, a weighted average of the possible outcomes, reduces the volume and gives us one figure which can form the basis for the decision. Expected value also has several problems. That firms typically, at any given moment, have a number of projects operating partially overcomes these problems. The fact that all firms and all industries are subject to an economy-wide systematic risk means that expected value remains incomplete. Expected value also fails to consider risk aversion, a phenomenon which characterises the human race.

Utility theory provides a useful means of representing personal attitudes of individuals to factors which they find desirable or undesirable. The concept of utility can be a useful one in the context of the attitude of individuals to risk. A risk-averse person is one who derives a decreasing amount of satisfaction from each additional increment of wealth.

Provided that the dispersion of possible returns is normal about the expected value, the expected value/variance criterion provides a useful decision rule for all risk-averse investors.

Overseas investments raise additional risk problems, which need to be addressed.

In practice, risk seems to be formally considered by most very large UK firms. It seems unlikely that this is the case with smaller firms. Sensitivity analysis and assessment of probabilities are fairly popular in assessing risk. Reduced payback periods and increased discount rates seem fairly popular responses to perceived risk.

FURTHER READING	Risk generally is dealt with very thoroughly in a number of texts, including those by Bierman & Smidt (1988) and Levy & Sarnat (1988). The subject of probabilities is well explained by Harper (1982), who also deals with expected values. The research studies of Ho and Pike (1991) and of Pike & Wolfe (1988), both of which were cited in the chapter, are well worth reading.
WORK-BASED ASSIGNMENT	(a) How does your organisation deal with the problem of risk in investment appraisal? (b) Are probabilities used? (c) If probabilities are not used, what is the reason for this?
QUESTIONS WITH ANSWERS (see Appendix 3)	**1** Easton Ltd needs to purchase a machine to manufacture a new product. The choice lies between two machines (A and B). Each machine has an estimated life of three years with no expected scrap value.

Machine A will cost £15 000 and machine B will cost £20 000, payable immediately in each case. The total variable costs of manufacture of each unit are £1 if made on machine A, but only £0.50 if made on machine B. This is because machine B is more sophisticated and requires less labour to operate it.

The product will sell for £4 each.

The demand for the product is uncertain but is estimated at 2000 units for each year, 3000 units for each year or 5000 units for each year. (Note that whatever sales level actually occurs, that level will apply to each year.)

The sales manager has placed probabilities on the level of demand as follows:

Annual demand	Probability of occurrence
2000	0.2
3000	0.6
5000	0.2

Presume that both taxation and fixed costs will be unaffected by any decision made.

Easton Ltd's cost of capital is 6 per cent p.a.

You are required:
(a) to calculate the NPV for each of the three activity levels for each machine A and B and state your conclusion.
(b) to calculate the *expected* NPV for each machine and state your conclusion.

2 In Question 1, assume that the 2000 level is the 'best estimate' of annual demand for Easton Ltd and that only machine A is available.
(a) Should the firm acquire machine A on the basis of its NPV?
(b) Carry out a sensitivity analysis on the decision recommended in (a).

3* Miles plc has the opportunity to produce a new product. Expected total sales volumes together with per unit sales prices and basic variable production costs of the new product are:

Per Unit

Year	Sales Quantities (000)	Sales Price £	Basic Variable Production Costs (Note 1) £
1	20	10	5
2	30	10	6
3	50	14	6
4	50	14	6

Note 1 Basic variable production costs exclude operating costs.

There are two alternative machines which Miles could purchase in order to manufacture the new product: machine A and machine B. Some details of each machine are as follows:

	Timing of Cash Flows (Year)	Machine A (£000)	B (£000)
Purchase price of machine	0	300	400
Salvage value of machine	4	60	40
Cost of machine housing	0	50	30
Salvage value of machine housing	–	Nil	Nil
Fixed annual operating costs (Note 2)	1–4	40	30

Note 2 'Annual operating costs' relate only to fixed-cash expenses and therefore exclude depreciation of the machine and its housing. Miles depreciates on a straight-line basis.

Machine A will require the installation of additional air conditioning and an existing air conditioning unit would be used for this purpose at an annual operating cash cost of £10 000. This air conditioning unit has a book value of £60 000 and if not utilised will be sold now for £25 000. Installation costs will amount to £15 000 and the salvage value of the unit at year 4 will be £10 000. The unit has previously been subject to 100% first year allowances.

Machine B utilises some advanced technology and uses fewer raw materials thereby reducing basic variable production costs by £1 per unit. A single routine overhaul of machine B will take place at the end of year 2 at a cost of £80 000. At this overhaul it will become apparent whether further repairs or modifications are needed. The costs of each possible level of repair or modification, together with their associated probabilities, are:

Note: * indicates a more complex question.

Level of further repair or modification	Cost, at year 2, of further repair or modification (£000s)	Probability
Nil	Nil	0.5
Minor	50	0.3
Major	140	0.2

The 'major' level of repair and modification will entail reverting to traditional technology for the remainder of the product's life with a consequent loss of the saving on future variable production costs as well as a reduction of the year 4 salvage value to only £20 000. The 'minor' level of repair or modification will not entail reverting to traditional technology and will not alter the salvage value of machine B. None of the repairs will alter other operating costs. It is expected that no further overhaul or repairs will be required after year 2.

For each machine all cash operating expenses will be paid for at the end of the year to which they relate. However, sales revenues will be received as cash flows in the following manner:

70% of each year's sales received at the end of that year,
30% of each year's sales received one year later.

The corporation tax rate is 50% and there is a one year tax delay. All capital expenditure and installation costs, except those relating to machine housing, are eligible for 100% first year allowances and all salvage values are subject to tax. Expenditure on the type of machine housing to be used is not eligible for any tax relief. All other costs are tax deductible expenses. Miles can take full advantage of any tax allowances at the earliest opportunity.

An appropriate after tax discount rate is 14% per annum.

Required:

(a) Ascertain the expected net present value of producing the new product by each of the two alternative methods.
   On the basis of expected net present value, advise Miles on which, if any, of the two alternative machines should be purchased.
(b) By paying a single lump sum now, Miles could obtain the services of a credit consultant who would ensure that all sales revenues were received in cash in the year of sale. Ascertain the maximum amount it would be worth paying to obtain the services of the credit consultant if such a payment were not a tax deductible expense.

(ACCA)

QUESTIONS FOR CLASS USE   Devonia (Laboratories) Ltd has recently carried out successful clinical trials on a new type of skin cream which has been developed to reduce the effects of ageing. Research and development costs incurred by the company in relation to the new product amount to £160 000. In order to gauge the market potential of the new product an independent firm of market research consultants were hired at a cost of £15 000. The market research report submitted by the consultants indicates that the skin cream is likely to have a product life of four years and could be sold to retail chemists and large department stores at a price of £20 per 100 ml container. For each of the four years of the new product's life sales demand has been estimated as follows:

Number of 100 ml containers sold	Probability of occurrence
11 000	0.3
14 000	0.6
16 000	0.1

If the company decides to launch the new product it is possible for production to begin at once. The necessary equipment to produce the product is already owned by the company and originally cost £150 000. At the end of the new product's life it is estimated that the equipment could be sold for £35 000. If the company decides against launching the new product the equipment will be sold immediately for £85 000 as it will be of no further use to the company.

The new skin cream will require two hours' labour for each 100 ml container produced. The cost of labour for the new product is £4.00 per hour. Additional workers will have to be recruited to produce the new product. At the end of the product's life the workers are unlikely to be offered further work with the company and redundancy costs of £10 000 are expected. The cost of the ingredients for each 100 ml container is £6.00. Additional overheads arising from production of the product is expected to be £15 000 p.a.

The new skin cream has attracted the interest of the company's competitors. If the company decides not to produce and sell the skin cream, it can sell the patent rights to a major competitor immediately for £125 000.

Devonia (Laboratories) Ltd has a cost of capital of 12 per cent.

Ignore taxation.

Required:

(a) Calculate the expected net present value (ENPV) of the new product.
(b) State, with reasons, whether or not Devonia (Laboratories) Ltd should launch the new product.
(c) Discuss the strengths and weaknesses of the expected net present value approach for making investment decisions.

(Certified Diploma)

CHAPTER 7

The pricing of securities and its relevance to real investment decisions

OBJECTIVES

In this chapter we shall deal with the following:

● the effect on risk and return of holding risky assets in portfolios
● efficient portfolios and the efficient frontier
● the risk-free rate and two-fund separation
● the relationship between the risk and expected return on individual assets
● the implications of this relationship, particularly on the discount rate which must be applied to expected cash flows to assess real investment projects through NPV
● the arbitrage pricing model

INTRODUCTION

The relevance of security prices

Most of the developed countries of the world have a market in which the owners of shares in particular local and international companies may be bought and sold. These capital markets, known typically (in English) as stock markets or stock exchanges, also provide a forum for the purchase and sale of loan stock, both of private sector companies and of governments and public utilities. Research evidence shows that in many of these markets (including the UK one), the market forces which set the prices of individual securities (shares and loan stocks) cause pricing efficiency to occur. 'Efficiency' in this context means that all available information concerning a particular security's future prospects is at all times fully and rationally reflected in the security's price. In Chapter 9 we shall take a more detailed look at the workings of the UK capital market and at the evidence for the efficiency of its pricing. At present it is sufficient that we appreciate that such a market does exist and that its pricing mechanism tends to be efficient.

In this chapter we are going to consider how securities traded in capital markets seem to be priced. We might feel that this is at most only of passing interest to us in the study of business finance since our main concern is that of firms' investment and financing decisions. That would, however, be an incorrect view of the topic, since:

(a) Financial managers are concerned with the way in which their firm's securities are priced in the free market as this might well have some impact on their financing decisions, e.g. at what price to issue new securities.

(b) Financial managers are also concerned with the relationship between how securities are priced in the capital market and firms' investment decisions. Firms make decisions concerning investment in real assets on the basis of anticipated returns and of the risk attaching to those returns. The capital market is a free market which deals in precisely those two commodities: return and risk. Thus we have a free and apparently efficient market which sets prices for return and risk. A lot of historical data is available on security prices and dividends, so we can readily observe what has happened in the past and draw conclusions on how return and risk seem to be related. In other words we can see how risk is dealt with in the pricing mechanism of a free market. This should be useful to financial managers since there seems no logical reason why they should take a different view of return and risk from that taken by investors in the capital market.

The market's pricing mechanism for securities becomes even more relevant to us when we remind ourselves that managers are seeking through their investment decisions to increase the wealth of the shareholders, partly through the firm's value on the capital market. It seems even more logical, therefore, that managers should take a similar attitude to risk and return to that of the security investors in the market.

If we can come to some sensible conclusion on the way in which risk and return are priced in the capital market, this should provide us with a very useful basis for the firm to assess real investment opportunities.

A reminder

In the last chapter we saw that diversification can reduce investment risk. We also saw that, given the assumption that possible returns are 'normally' distributed around the expected value and that investors are risk-averse, then the mean (or expected value) and the variance (or its square root, the standard deviation) are valid and practical, though sometimes incomplete, bases on which to assess and rank investment opportunities.

SECURITY INVESTMENT AND RISK

If we were to select a number of marketable securities at random, form them into portfolios of varying sizes, measure the expected returns and standard deviation of returns from each of our various-sized portfolios and then plot standard deviation against size of portfolio, we should obtain a graph similar to that in Fig. 7.1.

Before we go on to consider the implications of Fig. 7.1, just a word of explanation on its derivation. The expected returns referred to are the monthly returns of a security or a portfolio of securities. This is calculated as:

$$r_t = \frac{P_t - P_{t-1} + d_t}{P_{t-1}}$$

Where P_t is the market value of the security or portfolio at the end of month t, P_{t-1} the value at the start of the month and d_t the dividend (if any) arising from the security or portfolio during the month. The expected value of returns for a security or portfolio is based on past experience, say of returns over the past 60 months. Thus the expected value could be the average (mean) of the monthly returns for the past five years.

**Figure 7.1
The risk of
various-sized,
randomly selected
portfolios**

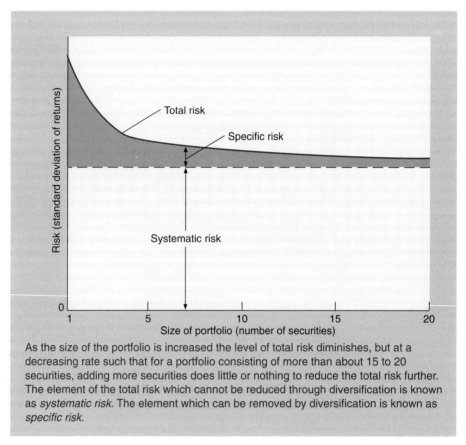

As the size of the portfolio is increased the level of total risk diminishes, but at a decreasing rate such that for a portfolio consisting of more than about 15 to 20 securities, adding more securities does little or nothing to reduce the total risk further. The element of the total risk which cannot be reduced through diversification is known as *systematic risk*. The element which can be removed by diversification is known as *specific risk*.

The various-sized portfolios are constructed randomly. Several portfolios of each size are constructed, and the standard deviation depicted in Fig. 7.1 is the average of the standard deviations of all of the portfolios for each size (see Evans & Archer, 1968).

As standard deviation of returns around the mean is a reasonable measure of risk, Fig. 7.1 suggests that large reduction in risk can be achieved merely by randomly combining securities in portfolios. This provides empirical support for the maxim 'Do not put all your eggs in one basket' which is often applied to investment in securities.

Two features might surprise adherents to the eggs and baskets maxim, however. These are:

(a) Very limited diversification yields large reductions in the level of risk. Even spreading the investment funds available into a couple of different securities successfully eliminates a large amount of risk. Each additional different security added to the portfolio yields successively less by way of risk reduction.

(b) Once the portfolio contains about 15 to 20 securities there is little to be gained by way of risk reduction from further increases in its size. There seems to be part of the risk which is impervious to attempts to reduce it through diversification.

That part of the risk which is susceptible to removal by diversification is of course specific risk; the stubborn part is systematic risk. Total risk is the sum of these two.

As we saw in the last chapter, specific (or unsystematic) risk arises from factors which are random as between one firm's securities and those of another. As these factors are random, a reasonably small amount of diversification will cause them to cancel one another.

The systematic (or portfolio) risk is concerned with economy-wide (macroeconomic) factors to which all firms are heir.

The implications of the phenomenon represented in Fig. 7.1 are:

(a) investors should hold securities in portfolios as, by doing so, risk can be reduced at little cost; and

(b) there is limited point in diversifying into many more than 15 to 20 different securities as nearly all the benefits of diversification have been exhausted at that size of portfolio. Further diversification means that the investor will have to pay higher dealing charges to establish the portfolio and then will have more cost and/or work in managing it.

If systematic risk must be borne by investors because it is caused by economy-wide factors, it seems likely that some securities are more susceptible to these factors than are others. For example, a high street food supermarket would seem likely to suffer less than would a manufacturer of capital goods, say, as a result of economic recession.

Is the level of risk attaching to the returns from all securities the same, even though no one is forced to bear any specific risk? This question and several others relating to it will now be examined.

PORTFOLIO THEORY

If we assume both that security returns are normally distributed about their expected value and that investors are risk-averse then we can completely describe securities by their means and standard deviations and so represent them graphically, as in Fig. 7.2.

In Fig. 7.2 all investors would prefer investment X to investment Y as it has a higher expected value for the same level of risk. All risk-averse investors would prefer investment Z to investment Y as it has lower risk for the same level of expected return. Thus both X and Z are said to dominate Y. The choice between X and Z, however, depends upon the personal attitude to risk of the investor making the decision (i.e. on the shape of the particular investor's utility curve).

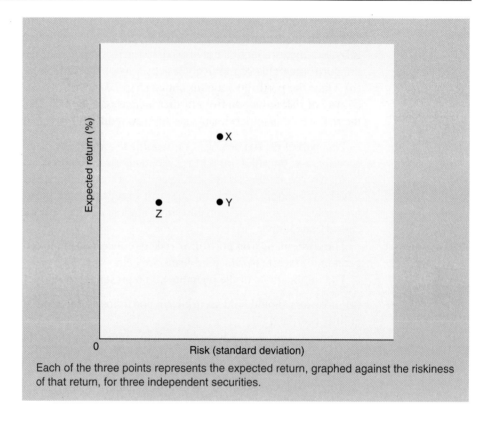

Figure 7.2
The risk/return profiles of three securities

Each of the three points represents the expected return, graphed against the riskiness of that return, for three independent securities.

A and B in Fig. 7.3 are securities whose positions on the graph are defined by their expected values and standard deviations. B is expected to yield higher returns than A (14 per cent as against 10 per cent) but it is also expected to be more risky (standard deviation of 12 per cent as against 10 per cent). Assuming that all investors have similar expectations of these and other securities, then they would all see these securities as occupying the same position on the graph depicted in Fig. 7.3.

Suppose that we were to form a portfolio containing a proportion (α) of each of A and B. (Note that since the entire portfolio consists only of securities A and B, α_B = 1 – α_A.) The expected return from that portfolio would be:

$$r_p = \alpha_A r_A + \alpha_B r_B$$

where r_p, r_A and r_B are the expected returns from the portfolio, security A and security B respectively, i.e. the returns of the portfolio is simply the weighted average of the returns of the constituent securities. The standard deviation of the portfolio would be:

$$\sigma_P = \sqrt{\alpha_A^2 \sigma_A^2 + \alpha_B^2 \sigma_B^2 + 2\alpha_A \alpha_B R \sigma_A \sigma_B}$$

where σ_P, σ_A and σ_B are respectively the standard deviation of the expected returns of the portfolio, security A and security B. R is the coefficient of correlation between the expected returns of the two securities.* If R were +1 it would mean that the expected returns would be perfectly correlated one with the other, e.g. an increase of x per cent in the returns of A would always imply a y per cent increase in the returns of B and vice versa. If R were –1 it would imply as close a relationship but a negative one, e.g. an x per cent increase in the returns of A would always mean a y per cent decrease in the returns from B. R of value between –1 and +1 means less direct relationships with a value of zero meaning that there is no relationship between the returns of the two securities. (Note that there would be a separate R for any two variables. The particular value of R for A and B would be peculiar to A and B and not the same, except by coincidence, for any other two securities C and D nor even A and C.)

**Figure 7.3
The risk/return
profiles of two
securities, A and B**

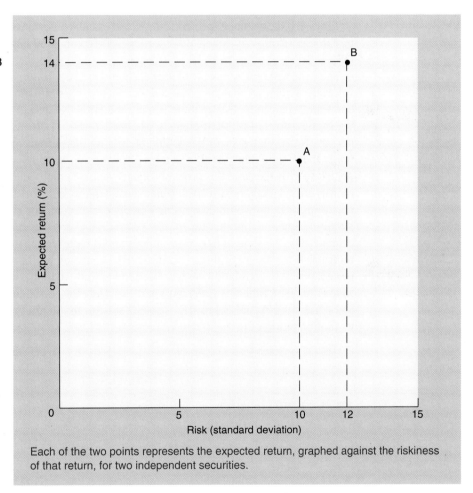

Each of the two points represents the expected return, graphed against the riskiness of that return, for two independent securities.

* $$R = \frac{\text{Covariance (A, B)}}{\sigma_A \sigma_B}$$

Readers who are not too confident with these statistical measures should refer to Harper (1991) or one of the other texts which cover the ground.

Table 7.1 Risk and expected returns for various portfolios of securities A and B with differing assumptions as to the correlation coefficient

Proportion of security A in portfolio %	Expected returns of portfolio (r_p) %	Standard deviation for various correlation coefficients (R)				
		−1.0 %	−0.5 %	0.0 %	+0.5 %	+1.0 %
0	14	12.0	12.0	12.0	12.0	12.0
25	13	6.5	8.0	9.3	10.5	11.5
50	12	1.0	5.6	7.8	9.5	11.0
75	11	4.5	6.5	8.1	9.4	10.5
100	10	10.0	10.0	10.0	10.0	10.0

Table 7.1 shows the expected returns and standard deviations for a selection of possible portfolios of A and B for a range of hypothetical correlation coefficients (R).

The expected return/risk profiles of each of these portfolios are mapped out in Fig. 7.4. Here we can see that the greatest risk reduction possibilities occur with negatively correlated securities. In fact there is a combination* of A and B which has no risk when the correlation coefficient is assumed to be −1. In reality such perfectly negatively correlated securities would be impossible to find. Their existence would imply that it would be possible to form portfolios possessing no risk at all, which is not likely to be the case. It is probably equally unlikely that securities whose expected returns are perfectly positively correlated exist in the real world. If they did, forming portfolios of them would do nothing to reduce risk, since the risk of the portfolio is simply a linear combination of the risks of the constituent securities. This is evidenced by the straight line connecting A and B representing the profile of expected return/risk for R= +1 in Fig. 7.4. In reality securities with positive, but less than perfect positive, correlation are what we tend to find. To that extent the second-from-right column of Table 7.1 is the most realistic. Here the correlation coefficient is +0.5 and combining A and B provides some reduction in the total risk but by no means total elimination of it.

* This is discoverable by finding the minimum value for σ_P by means of differential calculus, viz.:

$$\sigma_P^2 = \alpha_A^2 \sigma_A^2 + (1 - \alpha_A)^2 \sigma_B^2 + 2\alpha_A (1 - \alpha_A) R \sigma_A \sigma_B$$

(this is because $\alpha_B = 1 - \alpha_A$)

$$\frac{d\sigma_P^2}{d\alpha_A} = 2\alpha_A \sigma_A^2 + 2\alpha_A \sigma_B^2 - 2\sigma_B^2 + 2R\sigma_A \sigma_B - 4\alpha_A R \sigma_A \sigma_B$$

Setting this equal to zero and putting in the actual values for σ_A and σ_B and assuming $R = -1$ we get:

$$(2\alpha_A \times 100) + (2\alpha_A \times 144) - (2 \times 144) - (2 \times 10 \times 12) + (4\alpha_A \times 120) = 0$$

$$200\alpha_A + 288\alpha_A + 480\alpha_A = 288 + 240$$

$$\alpha_A = \frac{528}{968}$$

That part of the risk which reduces when A and B are combined in a portfolio is of course specific risk. As we saw from Fig. 7.1, combining two securities far from exhausts the possibilities of specific risk reduction. Introducing further securities in appropriate combinations into the portfolio would reduce the risk still further.

Figure 7.4
The risk/return profiles of various portfolios of Securities A and B, with differing assumptions regarding the correlation coefficient

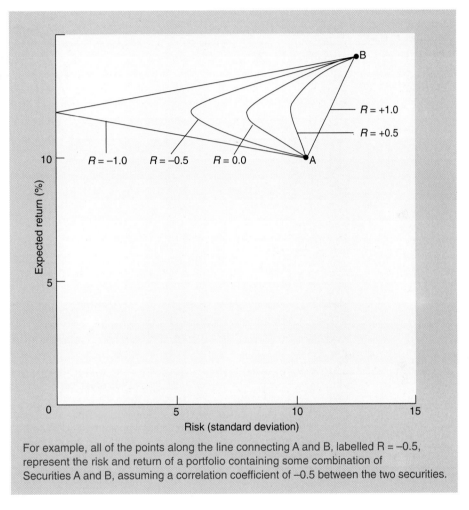

For example, all of the points along the line connecting A and B, labelled R = –0.5, represent the risk and return of a portfolio containing some combination of Securities A and B, assuming a correlation coefficient of –0.5 between the two securities.

Figure 7.5 shows three more securities C, D, and E brought into the reckoning. The various curved lines show the expected return/risk profiles of various combinations of any two of the five securities. The line XB furthest to the top left of the graph shows the expected risk/return profile of a portfolio containing various proportions of each of these five securities. Note that every combination of expected return and risk along this line 'dominates' any other position in which the investor could be with these five securities. Take point X along this line, for example. No other combination available will yield higher expected return for X's level of risk, nor less risk for X's expected return. Consider the portfolio represented by point Y; although this has a higher expected return than X, it also has higher risk. Thus X does not dominate Y, nor does Y dominate X.

Figure 7.5
The risk/return
profiles of various
portfolios of
securities A, B, C,
D and E

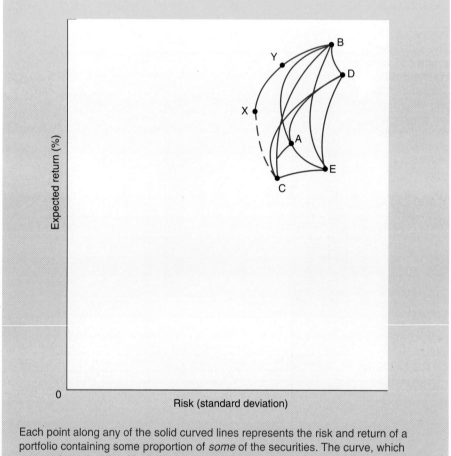

Each point along any of the solid curved lines represents the risk and return of a portfolio containing some proportion of *some* of the securities. The curve, which passes through points X and Y represents the risk and return of a portfolio containing some proportion of *all* of the securities. The portfolios which lie along this line between B and X are said to *dominate* all other possible combinations of these five securities. This means that either they have a higher expected return for the same or a lower level of risk or lower risk for the same or a higher expected return.

Efficiency

Of course these five securities do not represent the total of financial investment opportunities nor, therefore, the maximum specific risk reduction opportunities available. There is an efficient frontier for securities as a whole. This is represented in Fig. 7.6. Each point on the line EE represents some portfolio constructed from some or all of the securities available in the economy as a whole. 'Efficient' in this context means that there is no specific (unsystematic) risk present; it has all been diversified away.

None of the many portfolios represented by the efficient frontier has any specific risk; if they did, it would be possible to diversify further and get rid of it, thus pushing the frontier further to the top left.

**Figure 7.6
The efficient
frontier**

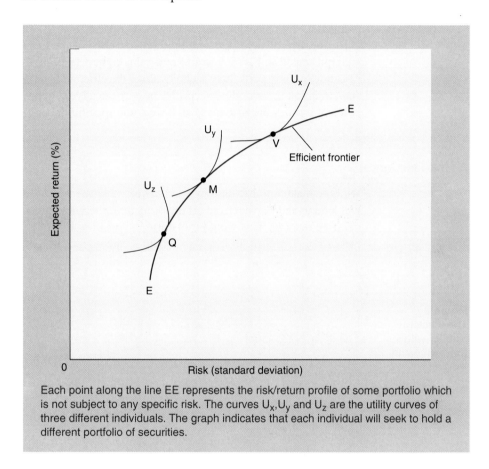

Each point along the line EE represents the risk/return profile of some portfolio which is not subject to any specific risk. The curves U_x, U_y and U_z are the utility curves of three different individuals. The graph indicates that each individual will seek to hold a different portfolio of securities.

Utility

Let us remind ourselves of what we discussed in Chapter 6 on the subject of utility. It is possible (in theory at least), in respect of any particular individual and of any two related factors, to represent that individual's preferences as regards the trade-off between the factors by a set of utility curves. If we assume both that investors are risk-averse and that they are expected utility of wealth maximisers, then they would have utility curves similar to those depicted in Fig. 7.6 (U_x, U_y and U_z).

Note that each of these utility curves (U_x, U_y and U_z) relate to different individuals all of whom are prepared to take on some risk, but require compensation in the form of increased expected returns for doing so. In each case the investors depicted require increasingly large increments in expected return for each successive increment of risk which they are prepared to accept. This is why each of these curves slopes upwards to the right.

The individual whose risk/expected return preferences are represented by U_z is rather more risk-averse than the individual represented by U_x. The latter is prepared to accept much more risk to achieve any given level of expected return than is the former. The U_x individual is still risk-averse and therefore needs increasing amounts of expected return for each additional increment of risk, but less so than the U_z individual.

Irrespective of their personal preferences, each of the investors whose attitudes are represented in Fig. 7.6 would reach the highest level of utility (satisfaction) by investing in some portfolio which lies along the efficient frontier (EE). No one would want to invest in individual securities or portfolios lying below or to the right of the efficient frontier because these all have some specific risk.

A risk-free asset

We now make another assumption which is that there is a financial market which will lend to and borrow from all investors unlimited amounts of money, at an equal, risk-free rate (r_f). This would transform the position from that shown in Fig. 7.6 to that of Fig. 7.7. Now all investors would locate on the straight line r_fS.

Figure 7.7
The efficient frontier with borrowing and lending

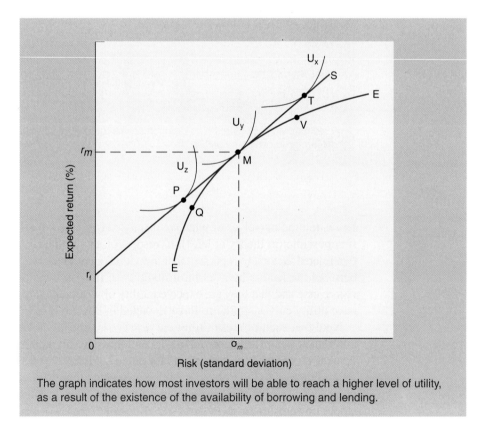

The graph indicates how most investors will be able to reach a higher level of utility, as a result of the existence of the availability of borrowing and lending.

An investor whose preferences are represented by a utility curve such as U_z in Figs 7.6 and 7.7 would choose to put some wealth into risky securities and lend the remainder at the risk-free rate. U_y is the utility curve of an investor who would invest entirely in risky securities despite the existence of the risk-free asset. This is because this person's utility curve is tangential to r_fS where r_fS itself is tangential to EE. The investor whose preferences are depicted in curve U_x (who is the least risk-averse of the three) would choose to borrow at rate r_f so that an amount even greater than that individual's wealth can be invested in risky securities.

Note that two of our investors will achieve a higher level of utility (a higher level of expected return for a given level of risk, or lower level of risk for a given level of expected return) through the existence of the risk-free borrowing/lending opportunity. Compare point P with point Q, or point T with point V in Fig. 7.7. For the third investor the position is unchanged. Only investors who happen to have preferences which cause their highest level of utility to be tangential with r_fS at M will be unaffected by the existence of the risk-free borrowing/lending opportunity. Every other investor will be better off.

Two-fund separation

The result of this is what is known as *two-fund separation*. Irrespective of the personal preferences of individuals they will all choose to invest their wealth in some combination of the portfolio M and the risk-free asset. This state of affairs is somewhat analogous to Fisher separation, which we encountered in Chapter 2. Fisher separation implies that irrespective of personal preferences as regards investment and consumption, all investors will concur about the optimum level of real investment provided that a borrowing/lending opportunity exists. Two-fund separation means that all investors will concur on the same portfolio of risky securities if a risk-free borrowing/lending opportunity exists.

What is portfolio M?

The foregoing raises the questions, 'What is this portfolio in which we all want to invest? What securities does it contain?'

Let us attack these questions from the other position. What happens to a security which does not form part of portfolio M? If we all want portfolio M, the prices of securities excluded from it will be zero. Any commodity which no one wants has a zero price (in a free market, at least). This means that there would be securities, with expectations of returns, which we can buy for nothing. Obviously this position would be too good to be true. Capital market efficiency, which we know at least broadly to exist, demands that such anomalies just could not occur in real life; such zero-priced or merely underpriced securities would offer superior returns for their risk and would enhance the portfolio M. Thus they would be bought until their price, relative to the prices of securities generally, was a reasonable one. The only logical conclusion from this is that the portfolio M strictly must contain a proportion of all securities on the market, i.e. it is the market portfolio.

More strictly still, since the capital market for securities is not a self-contained, sealed entity, the market portfolio should contain a proportion of all capital assets in existence. It is possible and often practical to sell securities and use the proceeds to buy (for instance) gold, land, a painting, some vintage wine, and thus such assets must be regarded as possible substitutes for securities and logically they must form part of the market portfolio.

Clearly, no one can hold the strict market portfolio. Most of what we know of capital market efficiency (and which we shall review in Chapter 9) suggests however that securities are priced logically one against another. To that extent they are substitutes for one another and so failure strictly to hold the market portfolio may not invalidate the principles so far established.

The capital market line

The line r_fS in Fig. 7.7 is known as the capital market line (CML). The CML defines the relationship between risk and return for efficient portfolios of risky securities. Note that this line will shift up and down, closer to or further from the horizontal, as interest rates change over time.

We can see from Fig. 7.7 that the expected return available to an investor is:

$$r_f + \text{risk premium}$$

The amount of the risk premium is dependent on how much of the investment is in the portfolio of risky securities.

CAPITAL ASSET PRICING MODEL

The CML defines the risk return trade-off for efficient portfolios. What is probably of more interest and value to us is the relationship between expected return and risk for individual securities. In fact this is:

$$E(r_i) = r_f + (E(r_m) - r_f)\frac{\text{Cov}(i, M)}{\sigma_m^2}$$

where $E(r_i)$ is the expected return from i, a particular individual security, r_f is the risk-free borrowing/lending rate, $E(r_m)$ the expected return on the market portfolio, $\text{Cov}(i,M)$ the covariance of returns of security i with those of the market portfolio and σ_m^2 the variance (square of the standard deviation) of the market returns.

This statement, known as the capital asset pricing model (CAPM), can be derived directly from what is known about the CML. (The Appendix to this chapter gives the detailed derivation of CAPM.)

Note that in using CAPM to discover the expected return for any particular security i, we only use one factor which refers specifically to i. This is $\text{Cov}(i,M)$. All of the other factors ($E(r_m)$, r_f and σ_m^2) are general to all securities. The only factor which distinguishes the expected returns of one security from those of another is the extent to which the expected returns from the particular security covary with the expected returns from the market portfolio.

This ties in pretty well with what we have discovered so far about specific and systematic risk. We know that specific risk can easily be avoided; it is not therefore surprising to find that the returns which we expect to get from a particular security bear no relation to specific risk. Even though higher risk usually engenders higher expectations of returns it is entirely logical that no higher return should be expected by someone who is needlessly exposed to specific risk.

Suppose that an office block window cleaner went to his employer to demand higher wages on the grounds that by choosing not to wear the safety harness provided by the employer, the window cleaner was exposed to greater risk than the other employees who wear the harness. No doubt the employer would answer emphatically that the window cleaner was not being asked to bear this risk and that it was unnecessary to bear it, since by the simple expedient of wearing the safety harness it could be completely avoided. In effect the capital market says the same to the misguided bearer of specific risk; consequently it will not compensate that investor for bearing it.*

CAPM tells us that expectations of returns will be enhanced by the extent of the covariance of expected returns from the particular security with those of the market portfolio. Again this ties in with what we already know in that systematic risk, which the investor is forced to bear, relates to factors which tend to affect all securities. The greater their effect on a particular security, the greater the systematic risk, and logically, the greater the returns expected from that security. It is not surprising that covariance with the generality of securities is a measure of systematic risk.

β: a measure of risk

CAPM tells us that the capital market prices securities so that no higher returns are expected for bearing specific risk. Bearing systematic risk is expected to be rewarded by a risk premium (over the risk-free rate) of

$$(E(r_m) - r_f) \times \text{Cov}(i, M)/\sigma_m^2$$

The last term is usually known as β (beta) so CAPM is typically written as $E(r_i) = r_f + (E(r_m) - r_f)\beta_i$; the greater the β which characterises a particular security, the higher are that security's expected returns.

Securities with high βs are by no means guaranteed high returns. It is in the nature of risk that nothing is guaranteed. However, before the event, high-β securities lead to expectations of higher returns than those from low-β ones. If the generality of investment in securities (the market portfolio) does well, then portfolios containing high-β securities will prosper – the higher the β, the more that they will prosper. On the other hand, should securities generally fare badly, high-β securities will fare particularly badly. In other words, β is a measure of volatility of returns relative to

*Some readers might be mystified as to how the capital market sets the returns from a particular security.

Remember that return in this context is dividend (if any) plus appreciation in value of the security over a period divided by the value of the security at the start of the period. The capital market, through the actions of buyers and sellers, sets the current market price of each security. If investors feel that 15 per cent p.a. is the appropriate level of return for the level of risk involved, the capital market will set the price of the security accordingly.

After the event, the actual return may prove to be other than 15 per cent. This difference is in the nature of risk; what is anticipated may not occur.

those of the market portfolio. βs above unity are regarded as high and those below unity as low. High-β securities are sometimes referred to as *aggressive* and low-β ones as *defensive*. In real life, equity shares can be found having βs of up to about 2.0; they can also be found with βs as low as around 0.4.

There is no reason of principle why some securities should not have a negative β. Systematic risk is caused by a number of macroeconomic factors, such as the level of interest rates, the price of fuel, etc. Some securities are greatly affected by most of these in an adverse way (high-β securities). Other securities are little affected by those factors (low-β securities). There could be some securities which are favourably affected by these factors, at a time when the factors are adversely affecting most securities; such securities would have a negative β.

Probably most firms are adversely affected by high interest rates and high fuel prices. However, banks and fuel-producing firms, respectively, might tend to be favoured by high levels of those two factors. This does not necessarily mean that the securities of banks and fuel producers have a negative β. A security's β is related to all of the macroeconomic factors affecting it. In the case of a particular security, whilst there may be one or two of these factors which have the opposite effect to the one they have on the majority of securities, most factors will have a similar effect to their effect on the majority. The bank may be favoured by high interest rates, but it is still adversely affected by high fuel costs, high labour costs, trade recession, etc. In practice, negative-β securities seem not to exist.

**Figure 7.8
The graphical
representation
of CAPM – the
security market line**

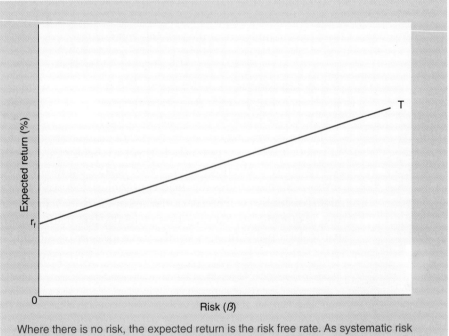

Where there is no risk, the expected return is the risk free rate. As systematic risk (measured by β) increases, an increasingly large risk premium, over the risk free rate, is expected.

It should be particularly noted that βs only indicate the effect of a particular security on a well diversified portfolio. A security with a low β may be very risky, but much of its risk may be specific risk.

Figure 7.8 shows CAPM represented diagrammatically. Here risk is measured by β. The risk/return profile of all assets should lie somewhere along the line r_fT, which is known as the security market line (SML).

It is important to recognise the difference between the capital market line and the security market line. The CML shows expected returns plotted against risk, where risk is measured in terms of standard deviation of returns. This is appropriate because the CML represents the risk/return trade-off for efficient portfolios, i.e. the risk is all systematic risk. The SML on the other hand shows the risk/return trade-off where risk is measured by β, i.e. only by the systematic risk element of the individual security. No individual security's risk/return profile is shown by the CML because all individual securities have an element of specific risk, i.e. they are inefficient. Thus all individual securities (and indeed all inefficient portfolios) lie to the bottom-right of the efficient frontier (Fig. 7.6).

CAPM was developed by Sharpe (1963), though others independently reached similar conclusions.

CAPM: AN EXAMPLE OF BETA ESTIMATION

EXAMPLE

The year end level of a representative Stock Exchange index and of the price of an ordinary share of Ace plc were as follows:

Year	Index	Ace plc (£)
1985	218	1.09
1986	230	1.20
1987	248	1.33
1988	250	1.40
1989	282	1.80
1990	297	1.99
1991	288	1.81
1992	290	1.98
1993	320	2.25
1994	356	2.55
1995	371	2.80

You are required on the basis of the above to calculate β. (Ignore dividends throughout.)

SOLUTION

Estimation of market factors

Year (1)	Index (2)	Return (3)	Return deviation (4)	Return variance (5)
	p_{mt}	$r_{mt} = \dfrac{p_{mt} - p_{mt-1}}{p_{mt-1}}$	$r_{mt} - \bar{r}_m$	$(r_{mt} - \bar{r}_m)^2$
1985	218			
1986	230	0.055	(0.001)	0.0000
1987	248	0.078	0.022	0.0005
1988	250	0.008	(0.048)	0.0023
1989	282	0.128	0.072	0.0052
1990	297	0.053	(0.003)	0.0000
1991	288	(0.030)	(0.086)	0.0074
1992	290	0.007	(0.049)	0.0024
1993	320	0.103	0.047	0.0022
1994	356	0.113	0.057	0.0032
1995	371	0.042	(0.014)	0.0002
		0.557		0.0234

$$\bar{r}_m = \frac{0.557}{10} = 0.056, \ \text{var} \ r_m = \frac{0.0234}{9} = 0.0026$$

(Note that to find the var r_m we divide by 9 as there are 10 readings but one *degree of freedom* has been lost in the calculation of the mean.)

Estimation of β of Ace plc

Year (1)	Share price (2)	Return (3)	Return deviation (4)	Covariance with market (5)
	p_{it}	$\dfrac{p_{it} - p_{it-1}}{p_{it-1}}$	$r_{it} - \bar{r}_{it}$	$(r_{it} - \bar{r}_{it})(r_{mt} - \bar{r}_{mt})$
	£			
1985	1.09			
1986	1.20	0.101	(0.002)	0.0000
1987	1.33	0.108	0.005	0.0001
1988	1.40	0.053	(0.050)	0.0024
1989	1.80	0.286	0.183	0.0132
1990	1.99	0.106	0.003	(0.0000)
1991	1.81	(0.090)	(0.193)	0.0166
1992	1.98	0.094	(0.009)	0.0004
1993	2.25	0.136	0.033	0.0016
1994	2.55	0.133	0.030	0.0017
1995	2.80	0.098	(0.005)	0.0001
		1.025		0.0361

$$\bar{r}_i = \frac{1.025}{10} = 0.103, \ \text{Cov}(i, M) = \frac{0.0361}{9} = 0.0040$$

(Here again we divide by 9 to find the covariance, since one degree of freedom has been lost in the calculation of r_{it} and r_{mt}. If the reader is confused by this, reference should be made to a statistics text such as Harper, 1991).

$$\text{Since } \beta_i = \frac{\text{Cov}(i, M)}{\text{Var } r_m}$$

$$\text{Then } \beta_{\text{Ace}} = \frac{0.0040}{0.0026} = 1.54$$

Thus Ace plc equity has a fairly high β.

ASSUMPTIONS OF CAPM

In developing CAPM several assumptions need to be made. These are:

(a) investors are risk-averse, and maximise expected utility of wealth;
(b) the capital market is not dominated by any individual investors;
(c) investors are only interested in two features of a security, its expected returns and its variance (or standard deviation);
(d) the existence of a risk-free rate at which all investors may borrow or lend without limit at the same rate;
(e) the absence of dealing charges, taxes, and other imperfections;
(f) all investors have identical perceptions of each security.

Let us briefly consider these in terms of their validity: (a) seems to be true; certainly most people seem to prefer more wealth to less (all things being equal) and most of us are risk-averse. (b) also is broadly true, with investors, even the large ones, not usually dominating the market in any one security. There has been much discussion of the validity of the *mean variance* criterion in the literature (e.g. Levy & Sarnat, 1988) and it seems that in the context of security returns, assumption (c) is probably not too far-fetched. Fama (1972) discusses evidence which suggests that while security returns are not strictly 'normal' in their distribution, they are roughly so.

Clearly (d), (e) and (f) are invalid. Whether or not their invalidity seriously weakens the model is probably only discernible by looking at how well CAPM works in practice.

TESTS OF CAPM

For most of us, certainly for most financial managers, the only important feature of a theoretical derivation like CAPM is how well it explains, and more particularly how well it predicts, real events.

β as an explainer of past events

CAPM has been subjected to a large number of empirical tests. Most of these have sought to calculate the β for a security by regressing the monthly returns (capital gain plus dividend expressed as a fraction of the security price at the beginning of the month) against returns from the *market portfolio*. Since the market portfolio is strictly unobservable (it contains some of every possible capital investment), a surrogate is used. Typically this is some representative capital market index (in the UK the 'Financial Times Actuaries Index' is sometimes used for this purpose). βs tend to be calculated on the basis of monthly returns over fairly protracted periods such as five years (60 months). The tests have then gone on to assess whether or not CAPM explains the returns for securities over the period observed.

Until recently it was possible to say that the various tests had broadly supported CAPM. Doubts had been expressed about the validity of using short-term bills of stable governments, like that of the UK and USA, as a risk-free rate, since it did not really fit with the evidence. Researchers found, however, β to be a valid and fairly complete measure of risk. Despite the fact that CAPM deals with expected returns (which are impossible to test) and tests had, of necessity, dealt with actual past events, it was concluded that CAPM was broadly valid as a useful explainer of what happened.

Recently, however, evidence has emerged which calls the validity of CAPM into question. Fama and French (1992) carried out a major study of US stocks covering the period 1962 to 1989. They found that β is not a useful explainer of investment returns. They found a correlation between β and returns, but they discovered that this was due to a correlation of both β and returns with other factors, such as the size of the firm whose shares were being considered. Thus, for example, they found a clear link between firm size and investment returns. The shares of large firms tend to give lower returns than those of smaller firms. Fama and French concluded that once they allowed for the effect of firm size and other such factors, the relationship between β and returns was, at best, weak.

It is probably too soon after publication of this research to conclude that CAPM is invalid. Other studies may cast more light on the subject. Meanwhile CAPM retains a fair degree of practical credibility.

β as a predictor of future events

An important issue, as regards the usefulness of CAPM to financial managers, concerns how well the β of a particular security calculated from past data predicts that security's β for a future period – in other words, how stable are βs over time.

The evidence suggests that βs of individual securities calculated over one time period are not very good predictors of the β for those individual securities over the following and subsequent periods. On the other hand, where securities are combined into portfolios, the β of the portfolio for one period seems a reasonable predictor of that portfolio's β during the next period. (Incidentally, the β of a portfolio is the weighted average of the βs of the constituent securities, i.e.

$$\beta_P = \sum_{i=1}^{n} \alpha_i \beta_i$$

where security i represents proportion α_i, by market value, of the portfolio.)

The stability of portfolio βs is particularly of interest to financial managers when it is considered that the portfolios concerned could be made up entirely of ordinary shares of firms in some particular industry. That is to say, there is a characteristic β for each industry which remains fairly stable over time.

Why should it be the case that βs of individual securities are not very stable, whilst those for a portfolio tend to be? There are perhaps two reasons for this:

(a) Measurement errors – the β calculated for a security may well not be the 'true' β for that security due to errors in estimating the β including, for example, using a capital market index as a surrogate for the market portfolio; and
(b) Actual changes in the security's risk profile over time – there is absolutely no reason why the capital market's perceptions of a security should remain constant when the firm concerned may, for example, be changing its real investment patterns. As we shall see in Chapter 11, the extent to which the particular firm is reliant on long-term borrowings also affects its securities' β, so changes in the extent of this reliance over time will tend to make the β look unstable.

Each of these factors will probably tend to be fairly random in nature (from one security to another), so that combining securities in portfolios would tend to give a more stable picture.

IMPLICATIONS OF CAPM

For security investors

These seem to be that:

(a) Investors should diversify sufficiently to eliminate most of the specific risk from their portfolios. There seem to be no rewards for bearing specific risk.
(b) They should decide whether they wish to invest in high-risk ($\beta > 1$), medium-risk ($\beta \simeq 1$) or low-risk ($\beta < 1$) securities. There is a list of βs of the leading Stock Exchange quoted equities published regularly by the London Business School which subscribers may use to help them to construct portfolios, reflecting their personal risk/return preferences. The published βs are updated quarterly and are believed to be derived from comparing monthly returns of the immediately preceding five years with those of a representative Stock Exchange index, acting as a surrogate for the market portfolio. (Several commercial organizations in the USA offer a similar service in relation to US securities.)

Whilst the evidence on capital market efficiency indicates that it is impossible to spot winners systematically, this does not mean that one firm's securities are much the same as those of another. The evidence on CAPM suggests that it is possible to distinguish between those securities which will perform better than average if the market does well – and worse if the market does badly – on the one hand, and less volatile, less risky securities on the other. Thus investors are able to select the level of risk which suits their situation and personality and to expect returns commensurate with that risk level.

The instability of βs for individual securities is probably not too significant here since investors are well advised to hold portfolios in any case.

For financial managers in deriving the discount rate for real investment projects

At this point it might be useful to ask ourselves how firms should select the rate at which to discount the expected cash flows of prospective real investment projects, in order to discover their NPVs.

In our discussion of shareholder wealth maximisation in Chapter 2 we introduced the idea that the appropriate discount rate is the borrowing/lending interest rate. In the real world such an approach is not tenable because the comparable alternative to real investment is not risk-free lending. The opportunity with which the project under consideration must logically be compared is one of equal risk to that project.

Let us remind ourselves of three factors which bear on the discount rate decision.

(a) The value of a firm is the sum of the NPVs of all of the projects which it currently has in operation, so that undertaking a new project with a positive NPV should increase the value of the firm by the amount of the positive NPV (see Chapter 4).

(b) Capital market efficiency research suggests that events of economic significance occurring within the firm reflect in the firm's share price so that taking on projects with positive NPVs should actually increase the market value of the firm's securities (see Chapter 9).

(c) CAPM tells us that expected return is directly proportional to the level of risk for each individual investment. Furthermore, the only part of risk which matters (assuming investors hold efficient portfolios) is systematic risk (measured by β).

Between them, these three lead to the assertion that the logical discount rate for an individual real (and inevitably risky) investment project should be derived from CAPM. The β value to be used would reflect the covariance of expected returns from the project with those from the generality of risky investments (the 'market' portfolio).

After all, the capital market is one where the commodities traded are risk and expected return, and to use a market-derived price of risk (which is what CAPM does) seems a reasonable way of pricing individual real investments. This is particularly logical where shareholder wealth maximisation is the firm's goal.

Whether it is very practical actually to seek to assess βs of individual real investment projects is less certain. It is difficult enough trying to estimate the cash flows, without trying to assess the degree of covariance these might have with the market portfolio.

A more practical approach probably is to try to use characteristic (average) βs for the industry in which the real investment is to be made, to derive the discount rate for the project. This might, at first sight, appear to be too much of a broad brush approach in that there are risks attaching to any particular project which may not apply to the area of activity more generally. A brief reflection, however, will reveal that the non-general factors relate, of course, to specific risk which the individual investor can diversify away.

For example, a firm, most of whose real investments are in newspaper publishing, intends to make a real investment in the manufacture of kitchen furniture. To derive the appropriate discount rate for the project it should use the average β of firms which are completely engaged in the same activity. By doing so the discount rate would reflect the capital market's perceptions of the systematic risk attaching to kitchen furniture manufacture.

Since the firm is seeking to enhance its shareholders' wealth, presumably, mainly through the market value of the shares, the perceptions of the market are all-important.

We should note that by advocating a capital market derived discount rate, we are saying that we should use an opportunity cost discount rate in the same way as the cash flows to be discounted are the opportunity cash flows. This is true since an investment alternative of equal systematic risk to the real investment under consideration is buying shares of another firm of equal β to that of the project. Thus we should only be prepared to make the real investment where we expect a positive NPV when expected cash flows are discounted at the expected rate of return from the security investment alternative.

LACK OF SHAREHOLDER UNANIMITY ON RISKY INVESTMENT

In the last chapter we identified a problem facing firms' managements in respect of selecting risky investment projects. The problem is that individual shareholders may not all see a particular risky project in the same light; whilst a project may increase the utility of one shareholder, it may reduce that of another.

Theoretically, discounting the expected cash flows (Σ[possible cash flows $\times$ each one's probability of occurrence]) using a discount rate derived from CAPM will overcome this problem. All shareholders, irrespective of their individual attitude to risk (provided that they are risk-averse), will be unanimous that projects having a positive NPV when expected cash flows are discounted at a CAPM-derived rate will increase their utility of wealth, and therefore should be undertaken. Note that this theoretical unanimity depends on the assumption that all shareholders hold the shares of the firm under consideration, as part of a well diversified portfolio.

USING CAPM TO DERIVE DISCOUNT RATES FOR REAL INVESTMENTS – THE PRACTICAL PROBLEMS

There are three factors which need to be estimated for the future in order that the logic of using CAPM to derive the discount rate can be carried into practice. We shall now take a look at each in turn to try to assess the difficulty of arriving at reasonable estimates for them. Really what we shall need to ask ourselves is whether the past is likely to be a useful guide to the future in respect of each of them and if it seems that it is not, what, if anything, can we use as an alternative?

The risk measure (β)

This is perhaps the least problematical of the three factors in that the average βs for ordinary shares of firms in particular industries do seem to be reasonably stable over time. It certainly seems that the β of a portfolio, calculated over a five-year period, is a fairly good predictor of the β of that same portfolio over the subsequent five years.

In practical terms, a reasonable approach seems to be to estimate, or better still, to use some commercial β service's estimate of the βs for several firms whose principal activity is similar to that in which the particular real investment under consideration lies. These individual βs should then be averaged.

The risk-free rate (r_f)

Here we should need to identify a risk-free asset and to make some estimation of its likely future value. Whilst there is strictly no such thing as a risk-free asset, short-dated UK Government bills probably are as safe an asset as we can find in the real world. The historical interest rates on these is readily accessible to us. Our problem remains one of estimating likely future rates. Fortunately Government bill rates are fairly stable from year to year and seem to be predicted with a fair degree of accuracy by the leading economic forecasters.

The expected return on the market portfolio ($E(r_m)$)

This is something of a problem area. This factor tends to be pretty volatile from year to year and difficult to forecast accurately. We could use an average of returns for the immediate past periods as a surrogate for future expectations but, as was shown by Ibbotson & Sinquefield (1979) on the basis of US data, vastly differing results could be obtained depending on which starting point is selected, e.g. annual rates of 6.5 per cent in the period 1960–1978, 4.5 per cent for 1970–1978 and 0.9 per cent for 1973–1978.

These same researchers also showed, however, that over long periods of time (e.g. 25 years) the average annual rates tend to be more, though not completely, stable. Merrett & Sykes (1966) showed fairly similar results in relation to the UK equities market, i.e. great volatility of returns from year to year, but greater – although by no means total – stability over longer periods.

One approach might therefore be to use the experience of the past 25 years, say, as a surrogate for the future expected market returns.

CAPM and tax

The point emerged clearly in Chapter 5, that, in practice, we should predict after-corporation tax cash flows and discount them at an after-corporation tax cost of capital. This raises the crucial question, in the context of using CAPM to derive the discount rate: is the CAPM derived rate before corporation tax or after corporation tax? The answer is that, as it is normally derived, it is after tax. This is because the expected return on the market portfolio $E(r_m)$, which is directly used in CAPM, is an after-corporation tax return. Returns on individual securities, and on portfolios of securities, are calculated using dividends (which are paid out of post-corporation tax income) and capital gains (which are based on future expectations of dividends). Thus the $E(r_m)$ is a post-corporation tax rate. It is essential that the risk-free rate (r_f) is also expressed in after-corporation tax terms.

CAPM and real life

Nothing that we have discussed so far in this chapter should lead us to the conclusion that CAPM is a perfect description of the real relationship between risk and return in the context of marketable securities. Tests of CAPM have found some inconsistency between fact and theory which seems unlikely totally, if at all, to be accounted for by inadequacies in the testing methods.

At the same time the logic of the derivation of CAPM and the reasonableness of the major assumptions on which that derivation is based, plus the general tendency of the evidence to support it, strongly suggest that its basic tenets are justified. It does seem reasonable for us to believe that risk is divided into that which is specific and susceptible to elimination and that which is systematic and unavoidable. There does seem to be a clear relationship between risk as measured by β and return.

Even if CAPM is less than perfect, its broad approach seems well worth taking into account.

When we come to consider how useful CAPM can be to us in the real investment appraisal context, it is then that our problems arise. As we have just seen, reliably estimating the three factors to plug into the model to obtain the expected return from an asset is rather difficult. This seems particularly problematical with the expected return on the market portfolio, or at least its proxy, a representative market index.

This probably means that CAPM is severely limited in its operational usefulness to financial managers when they are making real investment decisions. It is not easy to use it in practice to derive the discount rate. However, what is the alternative? If we are not to use CAPM, warts and all, what are we to do? The answer must be to make some guess at a discount rate, a guess based on no particular logic. In the face of this situation an approach which is logical, even if problematical, must be preferable.

Arbitrage Pricing Model

The fact that tests of CAPM have shown β not to be a perfect explanation of the relationship between the level of risk and the expected risk premium, caused researchers to look at other approaches. One such approach led to the development of the Arbitrage Pricing Model (APM). The logic of this model is that there is not a unique explanation of the risk/risk premium relationship, as is suggested by CAPM, but a number of them. The APM, which was developed by Ross (1976), holds that there are four factors which explain the risk/risk premium relationship of a particular security.

Basically, CAPM says that:

$$E(r_i) = r_f + \lambda \beta_i$$

where λ is the average risk premium $(E(r_m) - r_f)$.

However, APM holds that:

$$E(r_i) = r_f + \lambda_1\beta_{i1} + \lambda_2\beta_{i2} + \lambda_3\beta_{i3} + \lambda_4\beta_{i4}$$

where λ_1, λ_2, λ_3 and λ_4 are the average risk premium for each of the four factors in the model and β_{i1}, β_{i2}, β_{i3} and β_{i4} are measures of the sensitivity of the particular security i to each of the four factors.

The four factors in the APM relate to future macroeconomic factors, including industrial output and levels of inflation.

Tests conducted on APM appear to show it superior to CAPM as an explainer of historical security returns. However, because it contains four factors, rather than one, its practical usefulness in deriving a discount rate to be applied in NPV analyses is even more questionable than is that of CAPM.

DIVERSIFICATION WITHIN THE FIRM

CAPM and the principles from which it is derived tell us that specific risk may be eliminated by the investor holding securities in efficient portfolios. The same is true of APM. Evidence suggests that investors typically hold fairly well diversified portfolios.

As the typical individual or institutional investor in securities is diversified (not too exposed to specific risk), there seems no advantage to the shareholder in firms diversifying their own real investments across industries. Indeed it has been argued that firms should take on real investments which they know best how to manage (i.e. within their own area of expertise) and leave the diversification to their shareholders.

The fact that firms diversified across industries are very common may arise for one or both of two reasons.

(a) Managers are unfamiliar with the principles of modern portfolio theory and believe that the interests of shareholders are best served by inter-industry diversification.

(b) Managers are, not unnaturally, concerned with how risk affects themselves. Whereas shareholders tend to hold securities in portfolios this is not very practical for managers as regards their employments. They usually only have one employment at a time and are thus exposed to both the specific and the systematic risks of their firms. To individual shareholders the demise of the firm will be unfortunate but not fatal, to the extent that they each hold only perhaps 5 per cent of their wealth in that firm. To managers the failure of their employer firm will probably be something of a disaster, to the extent of loss of employment.

This second point identifies a possible area of conflict between the best interests of the shareholders and those of the managers.

SUMMARY Risks associated with investment in marketable securities consist of two types, specific risk and systematic risk. Most of the specific risk can be diversified away by holding diversified portfolios. Relatively little random diversification will eliminate nearly all specific risk, leaving a rump of systematic risk which is impervious to diversification.

Systematic risk affects securities differentially and the extent of particular securities' risk depends on the level of covariance with risky investments generally.

By making several simplifying assumptions it can be shown that all investors will choose to hold exactly the same portfolio of risky assets in conjunction with borrowing or lending at a risk-free rate. From this it is possible to derive a model relating expected returns to the level of systematic risk for individual securities. The capital asset pricing model, which is fairly robust to empirical testing, asserts that the expected returns from an asset are directly proportional to the level of covariance between those expected returns and those from a market portfolio. CAPM provides some insights into the risk/return *trade-off* relating to investment in risky assets, including real investment by firms. CAPM therefore provides a basis for the derivation of the appropriate discount rate to apply to the expected cash flows when assessing the potential NPV of real investment opportunities, though applying it in real life has its practical problems.

The arbitrage pricing model also shows insights on the risk/return relationship and has generally shown greater robustness to empirical testing than has CAPM. APM poses even greater problems than CAPM in the derivation of investment project discount rates.

FURTHER READING	Levy & Sarnat (1988) give a clear explanation of the derivation of CAPM and its implications for real investment appraisal. This is also clearly covered by Sharpe (1990). Puxty & Dodds (1991) are also worth reading on the derivation of CAPM and empirical tests of the model. Copeland & Weston (1988) give a rigorous coverage of CAPM and APM and discuss empirical tests of them. For an interesting and fairly detailed account of how one firm (Bowater–Scott Corporation Ltd) used CAPM to derive a discount rate, see Sizer & Coulthurst (1984).

WORK-BASED ASSIGNMENT	(a) If your organisation is a quoted company, deduce the β of the ordinary shares based on their monthly returns over the past year and those of the FT Actuaries Index.
	(b) If your organisation is not a quoted company, deduce the β of a quoted company of your choice.

QUESTIONS WITH ANSWERS (see Appendix 3)	**1** What sort of factors relating to a firm specialising in operating ferries crossing the English Channel would tend to give rise to:
	(a) specific risk; and
	(b) systematic risk?
	2 The following are the annual returns for the ordinary shares of Court plc and for a representative equity price index:

		Court plc	Index
		%	%
Year	1	19	13
	2	(8)	(7)
	3	(12)	(13)
	4	3	4
	5	8	8
	6	17	10
	7	14	15
	8	14	16
	9	14	16
	10	1	(2)

(The bracketed figures are negative returns.)

(a) What is the β for Court plc's ordinary shares?

(b) If the risk-free rate is 6 per cent p.a., what would be the expected return on Court plc's ordinary shares if the expected return for equities generally was 12 per cent p.a.?

APPENDIX – DERIVATION OF CAPM

**Figure 7.9
The relationship of an individual security *i* with the market portfolio M and the capital market line**

The line *i*M is a series of various combinations of individual security *i* and the market portfolio M.

In Fig. 7.9:
(a) EE is the *efficient frontier* of risky assets.
(b) r_f is the risk-free rate.
(c) $r_f S$ is the efficient frontier of possibilities once the risk-free asset is introduced.
(d) iM is the risk return profile of various portfolios containing proportions of an individual *inefficient* asset i and the *market* portfolio M.

Let α be the proportion of i in the portfolio (p) of i and M. Then,

$$E(r_p) = \alpha E(r_i) + (1 - \alpha)E(r_m) \tag{1}$$

and

$$\sigma_p = \sqrt{(\alpha^2 \sigma_i^2 + (1 - \alpha)^2 \sigma_m^2 + 2\alpha(1 - \alpha)\text{Cov}(i, M))} \tag{2}$$

The slope of iM at any point is given by

$$\frac{dE(r_p)}{d\sigma_p}, \text{ which equals} \frac{dE(r_p)}{d\alpha} \times \frac{d\alpha}{d\sigma_p}$$

$$\frac{dE(r_p)}{d\alpha} = E(r_i) - E(r_m)$$

If we let x = the expression within the square root sign in equation (2), then

$$\frac{d\sigma_p}{d\alpha} = \frac{dx}{d\alpha} \times \frac{d\sigma_p}{dx}$$

and $\quad \sigma_p = x^{1/2}$

$$\frac{d\sigma_p}{dx} = \tfrac{1}{2} x^{-1/2}$$

or $\quad \tfrac{1}{2} \times \dfrac{1}{\sqrt{[\alpha^2 \sigma_i^2 + (1 - \alpha)^2 \sigma_m^2 + 2\alpha(1 - \alpha)\text{Cov}(i, M)]}}$

$$\frac{dx}{d\alpha} = 2\alpha\sigma_i^2 + 2\alpha\sigma_m^2 - 2\sigma_m + 2\text{Cov}(i, M) - 4\alpha\text{Cov}(i, M)$$

so $\quad \dfrac{dE(r_p)}{d\sigma_p} = [E(r_i) - E(r_m)]$

$$\times \frac{2\sqrt{[\alpha^2 \sigma_i^2 + (1 - \alpha)^2 \sigma_m^2 + 2\alpha(1 - \alpha)\text{Cov}(i, M)]}}{2\alpha\sigma_i^2 + 2\alpha\sigma_m^2 - 2\sigma_m^2 + 2\text{Cov}(i, M) - 4\alpha\text{Cov}(i, M)}$$

If the market is in equilibrium, then M will already contain the appropriate proportion of i and so the portfolio of i and M will contain no excess i. Thus the only point on iM which would be expected to occur will be M, i.e. the point where $\alpha = 0$.

When $\alpha = 0$, $\dfrac{dE(r_p)}{d\sigma_p}$ (above) reduces to :

$$(E(r_i) - (E(r_m)) \times \frac{\sigma_m}{\text{Cov}(i, M) - \sigma_m^2} \tag{3}$$

At M the cord *iM* is tangential to (has the same slope as) the capital market line $r_f S$.

$$\text{The slope of } r_f S \text{ is } \frac{E(r_m) - r_f}{\sigma_m}$$

Equating this with (3) above and simplifying gives

$$E(r_i) = r_f + (E(r_m) - r_f) \frac{Cov(i, M)}{\sigma_m^2}$$

or $\quad E(r_i) = r_f + (E(r_m) - r_f)\beta \text{ where } \beta = \dfrac{Cov(i, M)}{\sigma_m^2}$

This is the CAPM which says, in effect, that the expected return from a risky asset depends on the risk-free rate of interest, the expected returns from the market portfolio and the degree of correlation between the risky asset's returns and those of the market portfolio.

PART 3

Financing decisions

Investment requires finance and there are many sources available. This part of the book considers how decisions are made on the most appropriate sources to finance particular investments. Chapter 8 reviews the principal sources of finance and their particular features. The role and effectiveness of the market for finance is discussed in Chapter 9. The theory that share prices always reflect the economic reality is examined in some detail. In Chapter 10, assessing the cost of finance is examined. The relationship between the investment and the financing decision is also considered. Chapter 11 is concerned with the extent to which it is likely to be beneficial for firms to borrow funds as an alternative to raising them from shareholders. Raising funds from shareholders can be done in broadly two possible ways. These are 'ploughing back' past profits, instead of paying them to shareholders as dividends, and raising fresh money from shareholders by asking them to buy new shares. Chapter 12 considers which of these two approaches, if either, is likely to be the most appropriate.

CHAPTER 8

Sources of long-term finance

OBJECTIVES

In this chapter we shall deal with the following:

- the major issues to consider in respect of each type of financing
- equity financing
- methods of raising equity finance
- preference shares
- loan stocks and debentures
- convertible loan stocks
- term loans
- the use of financial leasing
- financial grants from public funds and their importance
- the attitude that firms should take to deciding on their financing method

INTRODUCTION

In previous chapters we have seen that firms raise their long-term finance either from equity shareholders or from borrowings. Within each type of financing (equity or borrowing) are several sub-types. In fact one fairly important financing method (convertible loan stock) has elements of both equity and borrowing.

In this chapter we shall consider the various sub-types. Given the financial objective of maximisation of shareholders' wealth we shall consider each of them in the context of how they will affect the interests of existing equity shareholders. We shall also try to assess their attractions to potential investors.

The primary capital market

We shall in fact be considering the capital market in its primary function, as a market for *new* capital. The primary capital market does not reside in a single location. It is a somewhat nebulous market; in fact any point of contact between a supplier and a user of capital is part of the primary capital market. In the UK this includes the International Stock Exchange of the UK and the Republic of Ireland which, as well as its more familiar role as probably the most important part of the secondary market, is also a very important sector of the primary market. However, the primary market also includes a large number of other institutions and organisations.

An important financial source in the modern UK is grants given by the government and the European Community. We shall therefore be considering these in broad terms.

The factors

From the point of view of the firm and its existing shareholders there are several important factors relating to any particular source of new finance. These include:

(a) the administrative and legal costs of actually raising the finance;
(b) the cost of servicing the finance, e.g. interest payments;
(c) the level of obligation to make interest or similar payments;
(d) the level of obligation to repay the finance;
(e) the tax deductibility of costs related to the finance;
(f) the effect of the new finance on the level of control of the firm by its existing shareholders and on their freedom of action.

To the supplier of new finance to the firm the following are likely to be important factors:

(a) the level of return which is expected by investors;
(b) the level of risk attaching to the expected returns;
(c) the potential for liquidating the investment either through direct repayment by the firm or via the secondary market;
(d) the personal tax position of investors in relation to returns from their investment;
(e) the degree of control or influence over the firm's affairs which the investor is likely to acquire as a consequence of investing.

In this chapter we shall assess each of the financial sources reviewed in the context of these factors. We should note that those relating to suppliers of finance are of more than passing interest to the firm's financial managers and existing shareholders. Those factors have a considerable bearing on the attractiveness of any particular type of finance and therefore on the likely success of an attempt to raise new finance in that particular way.

Risk and return

Both intuition and the results of several studies suggest that investors expect and actually get, on average, higher returns where higher risk is involved. The relationship appears to be something like that depicted in Fig. 8.1.

To the firm the position is the corollary of that of the investors; sources of finance which are relatively risky to the firm tend to be cheap in terms of servicing cost, safe sources tend to be expensive. The level of returns required by secured lenders is relatively low but the existence of such loans represents, as we shall see, a potential threat to the welfare of the shareholders. Equity investors expect high returns, but issuing additional ordinary shares does not tend greatly to increase the risk borne by the original shareholders.

ORDINARY OR EQUITY CAPITAL

Equity financing is overwhelmingly the most important in the UK corporate private sector. Both as regards the cumulative financing arrangements and the raising of new capital, equity finance is by far the largest source (see Tables 8.1, 8.2 and 8.3). Equities seem to attract a wide range of investors, both private and institutional.

**Figure 8.1
The risk/return
relationship for
various types of
security**

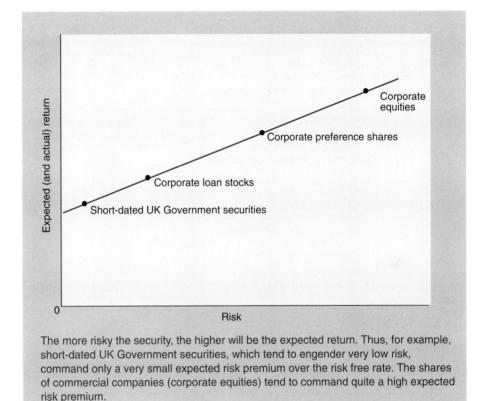

The more risky the security, the higher will be the expected return. Thus, for example, short-dated UK Government securities, which tend to engender very low risk, command only a very small expected risk premium over the risk free rate. The shares of commercial companies (corporate equities) tend to command quite a high expected risk premium.

The nature of equity

The ordinary shareholders are the owners of the firm, who, through the voting rights attaching to their shares, exercise ultimate control over the firm.

As owners of the firm the ordinary shareholders bear the greatest risk. If the firm trades unsuccessfully, the ordinary shareholders are the first to suffer in terms of lack of dividends and probably falls in the market value of their shares. If the firm collapses (it is put into liquidation) it is the ordinary shareholders who will be at the bottom of the list with a claim for repayment of their investment.

On the other hand, the fruits of the firm's success principally benefit ordinary shareholders; other participants in the firm – labour, lenders, suppliers, etc. – tend to earn returns not related to the firm's success. Thus once the claims of these other claimants are met the balance accrues to the ordinary shareholders.

Table 8.1   Balance sheet summaries of a sample of large UK firms, expressing the various elements as a percentage of the total long-term finance for each year

	1986 %	1987 %	1988 %	1989 %	1990 %
Fixed assets	77	79	82	85	85
Current assets:					
Stock in trade	27	26	24	23	20
Trade debtors	32	32	32	30	28
Cash and other liquid assets	15	16	14	13	13
	74	74	70	66	61
Current liabilities:					
Creditors and loans					
falling due within one year	42	43	43	42	39
Dividends, interest and tax owing	9	10	9	9	7
	51	53	52	51	46
Working capital	23	21	18	15	15
	100	100	100	100	100
Shareholders' interests (equity finance)	78	78	76	73	74
Long-term loans falling due after					
more than one year	22	22	24	27	26
	100	100	100	100	100

The figures are derived from the Business Statistics Office which aggregates the balance sheets of a representative sample of both listed and unlisted UK industrial and commercial firms. The number of firms involved varies from year to year, but exceeded 1600 in each of the above years.

Nominal values

When the firm is first established, a decision would have been made about how much equity finance (the law requires that there is some) it wishes to raise and into how many shares this is to be divided. If, for example, the decision is that £1m needs to be raised, it could be in the form of two shares of nominal value £500 000 each, 1m shares of £1 each, 200 000 shares of £5 each, or (more likely) 2m shares of £0.50 each. Which of these, or any one of the almost infinite number of other possibilities, is decided upon, is a matter of the judgement of the promoters of the firm.

Table 8.2   Sources of new finance for a sample of large UK firms*

	1980 %	1981 %	1982 %	1983 %	1984 %	1985 %	1986 %	1987 %	1988 %	1989 %	1990 %
Share and loan stock issues	7	13	0	1	12	37	25	29	22	20	35
Bank loans, short-term											
loans and credit	28	40	46	47	33	(15)	19	23	35	41	13
Retained profits											
(including depreciation)	65	47	54	52	55	78	56	47	43	39	52

Source: Business Statistics Office
* See footnote toTable 8.1.

Table 8.3 New security issues, net of redemptions, by UK firms (by type of security)*

| Year | Loan stocks | | | | | Preference | | Ordinary | | |
	Convertible loans £m	Other loans £m	Total loans £m	Percentage of total issues	£m	Percentage of total issues	£m	Percentage of total issues	Total issues £m
1985	320	121	441	9	414	8	4211	83	5066
1986	55	851	906	10	65	1	7 751	89	8 722
1987	186	(186)	0	0	659	4	14 717	96	15 376
1988	707	2 312	3019	38	612	8	4 352	54	7 983
1989	1 580	2 952	4 532	61	1 016	14	1 883	25	7 431
1990	1 763	1 046	2 809	46	515	8	2 852	46	6 176
1991	1 055	3 484	4 539	31	480	3	9 761	66	14 780
1992	679	3 115	3 794	42	25	0	5 272	58	9 091

Source: Bank of England
* This table gives information on issues to UK investors by Stock Exchange listed firms.

In making this decision, probably the major factor is marketability. Most investors would not find shares of very large nominal value very attractive as this would make it difficult to set aside an amount of money to be exactly invested in the firm. If the shares were of nominal value £50, an investor who wishes to invest £275 in the firm could not do so. The choice would be between five or six shares. Even if the shares were £10 nominal value the investor could get fairly close to the target of £275 (27 or 28 shares). It seems to be believed that large nominal value shares are not as readily marketable as those of smaller denomination. Certainly large-denomination shares are very rare in practice. Few ordinary shares have nominal values larger than £1 each.

Once the firm has invested its capital and has started to trade, the market value of its ordinary shares will probably move away from the nominal value, as a result of market forces. Further issues of ordinary shares will normally be priced by reference to current market prices, i.e. firms will seek to issue further ordinary shares at the highest price which the market will bear. In fact nominal values cease to have much significance once the firm has started trading. This is evidenced by the fact that in the USA, which has similar corporate financing arrangements to those encountered in the UK, shares of no par (or nominal) value are not unusual.

The decision on nominal value is not irrevocable; firms may subsequently *split* or *consolidate* nominal values. For example a firm whose ordinary shares have a nominal value of £1 each may split them into shares of £0.50 each. In practice this is easily accomplished and culminates in each ordinary shareholder being sent a replacement share certificate showing twice as many £0.50 shares as the investor previously had £1 ones. As we have seen, the objective of such a move seems to be to reduce the unit price to make the shares more marketable.*

*If the shares are in fact rendered more attractive by splitting, logically the market value of a particular investor's holding would be increased by the split. The evidence seems to indicate that this does not actually happen in practice. See Copeland & Weston (1988) for a discussion of some tests relating to this point.

Investment ratios

Several ratios are used by, or at least made available to, investors which give measures of some aspects of the ordinary shares' performance. These are published daily, together with the daily share price, by most of the more serious national newspapers. These ratios (which were introduced in Chapter 3) are:

(a) *Price/earnings ratio (PE)*. Here the current price per share is expressed as a multiple of the earnings per share (net profit available for ordinary shares divided by the number of ordinary shares which the firm has issued). The profit figure used in the calculation of the ratio is that for the most recently reported year.

Shares with large PEs are those which are highly priced for their historical earnings level, indicating the market's faith in the future of the firm and its ability to grow.

(b) *Dividend yield (DY)*. This expresses the gross equivalent of dividends per share paid in the most recent year as a percentage of the current market price. It gives some idea of the rate of return which the dividend represents. This may be compared with returns from other investments to try to assess the particular share. To the extent that over a period capital gains and losses are much more important in amount per share than dividends, DY is (to say the least) an incomplete measure of the benefits of ownership of the share.

(c) *Dividend cover (DC)*. This expresses the earnings per share, after prior claims have been satisfied, as a multiple of the actual dividend per share paid from those earnings. It gives some indication of the extent to which the firm pays its profits out as dividends and to what extent they are ploughed back.

Much of what we have already discussed in this book on such matters as the importance of risk calls into question the value of relying on the above ratios. It must be said, however, that such ratios are widely available to investors and so very possibly used by them. We shall discuss the issues relating to the choice of dividend levels in Chapter 12.

Factors for the firm to consider on equity financing

Issue costs

These vary considerably according to the method used to raise the new equity and the finance raised; ranging from virtually nothing up to about 15 per cent of the new finance raised (Jenkinson, 1990). We shall consider this in more detail when dealing with the various methods in the following section.

Servicing costs

Equity holders expect relatively high returns in terms of capital appreciation and dividends. Dividends represent an explicit cost. The capital appreciation results from the fact that sooner or later profits not paid out as dividends are expected to end up in the hands of the shareholders, even if they have to wait until the firm is liquidated before this happens. Thus one way or another, the entire profits will eventually be paid out to shareholders.

Obligation to pay dividends

Dividend levels are a question of the discretion of directors and financial managers. As we saw under 'Servicing costs' above, ultimately the dividend must be paid, but shareholders cannot directly force payment of a particular level of dividend in a particular year.

Obligation to redeem the investment

There is no such obligation unless (or until) the firm is liquidated. Because of this and to some extent because of the flexibility on dividend levels, finance provided by ordinary shareholders does not impose much by way of cash flow obligation on the firm.

Tax deductibility of dividends

In contrast with the servicing of virtually all other types of finance, dividends are not tax-deductible in arriving at the firm's Corporation Tax liability. This tends to make dividends more expensive than a similar gross equivalent loan interest rate (see the Appendix to this chapter for more details). In fact the advent of UK corporate tax rates close to the basic personal tax rate means that this point is not necessarily of great significance.

Effect on control and freedom of action

Where new equity finance is raised from other than the existing shareholders in the same proportions as their original investment, voting power will shift to some extent, perhaps to a large extent, and possibly with it control of the firm. This is not necessarily a feature of all increases in equity financing. In fact the two most important means of raising equity finance for most firms, retained profits and rights issues (each discussed below), generally avoid this problem.

It is somewhat doubtful whether this is really of much concern to typical ordinary shareholders, since they seem not to use their votes in any case. Most firms' annual general meetings are characterised by a distinct absence of most of those entitled to be present and to vote. Control is a factor which is more likely to be of concern to ordinary shareholders in small firms, a point which we shall discuss in Chapter 15.

Factors for the potential investor to consider on equity financing

Level of return

This would be expected to be higher than the level of return associated with 'safe' investments such as UK Government securities. This has historically been the case with real returns from UK equities averaging around 8 per cent p.a. since 1919, contrasting with an average real return from Government securities of about 2.5 per cent p.a. over the same period. Compared with other types of security, ordinary shares have on average provided the best, though nonetheless often an incomplete, hedge against inflation.

Equities provide an opportunity to make investments where returns are related fairly directly to commercial success. Most investment opportunities of this type require investors to spend time managing the assets in which their money is invested; they also expose investors to unlimited liability. However, equities enable delegation of day-to-day management to the directors and protect the investors' other assets.

Riskiness of returns

Returns both in terms of capital gains and of dividends are not certain by any means. Negative returns are very common over periods of a year or two (or less), though historically above-average positive returns compensate for these. A period of adverse trading could cause the value of a particular firm's ordinary shares to fall to zero, losing the shareholder the entire amount invested in those shares.

Ease of liquidating the investment

Typically, when investors take up part of an issue of new equity of a firm, they have no particular thoughts of the firm ever repaying that investment. However, the average investor would be reluctant to take up equities unless it were clear that there would be the opportunity to liquidate the investment, in some other way. This is where the secondary capital market comes in. It is clearly in the interest of the firm to have its ordinary shares regularly traded on a recognised stock exchange so that the facility to liquidate the investment exists.

Equities and personal tax

In the UK, dividends are taxed as *income* in the hands of the shareholder, at marginal rates up to 40 per cent. Capital appreciation is subject to the rather less severe Capital Gains Tax at rates similar to those applied to income.

Degree of control

Ordinary shares typically carry voting rights. This tends not to be too important to the typical shareholder but it does put him or her in a position, perhaps in concert with other shareholders, to apply pressure to the firm's senior management on any matter of concern.

METHODS OF RAISING ADDITIONAL EQUITY FINANCE

There are broadly three ways of raising new equity finance. These are retaining profits rather than paying them out as dividends, making issues of new shares to existing shareholders and making new share issues to the public. Table 8.2 shows the sources of new finance for a sample of large UK firms over recent years. From it we can see, despite some fluctuation from year to year, the clear dominance of retained profits over other methods. With new shares, over recent years, those issued to existing shareholders as rights issues have tended to be more important than issues to the general public (Bank of England).

Retained profit

It may seem surprising to mention retained profits as a source of new equity finance. However, profits certainly lead to a net increase in funds and retaining these, or part of them, rather than paying them out as dividends, is effectively a way of raising finance. After all, if the full profit were paid out as dividends and then shareholders bought new shares with their dividend money, this would have much the same effect as retaining the funds in the first place.

In fact retained profits are a very important source of finance, accounting for about half of all the long-term finance raised by UK firms over recent years (see Table 8.2).

A free source of finance?

At first sight, retained profits seem to be a source which costs nothing to service. A moment's reflection however shows this *not* to be true. From the ordinary shareholder's point of view, there is a clear opportunity cost in that, if cash dividends were paid, that cash could be invested in some income-yielding way. As the obvious comparison is an investment in equities of similar risk to those of the firm under consideration, retained profits logically have a cost similar to that of the original ordinary shares.

Bonus shares

In much the same way as firms can and do split nominal values, firms can convert retained profits into ordinary shares which are then distributed to existing shareholders free of charge.

EXAMPLE

The following is a highly abbreviated balance sheet of a firm which has been trading for some period of time and which has retained at least some of its profits.

Balance sheet as at 30 June 1993

Sources of finance (claims)	£m	Uses of finance (investments)	£m
Ordinary shares of £1 each	4	Fixed assets	5
Retained profits	3		
Total equity	7	Working capital	4
Long-term loan	2		
	9		9

It is open to the firm, with only the minimum of administrative difficulty, to convert all or part of the £3m retained profit to shares which may be issued *pro rata* to the ordinary shareholders. Let us assume for our example that £2m of the £3m retained profit is so converted. The revised balance sheet would be:

Balance sheet as at 30 June 1993

Sources of finance (claims)	£m	Uses of finance (investments)	£m
Ordinary shares of £1 each	6	Fixed assets	5
Retained profits	1		
Total equity	7	Working capital	4
Long-term loan	2		
	9		9

Note that the conversion of retained profits into shares leaves the uses of funds totally unaffected. It also leaves completely untouched the total equity figure, i.e. the contribution of the ordinary shareholders is not altered by the bonus issue. All that will occur is that for every two shares held before the bonus issue, the shareholder will hold three after it. As with splitting, the economic effect of a bonus issue should logically be zero. If in this example the price of an ordinary share were £1.80 before the issue, it should be £1.20 (i.e. £1.80 × ⅔) afterwards.

If they have no economic consequences, why do firms make bonus issues? Do managements believe that shareholders will be fooled into thinking that they have got something for nothing? If so, the evidence* suggests that they are wrong. Possibly bonus issues are intended to transmit information. Bonus issues are sometimes thought to indicate a confidence on the part of management in the investments which it has made. A third possible reason, as with splits, is simply to reduce the unit price of the shares to (what management may regard as) a more marketable size.

Factors to consider in respect of raising finance by retention of profits

Does dividend policy affect the net wealth of the shareholder?
If it does then retaining one proportion of the profit, rather than another proportion, will have some effect on the sum of the dividend paid and the ex-dividend price of the share. We shall review the debate and evidence on this topic in some detail in Chapter 12.

No issue costs
Other means of raising additional equity have explicit issue costs not applicable to retained profits.

Profits are uncertain
Once the need for raising further finance has been identified there is no guarantee that sufficiently large profits will subsequently be made to meet the requirements. On the other hand, once the funds have been generated from profits, their existence is certain and their retention just a matter of a management decision. This latter point contrasts with other methods of raising equity finance.

*See Chapter 9 for a discussion of tests of the effect of bonus issues on ordinary shareholders' wealth.

No dilution of control
Retaining profits does not alter the voting strength of any individual shareholder.

Rights issues

These are offers to existing ordinary shareholders to take up additional shares, for cash, at a price usually significantly below that at which the shares already issued trade in the capital market at the time.

Rights issues have generally represented by far the most important method of raising new equity finance in the UK, after retained profits, over recent years. In fact, the law requires, in normal circumstances, that any new equity issue must be offered first to existing shareholders in proportion to their individual shareholdings. Shareholders can agree to waive these 'pre-emption rights'. The existence of this point of law is sometimes seen as a restriction on the ability of directors to take advantage of some other source of equity finance.

Once the firm has decided on the amount of finance it needs and has set a price, it simply offers shares to existing shareholders. The number of new shares which any individual shareholder has the *right* to take up depends on the number of shares which he or she already owns.

EXAMPLE

A firm has in existence 4m ordinary £1 shares whose current market price is £1.80 each. The firm wishes to raise £1.2m by a rights issue at £1.50 per share. The number of shares to be issued will be £1.2m/£1.5, i.e. 800 000 shares. These will be offered on a 1 for 5 basis to existing ordinary shareholders. For example, a shareholder owning 200 shares will therefore be given the right to buy an additional 40 shares. If the shareholder wishes not to take up this entitlement, the rights may be sold to someone who does wish to take them up (irrespective of whether or not that someone is an existing shareholder). Usually rights may be sold in the capital market. Their buyer acquires the same right to take up the shares as did the shareholder to whom they were originally granted.

In the above example, the value of the entire equity of the firm immediately before the rights issue was £7.2m (i.e. 4m × £1.80). Immediately following the issue, this should rise by £1.2m (the amount of *new* money raised). The total value of the equity should now be £8.4m or £1.75 per share (i.e. £8.4m/4.8m).

This is the price at which the shares should trade immediately following the rights issue, assuming that everything else remains equal. Thus the value of the right to buy one share is likely to be £0.25 (i.e. the difference between the rights issue price, and the ex-rights price).*

Let us consider a shareholder who starts with 100 ordinary shares and as a result is offered 20 new shares in the rights issue. This person has three choices:

*Market forces would tend to ensure that this is broadly true since if it were not, it would imply that it would be possible either to make abnormal gains by buying rights on the one hand, or no one would be prepared to buy them on the other.

(a) Pay £30 (i.e. 20 × £1.50) to the firm and take up the entitlement. If this is done the value of the shareholding will go up from £180 (i.e. 100 × £1.80) to £210 (i.e. 120 × £1.75). This increase of £30 is exactly the amount which has just been paid to take up the rights, so the rights issue leaves the shareholder neither richer nor poorer than before.

(b) Sell the rights presumably for £5 (i.e. 20 × £0.25). This would leave a shareholding worth £175 (i.e. 100 × £1.75) and £5 in cash, a total value of £180, once again leaving the shareholder neither better nor worse off.

(c) Allow the rights to lapse, in which case the value of the shareholding will fall from £180 to £175. Thus the shareholder will lose wealth by failing to act either to take up the rights or to sell them within the time allowed by the firm to do so.

The importance of the rights issue price

How important is it that the firm gets the price right? In the above example, would existing ordinary shareholders be worse off, better off or unaffected if the rights issue price had been, say, £1 per share instead of £1.50?

Obviously to raise £1.2m would require issuing 1.2m shares if the issue price were to be £1 each. The value of the equity immediately following the issue would still be £8.4m but the market price per share would be £1.615 (i.e. £8.4m/5.2m). This would put the value of the rights at £0.615 per share. Let us again consider the position of a holder of 100 of the original ordinary shares who chooses to take up the entitlement of 30 new shares (remember that 1.2m new shares will now have to be offered to the holders of the original 4.0m shares, i.e. 3 for 10).

The value of our shareholder's increased holding will be £210. Again the increase from the original value of the holding (£180) is entirely accounted for by the cash which our shareholder has had to pay. Thus the wealth of the shareholder is not affected by the price at which the rights issue is made. It can equally well be shown that the shareholder who chooses to sell the rights will similarly be unaffected.

Firms typically price rights issues at about 20 per cent below the current pre-rights share price. As we have seen, doing this should not really advantage the shareholder. However, since allowing the rights to lapse disadvantages shareholders, a rights issue priced at a discount puts pressure on them either to take up the issue or to sell the rights. In either case this is likely to lead to the issue being successful in terms of all of the shares being taken up and the desired amount of money raised.

Another reason for pricing rights issues at a discount is to try to ensure that any fall in the market price of the shares already issued, between the date of the announcement of the rights issue (and of the rights issue price) and the date of the issue, still leaves the rights issue price below the market price. If, on the issue date, shares were cheaper to buy in the capital market than by taking up the rights, the issue would almost certainly fail.

Factors to consider in respect of rights issues

Rights issues are a relatively cheap way of raising equity finance
It is estimated that an issue of £2m costs about 4 per cent of that amount (Wilson

Committee report 1980). Note that since many of these costs are fixed, the cost will be proportionately more or less for smaller or larger issues respectively.

Pricing of issues is not a critical factor

As we have seen shareholders who either sell or take up their rights are left in more or less the same position as regards wealth irrespective of the issue price.

Rights issues are fairly certain

It is relatively rare in practice for a rights issue to fail. This is an important factor since many of the issue costs are committed in advance and are lost if the issue fails.

Existing shareholders are forced either to increase or to liquidate part of their shareholding

To shareholders given rights to take up additional shares, doing nothing is not a sensible option. In order to preserve their wealth they must either take up the shares and so increase their investment in the firm or sell the rights thus effectively liquidating part of their investment in the firm. Neither of these may be attractive to some shareholders which could cause the shares of firms which make frequent rights issues to become unpopular, thus adversely affecting their market value.

It is of course always open to an individual shareholder to sell some of the rights to obtain sufficient cash to take up the rest. This still requires action on the shareholder's part. In practice the vast majority of rights are taken up by existing shareholders (90 per cent according to the Wilson Committee, 1980).

Dilution of control

This need not occur with rights issues as existing shareholders are given the opportunity, usually accepted, to retain the same voting power after the issue as they had before.

Share issues in depressed markets

It is argued by some observers that it would be unfair to sell new shares to the public when either capital market prices generally, or the firm's shares in particular, are depressed. This is because it would allow outsiders to buy shares 'on the cheap' at the expense of the existing shareholders. If a rights issue is made under such circumstances, it is claimed, this advantage would only go to existing shareholders.

This seems an illogical view in the light of the evidence on capital market efficiency, which will be reviewed in the next chapter. Such evidence strongly supports the hypothesis that the current market price of a share is the consensus view of its value at the time. There is no reason to believe that because it has recently fallen in value it is about to increase, any more than it should cause us to feel that it is about to suffer a further decrease in value or to remain static.

Equity issues to the public

Such issues are relatively rare in practice and do not account for a very large proportion of total equity fund raising – probably less than 10 per cent of all new equity finance in the UK over recent years. Whilst there are not many such issues, those which do occur tend to be large in size. They seem to occur most with firms which have newly been listed by the Stock Exchange for a quotation and dealing, i.e. firms which are making their first significant public issue of ordinary shares.

Technically there are two ways of making public issues:

(a) The issuing firm can sell the shares to an *issuing house*, usually a merchant bank which specialises in such work. The issuing house then sells the shares to the public. This is known as an *offer for sale*.

(b) The issuing firm sells the shares direct to the public. Often such firms are advised by a merchant bank on such matters as the pricing of the issue. Here the offer is known as an *offer by prospectus*.

Irrespective of which of these methods is used, the general procedure is the same. Basically the shares are advertised in newspapers and/or in other printed forms. The advertisement is required by law and by the regulations of the Stock Exchange to give a large volume of detailed information. This is very expensive to prepare, including as it does reports from independent accountants, etc. The objective of including such voluminous and detailed information is to protect the public from the type of sloppy and sometimes fraudulent claims which were made by firms' managements in the earlier days of the Stock Exchange.

Smaller firms may not wish to be subjected to the rigours, and the accompanying cost, of obtaining a full Stock Exchange listing for their shares. For such firms the Stock Exchange provides a separate market in which shares may be traded. This is the *Unlisted Securities Market (USM)*, which tends to cater for firms whose shares have a total market value of between £1m and £5m.

The fact that a particular firm's securities are traded in the USM should warn potential investors that the requirements for the firm to obtain a full listing for its shares have not been met, though less rigorous ones will have been complied with. This implies that such securities represent a more hazardous investment than would those of a similar firm which had obtained a full listing.

Pricing of issues to the public

In contrast with the position with rights issues, the pricing of issues of ordinary shares to the public is of vital importance to existing shareholders.

If the new shares are priced at a discount on the value of the existing shares, unless existing holders were to take up such a number of new shares as would retain for them the same proportion of the total as they had before, it would be the equivalent of a shareholder allowing all or some of the allotment in a rights issue to lapse (see the example on page 207 for the effect of this).

Since issues to the public tend to occur where a firm is significantly extending its equity base, it is most unlikely that an existing shareholder will be able to take up sufficient new shares to avoid being penalised by an issue at a discount.

It is a matter of judgement as to how well the issue price strikes the balance between attracting the maximum amount of cash per share on the one hand, and avoiding a very costly failure to raise the required funds, after spending large amounts on promoting the issue, on the other. There are two ways in which the pricing problem can be mitigated. One is to have the shares underwritten. For a fee, underwriters will guarantee to take up shares for which the public do not subscribe. This ensures the success of the issue. The underwriters' fee or commission is fixed by them according to how many shares they are underwriting, the offer price and naturally, how high the underwriter believes the possibility to be that some shares will not be taken up by the public. Underwriters are in effect insurers. Most issues to the public are underwritten. Underwriting costs tend to be in the order of 2 per cent of the capital raised.

The second way of dealing with the pricing problem is for the shares to be open to tender. This is much like an auction where the shares are sold to the highest bidders, usually subject to a pre-stated reserve price (i.e. a price below which offers will not be accepted). When all of the offers have been received (the closing date for offers has been reached), the firm or the issuing house assesses what is the highest price at which all of the shares could be issued. This can probably best be explained with a simple example.

EXAMPLE

Suppose that a firm wishes to issue 10m shares by tender. After publishing the advertisement in the required form it receives offers as follows:

1m shares at £5.00 each
1m shares at £4.50 each
2m shares at £4.00 each
2m shares at £3.50 each
3m shares at £3.00 each
5m shares at £2.50 each
10m shares at £2.00 each

The highest price at which all of the 10m shares could be issued yet each offerer be required to pay the same price per share is £2.50. This is known as the *striking price*, i.e. the price at which all 10m shares will be issued, 9m to those who offered above £2.50 and the other 1m to some of those who offered £2.50 exactly. Note that all of the 10m shares are issued at £2.50 each.

Issues by tender seem to be increasingly popular, the late 1980s having seen several of them.

Factors to consider in respect of equity issues to the public

Issue costs

These are very large, estimated at 12½ per cent of the proceeds for a £5m issue (Jenkinson, 1990). This compares with 2 per cent for a rights issue and zero cost for retained profits. This probably explains the small number of public issues and why they tend mainly to occur in cases where there is not the rights or retained profits alternative.

Uncertainty of public issues

The relative certainty of success associated with rights issues does not exist with issues to the public. As we have discussed already, the use of underwriters and/or issuing by tender can overcome the problem to some extent, but at a cost.

Pricing of issues is critical

If the interests of existing ordinary shareholders are to be protected, the pricing question is one of vital importance. Issuing by tender does, to some extent, overcome the problem. Capital market efficiency suggests that offers will rationally and fairly price the issue.

Dilution of control

Clearly this is going to occur with issues to the public. It is probably the price which the original shareholders have to pay to obtain access to additional equity finance when rights issues and retained profits are not possibilities.

PREFERENCE SHARES

Preference shares form part of the risk-bearing ownership of the firm but since preference shareholders usually have the right to the first slice (of predetermined size) of any dividend paid, they bear less risk than do ordinary shares. Investors' expectations of returns from preference shares are therefore lower than expectations from ordinary shares in the same firm. Historically preference shares have been a significant source of corporate finance.

More recently they seem to have fallen from favour and have tended to be of very little importance (see Table 8.3).

Preference shares may be, and usually are, *cumulative*. This means that if the preference dividend is not met in full in any particular year, ordinary shareholders are not entitled to dividends in any future year until preference share dividends have been brought up to date.

Nominal value

Preference shares have a nominal value but, as with ordinary shares, its size is not usually of much importance. However, the preference dividend is usually expressed as a percentage of the nominal value (though it need not be).

Investment ratios

Dividend yield and dividend cover are important ratios to the preference shareholder. Dividends would normally be by far the most important part of the preference shares' returns, so the effective rate and its security are important matters.

Factors for the firm to consider on preference share financing

Issue costs

These are likely to be rather similar to those associated with raising new equity finance and similarly variable with the method used.

Servicing costs

These would tend to be somewhat lower than those relating to ordinary shares, since preference shares expose their holder to rather less risk.

Obligation to pay dividends

Preference shares do not impose on the firm the legal obligation to pay a dividend. They do, however, impose the obligation to meet the preference dividend before any dividend may be paid to ordinary shareholders. Where preference shares are cumulative, arrears of unpaid preference dividends must also be made good before ordinary shareholders may participate in dividends. In practice, despite the lack of legal obligation, firms seem reluctant to miss paying a preference dividend.

Obligation to redeem preference shares

Some preference shares are expressly issued as redeemable and where this is the case the firm must be mindful of the necessity to finance this redemption. By no means are all preference shares redeemable and where they are not, the position is similar to that of ordinary shares. Where preference shareholders cannot demand redemption this type of financing is a relatively safe one from the ordinary shareholders' viewpoint.

Tax deductibility of preference share dividends

The UK tax system does not distinguish between ordinary and preference dividends so they, like ordinary share dividends, are not deductible from the firm's profit for Corporation Tax purposes (see the Appendix to this chapter).

Effect on control and on freedom of action

Normally preference shares do not impose much by way of restriction on the ordinary shareholders. Many firms' preference shares give the holders the right to vote only where their dividends are in arrears. Generally preference shareholders have no voting rights.

Factors for the potential investor to consider on preference shareholding

Level of return

This tends to be low, significantly below that of equities of the same firm. It all tends to be in the form of dividends since preference shares do not normally experience significant changes in values.

Riskiness of returns

Typically this risk lies between that attaching to ordinary shares and to loan stocks. This is mainly because preference dividends have priority over ordinary ones.

Ease of liquidating the investment

Where preference shares are redeemable and/or traded in the capital market, liquidation is possible. Failure for at least one of these to be the case will usually make investors reluctant to take up preference share issues.

Preference shares and personal tax
Dividends are taxed as income.

Degree of control
Unless dividends are in arrears preference shareholders typically have no voting rights and hence no real power.

Methods of raising preference share capital

These are more or less identical to the options available with ordinary shares, including bonus issues to ordinary shareholders created from retained profits. In practice, rights issues seem to be the most popular methods of issuing preference shares.

LOAN STOCKS AND DEBENTURES

Many firms borrow by issuing securities with a fixed interest rate and a pre-stated redemption date. They are typically issued for periods within the range of 10 to 25 years, though some are issued for periods outside that range. Indeed, perpetual loan stocks (no redemption date) do exist.

The popularity of loan stocks to firms as a means of raising long-term finance seems to fluctuate rather wildly from year to year. In 1989, 61 per cent of the value of all securities issued by UK firms (net of redemptions) were loan stocks of some description or another, yet as recently as 1987, net of redemptions, the figure was zero (see Table 8.3).

Most loan stocks are secured either on specified assets of the borrowing firm, or on the assets generally. Alternatively, the loan stock holder may simply have the security which the law of contract gives any unsecured creditor to enforce payment of interest or capital if the firm defaults. Whether a loan stock is secured or not determines where in the queue for payment the loan stock holder will stand in the event of the liquidation of the borrowing firm.

Since it is not usually practical for individual loan stock holders to monitor their security at all times, trustees are often appointed by the firm to do this for them. Firms will be prepared to do this so that the issue will attract lenders.

Many firms seek and obtain a capital market quotation for their loan stocks so that potential lenders can *buy* a firm's borrowings from a previous lender. The new owner of the loan stock will, from the date of acquiring it, receive interest payments as well as the capital repayment if the stock is held until the redemption date.

Loan stocks attract all types of investors who seek relatively low-risk returns. Institutional investors are particularly attracted by them, especially those institutions which need regular cash receipts to meet recurring payment obligations, e.g. pension funds.

Investment ratios

Since profitability *per se* is of no direct interest to loan stock holders, ratios dealing with the effective rate of interest (yield) are likely to be of more concern to them.

Two ratios which tend to be widely reported (in newspapers, etc.) are:

(a) *Flat yield.* This is simply the gross interest receivable expressed as a percentage of the current market value of the relevant amount of loan.

(b) *Redemption yield.* Where, as is usually the case, the loan stock is redeemable, the effective return from owning it may include some capital gain or even loss. (A capital loss would arise where the current market price is above the redemption value. This would tend to occur where prevailing rates of interest are below the *coupon* rate for the loan stock.)

The redemption yield (r) would be given by the following expression:

$$\text{Current market value} = \sum_{t=1}^{n} I/(1+r)^t + \text{RV}/(1+r)^n$$

where I is the annual gross interest payment, RV is the redemption value and n is the remaining life (in years) of loan stock.

Methods of issuing loan stocks

Loan stocks can be issued in several ways, including direct issues to the public by newspaper advertisement, etc. Quite often firms wishing to issue loan stocks will approach a stockbroking firm and ask it to try to place part of the issue with its clients, often institutional ones.

Factors for the firm to consider on loan stock financing

Issue costs
These tend to be relatively low; they have been estimated at about 2½ per cent of the value of the cash raised on a £2m issue (Wilson Committee, 1980).

Servicing costs
Since loan stock represents a relatively low-risk investment to investors, expected returns tend to be low compared with those typically sought by equity holders. Historically this has been reflected in actual returns.

Obligation to pay interest
Loan stock holders have the basic right under the law of contract to take action to enforce payment of interest and repayment of capital on the due dates, should they not be forthcoming. Fairly typically, loan stock holders have the contractual right to take some more direct action (e.g. effective seizure of an asset on which their loan is secured), should the borrowing firm default on payments.

This clear obligation to pay interest, with potentially dire results for defaulting, can make servicing the loan stock finance a considerable millstone around the neck of the borrowing firm.

Obligation to redeem loan stocks
Irrespective of whether loan stocks are issued as redeemable or not, it is always open to the firm to buy its own loan stock, in the open market, and to cancel what it buys.

Thus loan stocks offer a level of flexibility not so readily available with ordinary and preference shares. On the other hand, if loan stocks are issued as redeemable with a stated redemption date, which will usually be the case, the firm is under a contractual obligation to redeem. This could put the firm into a difficult cash flow position as the due date for redemption approaches.

Tax deductibility of loan stock interest

Interest is fully deductible from the firm's profit for Corporation Tax purposes. This has tended in the past to make loan interest payments cheaper, £ for £, than ordinary and preference share dividends. This is now considerably less the case in the light of the recent downward movement of UK Corporation Tax rates.

Effect on control and on freedom of action

The severity of the consequences of failing to meet interest payments and capital repayments can considerably limit the freedom of action of the firm. Whilst control in the sense of voting rights is not usually involved with loan stock financing, control in the sense of being able to manage affairs without impediment may well be seriously eroded by the issuing of loan stocks.

It is common for those who lend money to a firm to impose conditions or covenants on the firm. Failure to meet these covenants could, depending on the precise contract between the lenders and the firm, give the lenders the right to immediate repayment of the loan. Typical covenants include:

- a restriction on dividend levels
- maintenance of a minimum current asset/current liability ratio
- a restriction on the right of the firm to dispose of its fixed assets.

We shall go more fully into the effect on the position of the ordinary shareholders as borrowings increase in Chapter 11.

Factors for the potential investor to consider on loan stocks

Level of returns

These tend to be relatively low, compared with those expected from equities and preference shares.

Riskiness of returns

Though the level of risk attaching to the physical receipts from the borrowing firm tends to be low, the loan stock holder is usually exposed to another risk, namely *interest rate risk*. This is the risk of capital losses caused by changes in the general level of interest rates.

EXAMPLE

An investor has £100 nominal value of perpetual (irredeemable) loan stock which has a coupon rate (the rate which the borrowing firm is contracted to pay on the nominal value of the stock) of 10 per cent. The prevailing interest rates and the level of risk attaching to the particular loan stock cause the capital market to seek a 10 per cent return from it. Since the loan stock's return on its nominal value is 10 per cent, the capital market would value the holding at £100 (i.e. the nominal value).

If the general level of interest rates were to increase so that the capital market now sought a 12½ per cent return from this loan stock, its value would fall to £80 (i.e. the amount on which the 10 per cent interest on £100 represents a 12½ per cent return). Thus our loan stock holder would be poorer by £20.

If the loan stock were not perpetual but redeemable at £100 at some date in the future, the price would probably not drop as low as £80 on the interest rate change. The closer the redemption date, the smaller the fall, but irrespective of the redemption position some loss of value would occur. Clearly the investor would gain similarly from a general fall in prevailing interest rates but a risk-averse investor (and most investors seem to be risk-averse) would be more concerned with the potential loss than with the potential gain.

The relatively lower interest rate risk associated with *short-dated* loan stocks tends to mean that lower returns are available from them, compared with those from stocks not due for redemption for some time.

Ease of liquidating the investment
Firms that wish to make public issues of loan stocks must seek a capital market quotation for them if they are to have any serious hopes of success. Thus publicly issued loan stocks can be liquidated by sale in the market.

Loan stocks and personal tax
Interest is subject to Income Tax in the hands of individual loan stock holders. Since all or almost all of the returns from loan stocks are in the form of interest, returns tend to be taxed at potentially quite high rates.

Degree of control
Loan stocks do not give their holders any control over the firm, except that which is necessary to enforce payment of their dues in the event of the firm defaulting.

Eurobonds

These are unsecured loan stocks denominated in a currency other than the home currency of the firm which made the issue. They are foreign currency loans. Firms are prompted to make Eurobond issues to exploit the availability of loan finance in an overseas country. Also Eurobonds can offer innovative features making them more attractive, both to the lenders and to the issuing firm. This latter point arises from the fact that the bonds are traded in an unregulated market.

Interest rate swaps

A firm may have borrowed money where the contract specified a floating interest rate, i.e. an interest rate which varies with the general level of interest rates in the economy. The firm may prefer to have a loan with a fixed rate, but was unable to negotiate such an arrangement.

Under these circumstances, it may be possible for the firm to find another firm with exactly the opposite problem, i.e. a fixed rate loan but a preference for a floating rate loan. Having identified one another, each of the firms might agree to service the loan of the other one. In practice the firms would probably make contact first and then issue the loan stock or undertake the borrowing in some other form.

Interest rate swaps have practical relevance because different firms have differing credit ratings. One may be able to negotiate a floating rate loan at a reasonable rate, but not a fixed rate one. The other firm may find itself in the opposite position.

CONVERTIBLE LOAN STOCKS

These are securities which bear all of the features of loan stocks, which we have just discussed, except that at a pre-stated date they may be converted by the holders into ordinary shares of the same firm. The conversion rate is usually expressed as so many ordinary shares in exchange for £100 nominal value of loan stock. If there are any splits or bonus issues of ordinary shares during the life of the loan stock, the conversion rights are usually adjusted to take account of them.

Convertible issues have wavered somewhat in their popularity recently. They accounted for as much as 28½ per cent of total long-term securities issued in 1990, yet they have been insignificant in other years (see Table 8.3).

Since convertibles are a hybrid of loan stocks and equities, the factors important both to the issuing firm and to potential investors will basically be those which we have already considered. However, a couple of features of convertibles are worth mentioning.

Issue costs
The fact that loan stocks are cheaper to issue than are equities means that convertibles may be a cheap way to issue ordinary shares, particularly where the firm is keen to have some loan finance in any case.

Loans are self-liquidating
There is no need for the firm to find cash to redeem the loan stock since it is redeemed with ordinary shares. This does not, of course, make it free. Issuing shares to redeem loan stock represents an opportunity cost to the firm.

TERM LOANS

Term loans are negotiated between the borrowing firm and some financial institution including clearing banks, insurance companies and merchant banks. This sort of finance is extremely important, perhaps accounting for as much as 25 per cent of new finance raised by firms other than through retained profits.

In many ways term loans are like loan stocks in that security is usually given to the lender and loans are made for up to 20 years. They differ from loan stocks in that they are not usually transferred from lender to lender in the way that loan stocks typically are. They are not traded in the capital market. Some term loans are repayable in instalments so that each monthly or annual payment consists of part interest, part capital repayment, in a similar manner to mortgage loan payments made by private house purchasers.

Term loans tend to be very cheap to negotiate, i.e. *issue costs* are very low since the borrowing firm deals with only one lender (at least in respect of each loan) and there is room for very much more flexibility in the conditions of the loan than is usually possible with an issue of loan stock.

Clearly, term loans so closely resemble loan stocks that, with the exception of the points concerning transferability and the possible spreading of capital repayment, the factors concerning both borrower and lender are much the same as those which we reviewed in respect of loan stocks.

LEASING

It may seem strange to see leasing appearing in a chapter dealing with sources of long-term finance, but in fact it is very close to being secured lending, which certainly justifies its place here.

Leases may be divided into two types:

(a) *Operating leases.* It is often possible to hire an asset, say an item of plant, which is perhaps required only occasionally, rather than purchasing it. Usually the owner carries out any maintenance necessary. The decision whether to buy the asset or to lease it will perhaps be affected by financing considerations. Basically, though, it is an operating decision which would be made according to which approach would be cheaper.

(b) *Financial leases.* Here the potential user identifies an asset in which it wishes to invest, negotiates price, delivery, etc., and then seeks a supplier of finance to buy it. Having arranged for the asset to be purchased the user leases it from the purchaser. Naturally the lease payments will need to be sufficient to justify the owner's expenditure, both in terms of capital repayment and of interest.

It is financial leases which concern us here since they are effectively term loans with capital repayable by instalments. This is an important source of finance which has been estimated as providing as much as 20 per cent of the total finance for new capital expenditure by firms over recent years (Drury & Braund, 1990).

In the past, financial leasing has been believed to be popular with users partly because, whilst it is tantamount to borrowing, neither the asset nor the obligation to the owner appeared on the balance sheet of the user firm. Such a source of *off balance sheet* finance could be overlooked by those trying to assess the financial position of the firm. However, a combination of changes in the law and in accounting practice has now put leasing *on the balance sheet*. Firms are now required to show both the leased assets and the capital value of the obligation to the owner on the face of the balance sheet.

Another feature of financial leasing, which was apparently a major reason for the growth in its popularity during the late 1970s and early 1980s in the UK, was its considerable *tax efficiency* in some circumstances. Lease payments are fully deductible for Corporation Tax purposes by the borrowing firm. This includes the capital portion of the payment.

Until 1984, the capital cost of items of plant attracted 100 per cent first-year capital allowance in their year of acquisition. As far as the borrowing firm was concerned, leasing rather than buying a fixed asset would deny it the opportunity to claim the first-year allowance. On the other hand, leasing would still enable the firm to claim 100 per cent of the cost of the asset, but over its life, rather than in the first year. In many cases, however, even where firms were to buy the asset, raising finance, say from a term loan, profits were insufficient for the full benefit to be gained from the large first-year allowance. This was particularly true where recession restricted profitability.

With leasing, the right to claim capital allowance passed to the 'lender'. If the profits were such as to put the 'lender' in a position to take full advantage of them, some of this advantage could be passed on to the 'borrower' in lower lease payments. Thus the 'borrower' could give up some of the advantage of the first-year allowance in exchange for a lower lease charge.

The advent in the mid-1980s of lower Corporation Tax rates and the abolition of the 100 per cent first-year allowance greatly reduced the benefit of financial leasing. This, taken together with the requirement for the 'borrower' firm to disclose in its annual accounts the extent of its indulgence in this source of finance seemed likely to reduce the level of use of financial leasing.

In fact, far from decreasing in popularity since the advent of the accounting and tax changes of the mid-1980s, financial leasing expanded massively in popularity in the late 1980s. The reasons for this fact are not obvious. Drury & Braund (1990) conducted a survey of UK firms of various sizes on the reasons why firms frequently prefer to acquire assets on financial leases, rather than buying them. There were two principal reasons given by firms for the popularity of leasing. The first was that the interest rate implied in leasing contracts was lower than the rate which the firms would have to pay to raise finance to buy the assets themselves. The other main reason given was that firms believed it still to be more tax-efficient to lease rather than to buy, despite the changes in the tax treatment of fixed assets.

Though in the case of some firms one or both of the principal reasons given in the survey could be valid, for the majority of firms this seems unlikely to be so. Drury & Braund discovered one factor which could cast some light on the subject. This was an alarmingly high incidence of mishandling of the analysis of the decision whether to lease financially, on the one hand, or to borrow and purchase, on the other. Even among larger, and presumably more financially sophisticated firms, about 30 per cent were taking an incorrect approach to the analysis such as to bias the results in favour of a decision to lease.

Though it would be unreasonable to conclude that the continued popularity of financial leasing is based on wholesale mishandling of the decision data, it remains far from clear as to why leasing is so popular.

To lease or not to lease – a financing decision

When a firm is considering the acquisition of an asset, it should estimate the cash flows which are expected to arise from its ownership. These should then be discounted at a rate which reflects the level of risk associated with those cash flows. If the NPV is positive the asset should be acquired, if negative it should not, at least from a financial viewpoint.

Whether the asset should be financed by a financial lease or by some other means is a completely separate decision. The first is an investment decision, the second a financing one.

Only by coincidence will the appropriate discount rate be equal to the rate inherent in the financial lease. This latter rate will tend to reflect the relative risk-free nature of lease financing from the lenders' point of view. To the user of the asset the level of risk is likely to be rather greater than that borne by the lender. It would therefore be illogical to discount the cash flows from the asset at the rate implicit in the financial lease.

We shall consider more fully the importance of separating the investment and the financing decision in Chapter 11.

Financial leasing is so similar in practical effect to secured borrowing that the factors which both *borrower* and *lender* need consider are pretty similar in respect of each of them.

GRANTS FROM PUBLIC FUNDS

In the UK there is a large number of different grants or sources of finance which are given at little or no direct cost to firms. The bulk of such finance emanates either from UK Government sources or from the European Union.

Each of the grants available is only available to encourage firms to act in a particular way. Examples of such action include:

- investment in new plant
- development of the microelectronics industry
- training and retraining staff
- energy conservation
- research and development

Many of the grants available apply only or particularly to businesses located in specified parts of the UK.

Since there are so many different schemes and since they tend to alter quite frequently, it is probably not worth our looking at any individual ones here. It must be emphasised, however, that the amounts which individual firms may claim can be highly significant and that every effort should be made by financial managers to familiarise themselves with the grants available and how to claim them. The Department of Trade and Industry is able and willing to provide information on most sources of grant finance. Local authorities, particularly County Councils, tend to produce guides to grants available in their own neighbourhood.

CONCLUSIONS ON LONG-TERM FINANCE

The apparent existence of an efficient capital market, coupled with the evidence on the relationship between risk and expected return, suggest that firms are unlikely to be advantaged significantly by selecting one type of finance rather than another.

Increases in equity financing, which does not expose existing ordinary shareholders to increased risk, tend to be expensive. Secured loan finance which does expose them to increased risk tends to be cheap. This suggests that there is no advantage or disadvantage to existing ordinary shareholders in raising further finance in one way rather than another. One method may increase expected returns of existing ordinary shareholders but it is also likely to increase their risk commensurately.

However, the situation in real life is probably not quite as suggested by Fig. 8.1 (page 199). There are anomalies in the primary capital market which can mean that using one form of financing rather than another can be to the advantage of equity holders. For example, loan finance attracts tax relief in a way that equity finance does not. Convertibles are probably a cheaper way of issuing ordinary shares than is a direct offer of equities to the public.

These points and those which will be discussed in the context of the gearing and dividend debates later in the book perhaps explain why we find that firms seem to devote much effort to deciding on the most appropriate means of raising long-term finance.

Perhaps we could generally conclude that firms should assess all possible methods of raising long-term finance. They should look for anomalies like the ones mentioned above and then seek to exploit them as far as is practical, given the particular circumstances of the firm.

SUMMARY   Firms obtain long-term finance from various sources, most of which are either in some form of equities or loans. All firms must have some equity finance but when considering increasing their long-term financing base they must assess the merits of the options open to them.

Equity finance has the advantage of not putting a financial millstone around the necks of existing equity holders but it tends to be expensive in terms of returns expected by investors. The cheapest method of raising equity finance (in terms of the issue costs) is by retaining profits; rights issues are relatively cheap, with issues to the public relatively costly.

Loan finance in the form of marketable (transferable) loan stocks tends to be relatively cheap to issue and can give a degree of flexibility. The existence of loan finance does however increase the risks attached to the returns to equity holders.

Term loans from financial institutions are a popular and relatively flexible financing method.

Convertible loan stocks, i.e. loan stocks which are exchanged for equities at some time after their original issue, can give a type of investment which could attract interest from potential investors.

Financial leases are in effect another type of loan finance. They used to be able to, and to some extent still can, exploit the tax system by transferring reliefs available to, but not usable by, one firm to another firm which can use them.

Grants from public funds can be an important source of finance to eligible firms. Financial managers should seek to exploit this source of free finance to the greatest extent possible.

Broadly (with the exception of grants), there is the usual risk/return trade-off in the cost of finance. Financing methods which are cheap are those which increase risk. Theoretically there is nothing to be gained by raising *cheap* finance, not at least from the viewpoint of the ordinary shareholders. However, anomalies exist which cut across this theory so managers should seek to exploit these as far as seems practical.

FURTHER READING

Weston & Copeland (1988) and Samuels, Wilkes & Brayshaw (1990) give full treatment, from both a theoretical and practical perspective, of corporate financing. Rutterford & Carter (1993) is a comprehensive collection of articles on various types of corporate finance sources. Drury & Braund (1990) give an account of their survey of financial leasing and a general discussion of the subject.

WORK-BASED ASSIGNMENT

(a) What are the sources of long-term finance used by your organisation?
(b) Does your organisation use financial leasing?
(c) If so, why does it?

QUESTIONS WITH ANSWERS (see Appendix 3)

1 Jackson plc is a medium-sized engineering company. It has decided to acquire a new plant costing £150 000. Previously it has always purchased plant. It has recently been approached by the officer of a leasing company with the following proposal. Lease payments of £35 000 per year would be required starting at the date of acquisition of the equipment and for the following four years. After that date the lease may be extended at the reduced rate of £200 per year.

Jackson has substantial tax losses. Profits from the project which has a life of 10 years are expected to be £40 000 per annum. The company's weighted average cost of capital is estimated at 16 per cent after tax. The marginal cost of debt is 12 per cent before tax.

Any residual value of the plant may be ignored.

Required:

Advise Jackson plc whether it should finance the acquisition of the plant by the lease proposal or by a bank loan costing 12 per cent.

(Certified Diploma)

2 On 5 April 19X4 Forward plc's shares were listed on the stock exchange at 100p. There were 25 million 25p shares in issue.

On 6 April 19X4 Forward announced to the press that it had unexpectedly discovered a new deposit of minerals.

The deposit was estimated to have a net present value of £8 million.

On 3 May 19X4 the company announced that it was intending to raise £4 million to finance development of the deposit by means of a rights issue which was to be priced at 80p. There were no other events which influenced Forward's share price during the period covered.

Required:

(a) Calculate the market capitalisation of the company after the announcement of the mineral deposit.
(b) How many shares will be issued to raise the £4 million?
(c) Calculate the market capitalisation of the company after the rights issue.
(d) At what price are the rights likely to be traded?
(e) Why do companies issue rights at a discount? Does this represent a 'give away' by the existing shareholders?
(f) Why do listed companies normally make rights issues for new equity capital rather than public issues?

(Certified Diploma)

QUESTIONS FOR CLASS USE

1 Shaw Holdings plc has 20 million ordinary shares of 50p in issue. These shares are currently valued on the stock exchange at £1.60 per share. The directors of Shaw Holdings believe the company requires additional long-term capital and have decided to make a one-for-four rights issue at £1.30 per share.

An investor with 2000 shares in Shaw Holdings has contacted you for investment advice. She is undecided whether to take up the rights issue, sell the rights, or allow the rights offer to lapse.

Required:

(a) Calculate the theoretical ex-rights price of an ordinary share.
(b) Calculate the value at which the rights are likely to be traded.
(c) Evaluate each of the options being considered by the owner of 2000 shares.
(d) Explain why rights issues are usually made at a discount.
(e) From the company's viewpoint, how critical is the pricing of a rights issue likely to be?

(Certified Diploma)

2 Securities can be issued using the following methods:
 (i) Offer for sale.
 (ii) Rights issue.
 (iii) Tender issue.

Describe briefly each method and state where its use might be appropriate.

(Certified Diploma)

APPENDIX – THE TAX POSITION OF DIVIDEND AND INTEREST PAYMENTS

Dividends

When a dividend is paid by a company to its shareholders (ordinary or preference) it is treated from a tax viewpoint as being paid out of the after-tax profit of the company for the accounting year in which the dividend payment is made. Arising from the dividend payment the company must pay an instalment towards its eventual Corporation Tax liability for the year concerned. This *Advance Corporation Tax (ACT)* is calculated by reference to the amount of the dividend paid; in fact it is $^{20}/_{80}$ of the dividend paid. ACT must be accounted for and paid to the Inland Revenue on a quarterly basis with payment being made on the 14th of the month following the end of the quarter.

For example, if a company paid a dividend on its shares in August 1994 of £16 000, then the ACT would amount to £4000 (£16 000 × $^{20}/_{80}$), due to be paid on 14 September 1994.

To the shareholders, the dividend receipt represents an amount received under deduction of the lower rate of Income Tax. A dividend receipt of, say, £80 represents to the shareholder a gross amount of £100 to which attaches an Income Tax credit of £20. To the recipients whose marginal rate of Income Tax is 20 per cent or 25 per cent the liability is completely discharged by the credit. Shareholders whose marginal rate is 40 per cent will subsequently have to pay an additional amount; if their marginal rate is zero (for example where a recipient is a registered charity) the tax credit can be claimed from the Inland Revenue and a repayment made.

Loan interest

Unlike dividends, payments of interest to the company's loan creditors are deducted in arriving at the Corporation Tax liability. When the company pays interest it must deduct basic rate Income Tax (25 per cent) at source which it must account for on a quarterly basis. To the recipient of the interest there is a 25 per cent tax credit (25/75 of the amount actually received).

CHAPTER 9

The secondary capital market (the Stock Exchange) and its efficiency

OBJECTIVES

In this chapter we shall deal with the following:

- the role of the capital markets in their secondary function
- the mechanisms of the British Stock Exchange
- efficiency of the secondary capital market
- tests of efficiency
- the implications of capital market efficiency

INTRODUCTION

The capital market is a title given to the market where long-term finance is raised by firms and by local and national governments. Firms raise this type of finance through the issue of equity (shares) and debt (loan stocks) to members of the public and to investing institutions (unit trusts, insurance companies, etc.), usually in exchange for cash. It is also a market where holdings of equity or debt (securities) may be transferred from one investor to another. The new finance market is known as the *primary capital market* whilst the market in which second-hand securities are traded is referred to as the *secondary capital market*. We have already considered this primary role in Chapter 8. In this chapter we shall confine ourselves to consideration of the secondary aspect.

The most important secondary capital markets throughout the world tend to be the official stock exchanges or stockmarkets. They are not the whole of the secondary capital market however – certainly not in the UK as we shall see later in the chapter, nor indeed in the USA. Nonetheless, the world's official stock exchanges are the major forums for trading local, and increasingly international, securities. Most of these official stock exchanges fulfil a primary function as well as a secondary one.

The existence of a secondary capital market is vital to firms wishing to raise long-term finance. Potential long-term investors will not generally be prepared to take up issues of shares or loan stocks, unless the opportunity exists to liquidate their investment at any time. Since it is not practical for firms themselves constantly to hold cash in readiness to redeem the securities, it is necessary for there to be a secondary capital market where security holders may sell their investments. The absence of secondary market facilities tends to make the raising of long-term finance impossible or, at best, very expensive in terms of returns demanded by investors. It is thought by some observers that underdeveloped countries are often restrained in their industrial and commercial development by the lack of an established secondary capital market and therefore by the lack of long-term investment finance.

Potential investors will not only require the existence of the opportunity to liquidate their securities as and when they wish, they will also be interested in whether their investment is *efficiently* priced. Efficiency in the context of pricing implies that, at all times, all available information about a firm's prospects is fully and rationally reflected in that firm's security prices. That is to say, the market price of a particular security is the present (discounted) value of the future economic benefits which ownership of the security will bestow on its owner. This will interest investors as they would generally prefer that the price at any particular moment is set rationally and not a matter of sheer chance. Perhaps more important is the fact that, as the capital market is the interface between managers and investors, efficiency means that financial decisions made by managers will reflect in the firms' security prices and so have a direct effect on shareholders' wealth. As maximisation of shareholders' wealth is generally accepted as one of the criteria for management decisions, this reflection of management action is a significant matter, with several implications.

In this chapter we shall look briefly at the mechanisms of the International Stock Exchange (the Stock Exchange) in its secondary role before going on to consider whether or not it seems to be efficient. Lastly we shall consider the implications for investors and for financial managers of the efficiency (or otherwise) of the Stock Exchange.

THE INTERNATIONAL STOCK EXCHANGE (OF THE UK AND THE REPUBLIC OF IRELAND)

As with all capital markets in their secondary role, the Stock Exchange is basically a market place where securities of private firms and public bodies may be bought and sold.

Stock Exchange members

Whereas with many types of markets members of the public may directly buy and sell on their own behalf, with the Stock Exchange they are barred from entry. Only members of the Stock Exchange have direct access to buy and sell securities. When members of the public wish to buy or sell securities through the Stock Exchange they can only do so by using a member as an agent.

The rules governing the conduct of the members are laid down and enforced by a Council elected by the membership. One of the functions of the Council is to authorise specific securities as suitable to be dealt on the Stock Exchange. Authorised securities are those which satisfy a number of criteria established by the Council. The object of screening securities before authorising them is to try to avoid members of the investing public from losing money by buying very hazardous securities.

Stock Exchange members have two roles:

(a) As market maker or dealer equivalent in principle to a trader in a street market. Each dealing firm specialises in a particular group of securities in much the same

way as traders in street markets tend to specialise in fruit, or meat, or fish, etc.
(b) As agent of the public who wish to buy or sell through the Stock Exchange (a stockbroker).

Until fairly recently (1986) these two roles were rigidly separated, with the dealing role being carried out by stockjobbers and the agency role by stockbrokers. Neither was generally allowed, by the rules of the Stock Exchange, to act in the other role. Since 1986 Stock Exchange members have been allowed to act in both ways. Now members may, on the one hand, have clients on whose behalf they buy and sell and, on the other, act as dealers.

Dealing on the Stock Exchange

Dealers will usually be prepared to buy or sell irrespective of whether they are immediately able to *close the deal*. Thus dealers will normally be ready to sell securities which they do not at the time possess or to buy those for which they have no immediate customer. It is only with very rarely traded securities and with exceptionally large orders that dealers may not be prepared to deal either as a buyer or seller. Any unwillingness on a dealing firm's part to make a market in a particular security on a particular occasion may damage its reputation. This could have an adverse effect on the future trade of that dealer. There is therefore a sanction against dealers who fail properly to fulfil their function as market makers.

The dealer's flexibility is facilitated by the existence of the Account system. The year is divided into about 24 periods or Accounts of usually ten working days each. The dealer has until the end of each Account to match purchases with sales. Delivery of securities sold and cash in payment for securities bought by the dealer takes place on Account Day, usually ten days after the end of the Account concerned. At any given time a particular firm of dealers will typically hold a *trading* stock, either a positive or a negative one, of some of the securities in which it deals. Where the stock is a positive one it is said to hold a *bull position* in that security, and where securities have been sold which the dealer has yet to buy in it is said to hold a *bear position*. In fact arrangements do exist whereby it is possible for the firm of dealers, provided that it can get the buyer's agreement, to delay delivery of securities sold, from one Account to the next.

Dealers are risk-taking market makers. When dealers buy some securities they judge that they can subsequently sell them at a higher price. Similarly, when they sell securities which they do not possess (where they take a bear position), their judgement is that they can buy the securities which they have an obligation to deliver, at a lower price. If they are wrong in this judgement it could be an expensive mistake as they may have to offer a very high price to encourage a seller into the market. Member firms who act only as dealers make their living through profits from trading.

Until the mid-1980s virtually all Stock Exchange transactions were conducted on the floor of the Exchange. Here each dealer firm would have its own 'stall' to which stockbrokers could go to deal on their clients' behalf. To deal at the most advantageous prices it would be necessary for the stockbroker to call at the stalls of all, or at least a good sample of, dealers who dealt in the particular security concerned, in order to compare prices. Now the 'floor' of the Stock Exchange is, in effect, a computerised dealing system, though essentially the system remains the same as it used to be. The Stock Exchange Automated Quotations system (SEAQ) allows dealers to display their prices to interested parties and constantly to update those prices. It also enables members of the Stock Exchange to deal directly using the terminal linked to SEAQ, without leaving their offices.

When members of the investing public wish to buy or to sell a particular security, they would typically telephone their firm of stockbrokers, or possibly visit the firm's premises. The stockbroker can immediately display the prices at which all dealers are prepared to trade. These prices will normally vary from one dealer to another. This is because estimates of the value of the particular security concerned will vary from dealer to dealer. The 'stockholding' position of the particular dealer at that particular moment will also influence the prices on offer. A dealer with a bear position may well be prepared to pay a higher price to buy the particular securities than one with bull position. In respect of a particular security and a particular dealer, the SEAQ screen will display two prices. At the lower of these the dealer is prepared to buy and at the higher one to sell. The same information is available to all member firms and to others who wish to subscribe. The stockbroker can tell the client what is the best price in the security according to whether the client is a potential buyer or a potential seller. The client can then immediately instruct the stockbroker to execute the trade at this best price or to do nothing. If the client wishes to go ahead with the deal the stockbroker, using the SEAQ terminal, executes the transaction immediately and without any direct contact with the relevant dealer firm. The effective contact between the stockbroker and the dealer is through SEAQ. The system automatically informs the dealer concerned that the trade has taken place and provides a record of the details of the transaction. Though it is open to anyone to be provided with the SEAQ information, only members of the Stock Exchange can actually use that information directly to trade through SEAQ.

By Account Day the client must deliver to the stockbroker the sold securities or the cash in respect of securities bought. On Account Day cash and securities are transferred from broker to dealer, dealer to broker, and from dealer to dealer in respect of transactions during the previous Account. Shortly after this the client will receive from the broker cash for securities sold or the certificate for securities bought. Stockbroking firms charge their clients a commission, which is the brokers' source of income. These dealing costs tend to be significant, particularly on small transactions, though they typically become proportionately cheaper on larger ones.

Stockbrokers offer their clients a range of professional services related to investment, rarely viewing their role in the narrow sense of buying and selling agent. They are, of course, in a competitive position one with another for investors' business. Those giving the best service, in terms of advice and guidance, are likely to attract most dealing commissions.

It is open for the public as well as members to exploit the Account system. It is possible during an Account for investors to sell securities which they do not own and to buy shares which they do not want to keep, making the opposite transaction to close the position before the end of that Account. This can be a very hazardous way of dealing, particularly for the investor taking a bear position, since there is no theoretical limit to the amount that may have to be paid to buy the security to close the position.

Options

Not only can investors buy and sell securities, they may also, through the Stock Exchange, buy the right (but not the obligation) to buy or sell specified securities at predetermined prices before a stated date. Where, for example, an investor believes that Trafalgar House shares are due to rise, an option to buy a certain quantity at a specified price before a stated date can be bought. This would be known as a 'call' option and the price of such an option would depend on the quantity, the call price and the exercise date. If, by the exercise date, the market price of Trafalgar House is above the call price, the investor would take up the option to buy the shares. An option giving the right to sell is known as a 'put' option. In certain securities the option itself may even be bought and sold (traded options).

The place of the Stock Exchange in the UK secondary market

There is no legal requirement in the UK that all secondary market activities must be carried out through the Stock Exchange. Whilst it has long been and still remains the case that the Stock Exchange dominates the UK secondary market in terms of business transacted, there are other markets, albeit limited ones.

There are for example commercial organisations which operate an *over the counter (OTC)* market, where the organisations act as a market maker in a range of securities. Securities are bought from and sold to the investing public, in much the same way as dealers in second-hand furniture do with their wares, without an agent being involved.

Whilst the Stock Exchange has been and still is regarded as pre-eminent in the UK secondary market, there is no special reason why it should continue to hold that position. There is some evidence – for example the recent emergence of the OTC market – which suggests that members of the investing public will readily look elsewhere if they feel that the Stock Exchange is not providing the service they need at a price they are prepared to pay.

CAPITAL MARKET EFFICIENCY

When security prices at all times rationally reflect all available, relevant information, the market in which they are traded is said to be *efficient*. This implies that any new information coming to light which bears on a particular firm will be incorporated into the market price of the security,

(a) quickly, and
(b) rationally, in terms of size and direction of security price movement.

To say that a secondary capital market is efficient is not necessarily to imply that the market is 'perfect' in the economists' sense, though to be efficient the market has to display most of the features of the perfect market to some degree. It is also important to note that efficiency does not mean perfect powers of prediction on the part of investors. All that it means is that the current price of a security is the best estimate of its economic value on the basis of the available evidence.

Why should capital markets be efficient?

Prices are set in capital markets by the forces of supply and demand. If the consensus view of those active in the market is that a security is underpriced, demand will force the price up.

In a secondary capital market such as the Stock Exchange, security prices are observed by large numbers of people, many of them skilled and experienced, nearly all of them moved to do so by that great motivator – financial gain. Information on the firm comes to these observers in a variety of ways. From the firm itself come accounting statements, press releases and leaks (deliberate or otherwise). Information on the industry and economy in which the firm operates will also be germane to assessment of the value of a particular security and this will emerge from a variety of sources.

Where observers spot what they consider to be an irrational price, they tend to seek to take advantage of it or to advise others to do so. For example, an investment analyst employed by a unit trust assesses the worth of a share in Marks and Spencer plc at £3.60 but notes that the current share price is £3.30. The analyst might then contact the investment manager to advise the purchase of some of these shares on the basis that they are currently underpriced and there are gains to be made. The increase in demand which some large-scale buying would engender would put up the price of the shares. Our analyst is just one of a large number of pundits constantly comparing the market price of Marks and Spencer shares with their own assessment of their worth. Most of these pundits will take action themselves or cause it to be taken by those whom they advise if they spot some disparity. The market price of the shares at all times represents the consensus view. If people feel strongly that this price is irrational they will take steps to gain from their beliefs; the greater they perceive the irrationality to be, the more dramatic the steps that they will take.

Efficiency and the consensus

Efficiency has been interpreted by some people as requiring that there is at least one person active in the market who has great knowledge, skill and judgement. This need not be the case. Beaver (1989) points out that all that is needed for efficiency is many observers with most having some rational perceptions even if their other perceptions about the security are misguided. He argues that the misguided perceptions will be random and probably not held by others. The rational perceptions, on the other hand, will be common perhaps not to all but nonetheless to a large number of observers. As the security price reflects a *weighted average* of the perceptions of all those active in the market for that particular security, the misconceptions, because they are random, will tend to cancel each other out and so have no overall effect on the price. The correct perceptions will not be random and so will not cancel each other and will therefore be reflected in the share price.

Beaver illustrates and supports this point with what is at first sight an irrelevant account of some predictions of results (win, lose or draw) of American football games. The *Chicago Daily News*, on each Friday over the period 1966 to 1968, reported the predictions of each of its 15 or 16 sports staff of the outcome of the games to be played over the forthcoming week-end. The newspaper also published the consensus view of the sports staff, i.e. the majority view on each game. When the success of the predictions was summarised for the three years the results were as shown in Table 9.1.

Table 9.1 Performance of forecasters of American football games

	1966	1967	1968
Number of forecasters (including the consensus)	15	15	16
Number of forecasts per forecaster	180	220	219
Rank of leading forecasters:			
J. Carmichael	1 (tie)	8	16
D. Nightingale	1 (tie)	11	5
A. Biondo	7	1	6
H. Duck	8	10	1
Rank of the consensus	1 (tie)	2	2

Source: Chicago Daily News

It is interesting to note that the consensus view outperforms all *individuals* over the three years and indeed outperforms all but one or two in any particular year (it tied with two individuals in 1966 and was beaten by one individual in 1967 and 1968). It is clear from the Table that the performance of the successful individuals is inconsistent, suggesting some element of luck in their successful year. Luck does not seem to be the only reason for the success as three of the four (J. Carmichael being the exception) performed better than average over the whole of the three years. Yet despite the apparent presence of skill in the individuals, over the three years the consensus easily beat them all.

It would appear that some forecasters are more skilled than others. It also seems that the consensus performs even better than the best individual. This is despite the fact that the consensus combines the forecasts of all the individuals, skilled and not so skilled. Far from having the effect of dragging down the quality of the forecasts of the best individuals, combining the forecasts, to find the consensus, actually improves the quality of forecasting. Beaver suggests that this is because idiosyncratic factors (e.g. personal loyalties to a particular football team, which might influence the forecasts of even the best forecaster) tend to cancel out when a reasonably large number of different individuals is involved in forming the consensus. Thus the consensus represents a rather more clear-sighted and objective forecast than any individual can provide, on a consistent basis.

Efficiency and speed of reaction

Efficiency requires not only that prices react rationally to new information, but that they react speedily. Certainly the rate at which data can be transmitted, received, analysed, the analysis transmitted, received and acted upon by buying or selling is very rapid, particularly in this era of cheap electronic data communication and processing.

Since there are large numbers of informed, highly motivated observers who are capable of quick action, we have good reason to believe that a sophisticated secondary capital market like the Stock Exchange could be efficient in its pricing of securities. The question now becomes, is it?

TESTS OF CAPITAL MARKET EFFICIENCY

Forms of efficiency

Attempts to assess efficiency have not so much addressed themselves to whether the capital markets are efficient or are not efficient but rather to what extent they are efficient. Fama (1965) suggested that efficiency and tests of it should be dealt with under three headings:

(a) *Weak form*. If the market is efficient to this level, any information which might be contained in past price movements is already reflected in the securities' prices.
(b) *Semi-strong form*. This form of efficiency implies that all relevant publicly available information is impounded in security prices.
(c) *Strong form*. If present this would mean that all relevant information, including that which is only available to those in privileged positions (e.g. managers) is fully reflected in security prices.

Approach taken by the tests

Propositions such as that relating to capital market efficiency are *not directly testable*. How can we test whether all available information is reflected in security prices? The researcher may not personally have all of the available information or even know that some of it exists. We can however test whether or not security price behaviour seems consistent with efficiency. All of the tests which have been carried out have tried to do this.

Most tests have sought to assess whether or not it seems possible to make *abnormal* returns by exploiting any possible inefficiency. Abnormal returns in this context means returns in excess of those which could be made over the same period in which the test was conducted, from securities of similar risk. Returns typically means capital gain plus dividend received over a period, expressed as a percentage of a security's price at the start of that period.

Tests of weak-form efficiency

It has long been popularly believed that security prices move in cycles which are predictable by those who study the matter closely enough. Many feel that past patterns of security price behaviour repeat themselves, so that spotting a repeat starting to occur can put the investor in a position to make abnormally large investment returns. Not surprisingly, adherents to this philosophy use graphs and charts of past security prices in order to facilitate recognition of the pattern early enough to benefit from it. These people are often referred to as *chartists*.

Others seek to develop trading rules which are perhaps easier to apply than those of the chartists. For example it is believed by some that the price of a particular security tends to hover around a particular value, rarely deviating from it by more than a small percentage. If the price starts to *break out* from the $\pm x\%$ band, they believe that this implies a large movement about to occur. This they feel can be taken advantage of by buying or selling according to the direction of the break-out. Such dealing rules are usually called *filter rules*. More generally the practitioners of techniques like filter rules and charts are known as *technical analysts*.

If the market is efficient this should mean that no gains could be made from technical analysis because there are so many observers at work that if any information were contained in past price movements it would be impounded in the current price as a result of buying and selling. Only new information would affect share prices. As new information is random, security prices would be expected to follow a random path or random walk. New information must be random or it would not be new information. That the sales of a Christmas card manufacturer were greater towards the end of some particular year than at other times during that year is not new information, because this pattern tends to occur each year and is predictable.

Let us suppose that the price of a particular security has followed the cyclical pattern shown in Fig. 9.1 over a number of years. There is obviously a regular pattern here. What should we do if we spotted this pattern at time t? Surely we should buy some of the securities and hold them until the next peak, sell them and rebuy at the following trough and so on until we became bored with making money! It seems too good to be true and of course it is. In real life we should not be the only ones to spot this repetition of peaks and troughs, in fact there would be a very large number of us who would notice it. As we try to sell at the peak, so would the others. Since few potential buyers would be interested at the peak price, the price would drop. Realising this, we should all try to sell earlier to try to beat the drop in price, which would simply cause it to occur still earlier. The logical conclusion of this is that the price would not in fact ever rise to the peak. Expecting the trough to be reached and eager not to miss it we should be buying earlier and earlier, thus keeping the price up and ensuring that the trough is never reached either.

The net result of all this is that if there are sufficient investors following past price patterns and seeking to exploit repetitions of them, those repetitions simply will not occur. In practice the more likely price profile of that security would approximate to the horizontal broken line in Fig. 9.1.

The first recorded discovery of randomness in a competitive market was by Bachelier when he observed it as a characteristic of commodity prices on the Paris Bourse as long ago as 1900. His discovery went somewhat unnoticed until interest in the topic was rekindled some years later.

Kendall (1953), accepting the popular view of the day that Stock Exchange security prices move in regular cycles, tried to identify the pattern, only to discover that there was none; prices seemed to move randomly.

Efficiency and randomness imply that there should be no systematic correlation between the price movement on one day and that on another. For example, it seems to be believed by some observers that if the price of a security rises today then it is more likely than not to rise again tomorrow, i.e. there are price trends. Similarly there are those who feel that the opposite is true and that a price rise today implies a fall tomorrow. These attitudes do not of course reflect any belief in efficiency.

**Figure 9.1
A graph of the daily share price against time, for a hypothetical security**

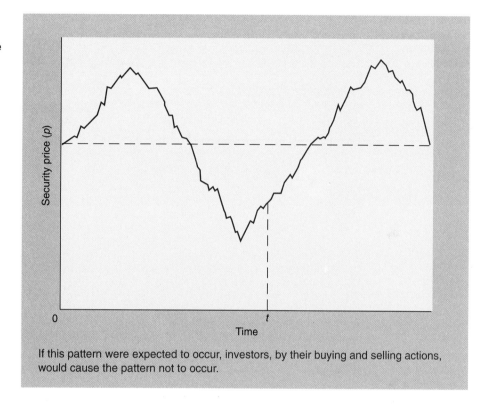

If this pattern were expected to occur, investors, by their buying and selling actions, would cause the pattern not to occur.

Figures 9.2, 9.3 and 9.4 depict the scatter of the price movement of one day (t) plotted against that of the following day ($t + 1$) for a particular security over a period. Figure 9.2 reflects a positive correlation, i.e. it suggests that an increase in the security price on one day will be followed by another increase on the following day. Figure 9.3 implies a negative correlation so that an increase in price on one day would mean a fall on the following day, and vice versa. Figure 9.4 shows what we should expect if the security were traded in a weak-form efficient market, i.e. there appears to be randomness between one day's price movement and that of the next. Sometimes an increase is followed by an increase, sometimes by a decrease, but with no patterns.

Many tests have sought to identify relationships between price movements on consecutive days, two or more days or weeks, and found no such relationships, either positive or negative, of significant size. This research shows that security price movements closely resemble the sort of pattern that would emerge from a random number generator. Probably the most highly regarded of these serial correlation tests was conducted by Fama (1965). Brealey (1970) and Cunningham (1973) conducted similar tests on security prices in the UK Stock Exchange and found evidence of weak-form efficiency.

Figure 9.2
A graph of a
security's price on
one day (day *t*)
against that of the
following day
(day *t* + 1) where
the two movements
are *positively*
correlated

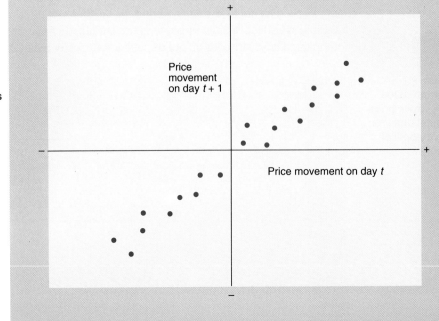

Figure 9.3
A graph of a
security's price on
one day (day *t*)
against that of the
following day
(day *t* + 1) where
the two movements
are *negatively*
correlated

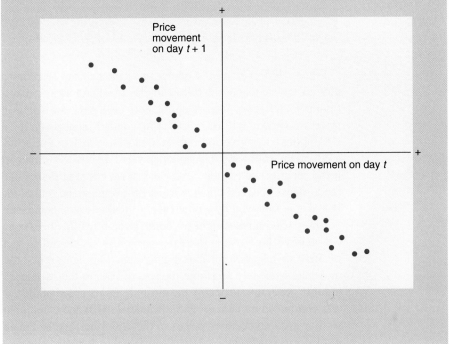

Figure 9.4
A graph of a security's price on one day (day *t*) against that of the following day (day *t* + 1) where the two movements are uncorrelated

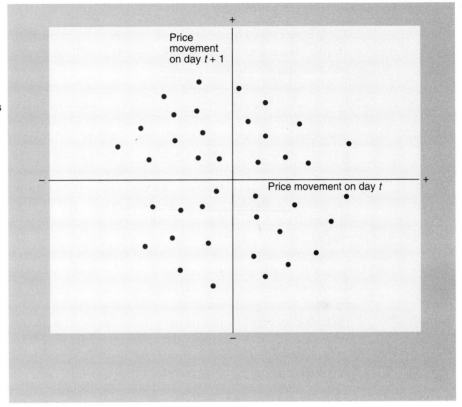

Most of the rules used by technical analysts have been tested. For example, Alexander (1961) used a filter rule and found that abnormal returns could be made but as soon as dealing charges are considered the gains disappear. Dryden (1970), using filter tests on UK security prices, came to similar conclusions.

The broad conclusion on weak-form tests is that the evidence on capital markets including the Stock Exchange is consistent with weak-form efficiency. Whilst there are minor inefficiencies, they are not of any economic significance since they cease to exist when dealing charges are considered. In a way this minor inefficiency is comforting to proponents of efficiency. The fact that the degree of inefficiency is not sufficient to yield gains to a potential exploiter implies that, were it significant, it would be exploited and eliminated.

It is particularly important to note that randomness does *not* mean that prices are set irrationally. On the contrary, since new information becomes available randomly, its reflection in security prices should also be random if the market is efficient. After a particular price movement it may well be possible to explain, by reference to real events, why the movement took place. Randomness should not be confused with arbitrariness here. Prices moving in trends and repeating past patterns would point to available information not being fully reflected in those prices, i.e. to inefficiency and arbitrary pricing.

Tests of semi-strong-form efficiency

These have centred on questions of whether new information, which could reasonably be expected to affect a security's price, actually does so, in the expected direction and with the expected rapidity.

Tests of this type pose several methodological problems. Such is the number of factors acting simultaneously on the price of a particular security, that it is difficult to know to what extent prices are affected by the specific factor in which the researcher is interested and to what extent other factors are involved. For our present purposes let us accept what is believed by most qualified observers, that the major researchers in this area, some of whose work we shall consider, have sufficiently well overcome the practical problems for their results to be regarded as providing significant insights. Readers who are interested in looking at the methodological problems in detail should take up some of the references given during and at the end of this chapter.

A fertile area for testing to see whether security prices react rationally to new information is where some action of management might superficially seem to indicate something which on closer examination is not the case. If security prices seem to reflect the superficial view of the action and not the rational one it would imply that the market was not efficient (in the semi-strong form) due to the naïvety of investors. In other words, it would imply the managers would be able to fool the investors by window-dressing activities.

One example of this is *capitalisation* or *bonus share issues*. This is little more than a bookkeeping entry which gives existing equity shareholders an increase in their holding of shares, without increasing each individual's slice of the ownership of the firm. For example, an investor owning 100 ordinary shares in a firm whose total shares issued is 1 000 000 owns one ten-thousandth of the equity value of that firm. If the firm makes a bonus issue of one for two, our shareholder now has 150 shares but as the total number of shares at issue will now be 1 500 000 this still represents one ten-thousandth of the equity. As the total value of the equity has not changed as a result of the bonus issue, logically share prices should adjust so that three shares after the issue are worth as much as two were before. Naïve investors might feel that this was a real gain and see the post-issue price of two-thirds of the pre-issue one as a genuine bargain. This would cause them to come into the market as buyers forcing the price up. Research conducted on the Stock Exchange and on Wall Street by Firth (1977a) and by Fama, Fisher, Jensen & Roll (1969) respectively found no such naïvety and that security prices reacted in the logical way.

Another example where the superficial interpretation of events could be a wrong one is where profits appear to improve as a result of a change in accounting procedures. Sunder (1973) looked at a number of US firms which had changed their method of stock-in-trade valuation so that they appeared to show higher profits than had the old method been adhered to. This would appear to be the perfect trap in which to catch the naïve investor, in that the economic consequences of the change would be adverse since the firms' tax charges (which are based on accounting profits) would increase. Rationally the change in accounting policy should cause a drop in equity share prices for those firms as the change would adversely affect the firms' cash flows (increased tax payments). Sunder found that reason appeared to have prevailed in that, for this group of firms, the change had an adverse effect on share prices. Sunder also took a group of firms which had altered their stock-in-trade valuation method in exactly the opposite way and found this had, as reason would demand, caused the opposite effect on share prices.

Using UK data Morris (1975) found that share prices had adjusted to take account of a reduction of earnings figures to adjust for inflation, even before the adjustment had been published.

Testing speed of reaction of security prices to new information presents great practical difficulties. It is hard to identify precisely when the new information becomes known and in some markets, including the Stock Exchange, difficult to know after the event precisely when the price movement occurred. On Wall Street records are available of all transactions and their timing, to the minute. Thus if a particular transaction is itself regarded as having possible informational content, researchers could know the timing of that transaction and the timing and price of subsequent transactions. Dann, Mayers & Raab (1977) conducted some research on the effect of trades of large blocks of shares of a particular firm, much larger than the number of shares traded in the typical stock market transaction. Amongst other things they noted that the *turbulence* caused by such trades, the period during which the market assessed the effect of the trade, lasted about 15 minutes at most. This is to say that an unexpected event, albeit an event occurring in the heart of the capital market (Wall Street in this particular case), had been assessed and was reflected in the new price within a quarter of an hour. Large block trades are felt to have possible informational content in that a purchase or a sale of a large quantity of the security might imply that the investor initiating the trade has some new information which has precipitated the action.

From the studies which we have reviewed here, the results of which are typical of the conclusions drawn from the research conducted on the world's secondary capital markets, the evidence seems consistent with the view that security prices adjust rationally and speedily to new information. Just as importantly, they seem to ignore bogus new information, i.e. data which appears to be relevant but which in fact is not. Thus the general conclusion is that the capital markets, including the Stock Exchange, are efficient in the semi-strong form.

Tests of strong-form efficiency

Strong-form efficiency would imply that there is no such thing as private information in the context of information relevant to the setting of security prices. As soon as information is available to any one person or group it is reflected in the price of the particular security or securities to which it relates.

Those who might have access to information which is not generally available include

(a) *insiders* who have privileged positions with regard to such information (this might include managers, staff, auditors and other professional advisers) and
(b) *expert and professional investors*.

Intuition suggests that managers who are privy to information not yet publicly available could turn this knowledge into investment returns that are abnormally high compared with those of investors not possessing the information. Similarly we might expect that investment fund managers would be more successful, given their experience and research resources, than if they were to select investments with a pin.

In the UK insider dealing is much frowned upon by public opinion, by law and by ethical standards of professional bodies. Thus, if insider dealing goes on, it is done furtively and is therefore not readily observable by researchers. In the USA a different attitude used to be taken (until the 1960s) to insider dealing, though insiders were required to register their status when dealing. Tests on the success of insiders dealing on Wall Street have been conducted. Both Jaffe (1974) and Finnerty (1976) found that insiders could consistently earn abnormal returns as a result of their greater access to information.

As regards professional investors, much research has been conducted into the performance of unit and investment trusts. These are organisations which attract funds from the investing public which are then invested predominantly in marketable securities. These studies, including one conducted by Firth (1977b) on UK unit trust performance during the period 1965 to 1975, have found no superior performance. Some researchers have found that the results of investment by these experts are in fact less good than would be the outcome of an investment strategy based on selecting securities at random.

The advice of professional investment advisers has also been assessed and found not generally to lead to consistently abnormal returns.

The conclusion on strong-form efficiency would seem to be that insiders who have genuine new information can use it to advantage, revealing an inefficiency of the capital markets. However, those not having access to such information are not, on a continuing basis, able to achieve better than average returns irrespective of whether they are 'experts' or not.

We have reviewed by no means all of the research which has been conducted; however, other studies have reached similar conclusions to those which we have considered.

CONCLUSIONS AND IMPLICATIONS OF CAPITAL MARKET EFFICIENCY

The conclusions of tests on the efficiency of the Stock Exchange and of capital markets generally is that the evidence is consistent with efficiency in all forms, except that only publicly available information seems to be reflected in security prices. Information not yet publicly available is not necessarily reflected. Results of research, emerging from the USA particularly, are showing some capital market inefficiencies. This may indicate that the application of more modern and sophisticated statistical techniques is revealing inefficiencies which were not previously apparent. However, for most practical purposes we can probably say that the Stock Exchange efficiently prices securities which are traded there.

Implications for investors

Capital market efficiency implies that investors should not seek either by regard to historical information on security price movements or by analysis of new economic information to obtain abnormally high returns from investment. Only where an investor has access to as-yet unreleased information can better-than-average returns be made – except by sheer chance. Even putting trust in investment analysts or investing through one of the investing institutions will not, on a regular basis, be advantageous and it may well be costly.

Why, if the above statement is true, do so many investors indulge in precisely the activities which appear to be futile? There are several possible explanations for this apparently irrational behaviour.

(a) *Ignorance of the evidence on efficiency.* Very few investors seem to be familiar with the evidence on capital market efficiency so, naturally enough, they do not take account of it. Few people or organisations have a vested interest in publicising the evidence and many have the opposite interest. Newspapers and journals which deal partly or mainly in giving advice on which specific securities to buy or sell do not have an interest in pointing out that this advice is only going to prove valuable by sheer chance so that on average it will be of no value. Other investment advisers, stockbrokers, etc., are similarly placed.

(b) *Close examination of charts of past security price movements shows patterns repeating themselves.* This is undoubtedly true in some cases, but it is equally true that plotting random numbers will also sometimes do exactly the same. In other words, chance alone will sometimes cause a pattern to repeat itself; this does not imply that gains can be made by trying to spot repeats.

(c) *Proponents of certain technical rules have been shown to be successful.* Efficiency does not imply that investment cannot be successful, simply that being more than averagely successful is a matter of good luck. During some particular periods and generally throughout the twentieth century, investment in securities dealt on the Stock Exchange will have given positive returns. The value of securities generally has increased, not to mention the dividends or interest receipts from which the investor will also have benefited. It should not therefore surprise us that, despite efficiency, following most investment advice over a substantial period yields positive returns. Indeed, efficiency implies that it would be impossible to find investment advice to follow which would yield lower-than-average returns in the long run, for the level of risk involved, except by sheer chance.

(d) *We all know of cases of people who have been extremely successful in capital market investment.* Those who are particularly successful tend not to hide their light under a bushel; those who are disastrously unsuccessful tend to keep quiet about it. In both cases it seems to be sheer luck – good and bad, respectively. Those who are unsuccessful tend to acknowledge this fact; the successful ones – being human – usually prefer to think that skill in selection and timing of investment was the cause.

Even in matters of sheer chance someone can still be successful, even staggeringly successful. Suppose that a coin-tossing championship of the UK were to be held and that all 60 million inhabitants entered. The rules are that we are all grouped into 30 million pairs; each of which tosses a coin. The member of each pair who calls correctly goes into the next round and the process is repeated until the winner emerges. We know that a winner must emerge, but would we really believe that skill was involved? We should more likely judge the winner to have had remarkably good fortune, in the face of a very small probability of success.

A notable paradox of capital market efficiency is that if large numbers of investors were not trying to earn abnormal returns by technical analysis and by the analysis of new information (fundamental analysis), efficiency would not exist. It is only because so many non-believers are actively seeking out inefficiencies to exploit to their own advantage that none exists which is, in practical terms, exploitable.

Implications for financial managers

These are vitally important and the main reason why we are discussing capital market efficiency at all in this book. Broadly the implications are:

(a) *It is difficult to 'pull the wool over the eyes' of investors*. Investors rationally interpret what the firm's management does and embroidering matters will not cause security prices to rise.

(b) *The market rationally values the firm*. If the management want to issue new equity shares, then the existing equity price is the appropriate issue price. If the general level of prices is low on a historical basis, it would be illogical for the firm to wait for a recovery before issuing new equity. If security prices follow a random walk, there is no reason to believe that just because prices have been higher in the past they will return to previous levels.

(c) *Management should act in a way which maximises shareholder wealth*. As this is the generally accepted criterion for making investment decisions within the firm, if managers make decisions which logically should promote it, then provided that they release information on what they have done, security prices will reflect the managers' actions. In other words, if managers act in a way which promotes the interests of shareholders, this will in fact promote their interests through the share price.

(d) *Managers may have an interest in withholding unfavourable information*. The strong-form inefficiency revealed by research shows that not all information which exists is impounded in security prices. Thus management might have a vested interest in withholding such information. Whether this would in fact be valid in the long run is doubtful since most information sees the light of day sooner or later. Probably a widespread feeling among investors that managers suppress unfavourable information would ultimately be detrimental to those managers.

(e) *The secondary capital markets rationally value assets which have risky returns*. In the same way that if we wish to value a second-hand car we might look at the price for similar cars in the second-hand car market, it is logical to try to assess the value of assets with particular risk and return expectations by looking at prices of similar assets in the secondary capital markets. This provides a major justification for the use of CAPM, in deriving an appropriate discount rate to apply to cash flows, in the assessment of real investment decisions made by firms.

The general position which efficiency engenders for management is that management and security holders are directly linked through security prices. Whilst this link may not be a rigid one where even relatively insignificant actions of management immediately reflect in security prices, nonetheless the evidence supports the view that security prices do react rapidly and rationally to new information. The implications of secondary capital market efficiency for managers will be referred to at various points throughout the remainder of this book.

SUMMARY

Capital markets have two functions: a primary finance raising one and a secondary security transfer function. The secondary function is vital to the interests of firms seeking to raise long-term finance as, without the facility to liquidate their investment, investors are reluctant to lay out funds. The Stock Exchange is, like most secondary markets round the world, closely regulated to promote fair treatment of all investors. Most capital markets, including the Stock Exchange, seem to be efficient in pricing the securities that are traded in them. Efficiency implies that prices at all times rationally reflect all available information which bears on the economic value of the security. Evidence suggests that the only manner in which capital markets show themselves to be inefficient is that they do not seem always fully to reflect information which is available only to insiders.

The implications of efficiency are important both to investors and to managers. Investors are wasting their time seeking out better-than-average investments; such investments are not recognisable until it is too late to benefit from their recognition. Managers should accept that the market at all times rationally values the firm and its securities. Efficiency also implies that managers' actions will be correctly interpreted by the market and reflected in security prices.

FURTHER READING

The role and operation of the Stock Exchange is covered by a number of texts including Samuels, Wilkes & Brayshaw (1990). Facts and figures on the Stock Exchange are published annually in *The Stock Exchange Fact Book*.

Capital market efficiency is well reviewed in the literature. Iveson, Moss & Simpson (1986) refer to a number of tests carried out on UK data. Copeland & Weston (1988) discuss much of the more important capital market research and the methodological problems which the researchers encountered. Comment on all of the research reviewed in this chapter and more besides is made in these last two texts. Keane (1983) gives a most interesting coverage of the topic, including discussion of the tests and, particularly, of the implications.

WORK-BASED ASSIGNMENT

(a) If your organisation is quoted on the Stock Exchange, try to find out whether the senior financial managers of your organisation accept the evidence on capital market efficiency.

(b) Does their position on capital market efficiency seem to affect their actions in any way?

QUESTIONS WITH ANSWERS (see Appendix 3)

1 'The shares of XYZ plc are underpriced at the moment.'
How logical is this statement about some Stock Exchange quoted securities?

2 Does capital market efficiency imply that all investors know all that there is to know about all securities traded in the market?

CHAPTER 10

Cost of capital estimations and the discount rate

OBJECTIVES

In this chapter we shall deal with the following:

- estimating the cost of individual sources of capital
- the difficulties of estimating the cost of equity finance
- target gearing ratios
- the weighted average cost of capital and its relevance as a discount rate
- WACC and CAPM derivation of cost of capital compared both in theory and practice

INTRODUCTION

In Chapter 8 we took a brief look at typical sources of long-term finance of UK firms. Now we shall see how it is possible to make estimates of the cost to the firm of each of these individual sources.

Since logically the discount rate to be applied to the expected cash flows of real investment opportunities within the firm should be the opportunity cost of finance to support the investment, this discount rate should be related to the costs of individual sources in some way. In fact, using an average cost of the various sources of finance, weighted according to the importance of each source to the particular firm, seems to be regarded as a standard means of determining discount rates. Evidence (Petty & Scott 1981; Corr, 1983) suggests that this weighted average cost of capital (WACC) approach is widely used in practice.

The approach to estimation of the cost of specific sources of capital which we shall consider in this chapter is based on the logic that the rate is implied by the current value of the financial asset concerned, and by future expectations of cash flows from that specific asset. This is probably the approach which is adopted in practice.

In Chapter 7 we saw that by making several assumptions it is possible to derive a logical device for deciding on the appropriate discount rate to apply to expected cash flows from investment possibilities to be able to assess each possibility's effect on the value of the firm (and therefore on the wealth of the shareholders). This device, the capital asset pricing model (CAPM), deduces the cost of capital from capital market information. CAPM deals explicitly with risk via a risk premium based on expected excess returns determined by covariance of specific security returns with those from the generality of risky investments.

The traditional WACC approach is also capital market based (we use current security values in the calculation), but it deals much less formally with risk than does CAPM.

After having considered the traditional approach we shall try to reconcile it with the CAPM approach, and attempt to reach some conclusion on the theoretical appropriateness of each and of their relative practicality.

COST OF INDIVIDUAL CAPITAL ELEMENTS

An economic asset (which loan stocks, equities, etc., are to their owners) has the current value

$$v_0 = \sum C_n /(1+r)^n \tag{1}$$

where C is the cash flow associated with the asset, r the rate of return, and n the time of each cash flow. To a loan creditor or shareholder, the future cash flows, at any given moment, will usually be the future interest or dividend receipts (payable annually, biannually, or perhaps quarterly) and perhaps a repayment of the principal at some future specified date.

Logically, a rate of return to the investors represents a cost to the firm in which they invested. Therefore we make the general statement that

$$p_0 = \sum C_n /(1+k)^n \tag{2}$$

where k is the cost of capital to the firm and p_0 is the security's current market price.

Loan stocks

With quoted loan stocks we should know the current market value of the loan stock, the contracted interest payments and dates, and the contracted amount and date of the repayment of the principal. Thus in the valuation expression above we should know all of the factors except k. Solving for k will give us the cost of capital figure which we require.

EXAMPLE

A loan stock which was originally issued at par is currently quoted in the capital market at £93 per £100 nominal value, repayment of the nominal value in full is due in exactly five years' time, and interest at 10 per cent on the nominal value is due for payment at the end of each of the next five years. What is the cost of the loan stock?

SOLUTION

The following statement holds true:

$$93 = \frac{10}{1+k_L} + \frac{10}{(1+k_L)^2} + \frac{10}{(1+k_L)^3} + \frac{10}{(1+k_L)^4} + \frac{110}{(1+k_L)^5}$$

Solving this equation for k_L will give us the required cost of capital figure. We have met this situation before in deducing the internal rate of return of an investment opportunity: k_L is of course the IRR of the loan stock and, as such, the solution is usually best discovered by a process of trial and error. The value of k_L is obviously above 10 per cent (if it were 10 per cent the current market value would be £100). Try 12 per cent:

	Cash flow	Discount factor	Present value
	£		£
Year 0	(93)	1.000	(93.0)
1	10	0.893	8.9
2	10	0.797	8.0
3	10	0.712	7.1
4	10	0.636	6.4
5	110	0.567	62.4
			(0.2)

Thus k_L is marginally under 12 per cent, which for our purposes and certainly for most practical purposes is near enough (the precise figure could be found by further trials). We can now say that the cost to the firm of this particular source of finance is 12 per cent.

Some readers may be puzzled as to why, when the original amount borrowed was £100, the amount to be repaid is equally £100 and the interest rate is 10 per cent, the cost of the loan stock is not 10 per cent.

We should remember that our purpose in calculating the cost of capital is to derive a discount rate to apply to investment projects. In previous chapters we have seen that the appropriate discount rate is the opportunity cost of capital. This means either the saving which would follow from repaying the capital source, or the cost of raising further finance from that source. At the present time this amount would be 12 per cent. If the firm wishes to cancel the loan stock, it can do so by buying the stock in the capital market at £93 (per £100 nominal). This would save the annual interest payments of 10 per cent on the nominal, and avoid the necessity to repay the capital after five years. If further finance is to be raised, presumably the same firm could raise £93 for a loan stock which pays £10 at the end of each of the next five years plus £100 at the end of the fifth year. So in either case 12 per cent is the appropriate rate.

We might also ask why investors were at one time prepared to pay £100 (for £100 nominal value) for a loan stock which yields £10 per annum in interest (a 10 per cent return) when they now obviously require 12 per cent. The 2 per cent difference must arise either from interest rates having increased generally and/or from the capital market having changed its perceptions of the risk of default (by the firm) in payment of interest or principal. Thus a firm's cost of capital is not necessarily static over time. Assuming capital market efficiency, the cost of any element of a firm's capital is the market's best estimate of that cost for the future.

Perpetual loan stocks are occasionally issued by firms. These are loan stocks which have no repayment date and which will, in theory at least, continue paying interest for ever. Their cost of capital calculation is similar to, though simpler than, the calculation at which we have just looked.

Where each of the C_n values is identical and n goes on to infinity,

$$p_{L0} = \sum_{n=1}^{\infty} \frac{C_n}{(1+k_L)^n}$$

can be rewritten as:

$$k_L = \frac{C_n}{p_{L0}}$$

Thus in the above example, if there were to be no repayment of principal but the annual £10 interest payments were to continue indefinitely, then

$$k_L = \frac{10}{93}$$

i.e.

$$k_L = 10.8\%$$

Tax relief and the cost of loan capital

Loan interest attracts Corporation Tax relief, so estimation of the true cost of loan stocks must consider it. Repayment of capital on the other hand is not tax deductible. The true cost of an interest payment is $i(1 - T)$ where T is the Corporation Tax rate (expressed as a decimal). When tax is brought into account, the expression for the current value of the loan stock becomes:

$$p_0 = \sum_{n=1}^{t} \frac{i_n(1-T)}{(1+k_L)^n} + \frac{C_n}{(1+k_L)^n}$$

where C_n is the amount of principal to be repaid after t years.

Since it is usual to identify the after-tax cash flows of investment projects, it is logical to discount them using an after-tax discount rate, so tax is usually taken into account in the cost of capital calculation.

Term loans

With term loans and in fact with unquoted loan stocks, there is no readily accessible figure for p_0 which can be put into the valuation model (equation (2), page 245) to deduce k. Logically p_0 should be the amount which the borrowing firm would need to pay immediately to induce the lender to cancel the loan contract. Alternatively it is the amount which could presently be borrowed by the firm given the future payments of interest and capital it is obliged to make under the terms of the loan in question. In theory these two should be alternative routes to the same value for p_0; in practice they may not be.

The real problem is that, equal or not, in practice p_0 is not readily observable, so some estimate of it needs to be made. In fact, unless the values of the loan are particularly large and/or there have been major changes in interest rates since the loan was negotiated, the contracted rate of interest would probably serve adequately as the present opportunity cost of the source. Alternatively an estimate, based on observation of current interest rates, could be made.

Financial leases

As we saw in Chapter 8, a financial lease is effectively a secured term loan with capital repayments at intervals during the period of the loan, rather than all at the end. Where it is not explicit in the lease contract, we can discover the interest rate fairly easily.

The value of the lease at the date of its being taken out is the cost of the asset which is the subject of the lease. Since this figure and the amount and timing of the future lease payments can be discovered, k can be discovered. To identify the present cost of a lease later in its life we should need to take a similar attitude to that which is necessary in respect of term loans and unquoted loan stocks. We could try to put some current value on the lease and solve for k in the valuation expression (equation (2) of page 245). We could however assume that the current opportunity cost of the lease finance is more or less the same as it was when the lease was first taken out.

Trying to value the lease at some date after it has been in operation for a while would be likely to be a fairly difficult task, so we are probably left with making the assumption that the interest rate implied by the original contract is still appropriate. Alternatively some estimate of rates applying to current new leases could be used.

Preference shares

The calculation of the cost of preference shares is almost identical to that for loan stocks. The major differences between the two financing methods are:

(a) loans stocks attract Corporation Tax relief, preference dividends do not; and
(b) loan interest is paid under a contractual obligation, preference dividends are paid at the discretion of the firm's directors.

The first point simply means that tax may be ignored in the calculation of the cost of preference shares. The second implies that rather more uncertainty is involved with predicting preference dividends than with predicting loan interest payments, though this creates no difference in principle.

Ordinary shares

These too are similar to loan stocks in the basic calculation of the cost of capital. Ordinary shares have a value basically because they are expected to yield dividends. How, if at all, the pattern of dividends affects the value of equities we shall discuss in Chapter 12.

To say that equities should be valued on the basis of future dividends is not to assume any particular investor intends to hold a particular share for ever, though the proceeds of any future disposal of the share will itself depend on expectations, at the date of disposal, of future dividends.

If a firm is expected to pay a constant dividend d per share, at the end of each year indefinitely, the value of each ordinary share will be:

$$p_{E0} = \sum_{n=1}^{\infty} \frac{d_n}{(1+k_E)^n}$$

to the investor who intends to hold the shares for ever.

Suppose that the investor intends to sell the share at time t; its value at that time will be

$$\sum_{n=t+1}^{\infty} \frac{d_n}{(1+k_E)^n}$$

This would mean that the value to our shareholder would be:

$$p_{E0} = \sum_{n=1}^{t} \frac{d_n}{(1+k_E)^n} + \left(\sum_{n=t+1}^{\infty} \frac{d_n}{(1+k_E)^n} \times \frac{1}{(1+k_E)^t} \right)$$

i.e. the value depends on the dividends to be received until time t (suitably discounted) plus the market value at time t (suitably discounted at $1/(1+k_E)^t$).

This expression reduces to

$$p_{E0} = \sum_{n=1}^{\infty} \frac{d}{(1+k_E)^n}$$

so irrespective of whether disposal at some future date is envisaged or not, provided valuation always depends on dividends, the current value will be unaffected.

Unlike loan interest, which is usually fixed by the contract between borrower and lender, and preference dividends, which firms usually endeavour to pay (and for which there is a defined ceiling), ordinary share dividends are highly uncertain as to amount. This poses a major problem in the calculation of the cost of equities. The prediction of future dividends is a daunting task. Two simplifying approaches may be taken however:

(a) assume that dividends will remain as at present;
(b) assume some constant rate of growth in them.

If the first of these is adopted, the model similar to that for a perpetual loan stock is used, i.e.

$$p_{E0} = \sum_{n=1}^{\infty} \frac{d_n}{(1+k_E)^n} \tag{3}$$

which when all dividends are equal means

$$k_E = \frac{d_n}{p_{E0}} \tag{4}$$

If we assume a constant rate of growth g, then

$$p_{E0} = \frac{d_1}{1+k_E} + \frac{d_1(1+g)}{(1+k_E)^2} + \frac{d_1(1+g)^2}{(1+k_E)^3} + \sum_{n=4}^{\infty} \frac{d_1(1+g)^{n-1}}{(1+k_E)^n} \tag{5}$$

which reduces to

$$p_{E0} = \frac{d_1}{k_E - g} \tag{6}$$

so

$$k_E = \frac{d_1}{p_{E0}} + g \tag{7}$$

where d_1 is the expected dividend per share, payable next year.

EXAMPLE

A firm's ordinary shares are currently trading at £2.00 each in the capital market. Next year's dividend is expected to be £0.14 per share and subsequent dividends are expected to grow at an annual rate of 5 per cent of the previous year's dividend. What is the cost of the ordinary shares to the firm?

SOLUTION

$$k_E = \frac{d_1}{p_{E0}} + g$$

$$= \frac{0.14}{2.00} + 0.05$$

$$= 12\%$$

The simplifying assumptions made with the constant dividend and constant growth of dividend models clearly are unrealistic. In practice dividends tend to increase from time to time, and to remain steady at the new level for a period before the next increase.

Retained profit

As was made clear in Chapter 8, retained profit is not a free source of finance. It has an opportunity cost to shareholders because, if such profits were to be distributed, shareholders could use them to make revenue-generating investments. It would be incorrect, however, to deal with retained profit separately in deducing its cost. When we derive the cost of equity, we are deriving the cost of the share capital *and* of the retained profit. For example, the current market price of a share (p_{E0}) used in the dividend valuation model (above) would reflect the fact, if it is a fact, that there are retained profits attaching to the particular share. Thus, provided that the cost of equity is properly derived, the fact that the equity is part share capital and part retained profit will automatically be taken into account.

Convertible loan stocks

These may be viewed as redeemable loan stocks on which interest will be paid until a date in the future when they will be *redeemed* by their conversion into equities. Estimating the cost of convertibles is therefore a basically similar operation to valuing loan stocks, except that the redemption amount is unknown, to the extent that we do not know what the equity share price will be at the conversion date. As with estimating the cost of equities, we can make some assumptions – for example, that the equity dividends (and therefore the equity price) will remain constant so that the current equity price may be assumed. Another possibility is the assumption that dividends will grow at a steady rate, and with them, the equity price.

EXAMPLE

A convertible loan stock of Tower plc currently trades in the capital market at £140 per £100 nominal. The stock pays annual interest of £11 per £100 nominal and may be converted in exactly five years' time at a rate of 50 ordinary shares in the firm per £100 nominal of loan stock. The present price of the ordinary shares is £2.20 which is expected to grow by 5 per cent per annum over the next five years. What is the cost of the convertible loan stock?

SOLUTION

The price of the convertible p_{C0} is given by:

$$p_{C0} = \sum_{n=1}^{t} \frac{i}{(1+k_C)^n} + \frac{P_{E0}(1+g)^t R_C}{(1+k_C)^t}$$

where i is the interest payment in each year until conversion in year t, P_{E0} is the current market price of an equity share, g is the growth rate of the equity price, R_C the conversion rate, and k_C the cost of the convertible. In this example we have:

$$£140 = \frac{£11}{1+k_c} + \frac{£11}{(1+k_c)^2} + \frac{£11}{(1+k_c)^3} + \frac{£11}{(1+k_c)^4}$$

$$+ \frac{£11}{(1+k_c)^5} + \frac{(1+0.05)^5 \times £2.20 \times 50}{(1+k_c)^5}$$

Solving for k_C (by trial and error) gives about 8 per cent as the cost of the convertible finance. Note that 8 per cent is an opportunity cost since:

(a) the firm should be able to issue some more convertibles with similar terms and expect to issue them at £140 per £100 nominal;

(b) if the firm were to buy back its own convertibles, for an investment of £140 it could gain £11 each year for five years and issue the shares for cash in five years instead of using them to 'redeem' the loan stock.

This would represent an annual return of 8 per cent to Tower plc.

THE COST OF CAPITAL TO THE FIRM

We have seen how the cost of individual elements can be estimated from current capital market prices and predictions of future cash flows associated with the element concerned. Most firms use at least two of the financing methods which we have considered and each is likely to have a different cost. For example, to the capital market investor loan stock tends to be a much less risky prospect than do equities in the same firm. Expectations of returns from equities are therefore higher. Given this disparity in the cost of the various elements, which discount rate should be applied to discounting estimated cash flows of prospective investment projects?

Target gearing ratios

It has been suggested by some observers (e.g. Modigliani & Miller, 1963) that firms may have some target ratio, based on capital market values, of the various financing elements. In other words a particular firm seeks to keep equity finance as a relatively fixed proportion (by market value) of the total finance. Similarly, it seeks to keep loan-type finance as more or less a fixed proportion. Minor variations may occur from time to time, but firms are believed to take steps to get back to target as soon as it is practicable to do so.

It is believed that such target ratios exist because firms, taking account of such factors as levels of interest rates, tax advantages of loan interest relative to dividends, and the stability of the firm's operating cash flows, decide on an optimal mix of financing methods which they then try to establish and maintain. Such targets are not established for all time; changes in interest rates, tax rules, etc., may cause a change to a new target which may then rule for several years.

Targets will also vary from firm to firm, partly because of differences of opinion from one set of management to another. Such differences may also partly, perhaps mainly, arise from differences in the nature of the trade in which the particular firm is engaged.

The objective of trying to establish and maintain an optimal balance between various sources of finance, indeed raising finance from other than equities at all, is presumably to try to minimise the cost of capital. Whether such attempts actually work is a matter to which we shall return in Chapter 11. Meanwhile let us go back to the question of the choice of the discount rate.

Weighted average cost of capital

Accepting the target ratio assumption for the time being, and bearing in mind the logic of the discount rate being the opportunity cost of capital, it seems reasonable to conclude that the appropriate discount rate is the average of the costs of the financing elements weighted according to the target. The easiest way to get this weighting is to assume that the present position is the target and to calculate a weighted average cost of capital (WACC) based on the current market values of the various elements.

Using opportunity cost implies looking at the savings in financing cost which would arise if finance were to be repaid instead of undertaking the investment project. Alternatively, it could be seen as the additional cost of raising the necessary finance to support the project. If there is a target, repayment of finance or additional financing would be carried out in accordance with the target. For example, suppose that a firm has a target debt/equity ratio of 50:50 (by market value). If the firm is to take on extra finance to support an investment project it will in principle do so in the same 50 : 50 proportion, otherwise it will disturb the existing position (presumably 50 : 50). Similarly, if the finance for the project is available but it could alternatively be repaid to suppliers, presumably 50 per cent would be used to cancel loan stocks and 50 per cent paid to ordinary shareholders, perhaps as a dividend. Thus, given the target rate assumption, the only logical opportunity cost of capital is WACC.

EXAMPLE

Calculation of WACC

Hazelwood plc is financed by:

(a) 1 million ordinary shares (nominal value £1 each) which are expected to yield a dividend of £0.10 per share in one year's time; dividends are expected to grow by 10 per cent of the previous year's dividend each year; the current market price of the share is £1.80 each; and

(b) £800 000 (nominal) loan stock which pays interest at the end of each year of 11 per cent (of nominal) for three years, after which the loan stock will be redeemed at nominal value; currently the loan stock is quoted in the capital market at £95 (per £100 nominal).

What is the firm's WACC? (ignore taxation)

SOLUTION

First we must find the cost of each of the individual elements.

(a) *Ordinary shares.* Here we can employ the standard dividend growth model (see equations (5)–(7), page 250)

$$\text{Cost of equity, } k_E = \frac{£0.10}{£1.80} + 10\%$$

$$= 15.6\%, \text{ say } 16\%$$

(b) *Loan stock.* We must use our IRR type trial and error here. We have the equivalent of an investment project where an investment of £95 now will bring in interest of £11 at the end of each of the next three years plus £100 at the end of the third year.

Clearly the discount rate which will give a zero NPV is above 11 per cent. Try 13 per cent:

	Cash flow £	Discount factor	Present value £
Year 0	(95)	1.000	(95.000)
1	11	0.885	9.735
2	11	0.783	8.613
3	111	0.693	76.923
			0.271

The appropriate discount rate lies above 13 per cent. Try 14 per cent:

	Cash flow £	Discount factor	Present value £
Year 0	(95)	1.000	(95.000)
1	11	0.877	9.647
2	11	0.769	8.459
3	111	0.675	74.925
			(1.969)

Clearly the appropriate rate lies very close to 13 per cent; a closer approximation may be obtained by linear interpolation. It is very doubtful whether there is any point in seeking more accuracy than the nearest whole percentage (13 per cent) since:

(a) the cost of the other element in the financing (ordinary shares) has been calculated making some fairly sweeping assumptions about future dividends; *and*
(b) the cash flows which will be discounted by the resulting WACC cannot be predicted with any great accuracy.

We may say then that the cost of the loan stock, $k_L = 13\%$.
Next we need to value the two elements:

(a) Ordinary shares. The total value of the ordinary shares,

$$V_E = 1 \text{ million} \times £1.80 = £1.80m$$

(b) Loan stock. The total value of the loan stock,

$$V_L = 800\,000 \times \frac{95}{100} = £0.76m$$

$$\text{WACC} = \left(k_E \times \frac{V_E}{V_E + V_L} \right) + \left(k_L \times \frac{V_L}{V_E + V_L} \right)$$

$$= \left(16 \times \frac{1.80}{1.80 + 0.76} \right) + \left(13 \times \frac{0.76}{1.80 + 0.76} \right)$$

$$= 11.25 + 3.86$$

$$= 15.11\% \text{ say } 15\%$$

Note that we used market values rather than the nominal values of the two elements as the weights. This simply reflects the fact that we are seeking the opportunity cost of capital. Market values reflect or indicate current opportunities, nominal values do not (not necessarily, at least).

Realities of raising (and repaying) finance and the discount rate

Even if, as we have assumed, firms establish and maintain a target gearing ratio, the practical realities of raising and repaying finance are that it is not always economic to raise (or repay) each £1 of additional (or reduction in) finance strictly in the target proportions. This is because, as we have already seen in Chapter 8, there are fairly large fixed costs associated with share and loan stock issues. In practice firms seem to raise fairly substantial sums from each issue in order to take advantage of the economies of scale regarding the issue costs. This would tend to have the effect that the target is a factor around which the actual ratio hovers.

In the last example, the current ratio of loan stock to total finance for Hazelwood plc is 29.7 per cent (i.e. 0.76/(1.80 + 0.76)). Equity currently accounts for 70.3 per cent of the total. This suggests a target ratio of about 70 : 30. If the firm wished to raise £100 000, say, in order to undertake a new investment project, it is most unlikely that it would raise £70 000 in ordinary shares and £30 000 in loan stock. It is much more likely that it would raise the whole £100 000 from one source or the other. This would move its gearing ratio away from the 70 : 30 (approximately) which currently exists. The firm would get back nearer its target by raising the following increment of finance from the other source. The pattern would probably be something like that which is depicted in Fig. 10.1. Here the broken line represents the target ratio with the points A to E representing consecutive actual financing configurations. The firm here starts by raising some initial equity capital (0A) followed by an issue of loan stock of amount AB. It presumably chooses not to raise amount Ab as sufficient economies of scale as regards loan stock issue cost would not be available on such a small issue.

The next issue is of equities (amount BC) and so on until the present position (E) is reached.

Specific cost or weighted average

The fact that a particular increment of finance is to be used in some particular project should not lead the firm to use the specific cost of that finance as the discount rate. Say, in the case of Hazelwood plc, that the £100 000 were actually to be raised from an issue of loan stock at a cost of 13 per cent. It would clearly be wrong to use 13 per cent as the discount rate in assessing the investment project any more than 16 per cent should be used were the finance to be raised by an ordinary share issue. To use 13 per cent would mean that a project which might be acceptable if the firm were moving from point C to point D in Fig. 10.1 might be rejected if it were moving from point D to point E, when a 16 per cent (cost of equity) rate would be used. This would clearly be illogical and could lead to some bizarre investment decisions. It would be much more logical to use WACC.

**Figure 10.1
A graph of the
capital structure of
a geared firm over
time**

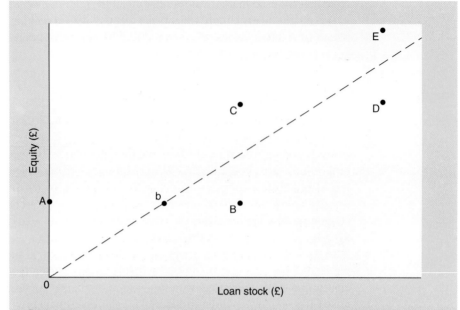

Since there are economies of scale in share and loan stock issue costs, firms tend not
to raise each tranche of new finance in the same proportion as the target gearing
ratio, but either totally from equities or totally from debt. This means that the actual
gearing ratio will tend to follow a path which wanders from one side of the target to
the other. Rarely will the actual and the target gearing ratios coincide. Points A,B,C, D
and E represent actual gearing at various times, whereas the dotted line represents
the target.

The target gearing ratio assumption

WACC weights the cost of each of the financing elements by its market value. When
WACC is used as the discount rate to apply to real investment projects, there is the
implicit assumption that the same weights will apply throughout the life of the
project. This in turn assumes that firms have a target gearing ratio.

Whilst it seems logical that firms will take a fairly consistent view of the advantages (if any) of capital gearing, we have little or no evidence that such targets actually
exist in practice. This is not to say that they do not exist, simply that there is no strong
evidence that they do. If in fact they do not exist, the logic of using WACC as the
discount rate must be called into question.

THE DISCOUNT RATE — CAPM VERSUS WACC

We have now seen two means of deducing an opportunity cost of capital which a
firm can use to discount the estimated cash flows of an investment project which it
is considering. The two means are:

1. CAPM, which uses as its inputs:
   (a) expected returns from the generality of risky investments;

(b) a risk-free interest rate; and

(c) a risk measurement factor based on expectations of the covariance of returns from the investment project with those from the generality of risky investments (β).

2. WACC, which uses as its inputs:

(a) expectations of future cash flows (dividends, interest and redemption values) from the various elements in the firm's capital structure; and

(b) the current market value of these various elements.

If we continue, as we did in the traditional approach to deriving the cost of capital, to assume that expectations of dividends is the only factor affecting equity prices, these two bases (CAPM and WACC) are not fundamentally in conflict. Both rely on expectations of returns to investors and on the capital market's reaction to those return expectations. Thus, used sensibly, both bases should give similar results.

Though WACC tends to be the title given to the more traditional means of deriving the discount rate, this is not to say that a CAPM derivation of it should fail to take account of the level of gearing. Since loan stocks typically have a much lower β than do the equities of the same firm, the CAPM derived cost of each of these will be different. Recognising the different level of cost is important, irrespective of how the individual costs are derived. We shall come back to the relationship of β and gearing in the next chapter.

In practice, when CAPM is used to discover the discount rate, it tends to be done without consideration as to how the firm is actually financed. In the next chapter we shall also consider whether or not this approach is justified, i.e. does the level of gearing affect the weighted average cost of capital?

WACC, since it does not deal with risk as explicitly as does CAPM, has the greater potential to be misused. Both intuition and modern portfolio theory tell us that risk and expected return are related. Since WACC is calculated on a firm-wide basis, as a discount rate it could only be valid if the particular project whose cash flows are to be discounted is in exactly the same risk class as the weighted (by value) average risk of the firm's existing projects.

In Fig. 10.2 the horizontal line represents the WACC for a particular firm. Logically the weighted average risk of the firm's existing projects must be β' as that is the risk level which, CAPM tells us, is consistent with the particular WACC. Only if projects under consideration are of exactly β' risk would WACC be the appropriate discount rate. If Project A (Fig. 10.2) were under consideration it should be accepted since it would have a positive NPV when discounted at r_A (the appropriate discount rate for its level of risk) even though if discounted at WACC its NPV would be negative. Similarly Project B, whose required rate of return is r_B, would have a positive NPV if discounted at WACC, yet a negative one if discounted at the more appropriate rate r_B. Thus use of WACC, irrespective of the risk attaching to the particular project under review, will cause some favourable projects (e.g. Project A in Fig. 10.2) to be rejected while others which would diminish the wealth of the shareholders (Project B) could be accepted.

In practice firms tend to specialise in similar projects with, presumably, similar risk, so that WACC might well be appropriate in most cases. Where a project under consideration is not of similar risk level to that of the existing projects, it might be possible to obtain the appropriate discount rate by looking at the WACC of firms whose activities (and therefore presumably risk) are all similar to the project under review. This is a similar approach to using the β of a firm whose activities are all of the same type as the project under review where the project is not typical of the existing projects of the investing firm, when deriving the discount rate via CAPM.

**Figure 10.2
A graph of the
expected return
against risk for a
firm**

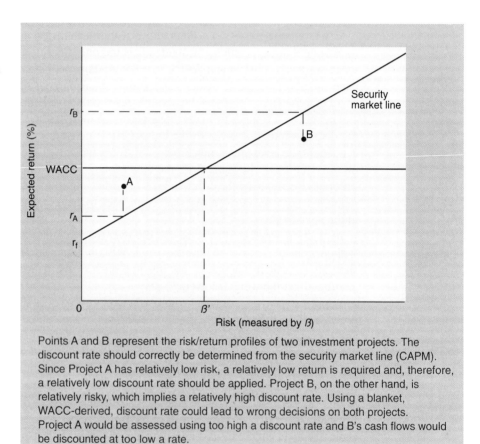

Points A and B represent the risk/return profiles of two investment projects. The discount rate should correctly be determined from the security market line (CAPM). Since Project A has relatively low risk, a relatively low return is required and, therefore, a relatively low discount rate should be applied. Project B, on the other hand, is relatively risky, which implies a relatively high discount rate. Using a blanket, WACC-derived, discount rate could lead to wrong decisions on both projects. Project A would be assessed using too high a discount rate and B's cash flows would be discounted at too low a rate.

The fundamental principle which must be remembered is that the value of a firm is the sum of the values of its various investments. Each of these investments will be valued according to its expected cash flows, their timing and the risk attaching to those cash flows. The same discount rate should be applied to a particular investment project irrespective of which firm is considering it. This is not to say that projects are equally valuable to all firms, as the cash flows may not be the same from firm to firm. This might be for a variety of reasons, not least of which would be different levels of efficiency in managing the particular project. Thus the 'same' project might be rejected by one firm but accepted by another.

Practicality of using WACC as compared with using CAPM

Traditionalists seem to regard CAPM as a rather fanciful approach to deducing discount rates, even though they may not disagree with CAPM in theory. The objection seems to lie in their recognition of the difficulty of estimating the parameters of CAPM (the risk-free rate, the expected market return and the β). The traditionalists are right to be sceptical of our ability reliably to estimate these (see Chapter 7). Where perhaps they are misguided is to believe that the estimates necessary to arrive at the WACC are any less susceptible to error than are those for CAPM.

Typically it would seem, WACC is estimated either from expectations of future cash flows from the various elements of long-term finance, or from recent history of what the costs of each element have been. If based on future expectations, WACC's estimation is not more reliable than is a discount rate derived from CAPM. If WACC to be used as a rate to discount future cash flows of a project is derived from evidence of the recent past, this too seems pretty dubious. Merely to extrapolate unquestioningly from the past to the future is not always a good idea and seems a particularly poor one in this context.

SUMMARY

Traditionally the costs of individual sources of finance have been derived from models which, logically enough, relate the current market value of a security or of a loan contract to the discounted value of future expected cash flows from that source. The cost of a particular source of finance is the discount rate. With some sources, for example quoted loan stocks, where the future cash flows can be reliably estimated, this is a fairly reliable way of deducing the cost of capital. Where we are dealing with less predictable areas such as dividends from equities, the resultant cost figure will be much less reliable.

The traditional means of discovering the rate at which to discount the predicted cash flows of potential investment opportunities is by finding the average of the costs of the firm's individual sources, weighted according to how much of each source is present in the firm's capital structure.

In principle this is as good a way as CAPM of finding the opportunity cost of capital, to which extent the two methods are interchangeable. The traditional method does however have more potential for misuse since it tends to make assumptions about the level of risk of a potential project which may very well not be justified. This could cause incorrect decisions to be made.

Traditionalists seem inclined to regard CAPM as not too practical a means of deriving discount rates, yet it seems not to require more by way of assumptions about the future than does the traditional means.

FURTHER READING

Most finance texts include fairly comprehensive treatment of the material discussed in this chapter. Samuels, Wilkes & Brayshaw (1990) give an interesting coverage of it; Levy & Sarnat (1988) and Copeland & Weston (1988) deal with it clearly. The last-mentioned goes into quite a lot of detail, particularly with regard to the costs of various types of finance.

(a) Try to deduce the weighted average cost of capital for your organisation.
(b) What does your organisation use as the discount rate in investment appraisal calculations (assuming that it uses NPV)?

---

1 The Directors of Milnthorpe Engineering plc are considering the feasibility of issuing 12 per cent Debentures at par to raise £1 000 000 for an investment to broaden their product range. The new plant is expected to produce a return of £240 000 per year indefinitely before tax and interest charges.

The company's existing capital structure is:

	£
Issued ordinary shares (£0.50 nominal value)	3 000 000
Issued 5% preference shares (£1 nominal value)	6 000 000
Reserves	6 000 000
	£15 000 000

The current market values of ordinary and preference shares are £2.00 and £0.80 respectively and the company's current maintainable earnings before meeting Corporation Tax at an effective rate of 50 per cent is £3 840 000 per year.

Required:

(a) Calculate the Weighted Average Cost of Capital before the issue of the Debentures.
(b) If there is no change in the cost of either Equity or Preference Capital what would you expect the Market Value of Ordinary Shares to be immediately after the issue of the Debentures and what would the Weighted Average Cost of Capital be at that time?

(Certified Diploma)

2 There are a number of methods which can be used to estimate the cost of equity. One of these is Gordon's growth model:

$$\left(\frac{D_1}{P_0} + g\right) = k_e$$

Required:

(a) Define each of the terms of the formula above. Using your own assumed or invented figures show an illustration of the calculation.
(b) Explain in general terms what the formula shows and how it can be used.
(c) What are the strengths and weaknesses of the model?
(d) Outline briefly any two other methods for calculating the cost of equity with which you may be familiar.

(Certified Diploma)

3 Spirax Holdings plc is a diverse group with interests in entertainment, property and machine tools. Its target capital structure is as follows:

	£ million
Ordinary share capital	30
Retained earnings	75
Debt	45
	150

The company's share price is 120p and it has just paid a net dividend of 12p. Dividends and profits have been growing at 10 per cent per year in money terms but a growth rate of only 3 per cent is expected in the future as it is anticipated that inflation will fall to zero. Currently debt interest is 8 per cent before tax and the Corporation Tax rate is 35 per cent.

The new office block is expected to cost £4.5 million and you can assume all this is to be spent at the end of 19X4. Rentals from the office block are forecast at £0.4 million per annum after taxation and these will be received at the end of each year for 50 years after construction is completed. The residual value of the building at that time is forecast to be £1.0 million. The project is to be initially financed by a bank loan costing 8 per cent per annum repayable over 15 years.

The directors have been arguing amongst themselves as to what cost of capital to use in their calculations. The marketing director reckons it is the cost of the bank loan since that is the actual cost of funds used. The financial director argues for the weighted average cost of capital since he says that is the overall cost of funds needed. The planning director has a slightly different argument. He says it is the risk of the project that is significant and he reckons that property investment is really pretty low risk and a reasonable cost of capital would be a rate 1 per cent above the post-tax cost of debt (8 per cent x (1 – 0.35)) = 5.2 per cent, say, 6 per cent post-tax.

Required:

(a) Calculate the weighted average cost of capital for Spirax Holdings.
(b) Comment on each of the directors' arguments concerning the appropriate discount rate.
(c) Compute the net present value of the project at the end of 19X4 using what you consider to be the most suitable rate. (You can ignore the delay between the collection of rental income and tax payments and other tax complications.)
(d) Describe how an expected inflation rate of 10 per cent would affect the project (you are not required to re-calculate your figures).

(Certified Diploma)

4* Summarised financial data for Univo plc is shown below:

Profit and loss accounts

£000

	19X9	19X0	19X1¹
Turnover	76 270	89 410	102 300
Taxable income	10 140	12 260	14 190
Taxation	3 549	4 291	4 966
	6 591	7 969	9 224
Dividend	2 335	2 557	2 800
Retained earnings	4 256	5 412	6 424

Balance sheet (£000)	*19X1¹*
Fixed assets	54 200
Current assets	39 500
Current liabilities	(26 200)
	67 500
Ordinary shares (50 pence par value)	20 000
Reserves	32 500
10% debenture 1996 (£100 par value)	15 000
	67 500

¹19X1 figures are unaudited estimates.

As a result of recent capital investment stock market analysts expect post tax earnings and dividends to increase by 25% for two years and then to revert to the company's existing growth rates.

Univo's asset (overall) beta is 0.763 and beta of debt is 0.20. The risk free rate is 12% and the market return 17%. The current market price of Univo's ordinary shares is 217 pence, cum 19X1 dividend, and the debenture price is £89.50 ex interest. Corporate tax is at the rate of 35%.

Required:

(a) (i) Using the dividend growth model, estimate what a fundamental analyst might consider to be the intrinsic (or realistic) value of the company's shares. Comment upon the significance of your estimate for the fundamental analyst.

Assume, for this part of the question only, that the cost of equity is not expected to change. The cost of equity may be estimated by using the CAPM.

(ii) If interest rates were to increase by 2% and expected dividend growth to remain unchanged, estimate what affect this would be likely to have on the intrinsic value of the company's shares.

(b) Explain whether your answer to (a) is consistent with the semi-strong and strong forms of the efficient markets hypothesis (EMH), and comment upon whether financial analysts serve any useful purpose in an efficient market.

(ACCA – part of question)

Note: * indicates a more complex question.

1 Riseley Chemicals Limited is considering installing a new reactor unit in one of its major chemical plants. The unit is of a revolutionary new design which has been developed and patented by the company and it is expected to give greatly improved raw material conversion efficiencies and lower manning levels. Riseley is planning to finance the purchase of this plant by a £14 000 000 bank loan. Interest on the loan will be payable at 3 per cent above bank base rate, currently standing at 10 per cent. Riseley's existing capital structure is as follows:

	£000
Share capital	60 000
Reserves	40 000
	100 000
Loans	6000
Total	106 000

It has a number of projects awaiting approval and it aims to increase the amount of its debt to 60 per cent of its equity within the next three years.

At present it is considering the cost of capital to use in its evaluation of the profitability of the new reactor. The finance director has discovered that various members of the management team have different ideas on this. The production director argues for using the rate of interest on bank borrowings as this is the rate that the company will have to pay. The marketing director has claimed that in his discussions with a competitor he had learned that they required a rate of 35 per cent. 'We should attempt to make at least 5 per cent more than them, if we are to expand and become one of the largest chemical companies.'

Riseley's shares are at present valued at 300p on the stock market. Its current dividend is 15p per share and this has been growing at 12 per cent per annum compound over recent years. The current rate of Corporation Tax is 35 per cent.

Required:

(a) Explain what you understand the term 'cost of capital' to mean. Why is it important for companies to try to estimate this figure carefully? Explain the difference between the cost of capital in real terms and the cost of capital in money terms.
(b) Comment on the remarks of the two directors.
(c) Compute the weighted average cost of capital for Riseley.

(Certified Diploma)

2 Blunsden Electronics plc is considering replacing one of its machines with more modern equipment. The existing machine has unit costs of production as follows:

	£
Labour	50
Maintenance	30
Depreciation	20
Apportioned overheads	100
	200

The new machine will have the following cost structure:

	£
Labour	20
Maintenance	20
Depreciation	40
Apportioned overheads	40
	120

Overhead costs are apportioned on the basis of labour cost. Maintenance is regarded as a variable cost. The cost of the new machine is £200 000 and development costs of £100 000 have already been spent. The new machine will be more flexible than the old machine, enabling working capital to be reduced by £50 000 after the new machine has been installed. You should assume that this saving lasts only for the life of the new machine. The level of overheads for the firm will remain unchanged as a consequence of introducing the new machine. The potential output of the new machine will be 25 per cent higher than for the old machine. However, for the foreseeable future production will be constrained by market conditions to the current level of 2000 units per annum. The lives of both the new and old machines are expected to be five years from today's date and their scrap values at that date, zero. Currently the cost of equity is estimated at 13 per cent per annum. The company aims to achieve a target debt ratio of 40 per cent (equity 60 per cent : debt 40 per cent). A bank has offered the company a loan at 10 per cent per annum to finance the project.

You can ignore taxation in your calculations.

Required:

(a) Prepare a statement showing those incremental cash flows of the project which are relevant to a decision concerning whether or not to proceed with the purchase of the new plant.

(b) Compute the cost of capital which should be used to discount the cash flows of the project.

(c) Write a short note explaining your answer to part (b) of the question, stating what other rate you might have used and why the one you have chosen is preferable.

(d) Compute the net present value of the project.

(e) Write a short report on the project giving your recommendations and stating what additional information you would require.

(Certified Diploma)

3 Trexon plc is a major oil and gas exploration company which has most of its operations in the Middle East and South East Asia. Recently, the company acquired rights to explore for oil and gas in the Gulf of Mexico. Trexon plc proposes to finance the new operations from the issue of equity shares. At present, the company is financed by a combination of equity capital and loan capital. The equity shares have a nominal value of £0.50 and a current market value of £2.60. The current level of dividend is £0.16 per share and this has been growing at a compound rate of 6 per cent per annum in recent years. The loan capital issued

by the company is irredeemable and has a current market value of £94 per £100 nominal. Interest on the loan capital is at the rate of 12 per cent and interest due at the year end has recently been paid. At present, the company expects 60 per cent of its finance to come from equity capital and the rest from loan capital. In the future, however, the company will aim to finance 70 per cent of its operations from equity capital.

When the proposal to finance the new operations via the rights issue of shares was announced at the annual general meeting of the company, objections were raised by two shareholders present.

Shareholder A argued:

'I fail to understand why the company has decided to issue shares to finance the new operation. Surely it would be better to re-invest profit as this is, in effect, a free source of finance to the company.'

Shareholder B argued:

'I also fail to understand why the company has decided to issue shares to finance the new operation. However, I do not agree with the suggestion made by Shareholder A. I do not believe that shareholder funds should be used at all to finance the new operation. Instead, the company should issue more loan capital as it is cheap relative to equity capital and would, therefore, reduce the overall cost of capital of the company.'

Corporation Tax is at the rate of 35 per cent.

Required:

(a) Explain the term 'cost of capital' and state why a company should calculate its cost of capital with care.
(b) Calculate the weighted average cost of capital of Trexon plc which should be used in future investment decisions.
(c) Comment on the remarks made by:
   (i) Shareholder A; and
   (ii) Shareholder B.

(Certified Diploma)

4* The directors of Denetter plc wish to make an equity issue to finance an £8 million expansion scheme, which has an expected net present value of £1.1 million, and to refinance an existing £5 million 15 per cent term loan which is due to mature in five years' time. There is a £350 000 penalty charge for early redemption of this loan. Denetter has obtained approval from its shareholders to suspend their pre-emptive rights and for the company to make a £15 million placement of shares which will be at the price of 185 pence per share. Issue costs are estimated to be 4 per cent of gross proceeds. Any surplus funds from the issue will be invested in commercial paper, which is currently yielding 9 per cent per year.

Note: * indicates a more complex question.

Denetter's current capital structure is summarised below:

	£000
Ordinary shares (25 pence par value)	8 000
Share premium	11 200
Revenue reserves	23 100
	42 300
15% term loan	5 000
11% debenture 1998–2001	9 000
	56 300

The company's current share price is 190 pence, and debenture price £102. Denetter can raise debenture or medium-term bank finance at 10% per year.

The stock market may be assumed to be semi-strong form efficient, and no information about the proposed uses of funds from the issue has been made available to the public.

Taxation may be ignored.

Required:

(a) Discuss the factors that Denetter's directors should have considered before deciding which form of financing to use.
(b) Explain what is meant by pre-emptive rights, and discuss their advantages and disadvantages.
(c) Estimate Denetter's expected share price once full details of the placement, and the uses to which the finance is to be put, are announced.
(d) Suggest reasons why the share price might not move to the price that you estimated in (c) above.

(ACCA)

CHAPTER 11

Gearing, the cost of capital and shareholders' wealth

OBJECTIVES

In this chapter we shall deal with the following:

- the use of loan finance as part of firms' long-term financial needs
- the effect of capital gearing on WACC, the value of the firm and the shareholders' wealth
- the traditional view of this effect
- the Modigliani/Miller view
- the empirical evidence of the effects of gearing
- gearing and CAPM
- a conjectural conclusion on gearing

INTRODUCTION

At several points in this book so far we have encountered the fact that many, probably most, firms raise part of their long-term financing requirements through borrowing, often by the issue of loan stocks or debentures. These give lenders contractual rights to receive interest, typically at a predetermined rate and on specified dates. Usually such loan stocks are redeemable; thus the contractual rights extend to the amount to be repaid and to the date of redemption. Loan finance could also be provided by a bank or similar institution, which would acquire similar contractual rights. The central point about loan finance, in the present context, lies in the fact that neither interest nor redemption payments are matters of the borrowing firm's discretion. Interest on such loans amounts to an annual charge on profits. This must be satisfied before the equity shareholders, who in the typical firm provide the larger part of the finance, may participate.

In Chapter 2 we found, subject to several assumptions, that financing through borrowing rather than equity does not seem to make any difference to the wealth of the shareholders. In this chapter we shall review the traditional view, that capital gearing does have an effect on shareholders' wealth, before we go on to develop the point raised in Chapter 2. After this we shall review the evidence and try to reach some conclusion on the matter.

IS LOAN FINANCE AS CHEAP AS IT SEEMS?

It is widely believed that the capital market prices securities so that expected returns from equities are higher than those from loan stocks. Historically this belief has been valid over all but fairly brief periods of time. Does the apparent cheapness of loan finance really mean that equity holders will benefit from the use of it in the firm's capital structure?

EXAMPLE

La Mer plc has one asset, a luxury yacht which is chartered to parties of jet-set holiday makers. Profits of the firm over the next few years are expected to be £140 000 p.a. La Mer is financed entirely by equity, namely 1 million ordinary shares whose current market value is £1 each. The firm is in the habit of paying all of the profit to shareholders by way of dividend. La Mer plc intends to buy an additional, similar vessel, also expected to generate annual profits of £140 000 p.a., at a cost of £1m. The finance for this is to be provided by the issue of £1m of 10 per cent loan stock. The loan is to be secured on the firm's two vessels.

Without the new yacht, the return per share is expected to be:

$$\frac{£140\ 000}{1\ 000\ 000} = £0.14 \text{ per share}$$

If the second yacht is acquired, the annual return per share will be:

Profit from chartering (2 × £140 000)	£280 000
Less: Interest (£1m @ 10%)	100 000
	£180 000

i.e. $\dfrac{£180\ 000}{1\ 000\ 000} = £0.18$ per share

Thus the expected return (and presumably therefore the value of the ordinary shares) is increased by the use of loan stock. (Note that if the finance for the new yacht had been raised by issuing 1 000 000 ordinary shares of £1 each, the annual return per share, with the second yacht, would have remained at £0.14.)

Since the ordinary shares are priced at £1 each when returns are expected to be 14p per share we may infer that investors regard 14 per cent as the appropriate return for such an investment. If the expected returns increase to 18p per share, as acquisition of the second vessel engenders, this seems likely to push up the price of an ordinary share to £1 × 18p/14p = £1.286 (18p represents a 14 per cent return on £1.286). This implies that, were the second vessel to be financed by an issue of equity, the value of each ordinary share would be £1, whereas if the second vessel were to be financed by loan stock, the firm's ordinary shares would be worth £1.286 each. In short, the shareholders' wealth would be increased by borrowing instead of issuing equity.

Too good to be true? Probably yes, yet there is nothing in the example which seems too far-fetched. Expected returns on equities tend to be greater than those on loan stocks, so the 10 per cent interest rate is not necessarily unrealistic. Surely though, such alchemy cannot really work. It cannot be possible in a fairly rational world, suddenly to turn a 14 per cent return into an 18 per cent one, to increase a share's price from £1 to £1.286, quite so simply – or can it?

To try to get to the bottom of this enigma, let us look at the situation from the point of view of the suppliers of the loan finance. If there are 14 per cent returns to be made from investing in yacht charting, why are they prepared to do so for a 10 per cent return? Why do they not buy ordinary shares in this firm? Are they so naïve that they do not notice the 14 per cent possibility? Perhaps they are, but this seems rather unlikely.

The difference between investing directly in yacht chartering (including buying shares in La Mer) and lending money on a fixed rate of interest is the different level of risk. In the example, of the £140 000 p.a. expected profits from the second yacht only £100 000 would be paid to the providers of the new finance. The other £40 000 goes to the equity holders, but with it goes all of the risk (or nearly all of it).

As with all real investment, returns are not certain. Suppose that there were to be a recession in the yacht charter business, so that the profits of La Mer plc fell to £70 000 p.a. from each vessel. This would mean:

Profit from chartering ($2 \times$ £70 000)	£140 000
Less: Interest (£1m @ 10%)	100 000
	£40 000

$$\text{i.e. } \frac{\text{£40 000}}{\text{1 000 000}} = \text{£0.04 per share}$$

(Note that had the second yacht been financed by equity the return per share would in the circumstances be £140 000/2 000 000 = £0.07, not quite such a disastrous outcome for equity holders.)

From this it seems clear that loan stocks provide an apparently cheap source of finance, but they have a hidden cost to equity shareholders.

BUSINESS RISK AND FINANCIAL RISK

Table 11.1 shows the annual dividend per share for La Mer (assuming the second vessel is acquired and that all available profit is paid as dividend) for each of the two financing schemes referred to above (all equity and 50 per cent loan financed) for various levels of chartering profits.

The inclusion of loan finance enhances returns on equity over those which could be earned in the all-equity structure, where annual profits are above £100 000 per vessel. Where annual profit per vessel falls below £100 000, however, the existence of loan finance weakens the ordinary shareholder's position. In fact, below a profit of £50 000 per vessel there would be insufficient profit to cover loan interest payments. Presuming that no other assets exist, the firm might have to dispose of one of the vessels to provide the finance to meet the interest payments.

At virtually all levels of profit the loan stockholders could view the situation philosophically. After all, not only do they have the right legally to enforce payment of their interest and repayment of their capital, they even have the vessels as security. Only if major losses to the market value of the yachts were to occur, would the loan stockholders' position seriously be threatened.

Where gearing exists, the risk to which equity holders are exposed clearly is increased over that which they would bear in the all-equity firm. To business risk, the normal risk attached to investing in the real world, is added financial risk, the risk caused by being burdened with the obligation to meet fixed charges illustrated in Table 11.1.

Table 11.1 Returns per share in La Mer plc for various levels of profit under each of two different financial structures

(a) Annual profit per vessel		0	£50 000	£100 000	£150 000	£200 000
All equity						
(b) Profit [(a) x 2]		0	£100 000	£200 000	£300 000	£400 000
(c) Return per share [(b) ÷ 2 000 000]		0	£0.05	£0.10	£0.15	£0.20
50 % loan finance						
(d) Profit [(a) x 2]		0	£100 000	£200 000	£300 000	£400 000
(e) *Less*: Interest (£1m @ 10%)	100 000	100 000	100 000	100 000	100 000	100 000
(f) Net profit	(£100 000)		0	£100 000	£200 000	£300 000
(g) Return per share [(f) ÷ 1 000 000]	(£0.10)		0	£0.10	£0.20	£0.30

Figure 11.1 depicts the relationship between business and financial risk where operating returns fluctuate. The amount of business risk depends on the area of activity in which the firm is invested; financial risk depends on how the firm is financed.

Figure 11.1
The return on equity over time for a financially geared firm with fluctuating profits

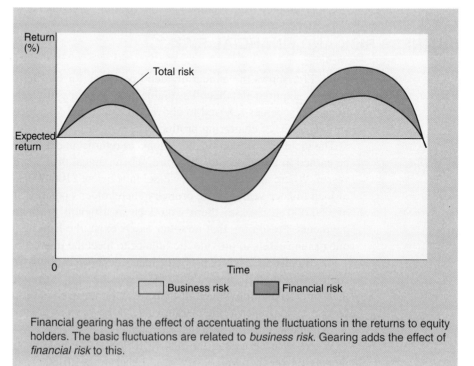

Financial gearing has the effect of accentuating the fluctuations in the returns to equity holders. The basic fluctuations are related to *business risk*. Gearing adds the effect of *financial risk* to this.

Intuition and modern portfolio theory both tell us that risk and return are related. Where investors perceive high risk they require high returns. Hence, referring back to the above example, while gearing will lift expected dividend per share to ordinary shareholders from 14p to 18p, this will not necessarily increase the share price (and therefore the wealth of the shareholder). Accompanying the increased expected dividend is a wider range of possible outcomes (see Table 11.1).

Not all of the new possibilities which gearing brings to the returns to equity holders are bad news. For example, for La Mer, Table 11.1 shows that for any chartering profit per vessel above £100 000 p.a., ordinary share dividends would actually be enhanced. Most investors, however, are risk-averse, which means that the possibility that profit per vessel could be below £100 000 tends to be more important to them than the possibility that profits could be greater.

La Mer's ordinary shareholders will only be better off through the introduction of gearing if the capital market, when it reassesses the situation following the loan stock issue and the purchase of the second yacht, prices the ordinary shares so that their expected yield is less than 18 per cent.

Before the firm's expansion these ordinary shares had an expected yield of 14 per cent. If, as a result of the higher risk level, after the expansion the market expected a return of 16 per cent, the price per share would be

$$\sum_{n=1}^{\infty} \frac{£0.18}{(1+0.16)^n} = £1.125$$

i.e. an increase in value per share.

If on the other hand capital market requirements for the level of risk rose to 20 per cent, the price per share would become

$$\sum_{n=1}^{\infty} \frac{£0.18}{(1+0.20)^n} = £0.90$$

Put another way, will the introduction of gearing lower the weighted average cost of capital (WACC) and therefore make more valuable the investments in which the firm is involved, or not? Before the introduction of gearing in La Mer, WACC was 14 per cent (the return on the ordinary shares). If, after the issue of loan stock, the capital market required return on equity shares rose to 16 per cent, then

$$\text{WACC} = \left(\frac{£1m}{£2.125m} \times 10\% \right) + \left(\frac{£1.125m}{£2.125m} \times 16\% \right)$$

$$= 4.71 + 7.53$$

$$= 12.24\%, \text{ i.e. a lowering of WACC through gearing.}$$

(Remember that :

WACC

$$= \left(\frac{\text{Market value of loan stock}}{\text{Market value of equity} + \text{Loan stock}} \times \text{Cost of loan stock} \right)$$

$$+ \left(\frac{\text{Market value of equity}}{\text{Market value of equity} + \text{Loan stock}} \times \text{Cost of equity} \right)$$

Also remember that the price per equity share will be £1.125 if required return is 16 per cent.)

If the capital market required a return of 20 per cent then

$$\text{WACC} = \left(\frac{£1m}{£1.9m} \times 10\%\right) + \left(\frac{£0.9m}{£1.9m} \times 20\%\right)$$

$$= 5.26\% + 9.47\%$$

$$= 14.73\%, \text{ i.e. an increase of WACC through gearing.}$$

Given the firm's overall objective of maximisation of shareholder wealth, how the capital market reacts, in terms of required returns, to the introduction of gearing is a very important matter. Gearing is presumably only undertaken with the objective of increasing equity shareholders' wealth.

THE TRADITIONAL VIEW

The traditional view seems to be that if the expected rate of return from equity investment in yacht chartering is 14 per cent, this will not be greatly affected by the introduction of capital gearing, not at least up to moderate levels. This view of the effect of gearing on capital market expectations of returns from equities, loan stocks and WACC is depicted in Fig. 11.2.

**Figure 11.2
The cost of capital for varying levels of gearing – the traditional view**

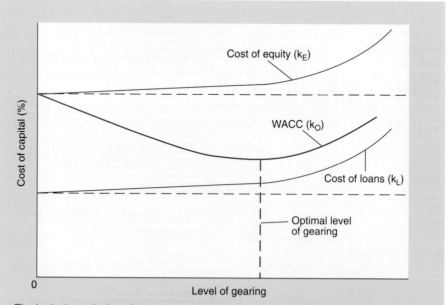

The logical conclusion of this view is that there is an optimum level of gearing, where there is a minimum weighted average cost of capital. This arises from the assumption that the cost of equity does not increase sufficiently to outweigh the advantage of the low cost loan finance until some significant level of gearing is achieved.

Figure 11.2 shows that, as gearing is increased, both equity investors and lenders perceive additional risk and require higher returns. At lower levels of gearing, however, neither group requires greatly increased returns to compensate for this risk, and WACC reduces. When gearing reaches higher levels, the risk issue becomes increasingly important to both groups, so required returns start to increase dramatically. Now WACC starts to rise steeply. Although the point at which each group's required return starts this steep rise is not necessarily the same, there is a point (or a range of points) where, according to traditionalists, WACC is at a minimum. This is the *optimal level of gearing* in Fig. 11.2. At this point the shareholders' wealth is maximised, i.e. the price per share would be at its peak. Note that a graph of share price against the level of gearing would resemble an inversion of the WACC (k_0) curve in Fig. 11.2.

The rationale for the traditional view seems to be that it is felt that lenders would recognise that at high levels of gearing their security is substantially lost and would begin to demand successively higher levels of interest to compensate them. It seems also to be believed that, up to a certain level of gearing, equity shareholders would not see the increased risk to their returns as too significant. After that point, however, they would start to demand major increases in returns for further increases in gearing.

A traditionalist would argue that, with La Mer at 50 per cent loan financing there is still plenty of security in the value of the vessels for the interest and the capital repayment, even if market prices of yachts dropped considerably. However, if the level of loan financing increased to, say, 90 per cent, a drop of more than 10 per cent in the market value of the yachts would erode the security of lenders. At the same time La Mer's equity holders would not see their position too badly threatened by the existence of moderate levels of loan finance and would not require returns great enough to negate the advantage of the apparently cheap loan finance.

Broadly, the traditional conclusion was that gearing is a good thing, in terms of shareholder wealth maximisation, at least up to a certain level past which it would start to have an adverse effect on WACC and therefore on shareholder wealth.

During the 1950s some observers started to question the value of gearing, finding it difficult to reconcile the 'something for nothing' aspect of the traditional view with the rapidly growing belief that securities are efficiently and rationally priced.

THE MILLER & MODIGLIANI VIEW OF GEARING

In 1958 Miller & Modigliani (MM) published an article, now almost legendary, questioning the traditional approach to the issue of gearing. MM argued that, given rational pricing in the capital markets, it is not possible for a firm to increase its total market value (lower its WACC) merely by doing what it is theoretically open to any of us to do, namely to borrow money. They asserted that if a particular firm is expected to generate some level of income, this should be valued without regard to how the firm is financed.

EXAMPLE

To see how the MM assertion would work in the case of La Mer, let us assume that the firm raised the £1m for the second vessel by issuing a 10 per cent debenture (i.e. borrowing at 10 per cent p.a.). Let us also assume that there is another firm, Sea plc, identical in every respect to La Mer, but completely financed by 2m ordinary shares of £1 each.

Franco, a holder of 1 per cent of the equity of La Mer (i.e. 10 000 shares) would expect a return on them of £1800 p.a. since, as we have seen, each one is expected to yield 18p p.a. Franco could equally well obtain the same expected income by borrowing the equivalent of 1 per cent of La Mer's borrowings (i.e. £10 000) at the rate of 10 per cent p.a. and using this to help finance the purchase of 1 per cent of the ordinary shares in Sea (20 000 shares). The Sea shares would be expected to yield 14p each and so £2800 in total which, after paying interest on the borrowing, would leave £1800 p.a. of expected income of equal risk (business and financial) as that of the expected income from La Mer. Franco's situation may be restated and summarised as follows:

	Investment	Income
Present position		
10 000 shares in La Mer		
(i.e. 1% of total shares)	£10 000	£1800
Alternative position		
Borrow £10 000	(£10 000)	(£1000)
Buy 20 000 shares in Sea		
(i.e. 1% of total shares)	20 000	2800
	£10 000	£1800

Since securities (indeed, any economic assets) are valued by reference only to their expected return and risk, each of the above positions must be equally valuable to Franco, or to any other investor. Both positions offer identical risk/return expectations.

If in the above circumstances Sea's shares fell in price below that of La Mer's shares, Franco could make the switch from the original to the alternative position, have the same expected return and risk, but make a profit on the switch. Since the sale of the La Mer shares and purchase of the Sea shares could be achieved simultaneously (an action known as *arbitraging*), a risk-free gain would be available. The actions of Franco, and others spotting this opportunity, would increase both the demand for Sea's shares and the supply of those of La Mer. As a result, the price of the shares would equalise.

MM's central point is that if Franco wants to be involved with gearing, but wishes to hold shares in Sea, Franco can undertake the gearing personally, i.e. *homemade gearing*.

Similarly, another individual, Merton, who owns shares in Sea, but wishes to invest in La Mer though not to be involved with gearing, can easily *ungear* an investment in La Mer. Merton can do this by lending the same proportion of the money to be invested, as La Mer borrows of its total financing.

	Investment	Income
Present position		
20 000 shares in Sea	£20 000	£2800
Alternative position		
Lend £10 000	£10 000	£1000
Buy 10 000 shares in La Mer	10 000	1800
	£20 000	£2800

Once again, a switch from the present to the alternative position would result in the same expected return with the same risk.

It would seem illogical for firms to be able to increase the wealth of their shareholders merely by *packaging* the firm's income in a particular way.

This is made especially illogical by the fact that individual shareholders can adjust the packaging to their own convenience, merely by borrowing and/or lending. Income of similar risk and expected return should be similarly priced in a rational market, irrespective of the packaging.

It seems clear from these examples that:

$$\frac{\text{Total value of the equity of Sea}}{100}$$

$$= \frac{\text{Total value of the equity of La Mer}}{100}$$

$$+ \frac{\text{Total value of the borrowings of La Mer}}{100}$$

Rearranging this gives:

Total value of the equity of Sea = Total value of the equity and borrowings of La Mer

and more generally,

$$V_U = V_G$$

where V_U and V_G are the total value of the ungeared and geared firms respectively.

The implication of the MM proposition is that the value of the firm is not affected by the financing method (i.e. $V_U = V_G$), therefore the cost of capital is not reduced (or affected at all) by the introduction of gearing. The only matters on which the value of the firm and its WACC depend are:

(a) the cash flows which the firm's investments are expected to generate, and
(b) their risk (i.e. their business risk).

This is another phenomenon following the same pattern as Fisher separation (see Chapter 2). MM were in effect saying that management should concentrate all its efforts on finding and managing investment opportunities, leaving the financing arrangements for individual shareholders to decide for themselves.

The effect suggested by MM is shown graphically in Fig. 11.3. Here we can see that the potential which increasing amounts of *cheap* loan finance have for reducing

WACC is exactly offset by the increasing cost of equity. Thus WACC is impervious to the level of gearing.

We see from Fig. 11.3 that shareholders in geared firms expect a return equal to the expected return from the identical ungeared firm, plus a premium which is directly proportional to the level of gearing. Thus, whilst gearing increases earnings per share, it also increases capital market expectations of the share's returns because of higher risk. The net effect of these factors on the value of each share will be zero, i.e. the effects will be equal and opposite (according to MM).

According to MM the relationship between the return expected by the capital market and the level of gearing is:

$$E(r_{EG}) = E(r_{EE}) + (E(r_{EE}) - r_L)\frac{L_G}{S_G}$$

where $E(r_{EG})$ and $E(r_{EE})$ are respectively the expected returns from shares in the geared and all-equity firm; L_G and S_G are respectively the total market value of the loan stock and shares of the geared firm.

Figure 11.3
The cost of capital for varying levels of gearing – the MM (pre-tax) view

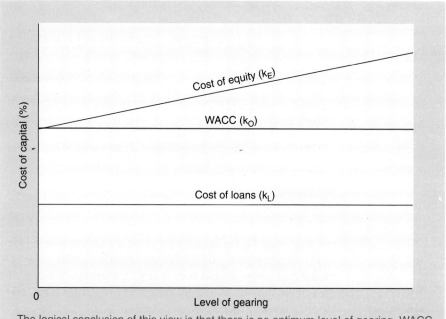

The logical conclusion of this view is that there is no optimum level of gearing. WACC will be identical at all levels of gearing. This arises from the assumption that the cost of equity rises at a rate which precisely cancels the advantage of the low cost loan finance at all levels of gearing.

Thus the introduction of 50 per cent gearing into the capital structure of La Mer would push the capital market's expected return on the firm's equities up to 18 per cent, $(E(r_{EG}) = 14 + (14 - 10)$ (£1m/£1m) = 18%). Thus the expected earnings per share of 18p (see page 268) would still only be worth £1.

MM's disagreement with the traditionalists was that MM saw the capital market's return expectations increasing as soon as gearing is introduced, and increasing in proportion to the amount of gearing. The traditionalists felt that this would not occur at lower levels of gearing.

The formal proof of the MM proposition is developed in Appendix I of this chapter.

The MM assumptions

(a) *Shares can be bought and sold without dealing costs*. This is obviously unrealistic: brokers' commissions and other costs are involved with trading in shares. It is doubtful, however, whether the weakness of this assumption seriously undermines the proposition. It might mean that investors would be unable to make a profit by exploiting minor instances of mispricing of shares of geared firms, relative to those of ungeared firms. The larger ones could be exploited despite the existence of dealing charges.

(b) *Capital markets are efficient*. The evidence seems to show that they are efficient, for practical purposes, in the weak and semi-strong form (see Chapter 9). This implies that investors would see through the financial packaging and realise that income of a particular risk class is equally valuable irrespective of how it is wrapped. It seems that this assumption is reasonable.

(c) *Interest rates are equal between borrowing and lending, firms and individuals*. Clearly this is invalid. In particular, there is usually a difference between the rate at which individuals and firms can borrow. Large firms, particularly, can often offer good security, can borrow large amounts, and can exploit borrowing opportunities not open to most individuals, e.g. borrowing overseas. The importance of this assumption lies in the question of homemade gearing, where the investor borrows on his or her own account and buys shares in the ungeared firm.

There is no reason, however, why the investor who exploits any mispricing of shares need be an individual; it could be a large firm, e.g. a large unit or investment trust. After all, most investment in securities, in the UK at least, is undertaken by the institutions rather than by individuals. Nor is it necessary that every investor in the economy seeks to exploit any mispricing in order to correct it. The action of a couple of investors, well placed to exploit the situation, would be sufficient. Probably the weakness of this assumption is not sufficient to call the MM proposition too seriously into question.

MM also made the implicit assumption that the corporate cost of borrowing does not increase with the level of gearing. This seems less plausible, a point to which we shall return later in the chapter.

(d) *There are no bankruptcy costs*. This assumption suggests that if a firm were to be liquidated the shareholders would receive, in exchange for their shares, the equivalent of their market value immediately before the liquidation. This assumption envisages a situation where, as a result of a firm defaulting on interest and/or capital repayment, it is liquidated at the instigation of loan stock holders. This sort of action would obviously be more likely with very highly geared firms.

The assumption is invalid since dealing costs would be involved in the disposal of the firm's assets, legal costs would arise in formally bringing about the demise of the firm and, perhaps most importantly, the market for real assets is not generally efficient in the same way that capital markets seem to be. This last point implies that a machine worth £1000 to firm A does not necessarily have that same value to firm B, because firm B, for some reason, may not be able to use it as effectively as firm A. Before the liquidation, firm A's equity value may have been based partially on a £1000 value for the machine, but when the machine comes to be sold it may only fetch £500.

This assumption's lack of validity undermines the MM proposition in its broad form. It is doubtful, however, whether the assumption is a very important one where gearing levels are moderate, which appears typically to be the case in practice. On the other hand the existence of bankruptcy costs may well be the reason for the modest gearing levels which we tend to see in real life.

(e) *Two firms identical in income (cash flow) and risk exist, one all-equity, the other geared.* This assumption is most unlikely strictly to be true. It seems not to be an important impediment to the validity of MM's proposition. CAPM, and modern portfolio theory in general, suggest that business risk can explicitly be dealt with so that it is possible to relate two firms of different risk. That is, there is an established mechanism for pricing risk which enables returns for one firm's shares to be reconciled with those of another firm. But even if CAPM, etc., is questioned, MM were really referring to one firm and making the point that if there were two firms identical except only for their financing method they would be equally valued. Stiglitz (1974) showed that it is not necessary for two such firms actually to exist in order for the proposition to be valid.

(f) *There is no taxation.* This is clearly invalid. MM were much criticised for this fact and were forced to reconsider their proposition because of it.

The revised *after-tax* version asserts that market forces must cause

$$V_G = V_U + T L_G$$

where L_G is the value of the firm's borrowings and T is the relevant Corporation Tax rate, at which loan stock interest will be relieved. The derivation of the above is shown in Appendix II to this chapter.

The after-tax proposition implies that the value of the geared firm is greater than the value of the all-equity one; also that the greater the level of gearing, the greater the value of the firm. The inevitable conclusion is that the value of the firm is highest and WACC lowest, when gearing is at 100 per cent, i.e. all finance is provided by loan stock holders.

Figure 11.4 shows the MM after-tax view of capital gearing. There is a contrast with the pre-tax position depicted in Fig. 11.3. In the after-tax case the cost of debt is low enough (due to higher tax relief on loan interest) for increasing amounts of loan finance to reduce WACC at a greater rate than the increasing demands of equity holders are raising it. Thus the WACC line slopes downward.

It is doubtful if this 100 per cent loan finance conclusion is tenable in practical terms, however. At very high levels of gearing the loan stock holders would recognise that their security had been substantially eroded and that while they might be lenders in name, as risk takers they are equity holders in reality. They would therefore seek a level of return which would compensate them for this risk, a level of return similar to that which the equity holders seek. This would mean that at very high levels of gearing, both in the pre-tax and in the more important post-tax propositions, the cost of loans would rise significantly. In order for MM conclusions to hold, this requires that the rate of increase in the cost of equity starts to fall. In Fig. 11.4, if the cost of loans line is going to start turning upwards at some high level of gearing, the WACC line can only continue its downward path if the cost of equity line becomes less steep. (Remember that the WACC line is the average of the other two.)

**Figure 11.4
The cost of capital
for varying levels
of gearing – the
MM (post-tax) view**

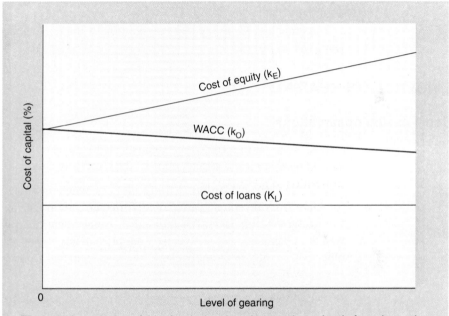

The logical conclusion of this view is that there is an optimum level of gearing and that this is located at 100% gearing. This arises from the assumption that the cost of equity rises at a rate which would precisely cancel the advantage of the low cost loan finance at all levels of gearing, were it not for the fact that loan interest is tax deductible. The fact that interest is deductible means that the greater the amount of loan finance the greater the tax benefit to the firm.

The idea of the rate of increase in the cost of equity, as gearing is increased, suddenly starting to reduce at high gearing levels seems to defy logic. Why should investors start to behave contrary to all the theories and evidence of investor reaction to increasing risk? This suggests a weakness in the MM analysis which perhaps means that their conclusion in the after-tax case is not all that logical.

OTHER THOUGHTS ON THE TAX ADVANTAGE OF LOAN FINANCING

Miller (1977), showed that the tax benefits of gearing for a particular firm will depend on the personal tax positions of both the loan stock holders and the shareholders. Thus firms will tend to attract investors (both lenders and shareholders) who are suited to the firm's capital structure. This is known as a 'clientele' effect, where particular policies attract particular types of investor. If Miller is right about this, the implication is that firms should probably try to avoid altering their capital structure because this would lead to investors selling their loan stocks or shares and investing their money in a firm which matches their preferences. This is because the dealing costs involved with selling and buying securities would have an adverse effect on the wealth of the investors.

More recently, Dempsey (1991) showed, in the context of the UK tax and financial environment, that in theory gearing has a relatively small *adverse* effect on the wealth of shareholders.

It is probably fair to say that the question of the tax benefits of gearing remains unanswered.

EVIDENCE ON GEARING

Some casual observations

Before going on to some of the sophisticated studies relating to gearing, it is well worth noting some important points which arise from casual observation. These are:

(a) A very large proportion of firms, perhaps even a large majority of them, go in for some level of capital gearing. Few firms raise all of their financial requirements from equity shareholders. Assuming that managements are pursuing a shareholder wealth maximisation objective, they are presumably using gearing to promote that objective. Rightly or wrongly, therefore, managements seem to believe that gearing lowers WACC.

(b) Very high levels of gearing are rarely seen. Managements seem not to believe that the value of the firm is maximised (WACC minimised) by very high gearing levels.

Some formal evidence

The questions to which the answers are of real interest are:

(a) Does WACC change with gearing as MM (post-tax) suggested and
(b) Does it move to a minimum at some level of gearing of less than 100 per cent and then increase as gearing is further increased?

The publication of the MM articles on capital structure was followed thick and fast by a number of studies bearing on the above questions.

Miller & Modigliani (1958) themselves took the lead with a study using data concerning a number of oil firms and of electrical utility firms and came to the conclusion that WACC is not dependent on the level of gearing (supporting their pre-tax proposition).

Weston (1963) criticised the MM results on the basis that they had made too many simplifying assumptions. Weston himself used data on electrical utility firms to show that the MM post-tax proposition was valid in that WACC seemed to decrease with increased gearing.

Miller & Modigliani (1966) returned to the scene and, again using the electrical utilities found evidence to support the after-tax propositions. This was further supported by Masulis (1980).

Hamada (1972), using CAPM to deal with risk differences, found that the cost of equity increases with the level of gearing.

The formal evidence seems to answer question (a); WACC decreases with increased gearing. It does not really deal with question (b) and so we do not know from the formal evidence whether or not WACC bottoms out at some point below 100 per cent gearing, after which it starts to increase.

GEARING AND THE COST OF CAPITAL – CONCLUSION

The central question on gearing is whether in reality it is the traditionalists or MM who best explain the effect of gearing.

The traditional view, that somehow equity shareholders do not pay much attention to the increased risk which rising amounts of gearing engender until it reaches high levels, seems naïve. It appears to conflict with most of the evidence on the efficiency of the capital market. Tests of capital market efficiencies indicate that little of significance goes unnoticed. It is difficult to believe that increased levels of gearing are insignificant to equity shareholders, since gearing increases the range of possible returns. As most investors seem to be risk-averse, increasing the range of possible outcomes will be unattractive to them.

The formal evidence on the effects of gearing cited above also cuts across the traditional view since it appears that gearing levels broadly affect equity returns and WACC in the manner suggested by MM (post-tax).

On the other hand, casual observation shows that firms' managements do not seem to believe in very high levels of gearing, which rather supports the traditional view.

There is a conflict here, though perhaps it is possible to reconcile these two factors.

The MM (post-tax) analysis relies on a number of assumptions, most of which seem not to be so far-fetched as seriously to weaken their conclusions. Two of them, however, call their proposition into question.

(a) *There are no bankruptcy costs*. The importance of this assumption lies in the fact that the existence of high levels of loan finance exposes the firm to the risk that it will not be able to meet its payment obligations to lenders, not at least out of its operating cash flows, if the firm should experience a particularly adverse period of trading. Whilst it is equally true that the all-equity firm might have difficulty paying dividends in similar economic circumstances, there is an important difference.

Lenders have a contractual right to receive interest and capital repayment on the due dates. If they do not receive these, they have the legal power to enforce payment.

The exercise of such power can in practice lead to the liquidation of all of the firm's assets and its winding up. For the reasons we have already discussed (principally through an apparently inefficient market in real assets), this will usually disadvantage the ordinary shareholder to a significant extent.

By contrast, neither in a geared, nor in an ungeared, firm do ordinary shareholders have any rights to enforce the declaration and payment of a dividend.

This bankruptcy risk is probably insignificant at low levels of gearing, if only because any shortage of cash for interest payments could be borrowed from some other source – a possibility probably not so readily available to highly geared firms in distress.

(b) *The interest rate demanded by lenders remains the same at all levels of gearing.* At very low levels of gearing the position of lenders is one of great security, with the value of their loan probably covered many times by the value of the firm's assets. As gearing increases, this position erodes until at very high levels lenders, because they provide most of the finance, bear most of the risk.

Going back to the La Mer example, suppose that the unexpanded firm (i.e. just one yacht worth £1m) were financed 90 per cent by equity shares and 10 per cent by loan stock. Here the value of the yacht would have to fall by 90 per cent before the security of the lenders would be threatened. Even if the equity/loan ratio moved to 80:20, the lenders' security, whilst in theory slightly weakened, is not less in practical terms than had they only supplied 10 per cent of the finance. If however the ratio moved to 10:90, only a small drop (10 per cent) in the value of the yacht would leave the lenders bearing all the risk. Naturally enough, lenders would demand high returns to induce them to buy loan stocks in such a highly geared firm, presumably something like the returns expected by equity shareholders.

Logically, the loan stock holders would not see risk (and required return) increasing significantly with increases in gearing at the lower end. After all, unless the asset on which security rests is extremely volatile in its value, an asset value/loan ratio of 5:1 is probably as good as 10:1; the lenders only need to be paid once. If this ratio increases to nearer 1:1, lenders would no doubt start to see things differently.

It is notable that neither of these two 'weak' assumptions of MM significantly affect the position at lower levels of gearing. At higher levels, however, they start to loom very large. In the light of this and taking account of the evidence which we briefly discussed, we may perhaps draw a tentative conclusion.

Up to moderate levels of gearing the tax advantages of loan finance will cause the WACC to decrease as more gearing is introduced. Beyond moderate levels, bankruptcy risk (to equity shareholders) and the introduction of real risk to lenders will push up the returns required by each group, making WACC a very high figure at high gearing levels.

Figure 11.5 depicts this conclusion with k_E, k_0, and k_L all following the same pattern as shown in Fig. 11.4 (MM post-tax) up to a moderate level of gearing and then all starting to take off to very high levels as further gearing is introduced.

It is more likely that, in real life, *moderate* is not a fixed point for any particular firm; it is rather a range below which MM's proposition holds, but above which it clearly does not. Of course the vital question is what does 'moderate' mean? The problem is that it is likely to be difficult to define and, as such, a matter of judgement of financial management. It must be the point at which the balance is struck between the tax advantage on the one hand and bankruptcy cost and rising cost of borrowing on the other. This will vary from industry to industry and will to some extent depend upon the business risk (perhaps measured by β) of the investments in which the particular firm is engaged.

Figure 11.5
The cost of
capital for varying
levels of gearing –
a possible
reconciliation of
the traditional view,
the MM (post-tax)
view and what
appears to happen
in practice

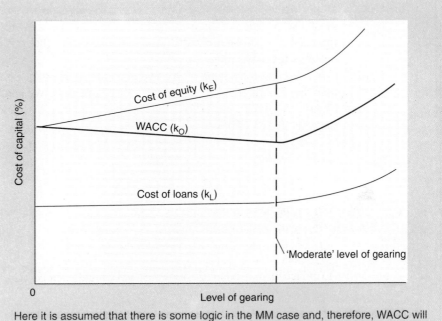

Here it is assumed that there is some logic in the MM case and, therefore, WACC will fall as gearing increases. As the level of gearing increases above a 'moderate' level of gearing, however, both equity holders and lenders will become increasingly conscious of the risk. As a result they will seek higher returns in compensation. This will drive WACC steeply up. Thus there will be an optimum level of gearing.

More formally the relationship between the value of the geared and ungeared firms can be expressed as:

$$V_G = V_U + TL_G - \text{Present value of the expected cost of bankruptcy.}$$

As gearing increases, the value of the tax shield (TL_G) increases but so does the expected cost of bankruptcy. At some point the latter will outweigh the former.

MM, MPT AND CAPM

Before leaving the subject of capital gearing and its effect on WACC, perhaps we should consider how these matters relate to modern portfolio theory in general and the capital asset pricing model in particular.

Earlier in this chapter we saw that the introduction of capital gearing exposes the ordinary shareholder to two types of risk, namely business risk and financial risk. The question now arises as to how these two relate to specific risk and systematic risk.

We should recall from Chapter 7 that business risk has two components, the specific or diversifiable part and the systematic part which the investor must bear. Figure 11.1 (page 270) depicts the relationship between business risk and financial risk; it shows that financial risk simply augments or accentuates business risk. It seems logical therefore that, if business risk is part specific and part systematic, this must also be true for financial risk. This means that, as with business risk, part of financial risk can be diversified away; it also means that part of it cannot be eliminated by diversification.

The logical conclusion of this is that equity shares in geared firms have higher βs than those in all-equity firms. Indeed, this is the case. We know that βs are additive. That is, the β for a portfolio is the average (weighted by market value) of the βs of the constituents of the portfolio. Therefore (ignoring tax):

$$\beta_{EE} = \beta_{EG}\frac{S_G}{S_G + L_G} + \beta_{LG}\frac{L_G}{S_G + L_G}$$

where

β_{EE} is the beta of the equities of the all-equity firm;
β_{EG} is the beta of the equities of the geared firm;
β_{LG} is the beta of the loan stock of the geared firm.

This assumes that the two firms are identical in all respects except their financing method.

If we take account of the 'tax shield' of debt, the relationship between the βs is:

$$\beta_{EE} = \beta_{EG}\frac{S_G}{S_G + L_G(1-T)} + \beta_{LG}\frac{L_G(1-T)}{S_G + L_G(1-T)}$$

where T is the Corporation tax rate.

If we assume that the loan stock is without risk ($\beta_{LG} = 0$), then

$$\beta_{EE} = \beta_{EG}\frac{S_G}{S_G + L_G}$$

Rearranging gives

$$\beta_{EG} = \beta_{EE}\left(1 + \frac{L_G}{S_G}\right)$$

$$\beta_{EG} = \beta_{EE} + \beta_{EE}\frac{L_G}{S_G}$$

or

$$\beta_{EG} = \beta_{EE} + \beta_{EE}\frac{L_G(1-T)}{S_G}$$

if we take account of Corporation tax.

In other words, the risk attaching to the equities in a geared firm is equal to the risk to equities in the equivalent all-equity firm plus a financial risk premium which depends on the basic all-equity risk and on the level of gearing.

This is simply another way of saying:

Total systematic risk (of equities in a geared firm)
= Systematic business risk + Systematic financial risk

Business risk can, as we know, be measured by β and financial risk is simply an accentuation of that same risk. This is entirely consistent with MM's assertions.

SUMMARY

Firms typically raise part of their finance from apparently cheap borrowings. The inclusion of a fixed commitment of interest payments and an obligation to repay the principal of the loan increases the risk to, and hence the return required by, ordinary shareholders.

Traditionalists argue that the net effect of gearing, at least up to a certain level, is to lower WACC and so increase the value of the equities. Modigliani & Miller, developing their argument with blinding logic (given certain assumptions), showed that, in the absence of all taxes, gearing made no difference. If the tax advantage of gearing is considered, MM showed that the introduction of a higher proportion of loan finance will always benefit ordinary shareholders, though subsequently Miller argued that the tax advantage of gearing does not exist.

Most of the assumptions made by MM seem reasonable, but those concerning bankruptcy cost and constant cost of loan finance seem highly questionable. The evidence, both formal and casual, of real life suggests that MM are correct up to a point. Beyond that point the unrealistic assumptions manifest their lack of reality.

It seems that increasing gearing does lower WACC but that it reaches its low point some time before 100 per cent gearing is reached and then starts to rise again.

FURTHER READING

The subject of capital gearing is well written up in the literature. There is good coverage of it by Lumby (1991), Levy & Sarnat (1988) and Davis & Pointon (1991). The empirical evidence on the effects of gearing is well covered by Copeland & Weston (1988). It is worth reading the original MM articles which are reprinted in Archer & D'Ambrosio (1967).

WORK-BASED ASSIGNMENT

What factors seem to affect the level of gearing at which your organisation operates?

QUESTIONS WITH ANSWERS (see Appendix 3)

1 Ashcroft plc, a family-controlled company, is considering raising additional funds to modernise its factory. The scheme is expected to cost £2.34 million and will increase annual profits before interest and tax from 1 January 19X4 by £0.6 million. A summarised balance sheet and profit and loss account is shown below. Currently the share price is 200p.

Two schemes have been suggested. Firstly, 1.3 million shares could be issued at 180p (net of issue costs). Secondly, a consortia of six city institutions have offered to buy debentures from the company totalling £2.34 million. Interest would be at the rate of 13 per cent per annum and capital repayments of equal annual instalments of £234 000 starting on 1 January 19X5, would be required.

Ashcroft plc

Balance sheet at 31 December 19X3

	£ million	£ million
Fixed assets (net)		1.4
Current assets:		
Stock	2.4	
Debtors	2.2	
	4.6	
Creditors: amounts falling due within one year		
Creditors	2.7	
Corporation tax	0.6	
Proposed final dividend	0.2	
	3.5	
Net current assets		1.1
Total assets *less* Current liabilities		2.5
Capital and reserves:		
Called up share capital, 25p ordinary shares		1.0
Profit and loss account		1.5
		2.5

Ashcroft plc

Profit and loss account year ended 31 December 19X3

	£ million
Turnover	11.2
Profit on ordinary activities before tax	1.2
Less: Taxation on profit on ordinary activities	0.6
Profit on ordinary activities after tax	0.6
Dividends (net)	0.3
Retained profit for the financial year	0.3

Assume corporation tax is charged at the rate of 50 per cent.

Required:

(a) Compute the earnings per share for 19X4 under the debt and the equity alternatives.

(b) Compute the level of profits before debenture interest and tax at which the earnings per share under the two schemes will be equal.

(c) Discuss the considerations the directors should take into account before deciding upon debt or equity finance.

(Certified Diploma)

2 Aspley Engineers plc, a medium-sized listed company, is considering two schemes to finance its next expansion. The first is to raise £80 million by means of a term loan from its bankers. Interest would be charged at 2 per cent above base rate which you should assume currently stands at 10 per cent. The loan would be repayable in equal annual instalments over five years starting on 1 January 19X0 and finishing on 1 January 19X4. The bank requires a floating charge on the company's assets and an agreement to the following covenants. Firstly, an interest cover of at least 2 times must be maintained and secondly the ratio of debt to equity is not to exceed 1 to 1.

The other scheme is to raise £80 million by issuing 20 million ordinary shares at 400p.

The following extracts have been taken from the company's records.

Year ended 30 June	19X8	19X7	19X6
No. of £1 ordinary shares (millions)	100	100	100
		£ millions	
Share capital and reserves	360	340	320
Loans	260	200	180
	620	540	500
Profit before interest and tax	93	52	80
Interest payable	30	28	24
Company share price – pence	480	281	546

Currently the chairman of the company and close family members own 42 per cent of its shares. Use a corporate tax rate of 35 per cent in your calculations.

Profit before interest and tax for 19X9 is expected to be £100 million and the net dividend 20p per share. The amount of interest on existing loans is likely to remain unchanged.

Required:

(a) Explain in general terms the purpose of covenants in term loan agreements.
(b) Calculate the following ratios for 19X9 for each of the debt and the equity alternatives.
(i) Interest cover.
(ii) Earnings per share.
(iii) Debt equity ratio.
(c) Using the information above, state with reasons which scheme you would recommend.

(Certified Diploma)

3* **(Taxation is to be ignored for this question.)**
The Harris Public Limited Company is about to raise finance by increasing its 12 million ordinary shares with a 1 for 3 rights issue. Total debt in the capital structure comprises:

Note: * indicates a more complex question.

	Book Value (£ millions)
16% Debentures	10.0
16% Bank loan	10.0
Various short term loans and overdrafts at current interest rates	0.2

The debentures have a further life of 9 years and are redeemable at par. The fixed interest 16% bank loan is guaranteed by the bank to be available for a further 9 years. Both the debentures and the bank loan were initially arranged several years ago when interest rates were high. Interest rates have since fallen.

The money raised by the rights issue will be used to:

(i) fund a new contract to which Harris is already committed and which requires an initial outlay of £1 million. The contract has a profitability index (present value of future net cash inflows ÷ present value of initial capital outlay) of 1.4, and full details of the contract have been public knowledge for several months; *and*

(ii) reduce borrowings by buying back, at current market value, and cancelling the £10 million debenture issue. The debentures are priced to yield 8% per annum, the current market rate for corporate debt, over the remaining 9 year life.

Total finance required in (i) and (ii) will be rounded up to the next whole £100 000 for the purpose of the rights issue. The excess funds raised will be used to reduce short term borrowings and overdrafts.

The company intends to announce full details of the rights issue on 1 July when the market price per share prior to the announcement is expected to be £5. The company is confident that the whole issue will be purchased but the Managing Director is concerned that the discount at which the issue is made may raise the cost of equity capital and hence the weighted average cost of capital.

Required:

(a) Calculate
   (i) the issue price per share;
   (ii) the theoretical ex rights price per share;
   (iii) the value of the right attached to each Harris share before being traded ex rights.

(b) Briefly explain whether the concern of the Managing Director is justified.

(c) Discuss whether this rights issue could be expected to alter the cost of equity and/or the weighted average cost of capital *in any way*.

(d) After setting the issue price (calculated in (a) above) but before announcing the rights issue, Harris decides to reduce borrowings by redeeming the 16% bank loan at its face value of £10 million rather than buying back the debentures at market value. The possibility of the redemption at face value is now known only to the company and its bankers but will become public knowledge when the rights issue is announced on 1 July. The market had expected the bank loan to run for its full remaining 9 years of life.

The excess cash generated by the rights issue, after reducing borrowings and funding the £1 million contract, will be invested in a project which has a profitability index of 1.2. The market is not aware of this project and will remain unaware until its details become public knowledge when the rights issue is announced.

Calculate:

(i) the share price on 1 July immediately after the announcement of the rights issue but before the shares are traded ex rights;

(ii) the theoretical ex rights price per share.

Briefly explain your calculations and also explain whether they assume that the market is displaying the weak, semi-strong or strong level of market efficiency.

(ACCA)

QUESTIONS FOR CLASS USE

1 Hesi Engineering Ltd produces and sells a pocket tape recorder which has been designed for business users. The company has been in operation for four years and has an issued share capital of 800 000 £1 ordinary shares. To date the company has produced only one product. For the year ended 31 May 19X1 the company sold 60 000 tape recorders to large retail outlets at a price of £30 per recorder.

The profit and loss account for the year to 31 May 19X1 is as follows:

	£000	£000
Sales		1800
Less:		
Variable expenses	720	
Fixed expenses	360	1080
Net profit before interest and taxation		720
Less interest payable		190
Net profit before taxation		530
Less corporation tax (at 35%)		186
Net profit after taxation		344
Dividend paid		160
Retained profit for the year		184

In recent months the company has been experiencing labour problems and, as a result, has decided to introduce a new highly automated production process in order to improve efficiency. The new production process is estimated to increase fixed costs by £120 000 (including depreciation) but will reduce variable costs by £7 per unit.

The new production process will be financed by the issue of £2 000 000 debentures at an interest rate of 12.5%. If the new production process is introduced immediately the directors believe that sales for the forthcoming year will be the same as for the year ended 31 May 19X1. Stocks will remain at the current level throughout the forthcoming year.

Required:

(a) Calculate the change in earnings per share if the company introduces the new production process immediately.

(b) Explain what is meant by the terms 'operating gearing' and 'financial gearing'. Why is it important for the directors of a company to consider the levels of operating and financial gearing?

(Certified Diploma – part of question)

2* The directors of Adsum Ltd are working on a three-year financial plan. Sales during the period will depend upon the state of the economy.

		Sales (£000 in current prices)		
Economic state:	Probability	Year 1	Year 2	Year 3
Slow growth	0.6	5300	5500	5800
Rapid growth	0.4	6000	7100	8200

If slow growth occurs inflation is expected to be 12% per year and if rapid growth occurs 5% per year. Return on sales (profit before tax to sales) is estimated to be 12% per year in both economic states.

In year 1 assets to the value of £200 000 (after all tax effects) will be disposed of, and in years 2 and 3 new fixed assets costing £1.7 million and £800 000 respectively will be purchased. Disposal and purchase values have been estimated at current prices.

Stock is expected to increase by 80% of the percentage increase in sales, debtors by 90% and creditors by 95%. For example, if sales in year 1 increase by 16% from current financial accounts values, stock at the end of year 1 is expected to increase by 16% x 80% = 12.8% of the current balance sheet value. Sales prices and dividends will be increased in line with inflation, except if this would lead to dividends being less than 22% or greater than 35% of before tax profits, in which case a minimum of 22% or a maximum of 35% respectively would be payable.

Corporate tax is at the rate of 35% and is payable at the end of the year in which profit arises. Capital allowances are expected to be £450 000, £530 000 and £620 000 for years 1, 2 and 3 respectively.

Adsum is not planning to raise external funds by equity or long-term debt issues. A £600 000 overdraft facility exists, which is expected to be available for the three year period, but cannot be increased due to the company's level of gearing.

Summarised current financial accounts of Adsum are shown below:

Balance sheet

	£000
Fixed assets	4400
Stock	2130
Debtors	2920
Cash	80
	9530
Creditors	(3210)
Overdraft	(420)
	5900
Financed by:	
Ordinary shares (25 pence par)	500
Reserves	2400
12% seven-year term loan	3000
	5900

Profit and loss account

	£000
Sales	5000
Profit before tax	600
Tax	210
	390
Dividend	150
Retained earnings	240

Required:

(a) Acting as a consultant to Adsum Limited advise the company on the financial implications of its forecasts as presented. Relevant calculations must be shown. Interest on cash balances or on additional overdraft may be ignored. State clearly any assumptions that you make.

(b) Discuss possible remedies for any problems that you identify.

(c) Advise Adsum Limited on other techniques that might be useful in the company's medium-term financial planning process and comment upon the assumptions that Adsum has used in its plans.

(ACCA)

3(a) Berlan plc has annual earnings before interest and tax of £15 million. These earnings are expected to remain constant. The market price of the company's ordinary shares is 86 pence per share cum. div. and of debentures £105.50 per debenture ex. interest. An interim dividend of six pence per share has been declared. Corporate tax is at the rate of 35% and all available earnings are distributed as dividends.

Berlan's long-term, capital structure is shown below:

	£000
Ordinary shares (25 pence par value)	12 500
Reserves	24 300
	36 800
16% debenture 31.12.X4 (£100 par value)	23 697
	60 497

Required:

Calculate the cost of capital of Berlan plc according to the traditional theory of capital structure. Assume that it is now 31 December 19X1.

(b) Canalot plc is an all equity company with an equilibrium market value of £32.5 million and a cost of capital of 18% per year.

The company proposes to repurchase £5 million of equity and to replace it with 13% irredeemable loan stock.

Canalot's earnings before interest and tax are expected to be constant for the foreseeable future. Corporate tax is at the rate of 35%. All profits are paid out as dividends.

Required:

Using the assumptions of Modigliani and Miller explain and demonstrate how this change in capital structure will affect:
- the market value
- the cost of equity
- the cost of capital
of Canalot plc.

(c) Explain any weaknesses of both the traditional and Modigliani and Miller theories and discuss how useful they might be in the determination of the appropriate capital structure for a company.

(ACCA)

APPENDIX I – PROOF OF THE MM COST OF CAPITAL PROPOSITION (PRE-TAX)

The following symbols will be used.

$V_U = S_U$ = market value of the ungeared (all equity) firm
S_G = market value of the equity of the geared firm
L_G = market value of the loan capital of the geared firm
$V_G = S_G + L_G$ = market value of the geared firm
i = interest rate
X = net operating income of both firms
α = the proportion of either firm's securities owned by an individual

Suppose that an individual owns proportion α of the shares of the ungeared firm. This is an investment valued at αV_U (or αS_U) which will produce income of αX.

The same income could be obtained (with, according to our assumption, the same risk) by buying proportion α of both the equity and loan stock of the geared firm:

	Investment required	Income produced
Buy proportion α of geared firm's equity	$\alpha S_G = \alpha(V_G - L_G)$	$\alpha(X - iL_G)$
Buy proportion α of geared firm's loan stock	αL_G	$\alpha i L_G$
Total	αV_G	αX

If $V_U > V_G$, the investor would sell the equity shares in the ungeared firm and buy equity shares and loan stock. Thus the investor would end up with the same income and make a profit on the difference between the price at which the equity shares of the ungeared firm could be sold and what would have to be paid to buy the equity shares and loan stock of the geared firm.

Such action by our investor (and by others similarly placed) will have the effect of reducing the value of the ungeared firm's equity and increasing that of the geared firm's securities. This would occur until the value of the two firms was equal. Efficient capital market research suggests that such a process would not take long.

The commodity which is being traded here (as far as our individual is concerned) is annual income of amount αX. MM argued that it would be irrational for this to be priced differently merely because it is not packaged in the same way. They contended that the packaging of the income is irrelevant since the individual investor can repackage it personally without (according to MM's assumption on frictionless capital markets) any personal cost.

MM also tackled the proof from the other starting point.

Suppose that an individual owns proportion α of the equity shares of a geared firm. This would have a market value of αS_G (or $\alpha(V_G - L_G)$, since $V_G = S_G + L_G$) and produce annual income $\alpha(X - iL_G)$.

In order to get the same income the individual could buy proportion α of the ungeared firm's equity and finance it partly by personal borrowing:

	Investment required	Income produced
Buy proportion α of ungeared firm's shares	$\alpha S_U = \alpha V_U$	αX
Borrow (personally) an amount equal to αL_G	$- \alpha L_G$	$- \alpha i L_G$
Total	$\alpha(V_U - L_G)$	$\alpha(X - iL_G)$

Thus by investing $\alpha(V_U - L_G)$ the investor can get the same income as had been obtained from an investment valued at $\alpha(V_G - L_G)$. If the market value of the geared firm (V_G) is greater than that of the ungeared one (V_U) it will benefit our investor to sell the equity stake in the geared firm and then go in for some 'personal' gearing.

Once again the action of investors in selling the geared firm's equity and buying that of the ungeared firm would, by the laws of supply and demand, quickly drive the two market values (V_U and V_G) back into equality.

The assumptions on which the above analysis is based are stated and discussed in the chapter.

APPENDIX II – PROOF OF THE MM COST OF CAPITAL PROPOSITION (POST-TAX)

It is proved below that

$$V_G = V_U + TL_G*$$

Suppose that an individual owns proportion α of the shares of an ungeared firm. This would be an investment valued at $\alpha(V_U)$ (or αS_U) which will produce income $\alpha X(1 - T)$, i.e. proportion α of the after-tax income of the firm.

The same income could be obtained by buying proportion α of the equity and proportion $\alpha(1 - T)$ of the loan stock of the geared firm:

	Investment required	Income produced
Buy proportion α of geared firm's equity	$\alpha S_G = \alpha(V_G - L_G)$	$\alpha(X - iL_G)(1 - T)$
Buy proportion $\alpha(1 - T)$ of the geared firm's loan stock	$\alpha L_G(1 - T)$	$\alpha i L_G(1 - T)$
Total	$\alpha(V_G - TL_G)$	$\alpha X(1 - T)$

If $\alpha(V_G - TL_G) < \alpha V_U$, i.e. if $V_G < V_U + TL_G$, it means that the investor could retain the same income ($\alpha X(1 - T)$) by selling the ungeared equities and replacing them with the cheaper geared firm's shares and loan stocks. The action of investors making this switch will tend to cause $V_G = V_U + TL_G$.

Tackling the proof from the other starting point, suppose that an investor holds proportion α in the equity of a geared firm. This would give an income of $\alpha(X - iL_G)(1 - T)$. (This is because the loan interest (iL_G) is tax deductible.) The investor could obtain the same income from selling these shares and buying proportion α of the shares of the ungeared firm and by borrowing amount $\alpha(1 - T)L_G$ to help finance the purchase of the shares.

	Investment required	Income produced
Buy proportion α of the ungeared firm's shares	$\alpha S_U = \alpha V_U$	$\alpha X(1 - T)$
Borrow (personally) $\alpha(1 - T)L_G$	$-\alpha(1 - T)L_G$	$-\alpha(1 - T)iL_G$
Total	$\alpha[V_U - (1 - T)L_G]$	$\alpha(X - iL_G)(1 - T)$

If $\alpha[V_U - (1 - T)L_G] < \alpha S_G$, then $V_U < S_G + L_G(1 - T)$, which would encourage holders of the geared firm's equity to switch to the ungeared firm's equity (with personal borrowing) since they could continue with the same income but make capital gains on the switch. Such switching would cause:

$$V_U = S_G + L_G(1 - T)$$

Therefore this equality must hold.

*Note that $\displaystyle\sum_{n=0}^{\infty} \frac{iTL_G}{(1 + i)^n} = TL_G$

i.e. the present value of the tax saving on loan interest (iTL_G) is TL_G.

CHAPTER 12

The dividend decision

OBJECTIVES

In this chapter we shall deal with the following:

- the nature of dividends
- the theoretical position of dividends as residuals
- the Miller/Modigliani view that the pattern of dividends is irrelevant to the value of shares (and WACC)
- the traditional view on dividends
- the evidence on dividends

INTRODUCTION

Dividends are payments made by firms to their shareholders. They tend to be viewed both by the firm's management and by the recipient shareholders as the equivalent of an interest payment to a loan creditor, a compensation for the shareholders' delaying consumption, etc. Dividends are also seen as a distribution of the firm's recent profits to its owners, the shareholders.

A share, like any other economic asset (i.e. an asset whose value is not wholly or partly derived from sentiment or emotion), is valued on the basis of future cash flows expected to derive from it. Unless a takeover or liquidation is seen as a possibility, the only possible cash flows likely to derive from a share are dividends. So it would seem that anticipated dividends are usually the only determinant of share prices and hence of the cost of equity capital.

It would appear then that management would best promote the shareholders' welfare by paying as large a dividend as the law will allow in any particular circumstances.

This attitude begs several questions, however. What if the firm sees advantageous investment opportunities; would it be beneficial to shareholders for the firm to fail to pay a dividend in order to keep sufficient finance available with which to make the investment? Alternatively, should the firm pay a dividend and raise the necessary finance for the investment opportunity by issuing additional shares to the investing public, perhaps including any of the existing shareholders who wish to be involved?

Even where the firm's management cannot see any particularly advantageous investment opportunities, should it err on the side of caution and pay less than the full amount of dividend which the law allows?

Just what should the firm's dividend policy be, and does it really matter anyway? We shall consider these questions during this chapter.

MILLER AND MODIGLIANI ON DIVIDENDS

In 1961 MM published another important article, this time dealing with dividends and their effect on shareholders' wealth. Their theme further developed the principle, Fisher separation, which we discussed in Chapter 2. In that chapter we looked at a very simple example, which suggested that firms' managers need not concern themselves with the payment of dividends. Provided that the firm takes on all available investment projects which have positive NPVs, when discounted at the borrowing/lending rate, shareholders' wealth will be maximised. Individual shareholders can, by borrowing or lending, achieve the pattern of receipts which maximises their personal utility of wealth.

MM took this slightly further by asserting that the value of a share in a firm will be unaffected by the pattern of dividends expected from it. If shareholders want dividends they can create them by selling part of their shareholding. If dividends are paid to shareholders who do not want to spend the money, they can cancel these dividends by using the cash received to buy additional shares in the firm, in the capital market.

Let us use an example to illustrate the MM proposition.

EXAMPLE

White plc has net assets whose net present value is £5.0m. This includes cash of £1.0m which the firm has identified could be invested in a project whose anticipated inflows have a present value of £2.0m. Assuming that the firm is financed by 1m ordinary shares (no gearing) and that the investment is undertaken and no dividend paid, the value of each share should be £(5 + 2 − 1)m/1m = £6. If instead of making the investment the £1.0m cash were used to pay a dividend, each share would be worth £(5 − 1)m/1m = £4 and the holder of one share would have £1 (the dividend) in cash.

Clearly it would be to the shareholder's advantage for the firm to make the investment and so it should be made. If White plc wants both to pay the dividend (using up all available cash) and to make the investment, it would need to raise new finance. Assuming that it wished to retain its all-equity status it would need to issue new shares to the value of the dividend. Since the value of the firm after paying the dividend and making the investment would be £5m, this engenders an issue price of the new shares of £5 each (200 000 of them to make up the £1m required).

It also means that the original shareholders would gain £1 per share by way of dividend and lose £1 per share as each share would have a value of £5 instead of the £6 which would apply if no dividend were paid. In other words, the dividend would make no difference to the wealth of the shareholders.

Note that, provided the new investment is undertaken, the worth of the original shares would be £6 each. This value is in some combination of share price and dividend. Irrespective of the amount of dividend paid by the firm, the individual shareholder can choose how much dividend to take. Suppose that no dividend is paid on the White plc shares, but a particular shareholder owning 100 of the shares wants cash of, say, £60? The shareholder can create a 'homemade' dividend by selling 10 shares (at £6 each, their current value).

Conversely, assuming that the firm pays a dividend of £1 per share (and creates an additional 200 000 shares to finance it), shareholders who do not want a dividend but prefer to keep their investment intact could negate the effect of the dividend payment by using the whole of the dividend receipt in buying new shares. Let us again consider the holder of 100 shares who receives £100 by way of dividend. This cash could be used to buy 20 new shares (at £5 each) increasing the investment to 120 shares in total. These will be worth £600, the same as the 100 shares would have been worth had no dividend been paid. Using the whole of the dividend to buy new shares will ensure that our shareholder retains the same proportion of the ownership (120 of the 1.2m) as was held before the dividend and the new issue (100 of the 1.0m shares).

This example illustrates MM's central point, which is that it would be illogical for the capital market to attach different values to otherwise identical firms, merely because their dividend policies were different. If it is costlessly possible for individual investors to adjust the firm's dividend policy to meet their own preferences it is not logical that investors would be prepared to pay more for the shares of a firm merely because the firm's dividend policy happens to match these preferences.

MM's assertion does of course rely on several assumptions of dubious validity in the real world. We shall consider the limitations of these assumptions later in the chapter.

A formal derivation of the MM proposition is contained in the Appendix to this chapter.

What MM really said

Before we go on to assess what MM said about dividends against the traditional view and against the evidence of what actually seems to happen in real life, it might be worth clarifying exactly what they really said.

What they did *not* say is that it does not matter whether dividends are paid or not as far as the value of the firm is concerned. If shareholders are never to receive a dividend or any other cash payment in respect of their shares, the value of those shares must be zero. What MM did say is that the pattern of dividends is irrelevant to valuation. Provided that the firm invests in real assets up to the point where all projects have a positive NPV when discounted at the firm's cost of capital, and provided that eventually all of the fruits of the investment are paid in cash to shareholders, it does not matter when payment is made. 'Eventually' may be a very long time, but this in principle does not matter. Even if no cash is expected to be forthcoming until the firm is liquidated this should not of itself cause the shares to be less valuable than were there to be a regular dividend until that time. Thus MM do not cast doubt on the validity of the dividend model for valuing equities, which we discussed in Chapter 10 (page 249).

In principle, the timing of a particular dividend does not matter to the shareholder, provided that the later dividend is $(1+r)^n$ times the earlier alternative, where r is the shareholder's expected return and n is the time lapse between the earlier and later dividends.

Suppose that a firm could pay a dividend now of amount D. Alternatively the firm could invest the amount D now in a project which will produce one cash inflow after n years which will be paid as a dividend at that time. The shareholders would be indifferent as to whether the dividend is paid now or in n years, provided that the later dividend is $D(1+r)^n$. This is because $D(1+r)^n$ has the present value D (i.e. $D(1+r)^n/(1+r)^n$). Thus dividend D now, or $D(1+r)^n$ in n years, should have equal effect on the value of the shares.

If the firm were able to invest in a project which yields an inflow of amount greater than $D(1+r)^n$ (i.e. a project with a positive NPV), this would enhance the value of the shares.

Of course, as MM pointed out, it is always open to individual shareholders to create dividends by selling part of their shareholding if the delay in the dividend does not suit their personal spending plans.

THE TRADITIONAL VIEW ON DIVIDENDS

Before MM made their assertion and presented a plausible proof of it, the view had been taken not only that dividends are the paramount determinant of share values but that £1 in cash is worth more than £1 of investment.

Going back to the White plc example (page 296), the traditionalists would value the shares differently dependent on whether a dividend were to be paid or not. Greater value would be placed on the situation where a dividend was to be paid (and a share issue undertaken) than where this was not the case. This is a view based on a 'bird in hand is worth two in the bush' approach, i.e. the notion that a certain receipt enhances the value of the asset from which it derives. So in the White plc example, if the shares are priced at £6 before a £1 per share dividend, the price of the share will not fall to £5 ex-dividend, but perhaps to £5.50. Thus the wealth of a shareholder will be enhanced by £0.50 per share as a result of the dividend.

The traditional view implies that the payment of actual dividends reduces the capital market's perceptions of the level of risk attaching to future dividends. This means that the discount rate to be applied to expected future dividends will be lower and the market price will be enhanced.

ARE MM RIGHT ABOUT DIVIDENDS?

The traditional view on dividends seems to suffer from a fundamental lack of logic. The only circumstances where shareholders should logically value £1 in cash more highly than £1 in investment, is where they feel that the firm is using retained cash to make disadvantageous investments (i.e. those which have negative NPVs when discounted at a rate which takes account of the level of risk attaching to the particular project). Since ultimately the shareholders must receive all of the fruits of the firm's investments, provided firms only invest in projects with positive NPVs then investment is to be preferred to present dividends.

MM seem to have logic on their side, yet firms appear to behave as if the pattern of dividends does matter. Financial managers seem to devote quite a lot of thought to fixing the levels of dividends. Most firms seem to maintain pretty stable levels of dividends, implying that they set aside a similar amount for dividends each year. Yet it would be a remarkable coincidence if each year there were a similar amount of cash for which profitable investment opportunities could not be found.

MM's assertion that the pattern of dividends does not matter is based, as we have seen, on several assumptions. The extent to which these weaken their analysis might explain why the logic of the MM proposition does not seem to be accepted in practice. We shall now review these assumptions.

(a) *There are frictionless capital markets, which implies that there are no transactions costs nor any other impediments to investors behaving in practice as they might be expected to do in theory.* Obviously this is invalid and probably sufficiently so to call the MM view into question. MM rely on the ability of individual shareholders to sell their shares to create dividends or to buy shares to eliminate dividends. The fact that dealing in the capital market involves real and significant cost (agents' fees, etc.) means, for example, that receiving a dividend and liquidating part of an investment in a particular share are not perfect substitutes for one another.

(b) *Securities are efficiently priced in the capital market.* The evidence (reviewed in Chapter 9) tends to support the validity of this assumption. The assumption is necessary, otherwise (in the above example) White plc undertaking the investment will not necessarily increase the share price by £1, nor the payment of the dividend necessarily reduce the share price by £1.

(c) *Shares may be issued by firms without any legal or administrative costs being incurred.* This assumption is not valid, and probably significantly so in the present context. MM see paying no dividend on the one hand, and paying a dividend and raising an equal amount by share issue on the other hand, as equivalent. This will not be true in practice; issuing new shares tends to involve the firm in fairly large legal and administrative costs (see Chapter 8). It seems likely that this is an important factor in making decisions on dividend payment levels.

(d) *Taxes, corporate and personal, do not exist.* Certainly this is untrue, but is it important? From the firm's point of view, its Corporation Tax liability is not dependent on the level of dividends provided that they are met from current taxable profit, which will usually be the case. There is a tax cash flow timing disadvantage to paying dividends due to the incidence of ACT (see Chapter 8) but this is probably not very significant.

On the personal tax front the main question is whether it is more *tax efficient* to receive dividends or to make capital gains. The answer depends on the individual's level of income and capital gains for the year concerned. If both of these are modest then neither dividend nor capital gains will attract tax, at least no more than will already have been paid by the firm. For shareholders whose income and capital gains are less modest, personal Income Tax and Capital Gains Tax become significant. To the extent that it is possible to generalise, it is probably true to say that for individuals with high levels of dividends and capital gains, further dividends are probably taxed more penally than are further capital gains.

A feature of the UK investment scene is the increasing tendency for equities to be owned by the investing institutions. Many of these, for example pension funds and life assurance funds, are exempt from taxes both on income and on capital gains. As a result they are able to reclaim some of the Corporation Tax paid by the firm whose dividends they receive. For such investors, dividends are more tax efficient than are capital gains. The situation is complicated still further by the fact that the firm's Corporation Tax liability will, to a large extent, depend on what it does with any funds which it retains. From the firm's point of view, some investments in real assets are more tax efficient than are others, e.g. an investment in a factory attracts tax relief, an investment in an office block does not.

MM's 'no tax' assumption is perhaps not significant provided that firms show some consistency in their dividend policy, a point to which we shall shortly return.

The deficiencies of the individual assumptions do not seem sufficiently profound to destroy the MM case. Clearly the existence of non-trivial dealing and share issue costs must weaken it, but there seems no reason why MM's analysis should not reasonably represent the true position – not, at least, as far as their analysis goes.

OTHER FACTORS

There are some other factors which might bear on the position and explain why firms do seem to regard the dividend decision as an important one.

Informational content of dividends

The view is held by some that the level of dividends, perhaps more particularly changes in the level of dividends paid by a firm, conveys new information to the world. For example, an increased level of dividend might be (and seems often to be interpreted as) a signal that the firm's management views the future with confidence.*

Assuming this view to be correct, whether such a signal is meant as one or is inadvertent probably varies from case to case. Certainly a typical tactic of an unwilling target firm's management in a merger battle is to increase its dividend level; perhaps this is a deliberate signal to inspire the shareholders' confidence in the firm's future.

If dividend increases are meant to act as signals, it seems reasonable to ask why management does not simply issue a statement. Surely a statement would be much less ambiguous than an increased dividend. Perhaps managements feel that actions speak louder than words.

---

*This contrasts strikingly with the conclusion that might be reached by following MM's analysis. Paying any dividend, let alone one which showed an increase over the previous year, might well indicate that the firm's management cannot find sufficient investment opportunities to use all the finance available to it, so it is returning some to shareholders. This would not suggest too much confidence in the future on the part of management.

Incidentally if the signalling view of dividends is correct, it would be expected that an increased dividend would have a favourable effect on the share price in the capital market. Such a phenomenon would represent a further piece of evidence that the capital market is not efficient in the strong form (see Chapter 9), because it implies that information available to firms' managers may not be impounded in the share price.

Clientele effect

It is widely believed that investors have a *preferred habitat*, i.e. a type of investment which they feel best suits them. In the context of dividends, their preference might well be dictated by their personal tax position. A person with a high marginal Income Tax rate might well be attracted to shares of firms where dividend payouts are low. On the other hand an investor such as a pension fund which is tax exempt, but which needs regular cash receipts in order to be able to meet payments to pensioners, might go for shares in firms whose dividend payments are relatively high. Such an investor could, of course, generate cash by selling shares, but this would involve brokers' fees etc. which obviously are best avoided.

If there really is a clientele effect it means that at least a proportion of any firm's shareholders acquired that firm's shares, because they are suited by the firm's dividend policy. If the firm is inconsistent in its policy on dividends, many investors would be put off the shares as they would not know whether the levels of dividends would suit their preferences or not. The lack of popularity of the shares would have an adverse effect on the share price and therefore on the cost of capital. Even if a particular firm were to be fairly consistent in its dividend policy but then undertook a major change, those of its investors who particularly liked the previous dividend policy (perhaps this might be all of the shareholders) would probably seek to move to the shares of a firm with a dividend policy more acceptable to them. While it might well be the case that a new *clientele* would find the dividend policy attractive, the friction caused by one set of investors selling to a new set of investors would have a net adverse effect on the shareholders. Not only this, but the uncertainty in the minds of investors which the change may precipitate as to how consistent the firm was likely to be in future could also have a dampening effect on the share price.

Liquidity

It has been suggested that the level of dividends paid by a particular firm, at a particular time, is largely dictated by the amount of cash available. Certainly this is what MM suggest should be the case. On the other hand, if failure to pay a dividend is interpreted adversely by the capital market, the best interests of shareholders' wealth might be advanced by making sure that cash is available, perhaps by borrowing or even, by passing up otherwise beneficial investment opportunities.

DIVIDENDS: THE EVIDENCE

Stability of dividend policy

The evidence of casual observation is that financial managers treat the dividend decision as an important one. It also seems that firms try to maintain dividends at previous levels, reductions in dividends seem relatively rare occurrences.

These impressions are supported by some findings of Lintner (1956) arising from interviews with financial managers of 28 selected firms. He found evidence that firms are reluctant to change dividend levels, particularly to reduce them or to increase them to a level which cannot be sustained in the longer term.

Fama and Babiak (1968) analysed relevant data from 201 firms over a 19-year span and came to conclusions which broadly supported Lintner's findings.

Effect of dividends on share price

Friend and Puckett (1964) tested the relationship between share prices and dividend policy. Whilst they experienced some methodological problems they found no close correlation between dividends and share prices.

Black and Scholes (1974) undertook a similar study to that of Friend and Puckett but overcame some of the problems encountered. They too found no evidence that higher or lower dividend levels lead to higher or lower returns either before or after taxes.

A number of subsequent tests, conducted both on UK and US data, has failed to show a clear relationship between dividends and share prices.

Informational content of dividends

Pettit (1972) found clear support for the proposition that the capital market takes account of dividend announcements as information for assessing share prices.

This finding has fairly consistently been supported by subsequent studies, for example, Aharoney and Swary (1980). The evidence on the informational effect of dividends seems fairly conclusive.

Clientele effect

Elton and Gruber (1970) conducted a rather interesting study to test for the *clientele effect*. By looking at the fall in share price when a dividend is paid they were able to infer an average marginal Income Tax rate for any particular firm's shareholders. They found that the lower Income Tax rates were associated with high dividend shares and higher Income Tax rates with low dividend shares, i.e. they found a clientele effect.

Pettit (1977) gained access to information on the security portfolios of a large number of clients of a large US stockbroker. He found that low levels of dividends seemed to be preferred by investors with relatively high marginal Income Tax rates, by younger investors and by those who were less than averagely risk-averse (high β share owners).

However Lewellen, Stanley, Lease and Schlarmbaum (1978), using the same data but a different approach to that taken by Pettit reached the dissimilar conclusion that there is only a very weak clientele effect. Litzenburger and Ramaswamy (1982) undertook a study which produced results which seemed to support the clientele effect. Crossland, Dempsey and Moizer (1991), using UK data, also found clear evidence of a significant clientele effect. The various studies on the clientele effect broadly seem to support its existence.

CONCLUSIONS ON DIVIDENDS

As with capital gearing, we do not know whether the traditionalists or MM are correct in their assertions. We do, however, have a certain amount of empirical evidence on the subject and so we might be able to reconcile the two views.

MM's assertion that patterns of dividends are irrelevant has some credibility. The assumptions are not entirely convincing but they do not seem sufficiently wide of the mark totally to invalidate the irrelevancy assertion. Importantly the evidence seems to support the MM view in that valuation seems not to be closely related to levels of dividends.

From the evidence there does seem to be a clientele effect in that the dividend policy associated with particular shares appears to attract an identifiable group of investors. Recognition of the clientele effect by managers could well explain their reluctance to alter dividend payment levels.

Perhaps we can conclude that MM are broadly correct that dividends do not affect values provided that investors know the dividend policy of the firm. Probably the most effective way of informing investors of the firm's policy is to establish a fairly constant pattern and to stick to it. Failure to show consistency is likely to lead to uncertainty for investors and to the necessity for shareholders to leave one *habitat* in favour of another, more preferred one. In either case the effect of changes in dividend policy seems likely to lead to lower share prices and higher costs of capital. This implies that liquidity may not be a particularly important factor in the dividend decision, that firms will make sure that sufficient cash is available for the dividend, one way or another.

SUMMARY Dividends are payments made by firms to their shareholders. They are often portrayed as rewards to shareholders in terms of distributions of the previous or current year's profit and as a vital determinant of share prices. First principles suggest that this view is illogical as failure to pay dividends simply means that the wealth of individual shareholders will be more in the value of their shares and less in cash.

MM, depending on several simplifying assumptions, showed that the pattern of dividends is irrelevant to shareholders' wealth. Since it is open to firms to pay very large proportions of their profits as dividends and then to raise such finance as they need for investment purposes from new share issues, it would be illogical if managements could manipulate things and as a result increase the wealth of the shareholders.

The evidence on dividends tends to suggest that MM are broadly right. There does however appear to be a clientele effect which means that investors with particular dividend preferences are attracted to shares whose dividend record matches those preferences. Firms can probably best serve their shareholders by establishing a dividend policy and sticking to it as closely as possible.

FURTHER READING	Most business finance texts deal with the question of dividends and dividend policy. Brealey and Myers (1991) and Puxty and Dodds (1991) each contain interesting sections on it. Copeland and Weston (1988) discuss this topic, particularly the empirical evidence giving more detail of some of the particular studies mentioned in this chapter.

WORK-BASED ASSIGNMENT	What factors seem to affect the level of your organisation's dividend payments? Does senior management seem to believe that dividend levels affect share prices?

QUESTIONS WITH ANSWERS (see Appendix 3)

1 Feret Ltd has ten million shares at issue and has been paying dividends of 10p per share for a number of years and with its existing business is expected to be able to continue to earn sufficient profits to enable it to pay such a dividend for the foreseeable future. The company has been offered a new contract which would take two years to complete and would involve Feret in an investment outlay of £500 000 in each of the next two years. The board plan to finance the investment by a reduction of dividend.

If the project is undertaken, when it is completed it will increase the earnings of the company above their expected level by £350 000 per annum for the foreseeable future.

The current market price of an equity share of Feret Ltd is £0.90. The yield on company debentures is 10 per cent. The management of Feret believes that the market value of shares in the company is based on dividends. Taxation can be ignored.

Required:

(a) Would an announcement of a decision to reduce dividends with an explanation of why this was being done and with details of the proposed investment, lead to an increase or decrease in the current share price? Show calculations to justify your conclusion.

(b) Is it possible for an investor owning 100 shares in Feret Ltd who is dependent on the annual income from investments to increase his spending power during the next two years while still being able to maintain his spending potential in subsequent years? Illustrate your answer with appropriate figures.

(Certified Diploma)

2 Your board is considering its dividend policy.

Required:

(a) List and discuss the factors which would influence the amount of dividend paid by a medium-sized manufacturing firm.

(b) You have heard some academics claiming that at least in theory dividends don't count. Comment briefly on the truth of this statement in the real world.

(Certified Diploma)

3 The board of directors of Amalgamated Engineering plc, a company listed on the Stock Exchange, is due to meet soon to determine the level of final dividend to be paid to equity shareholders in respect of the financial year which has recently ended. Some directors, however, would prefer to withhold a final dividend payment and to use the available funds to re-purchase a proportion of the equity shares in the company. They believe this would represent a more attractive alternative to a final dividend.

Required:

(a) Discuss the advantages and disadvantages of share re-purchase as an alternative to dividends from the equity shareholders' viewpoint.

(b) Assuming the board of directors decide to pay a final dividend, what factors should be taken into account when determining the level of dividend payment?

(Certified Diploma)

QUESTION FOR CLASS USE

1 Some authorities have argued that dividend payments are irrelevant and have no value to shareholders.

Required:

(a) Explain the argument used to justify this statement. What are its shortcomings in the real world?

(b) Discuss the factors the directors of a medium-sized company, whose shares are listed on a stock exchange, should take into account when deciding on the amount of dividend to be paid.

(Certified Diploma)

APPENDIX – PROOF OF THE MM DIVIDEND IRRELEVANCY PROPOSITION

In the proof of their assertion MM considered firm j during a time period which starts at time t and ends at $t + 1$.

They used the following symbols:

D_{jt} is the total dividend paid during the period starting at time t.

d_{jt} is the dividend per share paid during that period.

P_{jt} is the price per share at time t.

r_t is the return per share during the period starting at time t.

n_t is the number of shares of the firm at time t.

m_t is the number of new shares issued during the period starting at time t.

V_{jt} is the value of the firm at time t (i.e. $V_{jt} = n_t \times P_{jt}$)

$$r_t = \frac{d_{jt} + P_{j(t + 1)} - P_{jt}}{P_{jt}} \qquad (1)$$

the return per share during the period is the dividend paid during it *plus* the increase in price per share $(P_{j(t + 1)} - P_{jt})$ expressed as a fraction of the price at the start of the period.

Rearranging (1) gives:

$$P_{jt} = \frac{d_{jt} + P_{j(t + 1)}}{1 + r_t} \qquad (2)$$

i.e. the price per share is the discounted value of the dividend for the period plus the price per share at the end of the period.

Market forces will tend to ensure that equations (1) and (2) hold to the extent that the current price P_{jt} will be such to cause r_t to be similar to that of other shares of similar risk to those of firm j.

$$n_{(t + 1)} - n_t = m_{(t + 1)} \qquad (3)$$

i.e. the difference between the number of shares at the start and end of the period is accounted for by those issued (or withdrawn) during the period

$$V_{jt} = \frac{D_{jt} + n_t P_{j(t + 1)}}{1 + r_t} \qquad (4)$$

From equation (2), the value of the whole firm is the discounted value of the total dividend payable during the period plus the value of the firm at the end of the period.

Expressed alternatively:

$$V_{jt} = \frac{D_{jt} + V_{(t + 1)} - m_t P_{(t + 1)}}{1 + r_t} \qquad (5)$$

i.e. the value of the firm at the start of the period is the discounted value of the dividend for the period plus the value of the firm at the end of the period less the value of any share capital raised during the period. This is because:

$$V_{(t + 1)} = n_t P_{(t + 1)} + m_t P_{(t + 1)} \qquad (6)$$

From equation (5) we can see that the value of the firm at time t is dependent upon anticipated dividends, the value of the firm at the end of the period and the value of any new shares issued. However, the quantity of new shares which it is necessary to issue is, in turn, dependent on the size of dividends paid.

$$m_t P_{(t+1)} = I_t - (X_t - D_t) \tag{7}$$

where I_t is the real investment and X_t the operating cash flow surplus during the period.

That is to say that the value of the finance which must be raised from new share issues is the excess of the funds invested over the operating cash flow surplus after dividends have been paid. In other words the value of the new issues depends on the extent to which new investment exceeds retained profit.

Substituting equation (7) into equation (5) for $m_t P_{(t+1)}$ gives:

$$V_t = \frac{D_t + V_{(t+1)} - I_t + X_t - D_t}{1 + r_t}$$

The D_t terms cancel each other out to give:

$$V_t = \frac{V_{(t+1)} - I_t + X_t}{1 + r_t}$$

Thus V_t is independent of the amount of dividend paid during the forthcoming period, but depends on the anticipated value of the firm at the end of the period, the anticipated level of investment and cash flow surplus.

Dividends can be at any level. Any cash deficiency caused by dividends being paid in excess of operating cash flows can be made up through capital issues of new equity.

The assumptions made and their validity are discussed in the chapter.

PART 4

Mixed decisions

There are some areas of business finance which do not fall distinctly into either invest-ment or financing decisions, but involve some combination of both. These areas are discussed in this part of the book. Working capital, the subject of Chapter 13, is such an area. Working capital consists of the firm's short-term assets and liabilities. Since these are in a constant state of change, as the firm carries out its normal activities, decisions on investment and finance are frequent and, for the most part, routine. Progressive firms in an open economy should be constantly seeking ways of reorganising themselves, so as best to be able to relate to their environment and to achieve their objectives. Such reorganisation, the subject of Chapter 14, typically involves altering some aspect, often a fundamental aspect, of their investment or financing strategy. Small firms are increas-ingly seen as a major part of the future of business. Chapter 15 considers to what extent, if at all, small firms should be treated differently from large ones, when making financial decisions.

CHAPTER 13

Management of working capital

OBJECTIVES

In this chapter we shall deal with the following:

- the nature of working capital and the working capital cycle
- its importance as a source and use of short-term finance
- liquidity of firms and working capital
- the management of the individual elements of working capital
  - stocks
  - trade debtors
  - cash (and bank overdrafts)
  - trade creditors
- the necessity for establishing policies on each element of working capital in order to provide a framework for its practical management

INTRODUCTION

When firms make investment decisions they must not only consider the financial outlay involved with acquiring the new machine or the new building, etc., they must also take account of the additional current assets which are usually involved with any expansion of activity. Increased production tends to engender a need to hold additional stocks of raw materials and work-in-progress. Increased sales usually means that the level of debtors will increase. A general increase in the firm's scale of operations tends to imply a need for greater levels of cash.

The current assets (stock-in-trade, debtors and cash) tend not to be financed entirely from the firm's long-term sources of finance. Most firms also have access to two major short-term sources of finance. The first of these is trade credit, arising from the fact that purchases of goods and services are usually on credit, i.e. the buying firm does not have to pay immediately on delivery but may be allowed to delay payment for a period, say 30 days. The second is a source with which many of us are all too familiar in our private lives, the bank overdraft.

Since the relationship between these short-term sources of finance (or current liabilities) and the current assets tends to be very close, it seems logical to deal with both of them in the same chapter.

It could be argued that it is wrong to separate discussion of current assets from that of the investment decision generally, and similarly to discuss short-term finance separately from long-term finance. The reason for taking the present approach is simply that there are features of the management of current assets and of current liabilities which particularly commend dealing with them together, yet separate from the longer-term investment and financing decisions. These features include the systematic nature of the management of the working capital elements and the frequency with which decisions have to be taken in respect of most of them.

Perhaps another reason for discussing current assets and current liabilities together is that care needs to be taken by financial managers to ensure a reasonable balance between the relative levels, so it is important not to lose sight of their interrelationship. In fact, so closely related are these two, that they are frequently netted against one another and considered as a single factor, namely working capital (current assets *less* current liabilities).

The working capital cycle

The upper portion of Fig. 13.1 depicts, in a highly simplified form, the chain of events in a manufacturing firm as regards working capital. The chain starts with the firm buying raw materials on credit. In due course this stock will be used in production, work will be carried out on the stock and it will become part of the firm's work-in-progress (WIP). Work will continue on the WIP until it eventually emerges as the finished product. As production progresses, labour costs and overheads will need to be met. Of course at some stage trade creditors will need to be paid. When the finished goods are sold on credit, debtors are increased. They will eventually pay, so that cash will be injected into the firm.

Each of the areas – stocks (raw materials, work-in-progress and finished goods), trade debtors, cash (positive or negative) and trade creditors – can be viewed as tanks into and from which funds flow. Most of this chapter will be devoted to questions of why any of these 'tanks' need exist at all and, if they are necessary, what attitude managers should take on the amounts which should be held in each tank at any given time.

Working capital is clearly not the only aspect of the firm which impacts on cash. The firm will have to make payments to governments, both central and local, for taxation. Fixed assets will be purchased and sold. Lessors of fixed assets will be paid their rent (lease payment). Shareholders (existing or new) may provide new funds in the form of cash, some shares may be redeemed for cash and dividends will normally be paid. Similarly long-term loan creditors (existing or new) may provide loan finance, loans will need to be repaid from time to time and interest obligations will have to be met by the firm. Unlike movements in the working capital items, most of these 'non-working capital' cash transactions are not everyday events. Some of them are annual or more frequent events (e.g. tax payments, lease payments, dividends, interest and, probably, fixed asset purchases and sales). Others (e.g. new equity and loan finance and redemption of old equity and loan finance) would typically be rarer events. A factor which most of these non-working capital transactions have in common is their size; they are likely individually to involve large amounts of cash.

It is obvious that the management of working capital, particularly of cash, is very closely linked to financing decisions and to decisions involving investment in fixed assets. This linkage involves both quantities of cash and the timing of cash flows. For example, if a particular long-term debt is to be redeemed under a contractual obligation, thought must be given to the question of the source of that cash. If cash has not been generated through the working capital cycle, some other source (e.g. new equity or loan finance) will need to be considered. These themes will be further developed later in this chapter.

Figure 13.1
The working
capital cycle for a
manufacturing firm

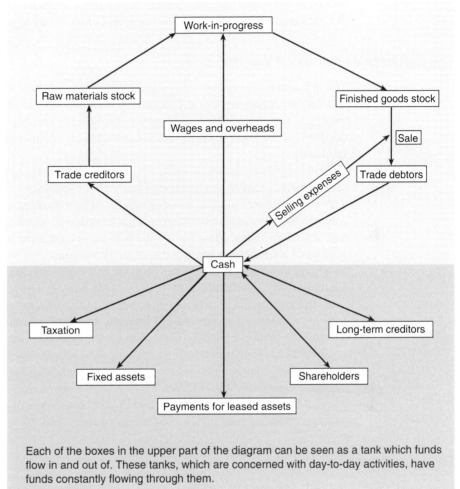

Each of the boxes in the upper part of the diagram can be seen as a tank which funds flow in and out of. These tanks, which are concerned with day-to-day activities, have funds constantly flowing through them.

The scale of working capital

It is tempting to believe that with working capital we are dealing with trivial matters. Such a view is very wide of the mark for the typical UK firm; the amounts involved tend to be vast. Table 8.1 (p. 200) shows the relative importance of the various elements in the balance sheets of a sample of large UK commercial and industrial firms over recent years. This clearly shows that, far from being trivial in financial terms, when compared with long-term investments and sources of finance the elements of working capital are in fact highly significant. For example, the Table shows that the investment in current assets is almost as large at each balance sheet date as that in fixed assets. This large investment is, of course, partly offset by the fact that it is financed substantially by 'free' trade credit.

A combination of the relative vastness of the typical firm's investment in working capital and the recent very high levels of interest rates, both in the UK and elsewhere, has led to the subject of management of working capital increasingly being treated as fundamental to the welfare of the firm and to its ability to survive.

The nature of decisions on working capital

The difference between working capital decisions and those involving fixed assets and long-term finance does not apparently lie in the amount of finance involved; to the extent that there is such a difference it lies in the tendency for working capital decisions to be short-term, reversible at relatively short notice, and made more frequently.

Whilst they may be made more frequently, many working capital decisions are easy since they tend to be repetitive. There will (or should be) a policy which creates a set of rules to be followed. For example, each time a customer seeks to buy goods from the firm on credit, a decision will be needed as to whether to grant credit at all and, if so, how much. Most firms will have decided on some formula which can be applied to help them to reach a decision. The existence of such formulae has the advantage that many decisions can be made by employees quite low in the management hierarchy and therefore they can be made fairly cheaply.

In establishing these formulae or sets of rules for the day-to-day management of working capital, great care should be taken to assess which approach will most advance the firm's objectives. Once a set of rules has been established it should be regarded as the framework within which all operating decisions must be made.

It is unlikely that rules established at one time will continue to represent the most beneficial approach over long periods of time. Circumstances, including the firm's competitive position, interest rates and the economic environment generally, alter over time. Policies must therefore be reviewed and, if necessary, revised periodically.

The use of budgets

Probably few areas of financial management can benefit as much as the control of working capital from the use of detailed plans in the form of budgets. The ability to assess in advance the calls which will be made on the various elements of working capital enables managers to ensure that the 'tanks' are always adequately full.

Few firms have steady and regular working capital requirements from week to week throughout the year; this is due, amongst other things, to seasonal factors. Prior knowledge of what the demands are likely to be at various times is of enormous value.

General attitude to working capital

Broadly, firms should seek to minimise the level of each type of current asset which they hold and to maximise the benefits of cheap short-term finance. This is, of course, subject to the costs involved with doing so to the extreme. For example, granting credit to customers is expensive (in lost interest on the funds, if nothing else), so ideally credit should not be given. However, failing to give credit is very likely to mean that the firm will be unable to make sales (perhaps because competitors do offer credit). Clearly the firm's credit policy must seek to strike a balance between the costs of taking one extreme view and those of taking the other extreme view.

Since working capital elements tend to be of high financial value, getting the balance between the extremes wrong tends to be an expensive matter. Indeed, as we shall shortly see, it can even be a fatal one.

WORKING CAPITAL AND LIQUIDITY

Not only do firms need to seek to strike a reasonable balance between the extremes in respect of individual working capital elements: a balance should also be sought between exploiting 'cheap' sources of short-term finance (current liabilities) to the fullest possible extent, and the risks and possible costs involved with being heavily reliant on suppliers of finance who can demand repayment at very short notice. That is to say, firms need to maintain sufficient current assets to enable them to be able to meet short-term claims as they become due. They need to be able to do this since failure to be able to meet them would entitle the short-term claimants (the current liabilities) to take steps to put the firm into liquidation. This would normally involve the forced sale of some or all of the firm's assets, including its fixed assets.

If bankruptcy costs were not significant and if the market for real assets were efficient, from a shareholder wealth maximisation perspective the liquidation threat would be unimportant. This is because shareholders could expect, on the liquidation of the firm, to receive for their shares an amount equal to the capital market price of the shares immediately before the liquidation. In other words, liquidation would not affect a shareholder's wealth. In reality, of course, since bankruptcy costs are likely to be significant and markets for real assets do not seem to be efficient, liquidation would usually be expected to have a severely adverse effect on shareholders' wealth.

One way to avoid the risk of liquidation is to maintain a large amount of cash on short-term interest-bearing deposit. In this way, should a need for cash to meet current liabilities suddenly arise, cash could quickly be made available to meet the demand. Obviously there would be no point in taking such an approach unless the funds used to establish the short-term deposit were provided from long-term sources. Otherwise the ploy would have the effect of solving the original problem by creating another group of short-term claimants who could create the same problem.

The approach of using long-term finance to create a short-term fund would offer the perfect solution to the liquidity problem but for imperfections in the capital market. These tend to mean, amongst other things, that firms usually cannot lend at as high a rate of interest as that which they have to pay to borrow. Also long-term interest rates are usually higher than short-term ones. So, for the average firm, borrowing long term and lending short term in order to maintain good liquidity and avoid the risk of liquidation is likely to be an expensive solution to the problem.

In practice firms seem to try to strike a balance between the levels of their current assets and current liabilities, i.e. a balance between exploiting cheap sources of short-term finance and the risk inherent in doing so.

It is probably fair to say that, irrespective of the root problem (e.g. lack of profitability), most business failures result from a deficiency in working capital.

The use of accounting ratios in the management of working capital

Accounting ratios are widely used in the management of working capital. The following are some of the ratios used to assist in the management of working capital. You may care to look back at Chapter 3 for more details of these ratios.

(a) The current ratio (current assets/current liabilities).

(b) Acid test ratio (liquid assets/current liabilities).

(c) No-credit period (liquid assets/average daily cash running costs).

Probably managers can best use these ratios by employing them to monitor their firm's actual liquidity position and constantly to compare it with some standard or target figure, taking steps to correct any significant deviations. The standard might be one which emerges from within the firm, or an industry average, or perhaps some combination of the two. One way or another, firms should actively seek to maintain liquidity and the confidence of short-term creditors that they will be paid.

OVERTRADING

A particular firm in particular circumstances will have particular working capital requirements, though what these are is a matter of managerial judgement. For example, the management of a retailing firm with a particular level of demand for its merchandise will decide on a level of stock requirement. If demand were to alter, a different level of stock holding would normally be required. A doubling of the level of demand would not necessarily imply a need to double stock levels, but it would normally imply a need for a significant increase in the amount of stock available to customers. The same point is broadly true for firms in any line of business in respect of all working capital aspects. It is obviously necessary, not only that management decides on the level of working capital which will be required, but that it also ensures that finance is available to provide for the investment in that amount of working capital. Not to be able to provide the level of working capital required to sustain a particular level of trading is known as *overtrading*.

Problems do arise in practice for firms who experience an expansion of trading activity due to an upturn in demand, particularly when the increase in demand is rapid and unexpected. The temptation for a firm to exploit profitable new trading opportunities is frequently overwhelming. Yet increased activity without increased working capital to sustain it can lead to serious overtrading problems, possibly culminating in complete financial failure of the firm. At first sight the problem seems capable of solving itself, since the increased profits from the additional business will provide the finance necessary to expand the working capital. This view is usually misleading, however, since the working capital requirement (additional stocks, additional cash for labour and other costs) generally precedes any additional cash flows from the increased business. This arises from the fact that the typical firm, irrespective of its line of business, has to pay cash to meet most of the costs of making a particular sale before cash is forthcoming from the customer. The extent of this problem varies from one type of business to another. Clearly it is a greater problem for a manufacturer (relatively large stock and debtor levels) selling on credit than it is for a firm providing services for immediate cash settlement, e.g. a hairdressing business. In fact, for a hairdressing firm rapid expansion of trading may pose no problems at all.

STOCK-IN-TRADE (INVENTORIES)

As we saw in Fig. 13.1, manufacturing firms typically hold stocks at various stages of completion, from raw materials to finished goods. Trading firms (wholesalers, retailers, etc.) by the nature of their business hold stock in only one condition. Broadly speaking, the level of investment in stocks by manufacturers tends to be relatively large compared with that of traders.

Even with traders there may be vast differences. A jeweller would normally hold much more stock (in value terms) than would a greengrocer with the same level of annual turnover. The perishable nature of the latter's wares would partly account for this, as would the high value of the individual items in the stock of the former. Another factor might be that when we buy jewellery we usually demand a choice, which is less likely to be the case when we buy potatoes.

With some firms the requirement for stocks varies with the time of year. Firework manufacturers in the UK who experience high sales in the period leading up to 5 November may well find it necessary to hold very large stocks during each summer as they *stockpile* Catherine wheels, etc., for the forthcoming period of high demand.

Irrespective of the nature of the trade, firms should seek to balance the costs of holding stock with those of holding no or low levels of stock. While the costs of holding stocks tend to be fairly certain, if difficult to identify, those of failing to hold stocks may or may not occur, i.e. there is a risk. Thus such costs are in the nature of *expected values*, where costs are combined with their probability of occurrence.

The costs of holding stocks

These include:

(a) *Lost interest*. This could be earned on the finance tied up in the stocks. This cost is partly mitigated by a certain amount of free credit granted by suppliers of the stock which would only be available if stock is bought. The existence of this aspect is very important to some types of business. High street supermarkets, because their stock turnover is rapid, typically have their entire stocks financed by suppliers of these stocks. For other types of business where this is not the case, the opportunity cost of interest should be based on the returns from an investment of risk similar to that of investing in stocks.

(b) *Storage costs*. These include rent of space occupied by the stock and the cost of employing people to guard and manage the stock. With some types of stock it might include the cost of keeping it in some particular environment necessary for its preservation. This is likely to be particularly true for perishables such as food.

(c) *Insurance costs*. Holding valuable stocks exposes firms to risk of fire, theft, etc., against which they will usually insure, at a cost.

(d) *Obsolescence*. Stocks can become obsolete, for example because they go out of fashion or lose their value due to changes in the design of the product in whose manufacture they were intended to be used. Thus apparently perfectly good stock can become little more than scrap. The firm holding no stock is clearly not exposed to the risk of this cost.

The costs of holding low (or no) stocks

These include:

(a) *Loss of customer goodwill*. Failure to be able to supply a customer due to having insufficient stock may mean the loss not only of that particular order, but of further orders as well. The extent to which this is important depends to a large degree on the nature of the trade and on the relative market power of supplier and customer.

(b) *Production dislocation*. Running out of raw materials when other production facilities (factory, machinery, labour, etc.) are available can be very costly. How costly depends on how flexible the firm can be in response to a *stock-out*, which in turn probably depends on the nature of the stock concerned. For example, a motor car manufacturer running out of a major body section probably has no choice but to stop production. If the firm runs out of interior mirrors, it is probably quite feasible for these to be added at the end of the production cycle rather than at the scheduled stage, without too much costly dislocation.

(c) *Loss of flexibility*. Firms which hold little or no stock inevitably lead a 'hand to mouth' existence where purchasing and manufacture must be very closely geared to sales. This may preclude maximising the efficiency of production runs or of buying materials in batches of economically optimum sizes. Such an existence also means that, unless things go precisely to plan, costly problems are likely to occur. For example, if there is even a slight increase in sales demand it will be unable to be met.

Stock holding creates a 'margin of safety' whereby mishaps of various descriptions can occur without major and costly repercussions.

(d) *Re-order costs*. Any firm existing on little or no stock will, among other things, be forced to place a large number of small orders with short intervals of time between each one. Each order gives rise to costs including the physical placing of the order (buyer's time, telephone, postage, etc.) and the receipt of the goods (storemen's time, costs of processing the invoice and making payment).

Stock management models

Models have been developed to aid managers in their task of balancing costs. Each of these models seems to have its strengths and its limitations.

**Figure 13.2
A graph of the
stock level against
time for some item
of stock**

An amount (E) of stock is delivered at time 0. This is steadily used, until the stock
level drops to 0, at which point a new consignment (amount E) arrives. The average
level of stock is E/2.

One such model can be used to identify the optimum size of order to be placed
for the purchase of new raw materials, given a particular rate of usage of stock and
other relevant factors. The model is based on the assumption that the level of each
stock item will be as shown in Fig. 13.2. This shows the stock level falling evenly
over time until just as the stock completely runs out it is replaced by quantity E. Since
the stock level falls evenly from E to zero, the average stock holding level is $E/2$.
The model seeks to balance stock holding costs with the cost of placing orders.

If C is the cost of placing each order, A the annual demand for (i.e. usage of) the
stock item, and H the cost of holding one unit of the stock item for one year, then
the annual cost of placing orders will be $(A/E \times C)$ and the cost of holding the stock
will be $(E/2 \times H)$. The total costs associated with placing orders and holding stock
is the sum of these two. (Note that we are not interested in the actual purchase price
of the stock itself as this is defined by the annual usage and the price per unit and is
independent, except for the question of possible discounts for bulk orders, of the size
of each order and the average stock level.)

Figure 13.3 shows the behaviour of the costs with various levels of stock. As stock
levels and, following our assumptions depicted in the graph in Fig. 13.2, order size
increase, the annual costs of placing orders decrease but holding costs increase. Total
cost drops as stock level increases until at point M it reaches a minimum and starts
to increase. What we want to know is the size of order quantity E which will minimise
the total cost, i.e. identify point M.

The total cost, and therefore the expression plotted as such in Fig. 13.3, is

$$\frac{AC}{E} + \frac{HE}{2}$$

This will be a minimum where the differential of the expression (with respect to E)

**Figure 13.3
A graph of the
stock holding
costs and stock
order costs
against the average
stock level for
some item of
stock**

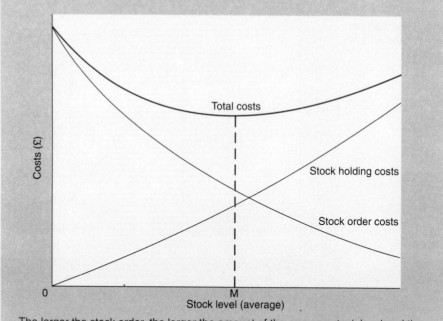

The larger the stock order, the larger the amount of the average stock level and the
higher the stock holding costs. On the other hand, large stock orders mean relatively
infrequent orders and, therefore, relatively low total order costs. There seems likely to
be an optimum stock order size, which will balance the two types of cost.

is equated to zero (the point of zero slope, M in Fig. 13.3), i.e. where

$$\frac{-AC}{E^2} + \frac{H}{2} = 0$$

so

$$E = \sqrt{\frac{2AC}{H}}$$

EXAMPLE

A firm uses 1000 units of a particular stock item each year. The costs of holding one
unit of it for a year are £3 and the cost of placing each order is £30. What is the most
economical size for each order?

SOLUTION

$$E = \sqrt{\frac{2AC}{H}}$$

$$= \sqrt{\left(\frac{2 \times 1000 \times 30}{3}\right)}$$

$$= 141.4, \text{ say } 141 \text{ units}$$

Thus each order will be placed for 141 units (or perhaps a round figure like 140 or 150), necessitating about seven orders being placed each year.

We should note the weaknesses of this model, the most striking of which are:

(a) Demand for stock items may fluctuate on a seasonal basis, i.e. the diagonals in Fig. 13.2 may not all be parallel, or even straight.

(b) Annual demand may be (almost certainly is) impossible to predict with certainty, though it may be possible to ascribe statistical probabilities to possible levels of demand.

(c) Many costs associated with holding and failing to hold stocks are ignored by the model. This particularly applies to some of the costs of holding low levels of stock such as loss of customer goodwill, production dislocation and loss of flexibility.

Virtually all of these deficiencies are capable of being accommodated by increasing the sophistication of the model. For example, the loss of customer goodwill and production dislocation problems can to some extent be dealt with by revising the model by incorporating a safety margin reflecting a pattern of stock levels over time, following more closely that which is depicted in Fig. 13.4 than the one shown in Fig. 13.2. How large this margin of safety should be must be a matter of managerial judgement. Some estimate of the costs of holding the additional stock, the costs of a 'stock-out' and the probability of its occurrence, must give some guidance in the exercise of the judgement.

Note that incorporating a safety stock means that the average stock holding level is no longer $E/2$ and so the basic model is not strictly valid; however, the model can quite easily be adjusted to cope with this.

Let us be clear that the model which we derived is a highly simplified, even simplistic, attempt to balance the two types of cost. However, the model can be extended to deal with most factors which the simpler version glosses over. Several of the references at the end of this chapter go into some of the sophistications which can be incorporated. The model may also be used with a little adaptation for WIP and finished stocks as well as for bought-in raw materials.

Some practical points on management of stocks

Optimum order quantities
These should be established for each item of stock, using either the model which we derived (above) or some more sophisticated version. These quantities should be periodically revised, but between revisions should be regarded as the size of order which should be placed, except in most unusual circumstances.

Stock re-order levels
The level of stock at which the next order must be placed should also be established and adhered to. The actual level for a particular stock item largely depends upon the

lead time, i.e. how long it takes between placing the order and the stock actually arriving at the factory, and the rate of usage of stock. One way or another, the order should be placed early enough for the stock to arrive just as the safety level is expected to be reached. This is depicted in Fig. 13.4.

Figure 13.4
Graph of the stock level against time for some item of stock, assuming a safety margin

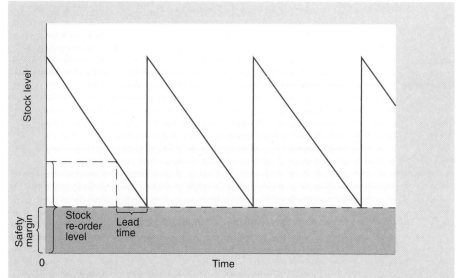

An amount of stock is delivered at time 0. This is steadily used, until the stock level drops to the stock re-order level, at which point a new consignment will be ordered. The stock re-order level should be set at such an amount that there is enough stock to maintain operations until the new consignment arrives, and to provide a margin of safety. The size of the margin of safety will probably depend on the reliability of the supplier in delivering within the expected time period. It will also depend on the predictability of the rate at which stock will be used during the lead time. The lead time is the period which elapses between placing the order and receiving the stock.

To illustrate this, let us assume that in the economic order quantity example (above) the lead time is three weeks. As the weekly usage is about 20 units (i.e. 1000/52), if the order is placed when the stock level drops to about 60 units and all goes according to plan the new stock will arrive just as existing stocks are running out. This, of course, leaves no safety margin, but as we have already seen such devices can easily be incorporated.

Most computer packages dealing with stock records have a facility for incorporating re-order levels for each stock item so that the computer's output will draw attention to the need to place the next order.

Budgeting and planning

Much of successful stock management is concerned with knowing what to expect in terms of levels of demand for and costs associated with stocks. The importance of forward planning and budgeting probably cannot be overestimated.

Reliable stock records

Unless firms know what they have in stock, stock management becomes very difficult. It is rarely possible in practice to gain sufficient information on stocks from physical observation.

Ratios

These can be useful in managing stocks, particularly the *stock holding period* ratio (average stock × 365/annual stock usage), which indicates the average period, in days, for which stock is held. The inputs for calculating the ratio may be stated either in terms of physical units of stock or in money terms. It is important that both inputs are stated in similar terms; usually cost is used.

The ratio may be calculated for a firm's entire stock (in which case the inputs would need to be expressed in money terms), for a section of the stock (e.g. stocks of tyres of a motor car manufacturer) or for specific items (e.g. stock of a particular size and quality of tyre). Such figures may be used as a check that policies laid down are in fact being followed.

Security and authorisation

Routine systems should be established to ensure that stock may only be ordered (or manufactured) and used on the authority of some fairly senior employee. This involves specifying the employees who are empowered to authorise the placing of orders and ensuring that stock is kept in some enclosed area, only to be issued on the authority of other specified employees. Clearly management needs to use some common sense here so as not to make the purchase and issuing of stock a major obstacle to the firm's activities. However, a system where anyone can order stock and where it can be used without authority is likely to lead to chaos.

To summarise, these practical points are really concerned with establishing routines to be applied systematically. Stock management should not be (though, perhaps inevitably, sometimes it is) a haphazard operation.

'JUST IN TIME' STOCKHOLDING

There is a tendency, which seems to have originated in the USA but to have been developed in Japan, for manufacturing firms to operate a system where there is a fairly continuous flow of raw material stock into the factory, of work-in-progress through the factory and of finished stocks to the customer. In such a system, large amounts of stock (raw materials, work-in-progress and finished stock) would never build up. Finished goods stocks would be produced just as they are needed to supply to customers, inputs of internally manufactured components and sub-assemblies would pass to the next stage of production just as they are needed to be used and raw material deliveries would arrive from suppliers just as they are needed in production. In essence the just in time (JIT) approach means that production and purchasing are linked closely to sales demand on a week-to-week basis, obviating the necessity to hold 'buffer' stocks to see the firm through unexpected demand peaks.

Though at first sight JIT is a technique of stock and production control, its effective implementation requires the acceptance of a particular philosophy and culture. An effective JIT system requires a flexible attitude on the part both of suppliers and of the internal workforce to expand and contract output at short notice. It also requires a concentration on quality of outputs at each stage, both by suppliers and by the internal workforce. If raw material stocks are to arrive just in time to go straight into production, those stocks must be of guaranteed quality which need not be tested or checked before being taken into production. The same general point about quality follows through each stage of production and into sales.

The JIT system can only be reliably established where there are very close relationships between users and suppliers. This requires that the user is prepared to guarantee only to buy from the one supplier in respect of a particular stock item and to give the supplier access to the user's production/sales plans. This enables the supplier to match its production to the needs of the user in much the same way as would a department of the user firm supplying components or sub-assemblies to another internal department. To work well, the system probably requires that supplier and user are geographically fairly close to one another so that deliveries can be made frequently and, when necessary, at short notice.

Achievement of low stock levels of internally produced components and sub-assemblies, and of finished stocks, normally requires short production runs, i.e. each production batch of a particular product or component is fairly small. To be economical this normally means that the costs of setting up each production run are fairly low. High-technology production methods (robots and computer-controlled manufacturing) typically have low set-up costs and considerable flexibility. This makes the achievement of an effective JIT system something which was not really achievable in the past.

An effective system of JIT also requires a workforce willing to increase and decrease its working hours from one period to another. This can pose serious problems for implementing a JIT system, particularly in a UK or US environment where regular weekly working hours are an established feature of industrial employment. The existence of a pool of labour willing to come in at short notice to supplement the 'core' workforce during production peaks may provide a solution in some cases.

Clearly a JIT policy will tend to lead to lower stock levels from the user's point of view and therefore to stock holding cost savings. The concentration on quality control and assurance is also likely to lead to net financial benefits. On the other hand, there may be additional opportunity costs arising from the fact that the user cannot, in the short term at least, buy from different suppliers according to price. Also, a flexible workforce may be a fairly expensive workforce. However, the increasing popularity of the JIT approach implies that many firms regard the policy as having net benefits for them.

TRADE DEBTORS (ACCOUNTS RECEIVABLE)

With the exception of the retail trade, where immediate cash settlement predominates, most commercial sales are made on credit. When the goods or service pass to the customer firm it becomes a trade debtor of the supplying firm until such time that it settles its debt by paying cash.

It appears that attitudes to the granting of credit vary from trade to trade, with time-honoured credit policies being perpetuated by virtue of the fact that individual firms find it hard to break patterns with which their competitors intend to continue.

In determining credit policy the financial manager must try to strike the balance between the costs of granting credit and those associated with denying or restricting credit.

The costs of granting credit

These include:

(a) *Lost interest*. Granting credit is tantamount to making interest free loans. Since trade debtors are not usually secured they tend to be fairly risky loans, thus the interest lost is at a fairly high rate.

(b) *Loss of purchasing power*. Where price inflation is present, which in the UK has been much of the twentieth century including every single year since the Second World War, value transfers from lender to borrower. This is because the borrower (trade debtor in this context) pays the debt in £s of lower value than those which were borrowed. To some extent this point is covered in (a) but recent experience of very high inflation rates showed that at such times interest rates do not necessarily increase fully to compensate lenders for the erosion of their money's purchasing power. Those granting trade credit should be aware that they are likely to be forgoing more than just interest in times of inflation.

(c) *Assessing the potential customer's creditworthiness*. It is usual before granting credit to a new customer or perhaps when increasing the credit limit of an existing customer to assess creditworthiness. This would usually be done by some combination of references from the customer's bank and other traders who have already granted credit to that customer. It might also include examination of the customer's published accounts for clues as to liquidity and financial rectitude and paying a credit rating agency for a report on the customer.

Carrying out these procedures costs money, though to a large extent the cost, once incurred, is unlikely to need to be repeated. Typically firms, once having granted credit to a particular customer, reassess that customer on the basis of their own experience of the customer's 'track record' of payment.

(d) *Administration and record keeping costs*. Most firms which grant credit find it necessary to employ people to act in the role of credit controllers, i.e. to devote themselves to the administration and collection of trade debts. The granting of credit usually involves a greatly increased volume of accounting transactions.

(e) *Bad debts*. Unless the firm is adopting an extremely cautious credit granting policy it is almost inevitable that some trade debts will never be paid, due for example to the defaulting customer's financial collapse. This risk can be insured against though typically it is borne by the supplier, either way there is a cost.

(f) *Discounts*. It is quite common for firms to offer their credit customers a discount if they settle their debts quickly. For example, a 2½ per cent discount may be offered if customers pay within 30 days of receipt of the goods or service. What the effective cost of such a ploy would be of course depends upon how long the customers who pay quickly and claim the discount would take to pay were no discount available. If, say, in the above example they would on average take 40 days but the discount causes them to pay exactly on day 30, the effective cost of the discount is 2½ per cent per 10 days or about 100 per cent per annum (compounded). Obviously the allowing of discounts for prompt payment can be a tremendous cost so its use should be treated with caution. We should bear in mind however that discount-induced prompt payment may well reduce some of the costs which we have already discussed, particularly those associated with bad debts and administration of debtors.

The costs of denying credit

These include:

(a) *Loss of customer goodwill*. If its competitors grant credit it will be very difficult for a firm to deny credit, not at least without offering some special inducement (e.g. discounted prices) which itself may be as expensive as granting credit. Where the supplier is in a monopolistic or near-monopolistic position it may be able to sell as much of its wares as it wishes without offering credit. In a competitive market, however, credit may be used as a basis of competition, so that it may be necessary to offer unusually extended credit in order to attract large and recurring orders.

(b) *Inconvenience and loss of security of collecting cash*. Administratively supplying goods or services on credit can be very convenient. Cash is not usually paid until the customer is satisfied that the goods are as ordered, etc., which avoids the necessity for refunds in respect of defective goods. Cash is collected centrally, usually by cheques received by post, or by direct bank credit. It is unnecessary for delivery drivers to collect cash, thus the delay and potential administrative and security problems likely to arise from such decentralised cash collection may be avoided. The existence of trade credit tends to allow specialisation and segregation of duties; delivery drivers deliver the goods and credit controllers collect the cash.

Some practical points in management of trade debts

(a) *Establish a credit policy*. The firm should consider whether it judges it appropriate to offer trade credit at all, and if so how much, to whom and under what circumstances. A firm might, for example, decide generally that trade credit is not a good idea, but nonetheless identify specific circumstances where it is prepared to offer it. For example, a retailer may be prepared to offer credit only for orders above, say, £100.

One way or another firms should establish a policy, not merely accept that credit is inevitable.

(b) *Assess customers' creditworthiness.* Even though in principle the firm may have decided that it is in its best interests to offer credit, it should not offer unlimited credit to any potential customer who seeks it. Those seeking credit are in effect asking for a loan, and supplying firms should see matters in those terms.

The firm should establish a policy for investigating creditworthiness and should not be prepared to grant credit before satisfying itself that the risk of doing so in respect of each customer is an acceptable one. It is not just a question of either granting credit or not. Credit limits should be established and these will almost certainly vary from customer to customer depending on the supplying firm's confidence in each customer's individual creditworthiness. Once established, each customer's credit limit should be rigorously observed until such time as there is some fundamental review by a fairly senior employee.

The supplying firm should try to establish some 'ear to the ground' routines so that signs that any particular established credit customer is experiencing liquidity problems can be picked up quickly and some action taken. Such routines might include regularly monitoring the customers' financial accounts. Another approach which could also be used is to look out for customers who are taking longer than they usually do to pay their debts; this may indicate a weakening liquidity position.

(c) *Establish effective administration of debtors.* Systems should be established to ensure:
   (i) that no goods are dispatched until it has been confirmed that the present order will not take the customer above the predetermined credit limit for that customer;
   (ii) that invoices for goods supplied on credit go off to the customer as soon as possible after the goods, thus encouraging the customer to initiate payment routines sooner rather than later;
   (iii) that existing debtors are systematically reviewed and that slow payers are sent reminders.

Most computer packages for dealing with trade debtors can produce a list of debtors with each customer's debt analysed by length of time for which the debt has been outstanding. This (known as an ageing summary) and similar devices can usefully be employed by credit controllers in the pursuit of trade debts.

(d) *Establish a policy on bad debts.* At some stage it will often become more costly to pursue reluctant payers than their debt is worth. The firm should decide what its policy on writing off bad debts should be. Once having been established, the policy should be followed except in unusual circumstances.

It is important that writing off a bad debt only occurs when all the steps identified in the policy have been followed. It is also important that writing off bad debts can only be authorised by a fairly senior employee.

(e) *Consider offering discounts for prompt payment.* The costs and advantages of allowing discounts should be assessed. If the firm establishes a particular policy of allowing discounts, care should be taken to ensure that customers are allowed to deduct discounts only when they have in fact paid within the specified period.

(f) *Consider factoring debts.* It is possible to enter into an arrangement with a firm of debt factors (many are subsidiaries of commercial banks). Here the factor collects the debts on behalf of the supplier firm. The precise arrangements can vary considerably but, fairly typically, payment (at a discount) is made immediately after the sale by the factor, who then goes on to collect the debt and to manage all accounting and administrative matters concerned with it. This relieves the supplier firm of the administrative and financial burden of granting trade credit, but at a cost.

(g) *Manage exchange rate risk.* Where the firm is involved with credit sales in a foreign currency there is the danger that an adverse shift in the exchange rate during the period from the credit sale to its settlement will reduce the value of the debt. One way to avoid this is to make it a condition of the sale that settlement must be in sterling. This may not be commercially acceptable to some overseas customers, however. An alternative is to use 'derivatives' of the foreign exchange market to 'insure' against an adverse shift in exchange rates.

For example, it is possible to negotiate an option to sell a particular currency on a specified future date at a specified rate of exchange. Entering into an appropriate option contract has a cost. It is not certain that the option will need to be exercised by the firm. However, this is in the nature of 'insurance', in that we pay a fee to indemnify ourselves against the effects of an uncertain, adverse occurrence.

(h) *Ratios.* These can be useful in debtor management. Probably the most widely used is *debtor collection period* (average debtors × 365/annual credit sales) which indicates the average time taken between a sale being made and the cash being received. It gives an overall impression of what is actually happening with debtors, which can be compared with the firm's policy on debtor collection to provide a control device. Where collection periods are in fact exceeding those specified in the firm's policy, steps can be taken to try to correct matters.

In summary, the firm's management of trade debtors should be thought through in advance and conducted in a systematic manner. Incidences, by accident or by design, of departure from the firm's credit policy should be highly exceptional.

CASH (INCLUDING OVERDRAFTS AND SHORT-TERM DEPOSITS)

If we glance back at Fig. 13.1 on page 313, we see that cash is sooner or later involved in everything that the typical firm does. Some firms may not hold stock (perhaps because they sell services rather than goods), others may have no trade debtors or creditors (because they neither give nor receive credit), but all of them have cash. Admittedly some firms have negative cash balances (overdrafts) but a business with no cash balance at any given moment would be rare.

Cash tends to be held for three reasons:

(a) to meet planned needs to pay suppliers, labour, etc.;
(b) as a fund to meet unexpected obligations, e.g. a short-term creditor demanding payment earlier than expected; and
(c) to enable unexpected opportunities to be taken, e.g. to place a larger than planned order for stock to exploit some temporary price advantage.

As we saw in our discussion of Fig. 13.1 earlier in the chapter, cash is much more than just one of the elements of working capital. As the medium of exchange and store of value it provides the linkage between all financial aspects of the firm. More specifically it links short- and long-term financing decisions with one another and with decisions involving investment both in fixed assets and working capital.

Clearly, cash management is one of the key roles in any organisation of any size or description. Treasury management, as this role is increasingly being called, requires a specialism of skills, knowledge and experience. This has led to a tendency for treasury managers in larger organisations to be specialists whose career path lies exclusively in that functional area. Not surprisingly, in smaller organisations the role of treasury manager is likely to be filled by the accountant.

We shall firstly have a look at the costs involved with holding cash/not holding cash, before we go on to the closely related topic of the use of bank overdrafts to overcome temporary cash shortages.

The costs of holding cash

These include:

(a) *Loss of interest*. If cash is in its most liquid form (notes and coins), it will yield no interest at all. Even if it is in a current account with a bank it will not yield income at a very high rate. It may be possible for a firm to have some, perhaps most, of its cash on some very short-term deposit from which it can be withdrawn at short notice should the need arise. Even where this is done there is still a cost, since short-term interest rates tend to be lower than longer-term ones.

(b) *Loss of purchasing power*. As with trade debts, during a period of inflation there is an erosion in the value of money. This is not necessarily compensated by interest rates. Holding cash in one currency can lead to a loss of purchasing power in another one, where there is a movement in the exchange rate between the two currencies.

The costs of holding little or no cash

These include:

(a) *Loss of supplier goodwill*. 'Supplier' here is used in its widest sense to include employees as suppliers of labour. Failure to meet financial obligations on time due to cash shortages may mean the loss of further supplies from injured parties. This could be extremely damaging, especially where the particular commodity is one which is vital to the firm's continuing operations, e.g. labour. Failure to meet a financial obligation to a creditor puts that creditor into a position where it could take steps to instigate the defaulting firm's liquidation. Given the bankruptcy costs and an inefficient market for real assets, such an outcome must be a matter of great concern to shareholders seeking to increase or at least to maintain their wealth.

(b) *Loss of opportunities*. Cash shortages will tend to mean that it may be impossible to react quickly to an opportunity. For example, if a firm is offered a contract which must be fulfilled at short notice by overtime working, it may have to be refused if cash is not available to meet the additional labour costs.

(c) *Inability to claim discounts*. Discounts for prompt payment are very advantageous, in percentage terms, to the purchasing firm. Cash shortages may preclude the claiming of such discounts.

(d) *Cost of borrowing*. Shortages of cash may force the firm to borrow short term to be able to meet unexpected obligations. Interest costs for such borrowings can be expensive, particularly where the money has to be raised at very short notice and under pressure.

As ever, optimally balancing these two types of cost is the aim of the financial (treasury) manager. There are some models which can be helpful in this task.

Cash management models

A number of cash management models has been developed. The simplest one is substantially the same as the economic stock order quantity model which we derived on page 320. This cash model assumes that the firm keeps all of its cash on an interest-yielding deposit from which it can make withdrawals as it needs. It also assumes that all of the firm's receipts (from debtors, etc.) are put straight into the deposit and that cash usage is linear over time, following exactly the same pattern as Fig. 13.2 (page 319) does for stocks. The model derives the amount of money to withdraw from the deposit so that the costs of withdrawal are optimally balanced with those of interest, etc., forgone by holding cash. The model can be stated as:

$$C = \sqrt{\frac{2WP}{H}}$$

where C = the optimum amount of cash to be withdrawn each time;
W = the cost of making each withdrawal (a cost independent of the size of the withdrawal);
P = the planned payments for the forthcoming time period;
H = the interest forgone on the cash withdrawn (i.e. the interest rate of the deposit).

EXAMPLE

A firm plans to use £20 000 of cash during the forthcoming year. It holds most of its cash in a deposit account from which it costs £30 to make each withdrawal and pays interest at 10 per cent p.a. What is the optimal size for each withdrawal?

SOLUTION

$$C = £\sqrt{\left(\frac{2 \times 30 \times 2000}{0.10}\right)}$$

$$= £3464$$

So the firm should withdraw about £3464 from the deposit; when all that is spent, it should withdraw a similar amount, and so on.

As with its close relation, the economic order quantity, this model takes a very simple view of the world, though it is probably better than nothing.

Sophistications to the basic model have been proposed by Miller & Orr (1966) and another approach has been suggested by Beranek (1963).

Bank overdrafts

These are facilities allowed by commercial banks for firms to have negative balances on their current accounts. The bank overdraft is obviously therefore a form of borrowing for which the bank will charge interest, typically at 1 or 2 per cent above the relevant base lending rate. Banks usually make a fixed charge for establishing the facility as well.

Once the facility is established, the firm may continue to conduct its bank account as normal except that it can now incur a negative balance up to a specified limit. This tends to be a cheap form of finance, as the firm is only required to pay for the funds used for as long as they are being used. In fact, overdrafts are essentially short-term loans with fluctuating interest rates; the actual rate charged is likely to be relatively low compared with those associated with longer-term loans.

Firms seem to use overdrafts particularly to overcome temporary cash shortages, caused perhaps by seasonal fluctuations. For example, a firm whose main trading period is during the summer holiday season, will tend to stock up during the late spring. This will put a temporary strain on its cash resources which will gradually be relieved as the summer progresses. The alternative to overdraft finance may only be some long-term source. If the firm made a debenture issue, it would then be saddled with interest payments throughout the year on funds which it only needs for a month or two. The firm could, of course, put the spare cash on deposit for the other 10 or 11 months, but imperfections in the market for finance will tend to mean that interest received will not match interest paid on those funds.

Bank overdrafts have a major disadvantage compared with long-term loans: they are usually repayable at call (i.e. immediately) as a condition of the facility being granted. Where overdrafts are being used, as in our example, to overcome temporary shortages of cash, this is probably not a problem since, whatever 'at call' means in theory, in practice it probably means at a couple of months' notice. To the firm seeking to use a bank overdraft as a more permanent source of finance this can be a serious problem, however.

Some practical points in the management of cash and overdrafts

(a) *Establish a policy.* The firm should, with the aid of models and taking account of matters not covered by the models, establish a policy for cash. This policy should be adhered to, except in the most unusual circumstances, until such a time as the policy is reviewed.

(b) *Plan cash flows.* Forward planning is vitally important in this area; failure to balance cash inflows with cash outflows can be fatal.

The formal statement of financial plans, the budget, can probably best be explained through an example.

EXAMPLE

A firm has the following plans for the next few months:

1 *Sales:*

	£
September	60 000
October	60 000
November	70 000
December	90 000

All sales will be made on credit. Half of the creditors are expected to pay within the month of sale and to claim a 2 per cent cash discount. The remainder are expected to pay in the following month.

2 *Raw material purchases:*

	£
September	20 000
October	40 000
November	40 000
December	30 000

The firm plans to pay its creditors (in full) in the month following that of the purchase.

3 *Wages and salaries:*

	£
September	12 000
October	15 000
November	17 000
December	13 000

All employees are paid in full in the month in which the wage or salary is earned.
4 Rent of £10 000 each quarter is payable in March, June, September and December.
5 Other cash overheads of £2000 per month are payable.
6 Some new plant due for delivery in September will be paid for in November at a cost of £25 000.
7 On 1 October the firm plans to have £10 000 in the bank.

A cash budget for the months of October to December (inclusive) is to be prepared.

SOLUTION Cash budget for the three months ending 31 December:

	October £	November £	December £
Cash inflows:			
Debtors: Current month	29 400	34 300	44 100
Previous month	30 000	30 000	35 000
Total cash inflows (A)	59 400	64 300	79 100
Cash outflows:			
Creditors	20 000	40 000	40 000
Wages and salaries	15 000	17 000	13 000
Rent	–	–	10 000
Overheads	2 000	2 000	2 000
Plant acquired	–	25 000	–
Total cash outflows (B)	37 000	84 000	65 000
Cash surplus/(deficit) for the month (A–B)	22 400	(19 700)	14 100
Cumulative cash balance	32 400	12 700	26 800

Notes to the solution

1. The above statement reflects the timing and the amount of cash payments and receipts and the resultant balance. It is not, and is not intended to be, a profit and loss account. The profit or loss for these months will almost certainly be different from the cash surplus or deficit.

2. Knowledge of the projected cumulative cash balance enables plans to be made to use the surplus to effect; even if the most effective prospect is putting it on short term deposit, it is better than nothing.

(c) *Make judicious use of bank overdraft and deposit accounts.* Bank overdrafts should be avoided if possible, by scheduling payments and receipts with a view to staying in credit. Use temporary cash excesses by putting the money on deposit, even for very short periods. Where the cash surplus looks more permanent, thought should be given to whether it should be used in real investment or repaid to suppliers of long-term funds, thus saving the cost of servicing it.

(d) *Bank frequently.* Do not allow cheques received to gather dust in the accounts department when they could be in the bank saving overdraft interest or on deposit earning interest. Firms with large receipts of notes and coin (e.g. retailers) should consider banking several times each day, if only for security reasons.

(e) *Time transactions to the best cash flow effect.* There are several areas, particularly relating to tax payments, where with a little forethought a payment can legitimately be delayed or a receipt hastened. For example, Corporation Tax is based on the individual firm's accounting year and the timing of capital allowances is dependent on the date of acquisition of fixed assets. If a new piece of plant is purchased at the end of a firm's accounting period, the tax relief will first manifest itself in cash flow terms almost a year earlier than if the acquisition is delayed the short period until the start of the new accounting year.

TRADE CREDITORS (ACCOUNTS PAYABLE)

This is money owed for goods and services purchased on credit by the firm. It is the other side of the coin from trade debtors; one firm's trade debts are another firm's trade credit. Within an economy it will be true that:

$$\Sigma \text{ Trade debts} = \Sigma \text{ Trade credits}$$

Trade credit is a very important source of 'free' finance which firms should take very seriously. That trade credit is strictly free is doubtful, since firms will build the cost of granting credit into the pricing policy. However, unless suppliers are willing to discriminate in their pricing between those who settle their bills immediately and those who do not, there is no obvious differential cost of taking credit. There may be less obvious costs involved so, as ever, the balance must be sought between that cost and the cost of not taking trade credit.

The costs of taking credit

These include:

(a) *Price.* Some suppliers might offer cheaper prices for immediate settlement – in effect a discount for prompt payment. Cash-and-carry wholesalers in the grocery trade are examples of traders who are prepared to offer lower prices because they do not offer credit (or delivery). The small retail grocer has the choice of dealing with wholesalers who do offer credit but usually charge higher prices.

(b) *Possible loss of supplier goodwill.* If credit is overstepped, suppliers may discriminate against delinquent customers if supplies become short. As with the effect of any loss of goodwill, it depends very much on the relative market strengths of the parties involved.

(c) *Administration and accounting.* Taking credit almost certainly engenders administrative and accounting costs which would not otherwise be incurred.

(d) *Restrictions.* Many suppliers insist that in order to be granted credit, orders must be of some minimum size or even regularity.

The costs of not taking credit

These include:

(a) *Interest cost.* Trade credit is, in effect, an interest-free loan, so failure to exploit it has an interest cost. It may well be worth incurring some of the costs of taking credit in order to get it, particularly when interest rates are high.

(b) *Inflation*. In periods of inflation, borrowers are favoured over lenders with interest rates not seeming totally to redress the balance.

(c) *Inconvenience*. It may be inconvenient, for the reasons discussed in the context of trade debtors, to pay on delivery of the goods or performance of the service. It will probably also inconvenience the supplier. Indeed, insistence on paying on the nail may even be a cause of loss of supplier goodwill. If the supplier's systems are geared to deferred payment, a customer who insists on immediate settlement may not be welcome.

Some practical points in the management of trade credit

(a) *Establish a policy*. After weighing the two types of cost a policy should be established and followed. It may well be that suppliers are treated differently according to:
  (i) the discounts offered for prompt payment;
  (ii) the attitude to credit taken by individual suppliers;
  (iii) the weight of any possible repercussions arising from loss of supplier goodwill.

(b) *Exploit trade credit as far as is reasonable*. It is unlikely that, for the typical firm, the costs of claiming credit outweigh the considerable advantage of doing so.

(c) *Manage exchange rate risk*. Where the firm is involved with purchases on credit in a foreign currency, there is the danger that an adverse shift in the exchange rate during the period from the purchase to its settlement will increase the amount actually to be settled. This is the other side of the coin from the similar problem related to trade debtors which we discussed in that context earlier in the chapter.

   As with the trade debtor problem, one way to avoid this is to make it a condition of the purchase that settlement must be in sterling. Another possibility is to buy the required foreign currency immediately, thus fixing the exchange rate and removing the risk. This solution may be less than perfect, however, since it involves an immediate outflow of cash. Use of the foreign exchange market to purchase an option to buy a particular currency on a specified future date at a specified rate of exchange provides another possibility, but there is the cost of the options contracted to be considered.

(d) *Ratios*. The most useful ratio in the monitoring of trade credit is the *creditor payment period* (average trade creditors × 365/annual credit purchases). This gives a view of how long, on average, the firm is taking to pay its creditors, which can be compared with the planned period.

SUMMARY   The management of working capital is important to the firm. Very large amounts of resources tend to be involved in working capital, and its mismanagement can lead to dire effects on the firm. Poor liquidity tends to be seen as evidence of a firm in financial difficulties; thus poor management of working capital can cause pressure to be applied to the firm by those with whom it deals.

It is important that firms establish policies for the day-to-day management of each element of working capital and strive to follow those policies. The policies should not be regarded as immutable, but until some fundamental review takes place they should be adhered to. Broadly, firms should seek to establish and follow policies which seem best to balance the costs of having each of the working capital elements with the costs of not having them or having too little of them. The object of striking the balance is to maximise the shareholders' wealth.

FURTHER READING	Drury (1992) gives a full, yet clear, review of the various aspects of the management of working capital. Samuels, Wilkes & Brayshaw (1990), and Weston & Copeland (1988) each has one or more chapters covering the topics of this chapter and deal with them in a UK context. An interesting article by Moyes (1988) discusses the features and problems of JIT.

WORK-BASED ASSIGNMENT	(a) Ascertain the bought-in stock system (authorisations, re-order levels, order sizes, issues system, etc.) of your organisation and assess whether there are any aspects of it which could be improved to any significant extent. (b) How much would it cost to improve it? (c) How much would the improvement save?

QUESTIONS WITH ANSWERS (see Appendix 3)	1 Arcadia Ltd has only one product, a garden gnome, for which it plans to increase production and sales during the first half of next year. The plans for the next eight months are as follows:

Month	Production (gnomes)	Sales (gnomes)
November	700	700
December	800	800
January	1000	800
February	1200	1000
March	1200	1200
April	1400	1300
May	1500	1400
June	1500	1600

The selling price for each gnome will be £10. The raw materials will cost £4 per gnome, wages and other variable costs are expected to be £3 per gnome.

Salaries and other fixed overheads are expected to amount to £1400 per month during November and December, to rise to £1600 per month from January to April (inclusive) and to increase to £2000 per month for May and June.

Sixty per cent of the sales are made on a cash basis (paid on delivery). The remainder are sold on credit, debtors being expected to pay in full in the second month after the sale.

Payment is planned to be made for raw material purchases one month after delivery and materials are expected to be held in stock for one month before they are used in production.

Wages and other variable costs are expected to be paid during the month of production. Salaries and other fixed overheads are planned to be paid 80 per cent in the month in which they are incurred and 20 per cent in the following month.

In order to promote the expanded sales, an advertising campaign is to be undertaken. This will engender payments to the advertising agency of £1000 in January and £1500 in April.

A new machine, to help cope with the increased production, has been ordered and it should be delivered in February. The agreement is to pay the £6000 for the machine in three equal instalments of £2000 each in March, April and May.

The firm intends to pay a dividend of £600 to its shareholders in April.

The firm expects to have a bank current account balance (in funds) of £7500 on 1 January.

You are required to produce a cash budget for the firm for the first six months of next year, showing the net cash position at the end of each month.

2 Dixon plc uses a component, which it buys in, in its manufacturing process. The estimated annual usage is 23 000 and these are used fairly steadily throughout the year. It is estimated that the various stockholding costs amount to £1.50 per unit per year. Investigation indicates that it costs about £50 to process each order for the component. Experience shows that delivery always occurs within one week of placing an order.
(a) What is the economic order quantity for the component?
(b) At what stock level should the order be placed to be confident that delivery will occur before the existing stock of the components is all used?

3 Williams Wholesalers Ltd at present requires payment from its customers month end after month of delivery. On average it takes them 70 days to pay. Sales amount to £4 million per year and bad debts to £20 000 per year.

It is planned to offer customers a cash discount of 2 per cent for payment within 30 days. Williams estimates that 50 per cent of customers will accept this facility but that the remaining customers, who tend to be slow payers, will not pay until 80 days after the sale. At present the company has a partly used overdraft facility costing 13 per cent per annum. If the plan goes ahead bad debts will be reduced to £10 000 per annum and there will be savings in credit administration expenses of £6000 per annum.

Required:

(a) Explain and distinguish between the terms trade discount and cash discount and describe typical circumstances under which it is advantageous for a company to offer each type of discount.

(b) Calculate the approximate equivalent annual percentage cost of a 2 per cent cash discount which reduces debtors from 70 to 30 days sales outstanding. You need not refer to the data above to answer this question.

(c) Should Williams Wholesalers Ltd offer the new credit terms to customers? You should support your answer with any calculations and explanations which you consider necessary.

(Certified Diploma)

4 Control of working capital has always been thought to be the most important factor in the short-term financial management of companies.

Required:

(a) What are the most important components of net working capital? (You should ignore cash, marketable securities and bank overdrafts.)

(b) As a chief executive of a medium-sized manufacturing company how would you ensure that net working capital is kept under careful control?

(Certified Diploma)

5 Torrance Ltd was formed in 1988 in order to produce a new type of golf putter. The company sells the putter to wholesalers and retailers and has an annual turnover of £600 000. The following data relates to each putter produced:

	£	£
Selling price		36
Variable costs	18	
Fixed cost apportionment	6	24
Net profit		12

The cost of capital (before tax) of Torrance Ltd is estimated at 15%.

Torrance Ltd wishes to expand sales of this new putter and believes this can be done by offering customers a longer period in which to pay. The average collection period of the company is currently 30 days. The company is considering three options in order to increase sales. These are as follows:

	Option		
	1	2	3
Increase in average collection period (days)	10	20	30
Increase in sales (£s)	30 000	45 000	50 000

In addition to reconsidering its policy towards customers, Torrance Ltd is also reconsidering its policy towards trade creditors. In recent months the company has suffered from liquidity problems which it believes can be alleviated by delaying payment to trade creditors. Suppliers offer a 2.5% discount if they are paid within 10 days of the invoice date. If they are not paid within 10 days suppliers expect the amount to be paid in full within 30 days. Torrance Ltd currently pays suppliers at the end of the ten day period in order to take advantage of the discounts. However, it is considering delaying payment until either 30 days or 45 days after the invoice date.

Required:

(a) Prepare calculations to show which credit policy the company should offer its customers.
(b) Discuss the advantages and disadvantages of using trade credit as a source of finance.
(c) Prepare calculations to show the implicit annual interest cost associated with each proposal to delay payment to creditors. Discuss your findings.

(Certified Diploma)

6* At present the customers of the 'main' division of Jerome Public Limited Company take, on average, 90 days credit before paying. New credit terms are being considered which would allow a 5% cash discount for payment within 30 days with the alternative of full payment due after 60 days.

It is expected that 60% of all customers will take advantage of the discount terms. Customers not taking the discount would be equally split between those paying after 60 days and those taking 90 days credit. The new policy would increase sales by 20% from the current level of £100 000 per annum, but bad debts would rise from 1% to 2% of total sales. Main division's products have variable costs amounting to 80% of sales value.

Jerome's other division, the 'special orders' division, has received an order from Green Ltd, a private company. Green insists that the £50 000 of machinery ordered be supplied on 60 days credit. The variable costs of production and delivery which would be incurred by Jerome in meeting the order amount to £40 000. Green's credit worthiness is in doubt and the following estimates have been made:

Probability of Green paying in full in 60 days   0.6
Probability of Green completely defaulting   0.4

However, if the order is accepted by Jerome *and* if Green does not default then there is felt to be a probability of about 0.7 that a further 8 identical orders will be placed by Green in exactly one year's time, and further orders in later years may also be forthcoming. Experience has shown that once a firm meets the credit terms on an initial order the probability of default in the next year reduces to 0.1. Any work carried out on Green's order would take place in otherwise idle time and will not encroach upon Jerome's other activities. Should Green default the legal and other costs of debt collection will equal any money obtained.

Jerome finances all trade credit with readily available overdrafts at a cost of 12% per annum. An appropriate discount rate for longer term decisions is 15% per annum.

Required:

(a) In the absence of any changes in sales levels and bad debts etc., advise Jerome on the merits of offering the cash discount to 'main' division customers

Note: * indicates a more complex question.

who would otherwise have paid in
  (i) 60 days,
  (ii) 90 days.

Calculate the annualised implied interest cost of the cash discount terms. (Marks will not be lost for sensible rounding or approximation.)
(b) Advise Jerome on the merits of the new 'main' division credit terms after considering their effect on sales levels and bad debts etc.
(c) Provide information which will assist the 'special orders' division in deciding whether to accept Green's order and to offer 60 days credit if the order is expected
  (i) to be the only order from Green,
  (ii) to lead to the possibility of further orders from Green.

Explain the reasons for any differences in your conclusions and comment on any deficiencies inherent in your analysis.

(ACCA)

QUESTIONS FOR CLASS USE

1 Sound credit management can play an important role in the financial success of a business.

Required:

(a) Explain the role of the credit manager within a business.
(b) Discuss the major factors a credit manager would consider when assessing the creditworthiness of a particular customer.
(c) Identify and discuss the major sources of information that may be used to evaluate the creditworthiness of a commercial business.
(d) State the basis upon which any proposed changes in credit policy should be evaluated.

(Certified Diploma)

2 Prolog Ltd is a small wholesaler of microcomputers. It has in recent months been selling 50 machines a month at a price of £2000 each. These machines cost £1600 each. A new model has just been launched and this is expected to offer greatly enhanced performance. Its selling price and cost will be the same as for the old model. From the beginning of January, sales are expected to increase at a rate of 20 machines each month until the end of June when sales will amount to 170 units per month. They are expected to continue at that level thereafter. Operating costs including depreciation of £2000 per month, are forecast as follows:

	Jan.	Feb.	Mar.	Apr.	May	June
			£000			
Operating costs	6	8	10	12	12	12

Prolog expects to receive no credit for operating costs. Additional shelving for storage will be bought, installed and paid for in April costing £12 000. Corporation Tax of £25 000 is due at the end of March. Prolog anticipates that debtors will amount to two months' sales. To give their customers a good level of service Prolog plans to hold enough stock at the end of each period to fulfil anticipated demand from customers in the following month. The computer manufacturer however grants one month's credit to Prolog. Prolog Ltd's balance sheet appears below.

Prolog Ltd

Balance sheet at 31 December 19X4

	£000	£000
Fixed assets		80
Current assets		
Stock	112	
Debtors	200	
Cash	–	
	312	
Creditors: amounts falling due within one year		
Trade creditors	112	
Taxation	25	
Overdraft	68	
	205	
Net current assets		107
Total assets less current liabilities		187
Capital and reserves		
Share capital – 25p ordinary shares		10
Profit and loss account		177
		187

Required:

(a) Prepare a cash forecast for Prolog Ltd showing the cash balance or required overdraft for the six months ending 30 June 19X5.
(b) Compute at 30 June 19X5 Prolog's
   (i) Current ratio
   (ii) Acid test ratio
  You should ignore any possible tax liability or proposed dividend.
(c) State briefly what further information a banker would require from Prolog before granting additional overdraft facilities for the anticipated expansion of sales.

(Certified Diploma)

3 Salford Engineers Limited, a medium-sized manufacturing company, has discovered that it is holding 180 days' stock while its main competitors are holding only 90 days' stock.

Required:

(a) Discuss what you consider to be the most important factors which determine the optimum level of stockholding for the company.
(b) What action would you take if you were asked to investigate the reasons for Salford's high level of stock?

(Certified Diploma)

4 Your superior, the general manager of Plastics Manufacturers Limited, has recently been talking to the chief buyer of Plastic Toys Limited, who manufacture a wide range of toys for young children. At present it is considering changing its supplier of plastic granules and has offered to buy its entire requirement of 2000 kilos per month from you at the going market rate, providing that you will grant it three months' credit on its purchases. The following information is available:

(1) Plastic granules sell for £10 per kilo, variable costs are £7 per kilo and fixed costs £2 per kilo.
(2) Your own company is financially strong and has sales of £15 million per year. For the foreseeable future it will have surplus capacity and it is actively looking for new outlets.
(3) Extracts from Plastic Toys accounts:

	19X3	19X4	19X5
	£000	£000	£000
Sales	800	980	640
Profit before interest and tax	100	110	(150)
Capital employed	600	650	575
Current assets			
Stocks	200	220	320
Debtors	140	160	160
	340	380	480
Current liabilities			
Creditors	180	190	220
Overdraft	100	150	310
	280	340	530
Net current assets	60	40	(50)

Required:

(a) Write some short notes suggesting sources of information you would use in order to assess the creditworthiness of potential customers who are unknown to you. You should critically evaluate each source of information.
(b) Describe the accounting controls you would use to monitor the level of your company's trade debtors.
(c) Advise your general manager on the acceptability of the proposal. You should give your reasons and do any calculations you consider necessary.

(Certified Diploma)

5 Eurotech Ltd had credit sales of £1 800 000 and credit purchases of £1 260 000 during the year ended 31 May 19X1. The balance sheet at the year end was as follows:

Balance Sheet as at 31 May 19X1

	£000	£000	£000
Fixed assets			
Freehold premises at cost		228	
Less: Accumulated depreciation		50	178
Plant and machinery at cost		476	
Less: Accumulated depreciation		48	428
			606
Current assets			
Stock at cost		135	
Trade debtors		600	
Cash		1	
		736	
Less creditors: due within one year			
Trade creditors	520		
Corporation tax	14		
Dividend due	16		
Bank overdraft	560	1110	(374)
			232
Share capital and reserves			
£1 ordinary shares			50
Profit and loss account		68	
General reserve		114	182
			232

In recent months the company has experienced a serious decline in its liquidity position. The trade creditors are currently pressing for payment and the bank has asked the company to reduce the current level of its overdraft. The bank charges interest on the overdraft at 11 per cent per annum.

The management of Eurotech Ltd is considering two possible methods of raising finance to improve its liquidity. The first method is to factor the trade debtors. A factoring company has offered to provide an advance of 80 per cent of the approved value of trade debtors at an interest rate of 13 per cent per annum. Eurotech will also receive the factors sales and debt collection service for a fee of 2 per cent of sales turnover. The factoring service will mean that administration cost savings of £12 000 per annum can be made by Eurotech and it is also expected that the trade debtors will be reduced to an average of three months debtors. This will bring the company's credit period in line with the industry average and the advance will be based on this level of debtors.

The second method is to take out a long-term loan. A finance company has offered to lend Eurotech Ltd £360 000 using the freehold premises (currently valued at £650 000) as security. The rate of interest charged on the loan would be 14 per cent per annum.

Whichever method is adopted the finance raised will be used first to reduce the trade creditors to an average of two months outstanding and then any remaining balance would be used to reduce the overdraft at the bank.

In view of the problems referred to above, the management of Eurotech Ltd are concerned about the implications for additional working capital of launching a new product which it has recently developed. The product is a new type of car telephone which it intends to sell through small car accessory businesses, garages and large multiple stores. It is proposed that the new product should be launched in July 19X1.

Details of anticipated sales of the new product from each customer group for the foreseeable future are as follows:

Customer Type	July 19X1 sales £000	Monthly compound % sales growth	Credit period (months)
Car accessory businesses	6	5	1
Garages	12	10	2
Large multiple stores	18	20	3

Required:

(a) Based on the 19X0–19X1 figures, and assuming no new product is introduced:
  (i) Calculate the finance required to reduce the trade creditors to an average of two months outstanding.
  (ii) Calculate the net annual cost of each proposed financing method.
(b) Assuming the new product is introduced, prepare an ageing schedule of the monthly debtors balance relating to the new product for each of the first four months and comment on the information provided.

(Certified Diploma)

6 Babbage (Bearings) Ltd produces a single product which is sold to engineering businesses throughout the UK. The following financial data is available concerning the product:

	Per unit	
	£	£
Selling price		40
Variable costs	36	
Fixed cost apportionment	3	39
Net profit per unit		1

At present the company has an annual sales turnover of £4.8 million and an average collection period for debtors of one month. In order to stimulate sales the company is proposing a relaxation of its credit policy. By permitting all customers an average collection period of three months it is estimated that new markets in other parts of Europe could be developed. This would increase the total value of sales by 30%. The expected increase in sales will require an additional investment in stocks of £250 000 and there will be an increase in trade creditors of £300 000. There will be no increase in fixed costs as a result of the increase in sales. The company requires an 18% return on its investments.

Required:

(a) Evaluate the proposed change in credit policy assuming:
  (i) all customers take on average three months to pay.
  (ii) only new customers in Europe take on average three months to pay and UK customers continue to take an average of one month to pay.
(b) Identify and discuss the major sources of information that may be used by Babbage (Bearings) Ltd to evaluate the creditworthiness of its customers.
(c) Outline the major elements of a company's credit policy.

(Certified Diploma)

7* Comfylot plc produces garden seats which are sold in both domestic and export markets. Sales during the next year are forecast to be £16 million, 70% to the UK domestic market and 30% to the export market, and are expected to occur steadily throughout the year. 80% of UK sales are on credit terms, with payment due in 30 days. On average UK domestic customers take 57 days to make payment. An initial deposit of 15% of the sales price is paid by all export customers. All export sales are on 60 days credit with an average collection period for credit sales of 75 days. Bad debts are currently 0.75% of UK credit sales, and 1.25% of export sales (net of the deposit).

  Comfylot wishes to investigate the effects of each of three possible operational changes:

  (i) Domestic credit management could be undertaken by a non-recourse factoring company. The factor would charge a service fee of 1.5% and would provide finance on 80% of the debts factored at a cost of base rate + 2.5%. The finance element must be taken as part of the agreement with the factor. Using a factor would save an initial £85 000 per year in administration costs, but would lead to immediate redundancy payments of £15 000.

  (ii) As an alternative to using the factor a cash discount of 1.5% for payment in seven days could be offered on UK domestic sales. It is expected that 40% of domestic credit customers would use the cash discount. The discount would cost an additional £25 000 per year to administer, and would reduce bad debts to 0.50% of UK credit sales.

  (iii) Extra advertising could be undertaken to stimulate export sales. Comfylot has been approached by a European satellite TV company which believes that £300 000 of advertising could increase export sales in the coming year by up to 30%. There is a 0.2 chance of a 20% increase in export sales, a 0.5 chance of a 25% increase and a 0.3 chance of a 30% increase. Direct costs of production are 65% of the sales price. Administration costs would increase by £30 000, £40 000 and £50 000 for the 20%, 25% and 30% increases in export sales respectively. Increased export sales are likely to result in the

Note: * indicates a more complex question.

average collection period of the credit element of all exports lengthening by five days, and bad debts increasing to 1.5% of all export credit sales.

Bank base rate is currently 13% per year, and Comfylot can borrow overdraft finance at 15% per year. These rates are not expected to change in the near future.

Taxation may be ignored.

Required:

(a) Discuss whether any of the three suggested changes should be adopted by Comfylot plc. All relevant calculations must be shown.

(ACCA – part of question)

CHAPTER 14

Corporate restructuring (including takeovers and divestments)

OBJECTIVES

In this chapter we shall deal with the following:

● the nature of corporate restructuring
● the background to mergers
● the technicalities of mergers
● the regulation of mergers in the UK
● the economic success of mergers
● a review of two recently contested mergers
● divestments and the various means of achieving them
● the means of financing divestments
● other corporate restructuring devices

INTRODUCTION

A striking feature of the post-war business scene, throughout the world and particularly in the UK, is the extent of the use of various corporate restructuring devices. This feature has become more evident over time, perhaps promoted by the emergence of increasingly sophisticated techniques for achieving corporate restructures.

Changes in the economic environment and in the objectives being pursued by a particular firm may be seen by its management as necessitating significant changes in the firm's structure. Such changes may be concerned with the assets employed by the firm; or with the manner in which those assets are financed, or by some combination of both of these. Whatever the precise nature of a particular corporate restructuring, logically it should be undertaken to work towards the achievement of the firm's objectives. On the assumption that the firm's major financial objective is the maximisation of the shareholders' wealth, it is against that objective that the effectiveness of any particular restructuring should be assessed. Corporate restructuring is clearly a necessary and desirable feature of any dynamic and flexible economic environment. Despite the bad publicity which has attached to some aspects of certain corporate restructures, for example aspects of the Guinness takeover of Distillers in 1985–1986, corporate restructuring should not be seen as anything but a means for firms to pursue their legitimate objectives.

We shall start our consideration of the major restructuring devices which are found at present in the UK by concentrating in a little detail on two of the more important areas, namely takeovers (mergers) and divestments. Following that we shall take a look at some other corporate restructuring devices found in the UK today.

TAKEOVERS AND MERGERS

In recent years, buying existing businesses in their entirety has become a very popular way of investing. Not all firms do this, nor do those firms which have done so necessarily do it habitually, yet scarcely a week seems to pass without the city pages of the national newspapers telling us of an attempt on the ownership of some firm or another, often with quite large ones as targets.

In practice this type of investment is typically effected by one firm (the *bidder*) buying sufficient ordinary voting shares in the other firm (the *target*) to be able to exercise control or even to have complete ownership.

Whether we refer to a particular situation as a *takeover* or as a *merger* is a matter of semantics. Where the two firms are of similar size and/or there is agreement between the two sets of management as to the desirability of the outcome then it tends to be referred to as a 'merger'; otherwise the expression 'takeover' tends to be used. In this chapter, for convenience, we shall use the word merger irrespective of the circumstances.

Despite certain apparent differences, from the bidder's viewpoint, between a merger and the more traditional investment opportunity, the same basic principles should be applied to its appraisal. That is to say, a merger which would represent a net increase in the current worth of the bidder (a positive net present value) should be pursued, if the firm's financial objective is to be achieved.

REASONS FOR MERGERS

Theoretically a firm will become a bidder when it sees an opportunity to make an investment with a positive incremental net present value. It is likely to perceive such an opportunity, either

(a) where it considers that the incremental cash flows from the investment, when discounted at a rate consistent with the level of risk associated with those cash flows, are positive; or

(b) where the reduction in the level of risk associated with the bidder's existing cash flows causes the appropriate rate for discounting those cash flows to fall, thus increasing the NPV of the existing cash flows of the bidder.

Frequently a particular merger is attractive to the bidding firm for both of these reasons.

EXAMPLE   Bidder plc has an existing business which is expected to generate net positive cash flows of £1m for each of the next five years. The level of risk associated with these cash flows is perceived by the capital market as justifying a rate of return of 15 per cent p.a. Thus the net present value of Bidder is: £1m × 3.352 = £3.352m (where 3.352 is the annuity factor relating to 15 per cent p.a. for five years).

Bidder sees an opportunity to acquire the entire equity of Target plc. Forecasts indicate that the annual net positive cash flows of the merged firm would be £1.5m for each of the next five years and that the required rate of return would be 12 per cent p.a. The net present value of Bidder after the merger, should it take place, would become: £1.5m x 3.605 = £5.408m (where 3.605 is the annuity factor relating to 12 per cent p.a. for five years).

This would imply that it would be worth Bidder paying any amount up to £2.056m (i.e. £5.408m – £3.352m) for Target. Note that part of this amount arises from the existing cash flows of Bidder being discounted at a lower rate than previously. This factor would only arise where the merger had the effect of reducing risk.

It is quite feasible that £2.056m exceeds the current market value of Target. The reasons why this could be the case include:

(a) the target's expected cash flows being less than £0.5m p.a., i.e. the merged business might be able to generate more expected cash flows than the sum of the expected cash flows of the separate firms;

(b) the possibility of the risk attaching to the combined firm being less than applies to the overall level of risk of the separate parts.

Over the years a number of observers has sought to identify the factors which make mergers attractive, particularly to the bidder. Let us now consider some of these factors and discuss each of them in the context of the overall risk reduction and cash flow expansion mentioned above.

(a) *Elimination or reduction of competition.* Where the bidder and target are in competition for the market for their output, a merger could lead to a monopoly or at least a larger market share for the merged unit. This strength in the market place might enable prices to be raised without loss of turnover – hence an increase in cash flows. (As we shall see later in this chapter, in the UK such a merger may well fall foul of the Monopolies Commission.)

(b) *Safeguarding sources of supply or sales outlets.* A bidder may be attracted to a merger where the target is a supplier of some vital raw material which is in short supply or which the target could stop supplying, beyond the control of the bidder. Similarly, where the target represents a major sales outlet for the bidder, the target could cause problems for the bidder if it started to promote sales of the product of one of the bidder's competitors. Here a merger may not increase annual cash flows but it may well lower the perceived risk because the cash flows of both parts of the combined business would become more certain.

(c) *Access to the economies of scale that a larger business could yield.* Such economies may be in a wide variety of areas: for example, a larger buying power may lead to lower prices being paid for raw materials, larger production runs may become possible leading to savings in set-up costs and other overheads; combining administration and accounting activities may lead to savings in the associated costs. The effect of these would tend to decrease total cash outflows.

(d) *Access to some aspect of the target which the bidder considers under-utilised.* These might include:

   (i) particular tangible assets, including land, plant and cash, which are not fully exploited; and

   (ii) particular intangible assets such as its standing in some market, perhaps an export market or a particular contract; or technological expertise, which could be better exploited.

Under-utilisation of assets suggests poor management and bidders will sometimes be attracted to such targets where they have an abundance of management skills themselves. Firms must seek ways of promoting rising management talent, and expansion through merger with mismanaged firms provides an excellent means of creating promotional opportunities. Under-utilisation of assets implies the possibility of acquiring assets at a discount on their potential economic value.

The overall effect of such mergers would be expected to be an increase in positive cash flows, though stronger management skills being brought to bear on the target's assets may also decrease uncertainty about the cash flows, i.e. reduce risk.

(e) *Risk spreading and reduction through diversification.* Merging two firms with different activities will reduce risk since the returns from the different activities are unlikely to be perfectly positively correlated with one another.

Though this fact is frequently put forward as the justification for such mergers, in the context of maximisation of shareholders' wealth, it is invalid in itself. This is because, as we saw in Chapter 9, such diversification could be, and probably is, undertaken by individual shareholders at little or no cost. Their wealth will not be increased by having this done for them, because security market prices seem to assume that such diversification will already have taken place.

As we saw in Chapter 2 this provides us with an example of possible conflict of interests between shareholders and managers. Shareholders are unlikely to be benefited by the merger because they will typically have undertaken such risk-reducing diversification on a 'homemade' basis.

The managers, on the other hand, do not hold portfolios of employments, so the only way that they can achieve this risk reduction is through diversification at the firm level. A popular, though by no means the only, way to diversify is through merger.

Legislation to protect the public interest from monopolies has meant that mergers within the same industry have sometimes been impossible to achieve. This could leave firms which are ambitious to expand with diversification as their only possibility. It should be noted that, irrespective of the benefits of diversification, the other reasons for merger could still apply to a particular merger between firms in different industries. Even economies of scale, particularly in the administration of the merged firm, could apply.

Synergy

We can see then that, in theory, mergers can bring real benefits to shareholders due to genuine increases in positive cash flows and/or risk reduction. These benefits are often referred to as arising from *synergy*, a 'two plus two equals five' syndrome with the whole being greater than the sum of the parts.

We should note that these synergy benefits should accrue to the shareholders of the target as well as to those of the bidder. Merger can only take place where target shareholders are prepared to sell their shares. They will only do this where they are offered something in excess of what they perceive to be the current value (usually the Stock Exchange quotation) of those shares. Unless the shareholders of the target and the management of the bidder are basing their valuations on different information from one another, this excess can only exist due to the synergy benefits perceived by the bidder's management.

Going back to our example, the excess of £2.056m over the current market value of the equity of Target is a measure of the value of the synergy benefits. If the current market value of Target's equity is as high as £2.056m then there will be no synergy benefits of merger and, from a financial viewpoint, it should not take place. If the market value of Target's equity immediately before the merger is below £2.056m but Bidder has to pay as much as this in order to persuade the shareholders to sell, then all of the benefits from synergy would accrue to Target's shareholders, and none of it to those of Bidder. It is therefore unlikely that Bidder would offer as much as the £2.056m.

FINANCING OF MERGERS

It is important to realise that mergers are basically open market transactions with one party buying assets belonging to another party. How much the bidder firm offers and how it proposes to pay are matters of judgement which must be decided by the management. In practice, often such decisions are only made after taking advice from experts, usually merchant bankers.

As regards financing, the bidder must seek a method which is both attractive to the target's shareholders and acceptable to itself.

The following are commonly-encountered merger financing approaches.

(a) *Cash*. Cash has its attractions to the recipients as it gives something which they can use immediately, for consumption or reinvestment, without having to incur any cost. Target company shareholders receiving shares or loan stock which they wish not to keep, must incur cost and effort to turn them into cash. The receipt of cash will, however, in most cases be treated as a disposal for Capital Gains Tax purposes and many shareholders would not welcome the possibility of a charge arising from this.

From the bidder's point of view, cash may not be available and can only be obtained by making a public issue of shares or loan stock for cash, or borrowing in some form – a course of action which, for various reasons including cost, the bidder may not wish to follow.

(b) *Ordinary shares in the bidder firm*. Ordinary shares may be attractive to the recipients, who would simply cease being shareholders in the target and become shareholders in the bidder. After all, before the merger they hold shares in one firm (the target) so are obviously not hostile to equity investment *per se*. This is not to say that they wish to hold shares in the bidder, in which case the problems of disposal, mentioned above, will come into play. From the bidder's viewpoint, issuing shares to exchange for those of the target, has its attractions. Cash will not need to be raised and the firm will not be taking on the contractual commitments to pay interest or to repay capital as would be the case with loan stock issues.

We should not feel that share issues cost the bidder's original shareholders nothing, however. Issuing shares as the consideration in a merger represents an opportunity cost to the bidder, since presumably the issue could alternatively be made for cash.

(c) *Loan stocks of the bidder firm*. Loan stocks have their part to play but have serious disadvantages from both viewpoints. As we have seen, they create binding contractual obligations on the bidder both as regards interest and capital repayment. To the equity holder of the target they represent a distinct change of investment, a change to a risk/return profile which they may find unacceptable. Switching back to equities will involve them in inconvenience and cost, possibly including a Capital Gains Tax liability. The advantages of loan stocks in the merger context would seem to be twofold. To the bidder they would not have the effect of diluting control as a result of extending its share ownership (loan stock holders do not usually have votes at the annual general meeting). To the recipient they may have the attraction that, as they will have fixed interest payments and usually have a fixed capital repayment date, their market value is supported. Where target shareholders are sceptical about the future success of the merged firm, they may prefer an investment in it whose returns are surer than are those from the equity capital.

As well as the specific factors referred to in respect of each financing method, the bidder will need to have regard to its desired level of gearing. Perceptions as to what this should be may well change with the merger. The bidder's management may feel that, due to perceived changes in risk caused by the merger, the merged firm's gearing potential is different from that of the bidder alone.

Table 14.1 Recent takeovers and mergers by industrial and commercial companies within the UK

Year	Total number	Mean value £m	Cash %	Ordinary shares %	Preference shares and loan stocks %
1985	474	15.0	40	52	8
1986	696	21.5	26	58	16
1987	1125	13.7	32	62	6
1988	1499	15.2	70	22	8
1989	1337	20.4	82	13	5
1990	779	10.7	77	18	5
1991	506	20.6	70	29	1
1992	426	13.7	63	36	1

Source: Central Statistical Office

Table 14.1 shows how recent UK mergers have been financed. Though the mix varies from merger to merger and over time, it is clear that cash and ordinary shares of the bidder company are very much more important than preference shares and loan stock. The decline in merger activity over recent years, which appears to have been continued in 1993, is almost certainly partly caused by the economic recession of the early 1990s.

Other possible reasons for the reduction in the number of takeovers since the late 1980s will be discussed later in this chapter when we are assessing the evidence on the success of mergers.

APPRAISAL OF THE MERGER

By the bidder

A merger is simply an investment and should be appraised as one. The expected cash flows from the merged firm must be estimated and discounted according to a cost of capital factor which incorporates consideration of market perceptions of the risk of the merged firm, i.e. the systematic risk. The cash flows which must be assessed will include all of the normal operating cash flows of the new undertaking. In addition any cash flows arising from disposing of any unwanted divisions of the target (or of the bidder) arising from the merger, including any cost of making employees redundant, must be taken into account. We must also include the amount paid to acquire the target's equity. Where payment is not all in cash, the amount should include the opportunity cost of the equity and/or loan stock issue, i.e. it should include the amount of cash that would have been received for the share/loan stock issue had it been made for cash, assuming that all other factors would have been the same.

If the net present value calculated from the above is positive, then logically the investment should be made.

There will usually be non-financial factors to consider such as the acceptability of declaring employees redundant in order to gain potential economies of scale. These will have to be balanced with the strictly financial aspects when reaching a decision.

By the target's shareholders

Appraisal of the offer by this group is just as much a capital investment decision as it is for the bidder. Each shareholder must assess whether future cash benefits from accepting the offer, suitably discounted, will exceed the discounted cash flow benefits of retaining the shares of the target.

What level of expertise and sophistication will be applied to this appraisal and whether it will be done at all, on the basis suggested above, depends on the individual shareholder. The large investing institutions will, it is presumed, reach their decisions on the basis of reason and logic. This may be less the case with the individual private investor.

HOSTILE AND FRIENDLY MERGERS

Many merger attempts are resisted by the directors of the target firm, i.e. they are 'hostile' mergers. This may be for a variety of reasons including:

- a belief that there is a lack of commercial logic in the merger;
- a feeling that the price being offered to the target shareholders for their shares is too low; and
- an understandable desire by the target firm's directors to protect their personal futures. The immediate outcome of many mergers is the departure of some or all of the target's directors.

Hostile mergers often capture the headlines. We shall shortly be reviewing two recent such mergers involving Burmah Castrol/Foseco and Rentokil/Securiguard.

An increasing number of mergers are 'friendly' rather than hostile. Here the directors of both firms negotiate the terms and conditions which will be offered to the target firm's shareholders. When the formal bid is made, it is recommended, by the target's directors, that it should be accepted. The weight of such a recommendation tends to be sufficient to sway the shareholders to accept. An example of a friendly merger occurred when two major brewery firms, Greenalls and Devenish, joined forces in 1993.

REGULATION OF MERGERS IN THE UK

In the UK mergers are regulated in two ways, each by a different agency. The way in which this is done provides an interesting example of statutory regulation and 'self'-regulation working hand in hand.

The Monopolies and Mergers Commission

This is a statutory body which derives its power from the Fair Trading Act 1973. It is concerned with the outcome of the merger, rather than the conduct of the merger operation itself.

The Monopolies and Mergers Commission is empowered by statute to delay and to investigate any merger referred to it by the Secretary of State for Industry. The Secretary of State will refer mergers to the Commission on the advice of the Director General of Fair Trading, where it is considered that it may be against the public interest for them to proceed. The Secretary of State will not usually refer a particular merger to the Commission unless a monopoly is likely to result. The Commission publishes its findings in reports that are sometimes long and detailed.

In fact, relatively few of the many mergers which have taken place since the Commission was established have been referred to it. Of those which have been investigated, few have resulted in the Commission exercising its statutory power of veto in respect of them.

It seems that the Commission has not had great effect in restricting merger activity, nor was it intended to. The general philosophy of the legislation and of the

Commission is that it is up to firms and shareholders to decide on the economic desirability of particular mergers, with the state stepping in only when it fears that the public interest is threatened by the outcome of a merger.

The City Panel on Takeovers and Mergers

The Panel is a self-regulatory body which includes in its membership representatives of most of the leading financial institutions of the City of London. These include the Stock Exchange and the Committee of London Clearing Banks. The Panel and the Code which it administers were established in 1968, following a number of merger battles in the 1960s, which many observers saw as involving tactics which did not reflect well on big business and the financial institutions. Many of the less savoury encounters involved firms which are (or were) household names, thus attracting a high level of press and broadcasting attention.

The main fears were that actions of bidders and of target management, particularly in cases where the bid was opposed by the target's management, were having adverse effects on shareholders, more particularly small shareholders, of the target. Specifically it seemed that there were differences in the treatment of different shareholders as regards the quality and quantity of information each received pertaining to the merger.

The Code, which is constantly under review, comprises a set of rules defining the steps to be followed by both bidder and target in the course of the merger negotiations. The Code does not really address itself to wider questions of the desirability of the merger *per se*, it deals only with the conduct of the merger operation. The Panel has no statutory powers to enforce the Code, but it is able to apply moral pressures on offenders. Ultimately it can request that one of its members – the Stock Exchange – excludes the offending firm from quotation.

Whether the Panel and the Code have achieved their objectives is a question of debate, though most observers appear to feel that much of the more extravagant behaviour evident in the 1960s is not obvious today.

PRACTICAL STEPS TOWARDS THE MERGER

Most mergers are effected by the bidder buying from the target's shareholders sufficient ordinary shares to give control or even total ownership of the equity. This is usually done in two stages:

(a) by the bidder buying shares, for cash, in the capital market; and then
(b) by its making a formal offer to remaining shareholders by direct mailing and therefore outside the established capital market.

It is not common for bidders to acquire a large proportion of the required shares by buying them in the capital market. Once investors realise that there is a large buyer in the market, the share price will tend to rise in anticipation of a formal offer, making it uneconomic for the bidder to proceed further in this way. The formal offer to each shareholder probably becomes cheaper at the point where the capital market quotation reaches the proposed formal offer price. Of course all capital market purchases have to be paid for in cash, which may be a disincentive to a bidder who wishes to finance the merger in some other way. The formal offer document, which is usually communicated to shareholders by post, contains the precise terms of the offer and a statement explaining why, in the view of the bidder's management, it should be accepted. The offer document must be submitted for the approval of the Director General of Fair Trading and of the City Panel.

Usually offers are made on condition that they are accepted by the owners of a specified percentage of the shares concerned. In this way the bidder can ensure that, in the event of insufficient acceptance being forthcoming, it will not end up being forced to buy shares which it may not want. If, for example, the bidder wishes to obtain a minimum of 60 per cent of the shares of the target, it would probably prefer not to be forced to buy, say, 25 per cent if the owners of the other 75 per cent decide not to accept the offer. 90 per cent is often the proportion stated on offer documents because UK company law gives any firm, which owns that percentage of the equity of another firm, the right to acquire the remaining 10 per cent, with or without the consent of their owners, on the same terms as those on which the others were acquired.

A question which the target shareholders must consider on receiving the offer is whether to accept this particular offer or to hope for an improved one. Whilst the failure of an offer can cause the bidder to withdraw, frequently the bidder's reaction is to make an increased offer. This can be a difficult question for the shareholder because withdrawal by the bidder will probably result in the quoted share price of the target dropping back, from the high figure which it will probably have reached in the light of the offer, to the pre-offer price. On the other hand, rejection of the first offer is quite likely to result in a better one. Perhaps, though, this is no worse than the dilemma which all shareholders experience when they see their shares quoted at a high price; should they sell and take advantage of it or should they wait, in the hope that the price will go even higher?

The management of the target is most unlikely to react passively to advances made by a bidder to the target shareholders. Quite often the bidder will seek the support of the target management in advance of its formal offer. If the management supports the offer, because for example it feels that there is commercial logic in such a merger, it is likely that the offer document will include a statement by the target's management to that effect.

Frequently, however, the target's management will be hostile to the offer and will oppose it with some vigour. Typical tactics employed by hostile target management include:

(a) issuing statements countering the claims of the bidder and putting forward the arguments for remaining independent;
(b) revaluing the target firm's assets in an attempt to show that the bidder's offer undervalues them;
(c) releasing other information relevant to the target's future as an independent firm.

The object of these tactics is probably to increase the share price of the target to a point where the bidder's offer looks low and will be rejected.

Quite often these battles are long and bitter with claims of one side being met with counter-claims from the other, and offers being increased, until eventually an offer is accepted or the bidder withdraws. The battles can be damaging; they are expensive and, if the merger finally takes place, much bitterness can be carried into the management of the merged firm.

The results of the battle are not necessarily all bad: much new information about both parties tends to be forthcoming in statements and this enables the market to value the firms better.

ARE MERGERS SUCCESSFUL?

Having looked at why and how mergers occur, it seems appropriate to ask whether or not they appear to be successful. A number of studies has considered this question. These have fallen into three types:

(a) those which have asked managers of merged firms whether they consider the merger to have been successful or not;

(b) those which have tried to measure the success of mergers in terms of accounting profits; and

(c) those which have looked at the returns available to the shareholders of merged firms to see if these were better than they were likely to have been had the merger not taken place. Returns in this context are capital gains, plus dividends for the period as a percentage of the share's market value at the start of the period.

Of the first type, the general conclusion of managers seems to be that the mergers had not been beneficial. Coopers and Lybrand (1993) undertook a study during 1992 which comprised in-depth interviews with senior managers of 50 large UK firms which had been involved in a merger. The conclusion was that 54 per cent of mergers were not financially successful. This was remarkably consistent with the result which Coopers and Lybrand found when they conducted a similar study in 1973 and with that which Newbould (1970) found. The 1993 study identified several major causes of failure. These are set out in Table 14.2.

Table 14.2 Causes of failure of UK mergers

Cause of failure	% of interviewees who mentioned the factor as a cause of failure
Management attitudes	85
Lack of post-acquisition integration planning	80
Lack of knowledge by the predator of the target and its industry	45
Poor management and management practices in the target	45
Little or no experience of the target management in acquiring other firms	30

Source: Coopers and Lybrand

Typical of the results of the second type were those shown by Meeks (1977). This study, again using UK data, found that average profitability prior to the merger exceeds that for the post-merger period, to a significant extent.

Generally the results from the third type of study are in conflict. Franks, Broyles & Hecht (1977) found significant gains to the target shareholders, particularly in the period leading up to the merger. They also found no detriment to the bidder's shareholders, either before or after the merger; in fact small gains were made by this group.

Franks and Harris (1989), using a large sample of UK mergers, found positive gains for both sets of shareholders during the pre-merger and immediate post-merger periods. They also found, however, post-merger losses by the bidder's shareholders. Limmack (1991) came to a similar conclusion to that of Franks and Harris.

Broadly, the results of these three types of study are in agreement. Generally mergers seem not to be successful. This fact may well explain why the number of mergers seems to have reduced fairly dramatically since the late 1980s (see Table 14.1). Other possible reasons include:

- a greater professionalism among corporate management leading to fewer cheap targets
- relatively depressed share prices of 1980s being increased, again leading to fewer cheaper targets
- a change in the perceptions of corporate managers of the desirability of large, diversified units. This point is raised again, in the context of divestment, later in this chapter.

CASE STUDIES

To give some impression of the way in which many mergers are conducted, it might be useful to consider two recent cases. It is important to recognise that there is nothing unusual or peculiar about these particular examples; they are fairly typical of such merger battles.

CASE STUDY 1   **Burmah Castrol and Foseco**

On 15 October 1990 Burmah made a formal offer to the shareholders of Foseco for their ordinary shares. The offer was £2.75 in cash or loan stock for each Foseco share. The Foseco board responded by claiming that the Burmah offer was wholly unwelcome and unsolicited and that it substantially undervalued Foseco's worldwide business. The shareholders were advised not to accept the offer.

The bidder and target firms

Burmah Castrol plc.   In the formal offer document Burmah described itself as 'a leading international marketer of specialised oil and chemical products'. Burmah was incorporated in 1886 as one of the earliest oil companies. The firm had expanded dramatically in the 1970s as a result of a number of conglomerate-style acquisitions, which history had shown mainly to have been ill-judged. Subsequently the firm undertook a massive asset disposal process which left it as a specialist lubricants business with minor interests in fuels and chemicals.

Foseco plc. Foseco describes itself as specialising in advanced materials technology in three areas: metallurgical chemicals, construction and mining chemicals, and abrasives. The company was formed in 1931.

Events before the formal offer

In the morning of the day on which the offer was formally announced (15 October 1990) Burmah had succeeded in buying 10.6 per cent of Foseco's ordinary shares, through the Stock Exchange, for the offer price of £2.75.

The offer

On 8 November 1990 Schroders (Burmah's merchant bankers and advisers in the Foseco bid) sent a copy of the formal offer document to each of Foseco's shareholders. The offer was of £2.75 in cash, or loan notes with a value of £2.75, for each Foseco ordinary share. The conditions included a closing date for acceptances of 29 November 1990 and the opportunity for Burmah to withdraw if sufficient acceptances were not forthcoming to meet the objectives of the offer.

The document set out the reasons why Burmah believed that the offer should be accepted. These included Burmah's belief that:

(a) Foseco had been a dismal investment over the preceding decade;
(b) Foseco's board was unlikely to provide the redirection required to improve Foseco's performance;
(c) the offer, in view of (a) and (b), provided good value for the Foseco shares; and
(d) Burmah had the credentials, skills and experience to ensure a sound future for Foseco's businesses.

The document, which ran to 56 pages, also contained considerable details on the bid and on Burmah itself.

Foseco's reaction to the offer

The immediate reaction of the Foseco board was to oppose the bid and it wrote to its shareholders on 9 November expressing that opinion. On 20 November 1990 Foseco sent a 30-page defence document to each of its shareholders. The document set out what Foseco believed to be the reasons why the bid should be rejected. Foseco's main arguments were its belief that:

(a) there was a lack of a commercial case for Burmah acquiring Foseco;
(b) Burmah did not have the management credentials to run Foseco;
(c) the performance of Burmah in running that part of its existing operation which resembled the businesses of Foseco had been uninspiring; and
(d) the offer price seriously undervalued Foseco's business.

The document included a profit forecast for the year due to end on 31 December 1990 and a forecast increase in dividend.

Third party reaction to the offer

The general view taken by the press seemed to be that the bid was too low and that it would not be successful. Immediately following the announcement of the bid, the Foseco share price rose from £1.84 to £2.80. The fact that the price rose to greater than the offer price (£2.75) implied that the market believed that a higher bid would be forthcoming.

On 26 November 1990 the Secretary of State for Trade and Industry announced that the bid would not be referred to the Monopolies Commission.

A revised offer

By the closing date for the original offer, acceptances by holders of only 1 per cent of the Foseco shares had been received. Even with shares that Burmah had bought through the Stock Exchange since the original offer date, this meant that Burmah only had 21.75 per cent of the Foseco shares. On 4 December 1990 Burmah increased its offer to £3.00 (in cash or loan notes) for each Foseco share under the same conditions as the original offer, except that the closing date was now 21 December 1990.

Foseco's reaction to the revised offer

On 14 December 1990 Foseco sent a circular to all of its shareholders in which it advised refusal of the new offer. In this document the firm set out its plans, assuming that the takeover were to be unsuccessful, to do the following:

(a) seek to sell off its construction chemicals division;
(b) use cash generated from (a) to offer shareholders the opportunity to have their shares repurchased by the firm; and
(c) pay a 'special' dividend in addition to that which it had forecast in its defence document in response to the original offer.

The logic for (b) was presumably to try to be able to offer those shareholders who wanted it a means of liquidating their shares without selling them to Burmah, either directly or through the Stock Exchange. (We shall consider the question of share repurchase, as a separate matter, later in this chapter.) The special dividend was presumably a ploy to increase the share price above the offer price.

Third party reaction to the revised offer

The general press view seemed to be that the revised offer was high enough to be successful, also that if the offer were to be unsuccessful the share price would fall back. Investors seemed to agree because the price rose to £2.96, just below the offer price.

In the end the efforts of the Foseco board to defend the bid proved unsuccessful. By the deadline for acceptance of the offer Burmah had control of 63.5 per cent of the Foseco shares and Burmah had won.

CASE STUDY 2   **Rentokil and Securiguard**

On 18 May 1993 Rentokil formally offered £2.70 for each share of Securiguard. The directors of the latter firm recommended that the shareholders refuse the bid.

The bidder and target firms

Rentokil Group plc   The firm was first formed in 1927. Its main activities were in the fields of environmental and property services. Its turnover is around £500 million, of which a little more than 50 per cent came from outside the UK. Rentokil had steadily expanded over recent years, some of it as a result of merging with smaller firms in the industry. It tends to be regarded as a well managed, progressive firm.

Securiguard Group plc   The target was a fairly new firm, having been formed in 1982. Its activities were in the fields of security (guarding services), commercial cleaning, parcel delivery and personnel agencies. Its annual turnover, at the time of the bid, was around £170 million, of which about two-thirds derived from the UK. It had expanded fairly rapidly in the 1980s, mainly as a result of mergers. There seems to have been a belief that the firm had 'lost its way' somewhat in the early 1990s and that its share price, before the bid, reflected this view.

Events before the formal offer

At the date of the offer, Rentokil owned few if any shares in Securiguard. It would appear that it had made no real attempt to buy shares through the Stock Exchange in advance of the formal offer.

The offer

The formal offer document, which was sent to each Securiguard shareholder, stated that Rentokil would pay £2.70, in cash, for each Securiguard share. The document required that acceptances had to be received by 11 June 1993. It was understood that the motivation for the bid was Rentokil's desire to acquire a guarding service division.

Securiguard's reaction to the offer

Securiguard's directors advised rejection of the bid at the outset. In their defence document, sent to shareholders, the offer was described as 'derisory'. No real criticism of Rentokil, or of the merger *per se*, was made. The price seemed to be the real objection of the directors. No profit forecast was made, but the results for the six months to May 1993 were announced much earlier than had been the case in respect of the first half-year results previously. These showed turnover and profit to be sharply higher than they had been recently. A higher interim dividend was also announced.

Third party reaction to the offer

The press seemed to agree with Securiguard's directors that the offer was too low. It also seemed to be the consensus view that an increased offer would emerge. The immediate post-offer share price was £3.02, compared with £1.85 immediately before the offer. The fact that the price settled well above the offer price of £2.70 clearly implied that the market was confident of an increased offer.

A revised offer

By the original closing date for acceptances, holders of only 1.35 per cent of

Securiguard shares had accepted. Though Rentokil extended the closing date to 18 June and then to 25 June, no further acceptances were received. On 2 July a revised and, according to Rentokil, final offer of £3.45 (cash) per share was made.

Securiguard's reaction to the revised offer

Following the revised offer, the directors of Securiguard sought a meeting with their counterparts at Rentokil. Following this meeting the Securiguard directors recommended acceptance of the offer.

Third party reaction to the revised offer

The press view seemed to be that the offer was a good one and that it should be accepted. By 16 July holders of 93.08 per cent of Securiguard's shares had accepted and the firm became a subsidiary of Rentokil.

Some comments on the battles

In most ways the events which we have just reviewed were very typical of the majority of merger battles and of the tactics employed by target and bidder firms. Among others, three particular issues seem to emerge from these two cases.

(a) When they first started their merger moves, did the bidders have a ceiling price in mind or were they carried along by events into making large final offers? Burmah paid 9 per cent above its original offer price and 63 per cent above the pre-offer stock market price for Foseco. More dramatically, Rentokil paid 28 per cent above the original offer price and 86 per cent above the pre-offer price for Securiguard.

Obviously bidders in free markets do not always open the bidding at their ceiling price, but it could be the case, particularly with Rentokil, that once they had set their sights on the target, they were unwilling to accept defeat and be seen to do so.

(b) Would the targets have given information about themselves and their future had the bid not existed? It is pretty unusual for firms to issue a profit forecast, yet Foseco did so. Foseco also announced divestment and future dividend plans, also unusual events. Though Securiguard was not quite so forthcoming, it did bring forward the announcement of its half-year profits. Firms normally stick rigidly to the same profit announcement dates from one year to the next.

Clearly these announcements were made in an attempt to enhance the target share price and to defeat the bid. If shareholder wealth maximisation is the objective pursued by firms and if this can be achieved by the release of such information, why are firms so reluctant to release information about themselves in more normal circumstances? If releasing such information were to be seen as a means of defeating a takeover bid, logically they could also be used as a means of preventing one. If disclosure of information has the effect of increasing share prices, it could have the effect of making the shares too expensive for a potential bidder to contemplate. These two targets, particularly Foseco, may have been able to avoid costly and, ultimately, unsuccessful defences against the bid.

(c) Would the increased dividends, announced by both of these target firms, really have enhanced the share price? Presumably this was the reason for the increases in dividends, yet the theories and evidence, which we examined in Chapter 12, do not support this at all. Could this imply that corporate managers are either not aware of, or that they do not believe, the theories and evidence on dividends and share prices?

INTERNATIONAL MERGERS

The increasing internationalisation of commerce has led to mergers between firms in different countries. The European Union's single market, which started in 1993, seems to have led to UK firms being particularly active in mergers with firms in other EU countries. It appears that, in 1993, UK firms were the most active mergers participants in the EU, both as bidders and as targets (Hollinger 1993). An example of a recent merger where the UK firm was the bidder involved Kingfisher, the owner of several UK retail chains including Woolworth and Comet, which, in February 1993, paid £560 million for Darty, the owners of a chain of electrical appliance retailers throughout France.

DIVESTMENTS

In some circumstances a firm may wish to sell off some part of its business, perhaps a division or subsidiary company. The reasons for this could include:

(a) *A desire to concentrate on its core activities*. A firm operating in a range of areas of business, either as a result of organic growth or following mergers, may decide that it would prefer to concentrate on its main area of expertise. Such rationalisations have become quite common recently and possibly reflect a view, which we shall discuss in Chapter 15, that the future lies with smaller, more focused businesses.

An example of a recent sell-off, where the reason given was a desire to concentrate on core activities, was provided by the Trustee Savings Bank when it sold its Eurodollar car rental subsidiary for £192 million in September 1993.

(b) *A wish to get rid of some part of its business which is causing problems*, such as a lack of an acceptable level of profitability. This, together with reason (a), perhaps provides an example of the opposite of synergy, i.e. a 'five plus one equals four' syndrome, where the sum of the parts is greater than the whole.

(c) *A need to raise cash*. The need to raise cash may arise from a desire to make investments in other parts of the business, perhaps including a merger. The reason given for many recent sell-offs has been the desire to raise cash to enable a reduction in the level of capital gearing. An example of the latter was when, in March 1993, United Biscuit, the UK confectionery manufacturer, sold Terry's, its chocolate division, to the US food and tobacco group Philip Morris for £220 million. United Biscuit also gave a desire to concentrate on its core activities, of biscuit and savoury snack manufacture, as part of the reason for the sale. Some sell-offs, particularly those involving smaller firms, might be caused by a need to raise cash to avoid being forced into liquidation (bankruptcy) as a result of an inability to meet financial obligations.

In effect, divestments are the opposite of takeovers. Indeed, many of the divestments which have occurred recently were of subsidiaries acquired by rash takeovers during the 1970s and 1980s. Burmah Castrol provides an example of this.

When assessing the effectiveness of a divestment, the corporate objectives of both seller and buyer should be the touchstone. Assuming that shareholder wealth is the major financial criterion, an NPV analysis of the financial benefits and costs should be undertaken by both parties.

There are various means which are used to effect divestments, the more important of which we shall briefly consider.

Management buy-outs

Here the management of the particular part of the business which is to be disposed of buy it from the firm. These, according to KPMG Corporate Finance, have grown enormously in number over recent years in the UK. In 1980 there were about 100, but during 1992 there were about 500. The average value has also dramatically increased from a mean value per buy-out of £0.4 million in 1980 to £5.1 million per buy-out in 1992. There is evidence that the number and mean size of management buy-outs has been rather lower in 1993 than in 1992, almost certainly the result of the economic recession.

Some management buy-outs have proved to be very successful and have led to successful stock market flotations of the bought-out undertakings. Some of these have made millionaires of the managers concerned. During 1992, there were flotations of two major and notable buy-outs. These were MFI (self-assembly furniture), the largest management buy-out so far, and Taunton Cider. In November 1993, Abacus, an electrical components distributor, was floated at a valuation of around £35 million. The firm was the subject of a £3.4 million management buy-out in 1989, by a team of four of its managers.

Since the managers are unlikely to be able to raise all of the cash necessary to make the buy-out, some fairly complicated financing arrangements have been developed. Loans have accounted for much of the finance, hence the label 'leveraged buy-out'. The high level of gearing required has engendered relatively high risk, high coupon rate lending, known in the US as 'junk bonds'. 'Mezzanine' finance has also been a feature of a number of management buy-outs. This is basically a high coupon rate loan with equity possibilities. Usually there is some right to convert the loan finance into equity, but only if the firm through which the buy-out is effected becomes quoted on the Stock Exchange. The evidence on the success of management buy-outs is thin and inconclusive; however, it appears that managers taking over the business which they run is likely to continue to occur.

Buy-ins

Here a group of individuals puts together an offer for part, or possibly all, of the business of a firm with which they have previously had no particular connection.

Like management buy-outs, buy-ins have become increasingly popular in the 1980s. According to the Centre for Management Buyout Research at Nottingham University, there was just one UK buy-in, worth £0.5m, during 1979. In 1989, however, there were 147 buy-ins, worth an average of £24.5m each. By 1990, no doubt as a result of the recession, there were 111 UK buy-ins, worth an average of £5.8m each. Many of the features of management buy-outs are present with buy-ins, including the means of financing such deals.

An example of a recent buy-in occurred in October 1993 when TI Group, specialist engineers, sold part of a business which it had taken over, in its merger with Dowty, in 1992. The leader of the buy-in team was a former Dowty manager. The £40 million proceeds have been used by TI to reduce its capital gearing.

Buy-ins seem to occur quite often where the majority shareholder of a small family-type company wishes to retire. An example of this occurred in 1992, when a former manager with Mars led a team to buy-in Granelli McDermott, an ice cream manufacturer based in Cheadle, whose owner wished to retire.

Sell-offs

Sell-offs involve one established firm selling part of its business to another established firm, normally for cash. This is probably what Foseco intended to do with its construction chemicals divisions, had it avoided the Burmah merger. Some sell-offs have occurred under threat of takeover.

OTHER CORPORATE RESTRUCTURING ARRANGEMENTS

Spin-offs

Part of a firm's business is floated (spun-off) as a separate (probably quoted) firm and the existing shareholders receive the appropriate number of shares in the new firm. There is no change in ownership, except that the shareholders directly own the spun-off part, instead of owning it through the intermediary of the original firm. The reasons for doing this might include:

(a) *A desire to give the spun-off firm its own distinct corporate identity.*

(b) *Avoidance of a takeover attempt on the whole firm.* The value of the spun-off portion may not have been noticed in the original firm, except perhaps by a potential predator. By spinning-off a particularly valuable part of the business, the market will have the opportunity to assess that part as a separate unit. This may make it unattractive to predators. This point does imply a lack of belief in the efficiency of the capital market.

A mammoth spin-off, which was driven by the desire to avoid a takeover, involved ICI, one of the UK's largest firms. The spin-off was finalised in June 1993. ICI divided itself into two parts. Chemicals, paints, etc. formed one part, which retained the ICI name. The other part, which was named Zenaca, now has the old ICI's bioscience activities. In exchange for their old ICI shares, the shareholders were given shares both in the new ICI and in Zenaca. Hanson, a well seasoned and successful bidder, had bought a number of old ICI shares. ICI management feared a bid from Hanson and considered that one could most effectively be avoided by restructuring in this way.

Share repurchase

The Companies Act 1981 gave firms the right, provided that certain conditions were complied with, to purchase some of their shares from existing shareholders, should those shareholders wish to sell. The reasons for this include:

(a) *The possibility that it will increase the share prices.* This is because the number of shares will be reduced, which reduces the potential supply. Repurchase could also increase earnings per share where the cash which has been used for the repurchase was previously not very effectively used.

(b) *The provision of a means for a particular shareholder in a firm not quoted, or not actively traded, to liquidate an equity investment.* It could therefore provide an 'escape route' for a financier who only wished to have a limited-term equity investment with the firm.

SUMMARY

Corporate restructuring is an increasingly significant aspect of the means by which firms seek to pursue their corporate objectives. All forms of restructuring should, in the context of a shareholder wealth maximisation goal, seek either to increase the firm's cash flows or to reduce the level of the riskiness of those cash flows. Any restructuring scheme should therefore be assessed by all parties on an NPV basis.

An important type of restructuring is the takeover or merger. Mergers are financed in a variety of ways, typically in a combination of some of these ways. Merger activity in the UK is regulated by the Monopolies and Mergers Commission and by the City Panel. Usually the bidder buys shares in the target firm through the Stock Exchange, before making the formal offer. Despite doubts about the commercial success of mergers, evidence suggests that on the whole they prove not to be beneficial to shareholders. The Burmah–Foseco and Rentokil–Securiguard merger 'battles' were typical of such battles in most respects. The behaviour of the managements of those firms raises several issues relating to business finance.

Divestments, of various types, are another increasingly important form of corporate restructuring. Means of achieving divestment include management buy-outs, buy-ins and sell-offs. The reasons for divestment are varied but include a desire on the part of many firms to rationalise their operations and to concentrate on their core activity.

Other types of corporate restructuring include spin-offs and share repurchasing.

FURTHER READING

Samuels, Wilkes & Brayshaw (1990) and Weston & Copeland (1988) both give good coverage of most aspects of corporate restructuring, in a UK context. Benzie (1989) reviews UK takeover activity in the UK during the 1980s, providing some useful statistics. Wright, Thompson & Robbie (1990) give an interesting discussion of management buy-outs. Rybczynski (1989) provides a very useful review of corporate restructuring generally, but also making comparisons between practice in the UK and in other countries, particularly the USA, Germany and Japan.

WORK-BASED ASSIGNMENT

(a) Has your organisation undertaken any corporate restructuring of the type discussed in this chapter? If it has, has the restructuring proved beneficial?

(b) If no corporate restructuring has taken place in your organisation, what suggestions do you have for possible beneficial arrangements?

QUESTIONS WITH ANSWERS (see Appendix 3)

1 Global Communications plc is a fast-growing company in the media industry. Over the past two years the value of its shares has more than doubled. Recently it has made a bid for Wessex Newspapers plc, an independent regional newspaper company, whose share price has shown only modest gains over the past two years. The bid offer is one share in Global Communications plc for every four shares held in Wessex Newspapers plc.

Financial information relating to each company is given below:

Profit and Loss Accounts for the year ended 31 October 19X9

	Global Communications £m	*Wessex Newspapers £m*
Turnover	500	150
Profit on ordinary activities before tax	52	11
Taxation on profit on ordinary activities	21	4
Profit on ordinary activities after tax	31	7
Dividends	4	4
Retained profit for the year	27	3

A merger of the two companies is expected to result in administration cost savings, after taxation, of £2m per annum.

Balance Sheets as at 31 October 19X9

	Global Communications £m	Wessex Newspapers £m
Fixed assets	200	100
Net current assets	60	25
	260	125
Less: Liabilities due beyond one year	100	30
	160	95
Capital and reserves		
Share capital – 50p ordinary shares	90	50
Reserves	70	45
	160	95
Price earnings ratio (prior to bid)	20	12

Following a series of detailed talks and negotiations between the two companies, including an exchange of information between the two companies, the board of directors of Wessex Newspapers has decided that the proposed takeover bid would not be in the interests of the Wessex shareholders.

Required:

(a) Calculate the total value of the proposed bid.
(b) Calculate the earnings per share of Global Communications following a successful takeover.
(c) State what investigations you would expect Global Communications to have undertaken before making its takeover bid.
(d) Outline three defensive tactics the directors of Wessex Newspapers might adopt in order to resist the proposed takeover.

(Certified Diploma)

2 Alpha plc, a dynamic fast-growing company in micro-electronics, has just made a bid of 17 of its own shares for every 20 shares of Beta plc who manufacture a range of electric motors.

Balance sheets and profits and loss accounts for the two companies are shown below.

Profit and Loss Accounts year ended 31 March 19X4

	Alpha plc £000	Beta plc £000
Turnover	3000	2000
Operating profit	300	140
Interest	100	10
Profit on ordinary activities before tax	200	130
Taxation on profit on ordinary activities	100	65
Profit on ordinary activities after tax	100	65
Dividends (net)	20	30
Retained profit for the financial year	80	35
Number of issued shares (million)	1.0	0.5
Earnings per share	10p	13p
Price earnings ratio	20	10
Market price per share	200p	130p
Capitalisation	£2m	£0.65m
Dividend per share (net)	2p	6p

Historical share prices have been:

31 March	19X9	19X0	19X1	19X2	19X3
Alpha plc	60	90	150	160	200
Beta plc	90	80	120	140	130

Balance Sheets at 31 March 19X4

	Alpha plc £000	Beta plc £000
Fixed assets	1200	900
Current assets	900	700
Creditors: amounts falling due within 1 year	300	600
Net current assets	600	100
Total assets less current liabilities	1800	1000
Less long term loans	800	120
	1000	880
Share capital		
25p ordinary shares	250	125
Profit and loss account	750	755
	1000	880

The merger of the two companies will result in after-tax savings of £15 000 per annum to be made in the distribution system of Alpha.

One of the shareholders of Beta has queried the bid and has raised the following points. Firstly he understands that Alpha normally only pays small dividends and that his dividends per share will decrease. Secondly he is concerned that the bid undervalues Beta since the current value of the bid is less than the figure for equity in Beta's balance sheet.

Required:

(a) Calculate the bid consideration.
(b) Calculate the earnings per share for the combined group.
(c) Calculate the theoretical post-acquisition price of Alpha shares assuming that the price earnings ratio of Alpha remains the same.
(d) What, if any, is the theoretical objection to this approach? What alternative approach might be adopted? (No calculations required.)
(e) Comment on the shareholder's two points.

(Certified Diploma)

QUESTIONS FOR CLASS USE

1 Dawn Raider plc has just offered one of its shares for two shares in Sleepy Giant plc, a company in the same industry as itself. Extracts from the accounts of each company for the year ended 31 May 19X8 appear below.

	Dawn Raider £ million	Sleepy Giant £ million
Profit and loss accounts		
Sales	150	360
Profits after tax	18	16
Dividends	4	14
Balance sheet data		
Fixed assets	150	304
Net current assets*	48	182
	198	486
Less: Loans	80	40
	118	446
Share capital †	50	100
Reserves	68	346
	118	446
* Includes cash/(overdrafts)	(60)	90
†	25p shares	50p shares

Stock market data for each company is as follows.

Dawn Raider plc

	31 May 19X6	31 May 19X7	31 May 19X8
Share price (pence)	120	144	198
Earnings per share (pence)	5.3	6.9	9.0
Dividends per share (pence)	2.0	2.0	2.0

Sleepy Giant plc

Share price (pence)	45	43	72
Earnings per share (pence)	8.4	7.4	8.0
Dividends per share (pence)	8.0	7.0	7.0

If the takeover succeeds Dawn Raider plans to combine Sleepy Giant's marketing and distribution channels with its own, with an after-tax saving of £1 million per annum. In addition it expects to be able to increase Sleepy Giant's profits after tax by at least £5 million per annum by better management. Dawn Raider's own profits after tax are expected to be £23 million (excluding the £1 million saving already mentioned), in the year ended 31 May 19X9.

One of the shareholders of Sleepy Giant has written to its chairman arguing that the bid should not be accepted. The following is an extract from his letter.

'The bid considerably undervalues Sleepy Giant since it is below Sleepy Giant's net assets per share. Furthermore if Dawn Raider continues its existing policy of paying only 2p per share as a dividend, Sleepy Giant's shareholders will be considerably worse off.'

(a) Calculate:
    (i) The total value of the bid and the bid premium.
    (ii) Sleepy Giant's net assets per share at 31 May 19X8.
    (iii) The dividends the holder of 100 shares in Sleepy Giant would receive in the year before and the year after the takeover.
    (iv) The earnings per share for Dawn Raider in the year after the takeover.
    (v) The share price of Dawn Raider after the takeover assuming that it maintains its existing price earnings ratio.
(b) Comment on:
    (i) The points that the shareholder in Sleepy Giant raises in his letter.
    (ii) The amount of the bid consideration.
(c) Explain briefly the advantages and disadvantages of a share exchange offer compared with a cash offer from both an acquiring company's, and an acquiree's shareholders', viewpoints.

(Certified Diploma)

2 Giant Holdings plc, on 5 December 19X5, made an offer of one of its ordinary shares for every two shares in Minnow plc, a company based in the west of England. If the offer was successful Giant would use Minnow's distribution facilities to expand its sales of agricultural machinery to farmers and this would result in an increased cash flow of £3 million per year after tax. Giant's financial analysts estimate that the capitalised value of this flow is £30 million.

Extracts from the accounts of the two companies appear below:

Balance Sheet at 30 June 19X5

	Giant plc £ million	Minnow plc £ million
Fixed assets	250	120
Current assets*	300	70
Less: Creditors due in under one year	200	70
Total assets less current liabilities	350	120
Less: Loans due in more than one year	100	60
	250	60
Issued share capital and reserves		
Share capital (£1 shares)		50
(50p shares)	100	
Reserves	150	10
	250	60
*Includes stock of	100	50

Profit and Loss Account for year ended 30 June 19X5

	£ million	£ million
Profit after taxation	50	10
Dividends	20	7
Retained	30	3

Currently the share price of Giant is 500p and that of Minnow 200p.

Required:

(a) Calculate the price earnings ratio of Giant and Minnow before the merger. What can you deduce from this information?

(b) What will the price earnings ratio of the group be if the value of Giant's shares increases by 50p after the merger?

(c) Calculate the market capitalisation of Giant after the merger assuming that the stock market is rational and that there are no events other than those in the question which would influence the share price. You should ignore the 50p increase in Giant's share price mentioned in part (b) of the question.

(d) Calculate the net dividend income the holder of 1 share in Minnow would receive before and after the merger, assuming that Giant maintains the same dividend per share as before the merger.

(e) If you were a shareholder in Minnow what would your reaction be to the merger? State your reasons.

(Certified Diploma)

3 The directors of Simonson Engineering plc have decided to diversify the activities of the company. To this end, the directors are currently considering the acquisition of HLA plc – a company which operates a chain of D-I-Y stores. The following financial information is available for each company:

Profit and loss accounts for the year ended 31 May 19X2

	Simonson	HLA
	£m	£m
Turnover	340	260
Profit on ordinary activities before taxation	54	25
Taxation on profits on ordinary activities	19	9
Profit on ordinary activities after taxation	35	16
Dividends	6	8
Retained profit for the year	29	8

Balance sheets as at 31 May 19X2

	Simonson	HLA
	£m	£m
Fixed assets	140	50
Net current assets	85	54
	225	104
Less creditors due after more than one year	62	36
	163	68
Capital and reserves		
Ordinary share capital	40	30
Retained profit	123	38
	163	68
Price/earnings ratio prior to bid	15	8

The share capital of Simonson is made up of 25p shares and the share capital of HLA is made up of 50p shares.

If the takeover bid is successful there is expected to be £3 million in after-tax savings arising as a result of economies in central administration services. In addition, it is believed that the after-tax profits of HLA plc can be increased by £2 million through a reduction in its work force.

Simonson plc has made a bid of two shares for every three shares held in HLA plc.

Required:

(a) Outline two reasons why a company may wish to diversify.
(b) State whether or not diversification is in the interests of the shareholders of a company.
(c) In relation to Simonson Engineering plc; calculate:
   (i)   the total value of the proposed bid;
   (ii) the earnings per share for Simonson plc following a successful takeover of HLA plc;
   (iii) the share price of Simonson plc after the takeover has occurred and assuming that the existing price earnings ratio is maintained and the economies achieved.
(d) Comment on the value of the bid from the viewpoint of shareholders in HLA plc.

(Certified Diploma)

CHAPTER 15

Small firms

OBJECTIVES

In this chapter we shall deal with the following:

- the importance of the small firm's sector of the economy and a definition of small
- the objectives of small firms
- the likely legal form of the small firm
- taxation and the small firm
- risk and the discount rate to apply in appraising real investment opportunities for the small firm
- problems experienced by small firms with raising external long-term finance
- valuing the shares of small firms
- gearing in the small firm
- dividends and small firms

INTRODUCTION

What people mean by *small* in the present context seems to vary widely: number of employees, total funds invested, and sales turnover are often used in the definition. For our present purposes a strict definition probably does not matter. The sorts of firms which we shall be discussing are those displaying the following features.

(a) They are more substantial than the very small businesses that act as the medium for the self-employment of their owners.

(b) The firm's securities are not quoted in any established capital market, i.e. they are not traded in an efficient market.

(c) The ownership of the firm's equity and hence its control lie in the hands of a small close-knit group, i.e. it is a *family-type* firm.

Small firms, as we have defined them, are an important part of the UK private sector. They probably account for over one-fifth of the private sector's output and over two-fifths of its employment opportunities. In the opinion of many, including the UK Government, it is a part of the UK economy which is likely to grow.

There are good reasons to believe that small firms will become increasingly important in the UK. The industrial restructuring which occurred in the 1980s shifted the balance still further away from the manufacturing, mineral extracting and power generation industries towards the service industries. Service industries, perhaps because they do not depend so much on the economies of scale, tend to operate in smaller units. Even in manufacturing, the new computer-based technologies have tended to make smaller firms more viable. This is because the flexibility of such technologies has meant that the economies of scale, in manufacturing, are much less profound than was the case with more traditional industrial methods. As we saw in Chapter 13 in the context of 'just-in-time' systems, flexibility is increasingly important in manufacturing industries. Small firms have probably shown themselves to be more flexible. Handy (1989) sees a future where firms of all sizes will increasingly subcontract or buy-in services and components, as they need them, from firms specialising in such work, rather than seeking to do virtually everything 'in house'. This will promote a need for many small firms, each one specialising in the provision of some product or service. Not only will it promote the need for the output of the small firms, this tendency will also have the effect of providing labour to staff the small firms. This is because larger firms will shed labour with skills other than in what those firms see as their 'core' activity. The restructuring, including management buy-outs, which we discussed in Chapter 14, may be seen as the start of a trend towards smaller units and a concentration on core activities.

Small firms are also seen as being particularly important in that they provide an environment in which innovation tends to flourish. Claims are made that a very high proportion, perhaps a majority, of new ideas emerge and are first tried in the small firm sector.

There are few areas of business finance where the broad principles which apply to large firms do not equally well apply to small ones, but there are certainly some areas where the emphasis is different and where small firms tend to have their own particular problems. In this chapter we shall consider some of these areas.

CORPORATE OBJECTIVES

In the context of larger firms we reached the conclusion that maximisation of shareholder wealth is a reasonable statement of the goal which most financial managers are likely to pursue. How different is this likely to be for smaller firms?

Management goals versus shareholder goals

With larger firms where the managers are probably not very substantial shareholders, conflict can arise between the objectives of each group.

In the case of the small firm the managers and the shareholders are likely to be substantially the same people or at least closely connected with one another. This might lead us to the conclusion that decisions are less likely to be made with a shareholder wealth maximisation goal as the major determinant, it being more likely that managers' welfare may be more important. On the other hand, it could equally well be argued that as managers are likely to be substantial shareholders they would make decisions following a pure wealth maximising goal more determinedly than would be the case with the typical large firm's management.

What we can probably say with conviction is that, whereas the vast majority of investors who buy shares in large firms do so with only an economic motive, those who involve themselves in smaller firms may well have other motives. These motives might include a desire to experience the satisfaction of building up a business, a desire to lead a particular way of life, or a desire to keep some (perhaps family) tradition alive. Since it is possible for managers to know the personal objectives of the shareholders of the smaller firm, decisions can probably be made with these in mind.

Irrespective of what other goals may be pursued by a small firm, decisions cannot be taken which consistently ignore the question of wealth. A firm which makes a series of decisions, each causing wealth to diminish, will sooner or later fail.

We may probably come to the conclusion that the wealth maximisation goal is very important to small firms and that, even where it is not necessarily the only objective, it cannot be ignored. This implies that the NPV investment appraisal technique is as relevant to small firms as it should be to large ones. In fact the evidence which we discussed in Chapter 4 suggests that NPV is not widely used by smaller firms.

ORGANISATION OF SMALL FIRMS

Typically the small firms which we are considering here will be organised as private limited companies. In essence these are identical to their public counterparts. The main differences are:

(a) Private companies need be of no minimum size; public companies must issue at least £50 000 of nominal share capital of which at least 25 per cent must be paid up. There is no upper limit on the size of a private company.
(b) Private companies are entitled to restrict the transfer of their shares, i.e. it is possible for the company's Articles of Association to contain a clause giving the directors the power to refuse to register a transfer, at their discretion.
(c) Whilst private companies must publish annual accounts, the volume of detail is rather less than that which the law requires of public companies.
(d) Private companies must generally include the word 'limited' or its abbreviation 'Ltd' in their names; public limited companies must include 'plc' in theirs.

Probably in practice the only one of these distinctions which is of any great significance is the second, concerning the restriction on transfer of shares. To the small firm the effect of the right of restriction can be something of a two-edged sword.

(a) It enables the majority of the shareholders to stop the minority, be it one or more shareholders, from transferring their shares to a third party unacceptable to the majority. In this way control, and even just influence through voting power, may be kept in the hands of those acceptable to the majority. In a family-type firm it may be important to the shareholders that ownership remains in the same hands, not necessarily for financial reasons.

(b) Potential equity investors would be reluctant to buy shares in a firm which effectively had the power to stop them selling the shares when they wished to. Not unnaturally most established secondary capital markets, certainly the International Stock Exchange, will not allow dealings in shares where there is a restriction on transfer. For small firms eager to expand, being a private limited company may be an impediment to growth.

It is not necessarily true that all small firms will be private limited companies, but given the attractions of the lesser requirement to account publicly and the ability to control their membership through share transfer restrictions, many of them are.

TAXATION OF SMALL FIRMS

As far as tax on corporate profits is concerned the only likely difference between large and small firms is the Corporation Tax rate. For firms whose profits are less than £250 000 p.a. the rate is 25 per cent, for firms with annual profits of £1 250 000 or more the rate is 33 per cent.

Note that 'large' and 'small' for tax purposes are defined entirely in terms of profit and that firms can and do move from being large to being small from one year to the next.

Tax avoidance

Perhaps where the distinction between small and large firms is likely to be most profound, in the context of taxation, is in the extent to which firms take actions purely for tax reasons.

Since small firms typically can know the personal circumstances of the share-holders, actions can be taken which will maximise the net (after-tax) wealth of their shareholders. For example, where all shareholders pay Income Tax at a high marginal rate it might be to their net advantage for profits to be retained by the firm instead of being distributed. This would possibly lead, in the long term, to a Capital Gains Tax liability on disposal of the shares, but this may be more tax efficient.

RISK AND THE DISCOUNT RATE

In the context of large firms it seems that discounting expected cash flows using a discount rate derived from CAPM is a reasonable way for considerations of risk to be incorporated into investment decision making. With small firms this would probably be invalid. It is thought to be true that investors in a large firm typically hold a relatively small proportion of that firm's total equity, as a relatively small proportion of a reasonably well diversified portfolio of equities.* For this reason investors would be exposed to relatively little specific risk, so a CAPM derived discount rate, i.e. one which deals only with systematic risk, is logical. Typically shareholders of small firms will not be well diversified. They may hold shares in many different firms but it is likely that their holding in the small firm will represent a large proportion (by value) of their total investment in equities. If the small firm were to fail, most of their wealth might be lost.

---

* Casual observation shows this broadly to be true. The majority of equities (about 80 per cent) quoted on the International Stock Exchange are owned by the investing institutions which tend to hold large, well diversified portfolios.

Since shares of small firms will tend not to be held in efficient portfolios, the discount rate which should be applied to the small firm's investment opportunities should take account of specific as well as systematic risk.

This means that there is no direct way of arriving at an appropriate discount rate, though CAPM can be used to discover a figure below which it should not lie. Probably the impressionistic devices such as sensitivity analysis and attempts to assess the worst possible outcome, best estimate and the best possible outcome could be used to gauge the level of risk.

Risk diversification within the firm

In our previous discussion of diversification and risk reduction the point emerged that, with large firms, the shareholders would probably not be advantaged by attempts by management to diversify its operations within the firm. This is because shareholders can and do diversify their security portfolios to achieve the same effect. For the reason mentioned above, shareholders in small firms may not be able to do this for themselves so there may be some point in the firm's management doing it for them, with the objective of reducing specific risk. Of course, because the firm is small, the practicality of internal diversification may be much less than would be the case with a larger firm.

SOURCES OF FINANCE

In modern times there have been four UK Government-sponsored inquiries which have dealt at least partly with the financing of small firms. These were:

(a) The MacMillan Committee on finance and industry (1931);
(b) The Radcliffe Committee on the working of the monetary system (1959);
(c) The Bolton Committee of inquiry on small firms (1971); and
(d) The Wilson Committee to review the functioning of financial institutions (1980).

Each of these discovered, to a greater or lesser extent, that small firms find it more difficult and more expensive to raise external finance than do larger firms. For this reason they are forced to rely on internally generated funds (retained profits) to a great extent.

If we look back to Table 8.2 on page 200 it seems that large firms also rely heavily on retained profits as a major source of finance, with capital issues averaging about 25 per cent of total new finance over recent years. Perhaps if a problem does exist it applies almost equally well to large firms.

No doubt small firms do experience some problems in raising external finance and, triggered off by the publication of the first three (particularly the first two) of the above committee reports, a number of schemes and agencies was established to make it easier for them. The Industrial and Commercial Financing Corporation (ICFC) is an example of one of the agencies.

The last two committee reports suggested not so much the absence of sources available to small firms, as an ignorance on the part of their management of the existence of those sources. Efforts to plug the *information gap* are manifest in the modern UK, with press and television advertising the Small Firms' Information Centres set up by the Department of Trade and Industry. These centres offer advice on and contacts with potential providers of finance.

Recently the Government has called the Income Tax system to the aid of small firms, offering potential investors relief from tax for making equity investments in small firms.

The emergence of the unlisted securities market over recent years has made it increasingly more practical for small public companies to make public issues of relatively modest size.

No doubt it remains more difficult and expensive for small firms to raise external finance, but at least their managers and shareholders may take comfort from the fact that just about everyone with any influence in the matter, most particularly the UK Government, seems eager to improve the situation.

VALUATION OF SMALL FIRMS

The existence of an apparently efficient market for the securities of large firms implies that unless we have access to 'inside information' there is no reason to believe that the current market price is not the best estimate of the security's value available to us. With small firms, as we have defined them, this will not be true since there is no current market price. Nonetheless it is sometimes necessary to value the ordinary shares of small firms, either to fix a price for a transfer for value (a sale) or where the transfer has been partly or fully gratuitous and a value is needed for Capital Gains or Inheritance Tax purposes.

There are basically three approaches which can be taken to such a valuation. We should bear in mind that we are seeking by each approach to value the equity of a firm. Since each one has the same objective, in theory they should if used correctly give the same result. This they will not usually do, possibly reflecting inefficiencies or imperfections in the market for real assets. We shall now look at each approach in turn.

Dividend yield

This approach is based on the notion that the ordinary shares of two different firms should have a similar dividend yield provided that the firms are roughly similar in size, activity, capital gearing and proportion of profit paid as dividend (dividend cover). If the shares of one of these firms are quoted and valued by an efficient market, this enables us to value the other one.

EXAMPLE

A plc and B Ltd are two firms similar in size, activity, gearing and dividend cover. A plc is a Stock Exchange quoted firm, B Ltd is not. The dividend yield (gross) for A is 10 per cent and B has recently paid annual dividends of £0.15 per share. What is the value of each B Ltd share?

SOLUTION

Bearing in mind that

$$\text{Dividend yield} = \frac{\text{Dividend paid (grossed up)}}{\text{Current market price per share}}$$

Then,

$$10\% = \frac{0.15 \times 100/75}{P_B}$$

(assuming a Basic Income Tax rate of 25 per cent) and

$$P_B = £2.00 \text{ per share}$$

The following points should be noted on using the dividend yield approach in practice:

(a) The difficulty of finding a quoted firm sufficiently like the unquoted one in the ways mentioned for the comparison to be valid.
(b) The doubts as to whether it is valid to assume that current dividend levels are the sole determinant of share values.
(c) The fact that prices are more likely to relate to future dividends; past dividends will tend only to be useful as a guide to the future.
(d) The lack of marketability of unquoted shares: this will tend to make them less valuable than apparently identical quoted ones.

Price/earnings

This approach is similar to the dividend yield approach but concentrates on earnings rather than dividends and takes the view that the shares of two similar firms will have equal PE ratios.

EXAMPLE

C plc and D Ltd are two firms similar in size, activity and gearing. C plc is quoted, D Ltd is not. The PE ratio for C is 12, the post-tax earnings per share for D have been £0.30 p.a. over recent years. What is the value of each D Ltd share?

SOLUTION Bearing in mind that:

$$PE = \frac{\text{Current market price per share}}{\text{Post - tax earnings per share}}$$

Then,

$$12 = \frac{P_D}{0.30}$$

$$P_D = £3.60$$

Clearly most of the points which apply to the dividend yield approach also apply to this approach. The PE approach does overcome the question of dividend policy, which MM assert is irrelevant in any case.

Net assets

Here the approach is to value the firm by reference to the individual values of its assets.

EXAMPLE The balance sheet of E Ltd is as shown below. What is the value of each E Ltd share?

Balance sheet of E Ltd at 31 December

Sources of finance (claims)	£m	Uses of finance (investments)	£m
Ordinary shares of £1 each	8	Fixed assets	11
Retained profit	7	Working capital	10
Total equity	15		
Long-term loans	6		
	21		21

SOLUTION

$$P_E = \frac{11 + 10 - 6}{8}$$

$$= £1.875$$

The above calculation is based on the *book values* of the assets and liabilities. It need not be done on this basis. Some current market value would be more logical, including a value for the firm's goodwill, if any. Since the assets concerned here are presumably purely economic ones, their value should be based on their ability to generate future benefits. For this reason there is no reason why the net assets basis should give us a different value than would the price/earnings approach.

Economic value (based on 'free' cash flows)

This approach is the most logical of them. It bases the valuation on the discounted (present) value of the estimated future net cash flows of the firm. Logical it may be, but it is problematical. Cash flows will be difficult to estimate, certainly beyond the first year or two. A discount rate will need to be identified which poses another problem. This might be able to be solved by using CAPM, with the average β for the industry in which the firm is engaged.

In practice, there tend to be differences between the values obtained from each approach. The dividend yield basis tends to be used to value minority shareholdings where the potential shareholder will not own sufficient shares to exercise any power nor perhaps any influence over dividend policy. Controlling shareholdings tend to be valued on the net assets or price/earnings bases.

Perhaps we should conclude this section by saying that valuing the shares of unquoted firms is a highly inexact science – value is in the eye of the beholder. In practice, the price at which a transfer occurs, or (for tax purposes) is deemed to have occurred, is likely to be the result of negotiation and compromise between the concerned parties.

GEARING

Once again the small firm is not in a fundamentally different position from that of the larger one on the issue of gearing. As we saw in Chapter 11, financial risk to which capital gearing gives rise, tends to emphasise business risk which will be present with or without gearing. Business risk is part specific and part systematic. Since small firms' shareholders may not be able to diversify sufficiently to eliminate most of the specific risk, they are likely to be more exposed to financial risk than would their typical large firm counterparts.

The relatively low Corporation Tax rates which apply to small firms mean that the effective relief for interest payments on borrowings is rather less than is the case with larger firms.

In Chapter 11 we suggested that there might be some optimal level of gearing which balances the increased risk to equity investors which gearing engenders, against the tax advantages. For the reasons which we have just reviewed this optimal level might be much lower for a small firm than for a larger one.

DIVIDENDS

Much of what is true concerning dividends in the context of large firms also applies to small ones, though there are differences. Perhaps most importantly it is feasible for the directors of small firms to know their shareholders' preferences as regards dividend policy and to make efforts to accommodate those preferences. This really is necessary; since typically it is not very practical for shareholders to sell their shares and replace them with those of another firm whose dividend policy appeals rather more.

SUMMARY

Small firms are an important sector of the UK economy and tend to have their own peculiarities as regards business finance while having most other features in common with large firms.

Corporate objectives are more likely to relate to aspirations of individual shareholders than is likely to be the case with large firms. Shareholder wealth maximisation is probably a fairly important objective for most small firms.

Many small firms are private limited companies, a status which gives them the benefits of corporate existence yet enables their directors to a great extent to control into whose hands the shares fall. It also limits the level of public accountability required of the small firm.

Small firms are taxed on their profits at a lower rate than are larger ones. They are also more likely than are large ones to take the personal tax position of their shareholders into account when making their decisions.

It is probably the case that shareholders in small firms do not hold efficient portfolios. CAPM as a device for deriving the discount rate for use in investment appraisal in the firm is therefore less appropriate than it would be for a larger firm. Perhaps the more impressionistic devices for assessing risk are particularly valid for small firms.

Observers have consistently noted the difficulty of small firms in raising external long-term finance. Past action to put them on equal terms with large firms has not been completely successful due, it would seem, to a lack of information on the part of small firms. Attempts to fill this information gap are being made.

For various reasons the shares of unquoted firms sometimes need to be valued and there are several approaches which can be taken to this. Ultimately the final agreed value is likely to be the outcome of a certain amount of 'horse trading' between the interested parties.

The optimum level of gearing should logically be lower for small firms than for large ones because the risk to equity holders caused by gearing is higher and the tax saving is lower. The dividend policy of a small firm is much more likely to reflect individual preferences of shareholders than will (or can) be the case with a large one.

FURTHER READING

Samuels, Wilkes & Brayshaw (1990) and Weston & Copeland (1988) provide quite good coverage of small firms generally. The references given at the end of previous chapters generally provide coverage of particular topics in the context of both large and small firms. The report of the Wilson Committee (1980) gives some relatively up-to-date information on financing problems of small firms.

For this assignment, consider a small firm with which you are familiar, either because you work in such an organisation or your organisation has dealings with it. Does this firm have problems raising finance which seem to be caused by its small size?

---

1 A colleague of yours has recently been considering leaving his position as sales manager of a medium-sized pharmaceutical business and purchasing a small chemical company, the summarised accounts of which appear below.

Balance Sheet at 31 December 19X3

	£ million	£ million
Fixed assets		8.2
Current assets	10.2	
Creditors: Amounts falling due within 1 year	7.8	
Net current assets		2.4
Total assets *less* current liabilities		10.6
Creditors: Amounts falling due after more than 1 year		
Long-term loans		4.2
		6.4
Capital and reserves:		
Called up share capital – 4 million 25p ordinary		
shares		1.0
Share premium account		2.0
Reserves		3.4
		6.4

Profit and Loss Account year ended 31 December 19X3

	£ million
Turnover	20.3
Profit on ordinary activities before taxation	2.2
Taxation on profit on ordinary activities	1.0
Profit on ordinary activities after taxation	1.2
Dividends (net)	0.7
Retained profit for the financial year	0.5

You ascertain that the gross dividend yield for a similar company is 7 per cent and its price earnings ratio is 8 times. Advanced Corporation Tax is ⅜th of the net dividend.

Required:

(a) Calculate the share price on the basis of:
   (i) dividend yield,
   (ii) price/earnings ratio, and
   (iii) net assets.

(b) Comment on the use of each of these methods in company valuation.

(Certified Diploma)

2 The following is a shortened version of the accounts of Woodhall Engineers plc, a company which is not listed on a stock exchange.

Woodhall Engineers plc

Profit and Loss Account year ended 31 December 19X4

	19X4	19X3
	£ million	£ million
Turnover	50	47
Operating costs	47	41
Operating profit	3	6
Interest payable	2	2
Profit on ordinary activities before tax	1	4
Taxation on profit on ordinary activities	–	–
Profit on ordinary activities after tax	1	4
Dividends (net)	1	1
Profit retained for the financial year	–	3

Balance Sheet at 31 December 19X4

	19X4	19X3
	£ million	£ million
Fixed assets (less depreciation)	20	21
Current assets		
Stocks	18	10
Debtors	17	16
Cash at bank	1	3
	36	29
Creditors: Amounts falling due within one year		
Short term debt	11	5
Trade creditors	10	10
	21	15
Total assets less current liabilities	35	35
Less: Long term loans (secured)	15	15
	20	20
Capital and reserves		
Called up share capital 25p ordinary shares	16	16
Profit and loss account	4	4
	20	20

The company is making plans to expand its factory. New plant will cost £8 million and an expansion in output will increase working capital by £4 million. Over the 15 years' life of the project incremental profits arising from the expansion will be

£2 million per year before interest and tax. In addition 19X5 profits before tax from its existing activities are expected to return to 19X3 levels.

Two alternative methods of financing the expansion have been discussed by Woodhall's directors. The first is the issue of £12 million 15 per cent debt repayable in year 2000. The second is a rights issue of 40 million, 25p ordinary shares which will give the company 30p per share after expenses.

The company has substantial tax losses so you can ignore taxation in your calculations. The 19X5 dividend per share is expected to be the same as that for 19X4.

Required:

(a) Compute the net asset value per share at 31 December 19X4 assuming that a value of £8 million is placed on goodwill and also fixed assets include land at a cost of £4 million. This is to be revalued to £10 million.
(b) Calculate the value of each of Woodhall's shares at the end of 19X4 on the following bases:
  (i) A similar company has a price earnings ratio of 8.
  (ii) The cash flows which are forecast for the company for the next 6 years are as follows:

	19X5	19X6	19X7	19X8	19X9	19X0
£ million	(6.0)	9.6	9.6	9.6	9.6	13.6

Woodhall's weighted average cost of capital is 12 per cent.
(c) Comment on the valuations which you have calculated in parts (a) and (b) of this question.

(Certified Diploma)

1 The chairman of Diversified Industries plc, a holding company which has interests in engineering, caravan manufacture and a chain of shops selling car accessories, has recently been approached by the managing director of Automobile Care plc, a smaller chain of accessory shops, who wishes to negotiate the merger of his company with Diversified Industries. The following information, which has been extracted from Automobile Care's accounts, is available.

| | Years ended 31 December | | |
| | 19X3 | 19X4 | 19X5 |
	£ million	£ million	£ million
Turnover	18.0	28.0	37.0
Profit before tax	3.2	4.1	7.3
Taxation	1.0	1.7	3.1
Profit after tax	2.2	2.4	4.2
Extraordinary items	(0.1)	(0.2)	1.4
Profit attributable to ordinary	2.1	2.2	5.6
Dividends (net)	0.9	1.1	1.3
Retained	1.2	1.1	4.3
Authorised share capital	6.0	6.0	6.0
Issued share capital			
16 million – 25p shares	4.0	4.0	4.0
Reserves	8.0	9.1	13.4

The market price per share at the end of November 19X6 was 315p per share.

Required:

(a) Calculate for 19X5 and explain the use of each of the following items.
  (i)   Earnings per share.
  (ii) Price earnings ratio.
  (iii) Dividend yield.
  (iv) Dividend cover.
  (v)   Net assets per share.
(b) Write some short notes on the factors the chairman of Diversified Industries should take into account when considering the bid. You should use the profit and loss details given in the question together with the figures you calculated in your answer to part (a) of the question.

(Certified Diploma)

2 Extracts from the accounts of Astwood Beverages plc, a company not listed on a stock exchange, appear below:

Astwood Beverages plc

Profit and Loss Account year ended 30 December

	19X4	19X5	19X6
	£000	£000	£000
Turnover	48 500	50 200	40 200
Profit before interest and taxation	4 700	5 000	3 200
Interest payable	2 100	2 200	2 300
Profit before taxation	2 600	2 800	900
Taxation	800	960	300
Profit after taxation	1 800	1 840	600
Extraordinary items	–	–	380
	1 800	1 840	220
Dividends (net)	480	480	120
Retained	1 320	1 360	100

Balance Sheet at 30 December 19X6

	£000
Fixed assets	
Cost	19 300
Accumulated depreciation	6 800
Net book value	12 500
Current assets	
Stock	5 200
Debtors	8 300
Cash	200
	13 700
Less creditors: Amounts falling due within one year	
Trade creditors and taxation	3 600
Bank overdrafts	9 600
Dividends payable	800
	14 000
Total assets, less current liabilities	12 200
Less: Long-term loans	6 000
	6 200
Capital and reserves	
12 million ordinary shares of 25p	3 000
Reserves	3 200
	6 200

Additional information:

(1) A competitor has offered to purchase Astwood's retail outlets and its current assets and assume responsibility for its current liabilities, but not its long-term

loan, for £10.0 million. If this deal goes ahead Astwood's only remaining asset, its factory, will be closed, its staff made redundant and the site sold to developers. It is estimated that this sale will give Astwood £8.0 million after all costs including redundancy payments.

(2) Similar companies have price earnings ratios of 13 and dividend yields of about 4 per cent, net of tax.

(3) An analyst from a firm of stockbrokers estimates that the net of tax cash flows attributable to Astwood's equity will be £1.2 million per year for the next 20 years. He ignores any cash flows arising after 20 years. He estimates that an appropriate discount rate will be 12 per cent, net of tax.

Required:

(a) Estimate the value of each share of the company by the following methods:
   (i) Assets valuation, assuming the competitor's offer is accepted.
   (ii) Using the price/earnings ratio of a similar company.
   (iii) Using the dividend yield of a similar company.
   (iv) On the basis of the cash flows estimated by the analyst.
(b) Comment on the relative merits of each valuation.

(Certified Diploma)

3 CDC Ltd owns a chain of tyre and exhaust fitting garages in the west of England. The company has been approached by ATD plc, which owns a large chain of petrol stations, with a view to a takeover of CDC Ltd. ATD plc is prepared to make an offer in cash or a share-for-share exchange.

The most recent accounts of CDC Ltd are summarised below:

Profit and Loss account for the year ended 30 November 19X1

	£m
Turnover	18.7
Profit before interest and tax	6.4
Interest	1.6
Profit before taxation	4.8
Corporation tax	1.2
Net profit after taxation	3.6
Dividend	1.0
Retained profit	2.6

Balance Sheet as at 30 November 19X1

	£m	£m
£m		
Fixed assets		
Freehold land and premises at cost	4.6	
Less accumulated depreciation	0.6	
		4.0
Plant and machinery at cost	9.5	
Less accumulated depreciation	3.6	
		5.9
		9.9
Current assets		
Stock at cost	2.8	
Debtors	0.4	
Bank	2.6	
	5.8	
Less: creditors amounts due within		
one year		
Trade creditors	4.3	
Dividends	1.0	
Corporation tax	1.2	6.5	(0.7)
Total assets less current liabilities		9.2
Less: creditors due beyond one year		
Loans		3.6
		5.6
Share capital and reserves		
Ordinary £1 shares		2.0
Profit and loss account		3.6
		5.6

The accountant for CDC Ltd has estimated the future free cash flows of the company to be as follows:

	19X2	19X3	19X4	19X5	Following 13 years
£m	4.4	4.6	4.9	5.0	5.4 per annum

The company has a cost of capital of 10%.

CDC Ltd has recently had a professional valuer establish the current re-sale value of its assets. The current re-sale value of each asset was as follows:

	£m
Freehold land and premises	18.2
Plant and machinery	4.2
Stock	3.4

The current re-sale values of the remaining assets are considered to be in line with their book values.

A company which is listed on the Stock Exchange and which is in the same business as CDC Ltd has a gross dividend yield of 5% and a price earnings ratio of 11 times.

Assume a basic rate of income tax of 25%.

Required:

(a) Calculate the value of a share in CDC Ltd using the following methods:
(i) Net assets (liquidation) basis
(ii) Dividend yield
(iii) Price earnings ratio
(iv) Free cash flows

(b) Briefly evaluate each of the share valuation methods above.
(c) Outline the major factors to be taken into consideration, from the point of view of the shareholders of CDC Ltd, when deciding between a cash offer and a share-for-share exchange.

(Certified Diploma)

REFERENCES

Alexander, S. 1961. Price movements in speculative markets, trends or random walks. *Industrial Management Review* (May).

Archer, S. H. & D'Ambrosio, C. A. (eds) 1983. *The Theory of Business Finance: A Book of Readings*, 3rd edn (Collier-Macmillan).

Beaver, W. H. 1989. *Financial Reporting: An Accounting Revolution* (Prentice-Hall).

Benzie, R. S. 1989. Takeover activity in the 1980s. In *Bank of England Quarterly Bulletin* (Feb.).

Beranek, W. 1963. *Analysis for Financial Decisions* (Irwin).

Bierman, H. & Smidt, S. 1988. *The Capital Budgeting Decision*, 7th edn (Collier-Macmillan).

Black, F. & Scholes, M. 1974. The effect of dividend policy on common stock prices and returns. *Journal of Financial Economics* (May).

Brealey, R. A. 1970. The distribution and independence of successive rates of return from the British equity market. *Journal of Business Finance*.

Brealey, R. & Myers, S. 1991. *The Principles of Corporate Finance*, 4th edn (McGraw-Hill International).

Boardman, C. M., Reinhart, W. J. & Celec, S. E. 1982. The role of the payback method in the theory and application of duration to capital budgeting. *Journal of Business Finance and Accounting* (Winter).

Carsberg, B. & Hope, A. 1976. *Business Investment Decisions Under Inflation* (Institute of Chartered Accountants in England and Wales).

Cole, W., Shears, P. & Tiley, J. 1990. *Law in a Business Context* (Chapman & Hall).

Coopers & Lybrand 1993. A review of the acquisitions experience of major UK companies (Coopers and Lybrand).

Copeland, T. E. & Weston, J. F. 1988. *Financial Theory and Corporate Policy*, 3rd edn (Addison-Wesley).

Corr, A. V. 1983. *The Capital Expenditure Decision*. (National Association of Accountants and the Society of Management Accountants of Canada).

Crossland, M., Dempsey, M. & Moizer, P. 1991. The effect of cum- to ex-dividend charges on UK share prices. *Accounting and Business Research*, vol. 22, no. 85.

Cunningham, S. W. 1973. The predictability of British stock market prices. *Applied Statistics*, vol. 22.

Cyert, R. M. & March, J. G. 1964. *A Behavioural Theory of the Firm* (Prentice Hall).

Dann, L., Mayers, D. & Raab, R. 1977. Trading rules, large blocks and the speed of adjustment. *Journal of Financial Economics* (Jan.).

Davis, E. & Pointon, J. 1991. *Finance and the Firm*, 2nd edn (Oxford University Press).

Dempsey, M. J. 1991. Modigliani & Miller again revisited: the cost of capital with unequal borrowing and lending rates. *Accounting and Business Research*.

Drury, C. 1992. *Management and Cost Accounting*, 3rd edn (Van Nostrand Reinhold (International)).

Drury, C. & Braund, S. 1990. The leasing decision: a comparison of theory and practice. *Accounting and Business Research*, vol. 20, no. 79 (Summer).

Drury, C., Braund, S., Osborne, P. and Tayles M. 1993. A survey of management accounting practices in UK manufacturing industries. (The Chartered Association of Certified Accountants).

Dryden, M. M. 1970. A statistical study of UK share prices. *Scottish Journal of Political Economy* (Nov.).

Elton, E. J. & Gruber, M. J. 1970. Marginal stockholders' tax rates and the clientele effect. *Review of Economics and Statistics* (Feb.).

Evans, J. & Archer S. H. 1968. Diversification and the reduction of dispersion: an empirical analysis. *Journal of Finance* (Dec.).

Fama, E. F. 1965. The behaviour of stock market prices. *Journal of Business* (Jan.).

Fama, E. F. 1977. *Foundations of Finance* (Basil Blackwell).

Fama, E. F. & Babiak, H. 1968. Dividend policy: an economic analysis. *Journal of the American Statistical Association* (Dec.).

Fama, E. F., Fisher, L., Jensen, M. & Roll, R. 1969. The adjustment of stock prices to new information. *International Economic Review* (Feb.).

Fama, E. F. & French, K. R. 1992. The cross-section of expected stock returns. *Journal of Finance* (June).

Finnerty, J. 1976. Insiders and market efficiency. *Journal of Finance* (Sep.).

Firth, M. 1977a. An empirical investigation of the impact of the announcement of capitalisation issues on share prices. *Journal of Business Finance and Accounting*.

Firth, M. 1977b. *The Valuation of Shares and the Efficient Markets Theory* (Macmillan).

Franks, J. R., Broyles, J. E. & Hecht, M. 1977. An industry study of mergers in the UK. *Journal of Finance* (Dec.).

Franks, J. & Harris, P. 1989. Shareholder wealth effects of corporate takeovers: the UK experience 1955–1985. *Journal of Financial Economics*, 23.

Friend, I. & Puckett, M. 1964. Dividends and stock prices. *American Economic Review* (Sep.).

Hamada, R. S. 1972. The effect of the firm's financial structure on the systematic risk of common stocks. *Journal of Finance* (May).

Handy, C. 1991. *The Age of Unreason* (Business Books).

Harper, W. M. 1982. *Operational Research*, 2nd edn (Macdonald & Evans).

Harper, W. M. 1991. *Statistics*, 6th edn (Pitman).

Hirshleifer, J. 1958. On the theory of optimal investment decisions. *Journal of Political Economy*, reprinted in Archer & D'Ambrosio (1983).

Ho, S. S. M. & Pike, R. H. 1991. Risk analysis in capital budgeting contexts: simple or sophisticated. *Accounting and Business Research*, vol. 21, no. 83.

Holinger, P. 1993. UK leads in European cross-border takeovers. *The Financial Times* (19 October).

Ibbotson, R. C. & Sinquefield, R. 1979. *Stocks, Bonds and Inflation* (Financial Analysts Research Foundation).

Iveson, S., Moss, C. & Simpson, M. 1986. *British Readings in Financial Management* (Harper & Row).

Jaffe, J. 1974. Special information and insider trading. *Journal of Business* (Jul.).

Jenkinson, T. J. 1990. New equity issues in the United Kingdom. *Bank of England Quarterly Bulletin* (May).

Keane, S. M. 1983. *Stock Market Efficiency* (Philip Allan).

Keenan, D. 1990. *Company Law for Students* (Pitman).

Kendall, M. G. 1953. The analysis of economic time series. *Journal of the Royal Statistical Society*, vol. 96, part 1.

Levy, H, & Sarnat, M. 1989. *Capital Investment and Financial Decisions*, 4th edn (Prentice-Hall International).

Levy, H. & Sarnat, M. 1988. *Principles of Financial Management* (Prentice-Hall).

Lewellen, W. G., Stanley, K. L., Lease, R. C. & Schlarbaum, G. G. 1978. Some direct evidence of the dividend clientele phenomenon. *Journal of Finance* (Dec.).

Limmack, R. J. 1991. Corporate mergers and shareholder wealth effects: 1977–1986. *Accounting and Business Research*, vol. 21, no. 83.

Lintner, J. 1956. Distribution of incomes of corporations among dividends, retained earnings and taxes. *American Economic Review* (May).

Litzenberger, R. & Ramaswamy, K. 1982. The effects of dividends on common stock prices: tax effects or information effects? *Journal of Finance* (May).

Lumby, S. 1991. *Investment Appraisal and Financing Decisions*, 4th edn (Chapman & Hall).

Masulis, R. 1980. The effect of capital structure changes on security prices. *Journal of Financial Economics* (Jun.).

McIntyre, A. D. & Coulthurst, N. J. 1985. Theory and practice in capital budgeting. *British Accounting Review* (Autumn).

Meeks, G. 1977. *Disappointing Marriage: A Study of Gains from Merger* (Cambridge University Press).

Merrett, A. J. & Sykes, A. 1966. Return on equities and fixed interest securities 1919–1966. *District Bank Review* (Jun.).

Miller, M. H. 1977. Debt and taxes. *Journal of Finance*, vol. 32, no. 2 (May).

Miller, M. H. & Modigliani, F. 1961. Dividend policy, growth and the valuation of shares. *Journal of Business* (Oct.).

Miller, M. H. & Modigliani, F. 1966. Some estimates of the cost of capital to the electrical utility industry 1954–57. *American Economic Review* (Jun.).

Miller, M. H. & Orr, D. 1966. A model of the demand for money by firms. *Quarterly Journal of Economics* (Aug.).

Mills, R. W. 1988. Capital budgeting techniques used in the UK and USA. *Management Accounting* (Jan.).

Modigliani, F. & Miller, M. H. 1958. The cost of capital, corporate finance and the theory of investment. *American Economic Review*, reprinted in Archer & D'Ambrosio (1983).

Modigliani, F. & Miller, M. H. 1963. Corporate income taxes and the cost of capital. *American Economic Review* (Jun.).

Moore, J. S. & Reichert, A. K. 1983. An analysis of the financial management techniques currently employed by large US corporations. *Journal of Business Finance and Accounting*, vol. 10, no. 4.

Morris, R. 1975. Evidence of the impact of inflation accounting on share prices. *Accounting and Business Research* (Spring).

Moyes, J. 1988. The dangers of JIT. *Management Accounting* (Feb.).

Newbould, A. 1970. *Management and Merger Activity* (Guthstead Press).

Parker, R. H. 1988. *Understanding Company Financial Statements* (Penguin Books).

Petit, R. R. 1972. Dividend announcements, security performance and capital market efficiency. *Journal of Finance* (Dec.).

Pettit, R. R. 1977. Taxes, transactions costs and clientele effects of dividends. *Journal of Financial Economics* (Dec.).

Petty, J. W. & Scott, D. F. 1981. Capital budgeting practices in large US firms. Reprinted in *Readings in Strategy for Corporate Investment*, ed. Derkinderin, F. G. J. & Crum, R. L. 1982 (Pitman).

Pike, R. H. 1982. *Capital Budgeting in the 1980s* (Institute of Cost and Management Accounting).

Pike, R. H. 1985. Owner–manager conflict and the role of the payback method. *Accounting and Business Research* (Winter).

Pike, R. H. 1992. Capital budgeting survey: an update. Bradford University Discussion Paper, cited in Pike, R. H. & Neale, C. W. 1993. *Corporate Finance and Investment* (Prentice Hall International).

Pike, R. H. & Ooi, T. S. 1988. The impact of corporate investment objectives and constraints on capital budgeting practices. *British Accounting Review* (Aug.).

Pike, R. H. & Wolfe, M. 1988. *Capital Budgeting in the 1990s* (Chartered Institute of Management Accountants).

Puxty, A. G. & Dodds, J. C. 1991. *Financial Management; method and meaning*, 2nd edn (Van Nostrand Reinhold).

Ross, S. A. 1976. The arbitrage theory and capital asset pricing. *Journal of Economic Theory* (Dec.).

Rutterford, J. & Carter, D. (eds) 1993. *Handbook of UK Corporate Finance*, 2nd edn (Butterworth).

Rybczynski, T. 1989. Corporate restructuring. *National Westminster Bank Quarterly Review* (Aug.).

Samuels, J. M., Wilkes, F. & Brayshaw, R. E. (1990). *Management of Company Finance*, 5th edn (Chapman & Hall).

Scapens, R. W., Sale, J. T. & Tikkas, P. A. 1987. *Financial control of divisional capital investment*. Chartered Institute of Management Accountants.

Sharpe, W. 1963. A simplified model for portfolio analysis. *Management Science* (Jan.).

Sharpe, W. 1990. *Investments*, 4th edn (Prentice-Hall).

Sizer, J. & Coulthurst, N. 1984. *A Casebook of British Management Accounting* (Institute of Chartered Accountants in England and Wales).

Stiglitz, J. E. 1974. On the irrelevance of corporate financial policy. *American Economic Review*, vol. 64, no. 6 (Dec.).

Stock Exchange Fact Book (annually) (The International Stock Exchange, London).

Sunder, S. 1973. Relationship between accounting changes and stock prices: problems of measurement and some empirical evidence. *Journal of Accounting Research* (supplement).

Taffler, R. 1991. Z-Scores: an approach to the recession. *Accountancy* (Jul.).

Watts, R. 1973. The information content of dividends. *Journal of Business* (Apr.).

Weston, J. F. 1963. A test of capital propositions. *Southern Economic Journal* (Oct.).

Weston, J. F. & Copeland, T. E. 1988. *Managerial Finance*, 2nd UK edn (Cassell).

Wilson Committee. 1980. *Committee to Review the Functioning of Financial Institutions* (HMSO, London).

Wright, M., Thompson, S. & Robbie, K. 1990. Management buy-outs: achievements, limitations and prospects. *National Westminster Bank Quarterly Review* (Aug.).

APPENDIX 1

Present value table

Present value of £1 in *n* years at discount rate r.

Discount rate (r)

Periods (n)	1%	2%	3%	4%	5%	6%	7%	8%	9%	10%	
1	0.990	0.980	0.971	0.962	0.952	0.943	0.935	0.926	0.917	0.909	1
2	0.980	0.961	0.943	0.925	0.907	0.890	0.873	0.857	0.842	0.826	2
3	0.971	0.942	0.915	0.889	0.864	0.840	0.816	0.794	0.772	0.751	3
4	0.961	0.924	0.888	0.855	0.823	0.792	0.763	0.735	0.708	0.683	4
5	0.951	0.906	0.863	0.822	0.784	0.747	0.713	0.681	0.650	0.621	5
6	0.942	0.888	0.837	0.790	0.746	0.705	0.666	0.630	0.596	0.564	6
7	0.933	0.871	0.813	0.760	0.711	0.665	0.623	0.583	0.547	0.513	7
8	0.923	0.853	0.789	0.731	0.677	0.627	0.582	0.540	0.502	0.467	8
9	0.914	0.837	0.766	0.703	0.645	0.592	0.544	0.500	0.460	0.424	9
10	0.905	0.820	0.744	0.676	0.614	0.558	0.508	0.463	0.422	0.386	10
11	0.896	0.804	0.722	0.650	0.585	0.527	0.475	0.429	0.388	0.350	11
12	0.887	0.788	0.701	0.625	0.557	0.497	0.444	0.397	0.356	0.319	12
13	0.879	0.773	0.681	0.601	0.530	0.469	0.415	0.368	0.326	0.290	13
14	0.870	0.758	0.661	0.577	0.505	0.442	0.388	0.340	0.299	0.263	14
15	0.861	0.743	0.642	0.555	0.481	0.417	0.362	0.315	0.275	0.239	15

	11%	12%	13%	14%	15%	16%	17%	18%	19%	20%	
1	0.901	0.893	0.885	0.877	0.870	0.862	0.855	0.847	0.840	0.833	1
2	0.812	0.797	0.783	0.769	0.756	0.743	0.731	0.718	0.706	0.694	2
3	0.731	0.712	0.693	0.675	0.658	0.641	0.624	0.609	0.593	0.579	3
4	0.659	0.636	0.613	0.592	0.572	0.552	0.534	0.516	0.499	0.482	4
5	0.593	0.567	0.543	0.519	0.497	0.476	0.456	0.437	0.419	0.402	5
6	0.535	0.507	0.480	0.456	0.432	0.410	0.390	0.370	0.352	0.335	6
7	0.482	0.452	0.425	0.400	0.376	0.354	0.333	0.314	0.296	0.279	7
8	0.434	0.404	0.376	0.351	0.327	0.305	0.285	0.266	0.249	0.233	8
9	0.391	0.361	0.333	0.308	0.284	0.263	0.243	0.225	0.209	0.194	9
10	0.352	0.322	0.295	0.270	0.247	0.227	0.208	0.191	0.176	0.162	10
11	0.317	0.287	0.261	0.237	0.215	0.195	0.178	0.162	0.148	0.135	11
12	0.286	0.257	0.231	0.208	0.187	0.168	0.152	0.137	0.124	0.112	12
13	0.258	0.229	0.204	0.182	0.163	0.145	0.130	0.116	0.104	0.093	13
14	0.232	0.205	0.181	0.160	0.141	0.125	0.111	0.099	0.088	0.078	14
15	0.209	0.183	0.160	0.140	0.123	0.108	0.095	0.084	0.074	0.065	15

APPENDIX 2

Annuity table

Present value of £1 receivable at the end of each year for *n* years at discount rate r.

Discount rate (r)

Years (n)	1%	2%	3%	4%	5%	6%	7%	8%	9%	10%	
1	0.990	0.980	0.971	0.962	0.952	0.943	0.935	0.926	0.917	0.909	1
2	1.970	1.942	1.913	1.886	1.859	1.833	1.808	1.783	1.759	1.736	2
3	2.941	2.884	2.829	2.775	2.723	2.673	2.624	2.577	2.531	2.487	3
4	3.902	3.808	3.717	3.630	3.546	3.465	3.387	3.312	3.240	3.170	4
5	4.853	4.713	4.580	4.452	4.329	4.212	4.100	3.993	3.890	3.791	5
6	5.795	5.601	5.417	5.242	5.076	4.917	4.767	4.623	4.486	4.355	6
7	6.728	6.472	6.230	6.002	5.786	5.582	5.389	5.206	5.033	4.868	7
8	7.652	7.325	7.020	6.733	6.463	6.210	5.971	5.747	5.535	5.335	8
9	8.566	8.162	7.786	7.435	7.108	6.802	6.515	6.247	5.995	5.759	9
10	9.471	8.983	8.530	8.111	7.722	7.360	7.024	6.710	6.418	6.145	10
11	10.37	9.787	9.253	8.760	8.306	7.887	7.499	7.139	6.805	6.495	11
12	11.26	10.58	9.954	9.385	8.863	8.384	7.943	7.536	7.161	6.814	12
13	12.13	11.35	10.63	9.986	9.394	8.853	8.358	7.904	7.487	7.103	13
14	13.00	12.11	11.30	10.56	9.899	9.295	8.745	8.244	7.786	7.367	14
15	13.87	12.85	11.94	11.12	10.38	9.712	9.108	8.559	8.061	7.606	15

	11%	12%	13%	14%	15%	16%	17%	18%	19%	20%	
1	0.901	0.893	0.885	0.877	0.870	0.862	0.855	0.847	0.840	0.833	1
2	1.713	1.690	1.668	1.647	1.626	1.605	1.585	1.566	1.547	1.528	2
3	2.444	2.402	2.361	2.322	2.283	2.246	2.210	2.174	2.140	2.106	3
4	3.102	3.037	2.974	2.914	2.855	2.798	2.743	2.690	2.639	2.589	4
5	3.696	3.605	3.517	3.433	3.352	3.274	3.199	3.127	3.058	2.991	5
6	4.231	4.111	3.998	3.889	3.784	3.685	3.589	3.498	3.410	3.326	6
7	4.712	4.564	4.423	4.288	4.160	4.039	3.922	3.812	3.706	3.605	7
8	5.146	4.968	4.799	4.639	4.487	4.344	4.207	4.078	3.954	3.837	8
9	5.537	5.328	5.132	4.946	4.772	4.607	4.451	4.303	4.163	4.031	9
10	5.889	5.650	5.426	5.216	5.019	4.833	4.659	4.494	4.339	4.192	10
11	6.207	5.938	5.687	5.453	5.234	5.029	4.836	4.656	4.486	4.327	11
12	6.492	6.194	5.918	5.660	5.421	5.197	4.988	4.793	4.611	4.439	12
13	6.750	6.424	6.122	5.842	5.583	5.342	5.118	4.910	4.715	4.533	13
14	6.982	6.628	6.302	6.002	5.724	5.468	5.229	5.008	4.802	4.611	14
15	7.191	6.811	6.462	6.142	5.847	5.575	5.324	5.092	4.876	4.675	15

APPENDIX 3

Suggested answers to end-of-chapter questions

CHAPTER 1

1 The reasons why so many firms operate as limited liability companies include the following:

- **Number of participants.** Partnerships (normally the alternative to a limited company where more than one person is involved with the ownership of the firm) are legally barred from having more than 20 partners, except in certain special cases. Thus a firm which wishes to attract equity finance from a large group of participants is, in effect, forced to operate as a limited company.
- **Limited liability.** Potential equity investors are much more likely to be prepared to participate in the firm if their liability for its losses is limited. Thus, all things being equal, it will be easier for a limited company to attract equity finance than it would be for a similar firm trading as a partnership or sole trader.
- **Perpetuity.** The continued legal existence of the firm does not depend on the continued existence of any particular participator. Where a particular partner leaves a partnership, the partnership legally comes to an end, though it is possible to form a new partnership to replace it from the existing partners.
- **Transferability.** Linked to the fact that a limited company can continue indefinitely is the ease with which one participator can be replaced with another. This means that it is practical for shareholders to sell their shares to other investors, perhaps through the Stock Exchange.
- **Credibility.** Since most firms operate as limited companies, not to do so may imply a lack of permanence or substance about a firm. This is not to say that because a firm is a limited company it can be relied on, but this may accord to some extent with public perceptions.

2 All legal persons are responsible for their own financial obligations. If they cannot or will not meet their obligations, creditors can invoke the law to help them to enforce payment. When the assets of a person have all been used to meet, or partially to meet, financial obligations, those still owed money by the person must suffer the loss. This position is as true for a limited company as it is for any other person. The fact that, legally, the company and its owners (shareholders) are separate means that the assets of the company are all that its creditors have access to meet the company's obligations. Shareholders cannot normally be required to provide additional finance should the company be unable to meet its obligations. This means that the company's liability, like that of any other person, is limited to the value of its assets. It also means that the maximum loss which a shareholder can normally incur is what that person has paid, or agreed to pay for the shares owned by that person.

CHAPTER 2

1 The separation theorem says that the investment should be made if it generates a higher rate of return than the rate which the firm has to pay for finance. Doing this will make the shareholders more wealthy.

How the investment is financed is a separate matter and, under the assumptions of the separation theorem, unimportant. Either the dividend could be paid and money borrowed to make the investment or the dividend not paid and the existing cash used to make the investment.

2 The separation theorem is based on four main assumptions. These are:

(a) Investments last only for one year.
(b) Returns from investment are known with certainty, i.e. there is no risk.
(c) All individuals wish to be as wealthy as possible.
(d) Borrowing and lending rates are equal to one another and apply equally to all lenders and borrowers.

Clearly these are not all realistic. Probably only **(c)** is realistic in that most of us would, all things being equal, prefer to be as wealthy as possible. It is evident from even the most casual observation of the real world that the other three are not realistic. This lack of realism must, to some extent, call the conclusions of the separation theorem into question in the real world.

CHAPTER 3

1 Blackstone plc

Table of ratios	*19X1*	*19X0*
Return on capital employed		

$$\frac{\text{Net profit before long-term interest and tax}}{\text{Total assets less creditors falling due within one year}} \times 100\%$$

$\frac{2309}{8235 + 65} \times 100\%$	27.8%	
$\frac{1050}{4300 + 937} \times 100\%$		20.0%

Return on shareholders' funds

$$\frac{\text{Net profit after long-term interest and tax}}{\text{Share capital and reserves}} \times 100\%$$

$\frac{1463}{4500} \times 100\%$	32.5%	
$\frac{624}{3437} \times 100\%$		18.2%

Gross profit margin	*19X1*	*19X0*

$$\frac{\text{Gross profit}}{\text{Sales}} \times 100\%$$

$\dfrac{5396}{11205} \times 100\%$	48.2%	
$\dfrac{3255}{7003} \times 100\%$		46.5%

Net profit margin

$$\frac{\text{Net profit before long-term interest and tax}}{\text{Sales}} \times 100\%$$

$\dfrac{2309}{11205} \times 100\%$	20.6%	
$\dfrac{1050}{7003} \times 100\%$		15.0%

Gearing ratio

$$\frac{\text{Borrowings (long and short-term)}}{\text{Total equity (shares plus reserves)}} \times 100\%$$

$\dfrac{3800+1625}{4500} \times 100\%$	120.5%	
$\dfrac{1800}{3437} \times 100\%$		52.4%

Current ratio

$$\frac{\text{Current assets}}{\text{Creditors falling due within one year}}$$

$\dfrac{3987}{3922}$	1.0 : 1	
$\dfrac{2178}{1241}$		1.8 : 1

Liquid ratio   *19X1*   *19X0*

$$\frac{\text{Liquid assets}}{\text{Creditors falling due within one year}}$$

Since this is an engineering firm, liquid
assets exclude stocks.

$$\frac{3987 - 2410}{3922}$$ 0.4 : 1

$$\frac{2178 - 1209}{1241}$$ 0.8 : 1

Days debtors

$$\frac{\text{Trade debtors}}{\text{Credit sales}} \times 365$$

$$\frac{1372}{11\ 205} \times 365$$ 44.7 days

$$\frac{807}{7003} \times 365$$ 42.1 days

Stock turnover

$$\frac{\text{Stock used}}{\text{Stock held}}$$

$$\frac{5809}{2410}$$ 2.4 times

$$\frac{3748}{1209}$$ 3.1 times

Comments could include the following:

   (a) Shareholder's perspective

- **Profitability**. This is much stronger in 19X1 than it was in 19X0, with return on capital employed, gross and net margins all being higher in the later year.
- **Gearing**. Things have altered dramatically over the two years, with the firm relying on significantly increased long-term borrowing, and overdraft finance being introduced. The stability of the company is weakened and a downturn in sales levels could seriously damage the shareholders' position.
- **Liquidity and activity**. The firm's liquidity position has considerably weakened.

For current assets to be equalled by current liabilities is a weakness for a manufacturing firm. The quick assets situation looks very weak. The considerable reduction in stock turnover and the use of overdraft finance are considerable contributors to this deterioration. The firm may well be overtrading, i.e. operating at a level beyond the capability of its working capital base.

- **General**. The firm has made considerable strides in its profitability, but at the expense of increasing the risk to which shareholders are exposed. The shareholder must ask him/herself whether the risk is worth bearing for the level of returns.

(b) Bank's perspective

The bank is currently owed £5.425 million by this firm. Though there are apparently assets to cover this, only £4.5 million is in the form of land and buildings (at book value). The bank must seriously consider its position and consider recalling the overdraft, as soon as possible. The bank may also be in a position to apply pressure to the firm to reign back on expansion and try to improve its liquidity and gearing.

2 Quardis Ltd

(a) Forecast Profit and Loss account for the year ending 31 May 19X1

		£000	£000
Sales	Credit	168	
	Cash	112	280
less	Cost of sales		
	Opening stock	24	
	Purchases	186	
		210	
	less closing stock	30	180
	$(24 \times 125/100)$		100
Gross profit			
less	Wages	34	
	Other overheads	21	
	Depreciation:		
	F & F $(60 \times 10\%)$ 6		
	Freehold $(460 \times 2\%)$ 9	15	
	Interest $(125 - 30 \times 13\%)$	12	82
	Net profit before tax		18
	Corporation tax $(18 \times 35\%)$		6
	Net profit after tax		12
	Dividend $(£0.05 \times 200\ 000)$		10
	Retained profit		2

(b)   Forecast Balance Sheet as at 31 May 19X1

	£000	£000	£000
Fixed assets			
Freehold premises, at cost		460	
less: Accumulated depreciation (30 + 9)		39	421
Fixtures & fittings, at cost (35 + 25)		60	
less: Accumulated depreciation (10 + 6)		16	44
			465
Current assets			
Stock	30		
Debtors (3/12 × 168)	42	72	
Creditors: Amounts falling due within			
one year			
Trade creditors (2/12 × 186)	31		
Accrued expenses (4 + 3)	7		
Taxation	6		
Dividend proposed	10		
Bank overdraft (balancing figure)	42	96	(24)
			441
Creditors: Amounts falling due			
beyond one year			
Loan–Highland Bank (125 – 30)			95
			346
Capital and reserves			
£1 ordinary shares			200
Retained profit (144 + 2)			146
			346

(c)   Without the 19X0 Profit and Loss account comments must be restricted.

- **Profitability**
  The return on equity is forecast at 3.5% (i.e. 12/346 × 100%). This compares poorly with the returns currently offered by very safe investments (e.g. building societies).

- **Liquidity**   *19X0*   *19X1*
  Current ratio   60/46 = 1.3:1   72/96 = 0.8:1
  Quick asset ratio   (60 – 24)/46 = 0.8:1   (72 – 30)/96 = 0.4:1
  The forecast liquidity is very weak compared with the 19X0 position.

- **Gearing**
  $$\frac{\text{Long and short-term borrowings}}{\text{Total equity}}$$
              125/344 = 36%   (95 + 42)/346 = 40%

Gearing overall will not greatly alter. It will, however, shift from being all long-term borrowing to a combination of short and long-term. This may not be a good development. Generally long-term borrowing is more satisfactory.

3

(a) (i) PBIT/CE $\quad$ = 11.6/100

$\quad\quad$ PBIT/18.0 $\quad$ = 0.116

$\quad\quad$ PBIT $\quad\quad\quad$ = 0.116 × 18.0

$\quad\quad$ PBIT $\quad\quad\quad$ = £2.088 million

$\quad$ (ii) PBIT/Sales $\quad$ = 16.0/100

$\quad\quad$ 2.088/Sales $\quad$ = 0.16

$\quad\quad$ Sales $\quad\quad\quad$ = 2.088/0.16

$\quad\quad$ Sales $\quad\quad\quad$ = £13.05 million

$\quad$ (iii) Equity/C E $\quad$ = 54/100

$\quad\quad$ Equity/18.0 $\quad$ = 0.54

$\quad\quad$ Equity $\quad\quad\quad$ = 0.54 × 18

$\quad\quad$ Equity $\quad\quad\quad$ = £9.72 million

$\quad\quad$ PAIT/Equity $\quad$ = 5/100

$\quad\quad$ PAIT/9.72 $\quad$ = 0.05

$\quad\quad$ PAIT $\quad\quad\quad$ = 0.05 × 9.72

$\quad\quad$ PAIT $\quad\quad\quad$ = £0.486 million

$\quad$ (iv) Equity $\quad\quad\quad$ = £9.72 million (see (iii) above)

$\quad$ (v) $\dfrac{\text{PAIT}}{\text{Number of shares}}$ = 0.60

$\quad\quad\dfrac{0.486(m)}{\text{Number of shares}}$ = 0.60

$\quad\quad$ Number of shares = $\dfrac{0.486(m)}{0.60}$

$\quad\quad$ Number of shares $\quad$ = 810 000

$\quad\quad$ Equity $\quad\quad\quad\quad$ = shares & reserves

$\quad\quad$ 9.72(m) $\quad\quad\quad$ = (810 000 × £1) + reserves

$\quad\quad$ Reserves $\quad\quad\quad$ = 9.72 – 0.810

$\quad\quad$ Reserves $\quad\quad\quad$ = £8.91 million

(b) The relationship is that:

NBIT/Sales × Sales/CE = NBIT/CE

i.e. Net margin × Activity = Return on capital employed

Thus ROCE is driven by a combination of margin and activity. In many cases firms develop marketing strategies which represent a trade-off between margins and activity.

(c) These two ratios are related in that:

Profit before interest and tax, less interest and tax, equals profit after tax

and

Capital employed equals debt plus equity

Thus ROCE tends to reflect the results of trading alone, whereas return on equity tends to reflect the results of trading taking account of tax and the level of gearing and interest rates.

(d) It does not mean this. Differences between the two EPS figures might reflect the following, as well as trading efficiency:

- The proportion of equity which is share capital as opposed to reserves.
- The level of capital gearing.

(e) ROCE is, subject to the general deficiencies of accounting and accounting ratios, a good indicator of effective management of the assets available. ROCE does not, however, reflect management's effective use of capital gearing and tax planning

---

CHAPTER 4   **1**   **Turners Ltd**

(a) NPV

Year	Discount factor	Machine A Cash flows £000	PV £000	Machine B Cash flows £000	PV £000
0	1.000	(120)	(120.00)	(120)	(120.00)
1	0.909	40	36.36	20	18.18
2	0.826	40	33.04	30	24.78
3	0.751	40	30.04	50	37.55
4	0.683	20	13.66	70	47.81
5	0.621	40	24.84	50	31.05
		net present value	17.94		39.37

Machine B shows itself to be significantly more desirable from an economic viewpoint than does Machine A. Since both machines have a positive NPV either would be worth buying.

(b) IRR
Clearly the IRR of both machines lies well above 10 per cent (the NPV at 10 per cent is fairly large relative to the initial outlay).

For our second trial, 10 per cent (above) being the first, let us try 20 per cent.

Year	Discount factor	Machine A Cash flows £000	PV £000	Machine B Cash flows £000	PV £000
0	1.000	(120)	(120.00)	(120)	(120.00)
1	0.833	40	33.32	20	16.66
2	0.694	40	27.76	30	20.82
3	0.579	40	23.16	50	28.95
4	0.482	20	9.64	70	33.74
5	0.402	40	16.08	50	20.10
			(10.04)		0.27

The IRR of Machine A lies below 20 per cent, but above 10 per cent. That of Machine B is just above 20 per cent. Further trials using other discount rates could be undertaken. Alternatively, a short-cut can be made to a reasonable approximation, i.e. linear interpolation.

Machine A

$$\text{IRR } 10\% + \left[(20 - 10) \cdot \frac{17.94}{17.94 + 10.04} \right]\% = 10 + 6.4 = \underline{\underline{16.4\%}}$$

Machine B

$$\text{IRR } 10\% + \left[(20 - 10) \cdot \frac{39.37}{39.37 - 0.27} \right]\% = 10 + 10.1 = \underline{\underline{20.1\%}}$$

On the basis of the IRR criterion Machine B would be preferred.

(c) ARR

The average 'profit' from each machine is:

Machine A	*£000*
Total labour savings	160
(40 + 40 + 40 + 20 + 20)	
Less: Depreciation (120 – 20)	100
	60

$$\text{Annual average} = \frac{60}{5} = 12$$

$$\text{Expressed as a percentage of original investment} = \frac{12}{120} = \underline{\underline{10\%}}$$

Machine B	*£000*
Total labour savings	190
(20 + 30 + 50 + 70 + 20)	
Less: Depreciation (120 – 30)	90
	100

$$\text{Annual average} = \frac{100}{5} = 20$$

$$\text{Expressed as a percentage of original investment} = \frac{20}{120} = \underline{\underline{16.7\%}}$$

On the basis of ARR Machine B is to be preferred.

(d) PBP

Machine A	3 Years
Machine B	3⅔ Years

Machine A is preferred as it has a faster payback.

2   **Silicon Ltd**

(a) and (b)

	19X7	19X8	19X9	19X0	19X1	19X2
Number sold (000)		100	100	100	80	80
Sale price per unit (£)		120	120	120	100	90
Contribution per unit (£) (i.e. SP – £65)		55	55	55	35	25
Incremental cash flows of manufacturing option	£000	£000	£000	£000	£000	£000
Total contribution	–	5 500	5 500	5 500	2 800	2 000
Less fixed costs		2 000	2 000	2 000	2 000	2 000
Profit before depreciation		3 500	3 500	3 500	800	0
Plant investment	(5 000)					
Working capital	(2 100)					2 100
Net cash flows	(7 100)	3 500	3 500	3 500	800	2 100
Discount factors	1.00	0.89	0.80	0.71	0.64	0.57
Present value	(7 100)	3 115	2 800	2 485	512	1 197
Net present value of manufacturing option	3 009					
Present value of sale of know-how option	3 100					
Incremental cash flows of royalties (annual sales × £10)		1 000	1 000	1 000	800	800
Discount factors	1.00	0.89	0.80	0.71	0.64	0.57
Present value	0	890	800	710	512	456
Net present value of the royalty option	3 368					

(c) The factors which should be taken into account include:

- The closeness of the three NPVs means that, though the royalty option is the best on the basis of the data used in the analysis, a fairly small mis-estimate of the data could cause the wrong judgement to be made. In short the NPVs do not give a clear basis for a judgement in this case.
- Silicon Ltd must consider its overall strategy. Is it prepared to give up manufacture and to become a research and development operation? Is the company happy to give a rival organisation the opportunity to manufacture a product developed by Silicon even if it may, in the short-term, be more profitable to do so?
- What other financial factors may be relevant here? Taxation has been ignored; would it alter the position? Would there be a need to lay off staff if the royalty or sale of know-how options are pursued and would this have financial implications?

3 (a)

	19X7 £000	19X8 £000	19X9 £000	19X0 £000	19X1 £000	19X2 £000
Sales revenue			450	470	470	470	470
Working capital recovered							180
			450	470	470	470	650
Materials			126	132	132	132	132
Labour			90	94	94	94	94
Overheads			30	30	30	30	30
Working capital		180					
New equipment		500					
		680	246	256	256	256	256
Incremental cash flows		(680)	304	214	214	214	394

Notes:

- Working capital invested in this project at the start will be recovered at the end of the project's life.
- The relevant overheads figure is £30 000 per year additional cost which the project is expected to cause.
- Depreciation is not a cash flow.
- Interest on the working capital investment and indeed on other aspects of this investment is dealt with by discounting.
- The development cost is not a relevant cost, since it has been incurred already and is not dependent on the decision under review.
- The cost of the equipment to enter this project is the £ 500 000 which will need to be spent. The book value of the old machine is not relevant since this does not represent an outlay or an opportunity cash flow.

(b)

(i) Payback period

	19X7	19X8	19X9	19X0	19X1	19X2
Incremental cash flows	(680)	204	214	214	214	394
Cumulative incremental cash flows		(680)	(476)	(262)	(48)	166

Thus the payback point occurs a little way into 19X1, i.e. after just over 4 years.

(ii) Net present value

	19X7	19X8	19X9	19X0	19X1	19X2
Incremental cash flows	(680)	204	214	214	214	394
Discount factor	1.000	0.893	0.797	0.712	0.636	0.567
Present values	(680)	182	171	152	136	223
Net present value	184					

(c) A memo to the board might include the following points:

- The fact that the project has a significant positive NPV and should be undertaken for that reason.

- The fact that the project has a relatively short payback period provides further support for undertaking it.
- The figures on which the analysis is based do not take account of the likely effects of taxation and this point should be examined before any final decision is made.
- The question of risk has not been considered, but should be before a final decision is taken.

4 (a)

Annual cash flows

Project 1 Year	0	1	2	3
	£000	£000	£000	£000
Net profit (loss)		29	(1)	2
Depreciation*		31	31	31
Capital cost	(100)			
Residual value				7
Net cash flows	(100)	60	30	40

*Annual depreciation
Project 1 (£100 000 – 7 000)/3 = £31 000

(i) *Net present value*

Net cash flows	(100)	60	30	40
10% discount factor	1.000	0.909	0.826	0.751
Present value	(100.00)	54.54	24.78	30.04
Net present value	9.36			

(ii) *Internal rate of return*
Clearly the IRR lies above 10%, try 15%

Net cash flows	(100)	60	30	40
15% discount factor	1.000	0.870	0.756	0.658
Present value	(100.00)	52.20	22.68	26.32
Net present value	1.20			

Thus the IRR lies a little above 15%, around 16%.

(iii) *Payback period*

Net cash flows	(100)	60	30	40
Cumulative cash flows	(100)	(40)	(10)	30

Thus the payback will occur after about 2 years, 3 months (assuming that the cash flows accrue equally over the year).

Annual cash flows

Project 2 Year	0	1	2	3
	£000	£000	£000	£000
Net profit (loss)		18	(2)	4
Depreciation*		18	18	18
Capital cost	(60)			
Residual value				6
Net cash flows	(60)	36	16	28

*Annual depreciation
   Project 2 (£60 000 – 6 000)/3 = £18 000

(i) *Net present value*

Net cash flows	(60)	36	16	28
10% discount factor	1.000	0.909	0.826	0.751
Present value	(60.00)	32.72	13.22	21.03
Net present value	6.97			

(ii) *Internal rate of return*
   Clearly the IRR lies above 10%, try 15%

Net cash flows	(60)	36	16	28
15% discount factor	1.000	0.870	0.756	0.658
Present value	(60.00)	31.32	12.10	18.42
Net present value	1.84			

Thus the IRR lies a little above 15%, around 17%.

(iii) *Payback period*

Net cash flows	(60)	36	16	28
Cumulative cash flows	(60)	(24)	(8)	20

Thus the payback will occur after about 2 years, 3 months (assuming that the cash flows accrue equally over the year).

(b) Assuming that Mylo Ltd is following the objective of wealth maximisation, Project 1 is preferable since it has the higher NPV. The difference between the two NPVs is not significant, however.

(c) The best approach to assessing investment opportunities is NPV because it fully addresses each of the following:

- The timing of the cash flows. By *discounting* the various cash flows associated with each project according to when it is expected to arise the fact that cash flows do not all occur simultaneously. Associated with this is the fact that by discounting, using the opportunity cost of finance (i.e. the return which the next best alternative opportunity would generate), the net benefit after financing costs have been met is identified (as the NPV).
- The whole of the relevant cash flows. NPV includes all of the relevant cash flows irrespective of when they are expected to occur. It treats them differently according to their date of occurrence, but they are all taken account of in the NPV and they all have, or can have, an influence on the decision.

● The objectives of the business. NPV is the only method of appraisal where the output of the analysis has a direct bearing on the wealth of the business. (Positive NPVs enhance wealth, negative ones reduce it.) Since most private sector businesses seek to increase their value and wealth, NPV clearly is the best approach to use, at least out of the methods we have considered so far.

CHAPTER 5

1 **(a)** Cost of capital is the cost of finance to support an investment. Thus it is the discount rate which will be applied to a firm's cash flows to deduce the project's net present value. The actual cost of capital will vary from project to project to take account of the level of risk involved with the particular investment.

(b) 'Real' in this context means adjusted for inflation. Interest rates in the market include an allowance for anticipated inflation, such rates are known as 'money' rates.

(c) This apparent anomaly can arise where we are considering projects of different scale and can be seen as an example of an important weakness in the use of the IRR technique. The data in the question tells us that the tunnel will yield a high rate of return on a relatively small investment (15 per cent on £2.0 billion investment). The bridge, on the other hand, will yield a lower rate of return on a much larger investment (12 per cent on £6.0 billion). Unless there is a shortage of available finance at the 10 per cent cost of capital the bridge investment would be preferred because it would make the investing company more wealthy (£3 billion as compared with £2 billion).

2   **United Conglomerates plc**

Close immediately

	Year 0 £m	Year 1 £m	Year 2 £m	Year 3 £m
Fixed assets disposal	4.0			
Recovery of working capital	2.5	2.5	1.0	–
Redundancy payments	(3.4)			
Sundry costs	(0.3)	(0.1)	–	–
	2.8	2.4	1.0	–
Discount factor	1.00	0.91	0.83	0.75
Present values	2.8	2.18	0.83	–
Net present value	5.81			

Gradual rundown

	Year 0 £m	Year 1 £m	Year 2 £m	Year 3 £m
Fixed assets disposal	–	–	2.0	3.0
Recovery of working capital	–	–	2.5	3.0
Redundancy payments	–	–	(1.1)	(2.0)
Operating losses	–	(0.9)	(0.7)	–
	–	(0.9)	2.7	4.0
Discount factor	1.00	0.91	0.83	0.75
Present values	–	(0.82)	2.24	3.00
Net present value	4.42			

(b) The incremental NPV is 5.81 – 4.42 = 1.39

Thus on the basis of NPV immediate closure is the preferred solution.

(c) Other considerations might include:

- Uncertainty. How confident can we be of the data used in the NPV analysis?
- Finality. Once the plant has been closed it will probably be too late to reverse the decision, whereas it may be possible to delay the closure decision until the situation becomes a little clearer.
- Social impact. The gradual closure option may have a less severe effect on the workforce in that they can be given time to find alternative employment.

(d) On the basis of the figures deduced in part **(a)** and assuming the firm is wealth maximising, the plant should be closed immediately.

3   **Beacon Chemicals plc**

(a) Incremental cash flows

	19X6 £000	19X7 £000	19X8 £000	19X9 £000	19X0 £000	19X1 £00
Sales revenue	–	80	120	144	100	64
Loss of cont.		(15)	(15)	(15)	(15)	(15)
Variable costs		(40)	(50)	(48)	(30)	(32)
Fixed costs		(8)	(8)	(8)	(8)	(8)
Operating cash flows		17	47	73	47	9
Working capital	(30)					30
Capital cost	(100)					
Incremental net cash flows	(130)	17	47	73	47	39

(b) Payback period

Cumulative cash flows	(130)	(113)	(66)	7

Thus the investment will pay for itself in just under 3 years.

(c) Net present value

Discount factor	1.00	0.93	0.86	0.79	0.74	0.68
Present value	(130)	16	40	58	35	27
Net present value	46					

(d) The report should include the following points:
- The positive NPV implies a viable investment to a wealth-maximising firm.
- The payback period is relatively short.
- Taxation has been ignored in the analysis.
- Some form of risk analysis should be undertaken.

(e) Taxation should always be taken into account since most investment decisions will have taxation effects. These may very well vary from one investment project to the next.

4

Year	Cash flows	Cumulative cash flows	Discount factor (14%)	NPV (14%)	Discount factor (20%)	NPV (20 %)
	£	£		£		£
19X7	(4470)	(4470)	1.000	(4470)	1.000	(4470)
19X8	1050	(3420)	0.877	921	0.833	875
19X9	1102	(2318)	0.769	848	0.694	765
19X0	1157	(1161)	0 675	781	0.579	670
19X1	1216	55	0 592	720	0.482	586
19X2	1276	1331	0 519	662	0.402	513
19X3	1340	2771	0 456	611	0.335	449
				73		(612)

(a)

    (i)   The payback period is just under 4 years.

    (ii) The NPV at the appropriate discount rate of 14% is just positive at £73.

    (iii) The IRR lies between 14% and 20%. An approximate value of it is 14% + [6% × (73/(73 + 612))] = 14.6%.

(b) Of the three methods in part (a), only NPV satisfies the important criterion of relating directly to what is usually taken to be the principal financial objective followed by most firms; wealth maximisation. To that extent the other two methods are seriously flawed. On the other hand IRR tends to give the same signals as does NPV, perhaps in a form more acceptable to managers i.e. in percentage terms. PBP is not really related to wealth maximisation at all. On the other hand it does highlight liquidity which many people feel is an important factor.

(c) Methods which could be used to allow for risk in a project are:

    ● Ascribing probabilities to the various cash flows and working out an expected value.

    ● Carrying out a sensitivity analysis of the project by taking each of the variables in turn and looking at how sensitive a favourable predicted outcome is to forecast errors in the variables.

5

Year	0	1	2	3	4	5
	£000	£000	£000	£000	£000	£000
Machinery cost	(120)					
Sales revenue		200	300	400	300	
Stock purchases	(20)	(100)	(120)	(150)	(90)	
Labour		(40)	(60)	(60)	(40)	
Other overheads		(30)	(30)	(31)	(40)	
Advertising	(20)	(5)	(5)	(5)		
Proceeds of old machine	10				(4)	
Operating cost savings		6	6	6	6	
Lost contributions from calculators (*see Note 1*)		(25)	(45)	(20)		
Corporation tax (*see Note 2*)		65	(13)	(23)	(65)	(51)
Net cash flows	(150)	71	33	117	67	(51)
Discount factors @14%	1.000	0.877	0.769	0.675	0.592	0.519
Present values	(150.0)	62.3	25.4	79.0	39.7	(26.5)

Net present value   29.9 (i.e. £29 900).

Note 1

Loss of profits from calculators

Year 1	Original contributions	$5000 \times (80 - 60)$	100 000
	Revised contributions	$5000 \times (75 - 60)$	75 000
	Lost contributions		25 000

Year 2	Original contributions	$4000 \times (60 - 45)$	60 000
	Revised contributions	$3000 \times (50 - 45)$	15 000
	Lost contributions		45 000

Year 3	Original contributions	$2000 \times (40 - 30)$	20 000
	Revised contributions		zero
	Lost contributions		20 000

Note 2

Tax cash flows

Year	0	1	2	3	4
	£000	£000	£000	£000	£000
Machinery cost	(120)				
Sales revenue		200	300	400	300
Stock used		(80)	(120)	(160)	(120)
Labour		(40)	(60)	(60)	(40)
Other overheads		(30)	(30)	(31)	(40)
Advertising	(20)	(5)	(5)	(5)	
Proceeds of old machine	10				(4)
Operating cost savings		6	6	6	6
Lost contributions					
from calculators		(25)	(45)	(20)	
Net tax cash flows	(130)	26	46	130	102
@ 50%	65	(13)	(23)	(65)	(51)

6 Calculation of present cost of operating the machine for its expected life.

	Machine	
	A	B
	£	£
Initial cost	50 000	90 000
Salvage value 5000 × 0.683	(3 415)	
7000 × 0.513		(3 591)
Annual running costs		
10 000 × 3.170	31 700	
8 000 × 4.868		38 944
Present cost (a)	78 285	125 353
Annuity factor (b)	3 170	4 868
Equivalent annual value (a)/(b)	£24 696	£25 750

Were the equivalent annual cost of A the same as B, then the present cost of operating A for four years would be £81 628 (i.e. £25 750 × 3.170). Thus the initial cost would be £53 343 (i.e. £81 628 – 31 700 +3415), so the increase would be £3343.

CHAPTER 6

Easton Ltd

1 *Different cash flows of Machine A*

		2000 demand £	3000 demand £	5000 demand £
Year 0		(15 000)	(15 000)	(15 000)
1	(£4–£1)/unit	6 000	9 000	15 000
2		6 000	9 000	15 000
3		6 000	9 000	15 000
Discounted: Factor		£	£	£
Year 0	(1.00)	(15 000)	(15 000)	(15 000)
1	(0.94)	5 640	8 460	14 100
2	(0.89)	5 340	8 010	13 350
3	(0.84)	5 040	7 560	12 600
		£1 020	9 030	25 050

Expected value = (0.2 × 1020) + (0.6 × 9030) + (0.2 × 25 050)
= £10 632

Differential cash flows of Machine B

		2000 demand £	3000 demand £	5000 demand £
Year 0		20 000	20 000	20 000
1	(£4–£0.5)/unit	7 000	10 500	17 500
2		7 000	10 500	17 500
3		7 000	10 500	17 500
Discounted: Factor		£	£	£
Year 0	(1.00)	20 000	20 000	20 000
1	(0.94)	6 580	9 870	16 450
2	(0.89)	6 230	9 345	15 575
3	(0.84)	5 880	8 820	14 700
		(1 310)	8 035	26 725

Expected value = (0.2 × 1310) + (0.6 × 8035) + (0.2 × 26 725)
= £9904

A more direct route to expected values would be to take the 'expected' demand [(0.2 × 2000) + (0.6 × 3000) + (0.2 × 5000) = 3200] and then find the NPV assuming that level of demand.

2 **Easton Ltd**

(a) The expression for the NPV may be put as follows:

$$\text{NPV} = D(S - V)A_n^r - I$$

> *Where* D is annual demand (in units)
> S is the selling price per unit
> V is the variable cost per unit
> A_n^r is the annuity factor at rate r over n years
> and I is the initial investment

Thus NPV $= (2000(4-1)2.673) - 15\,000$
$$= \underline{\underline{£1038}}$$

Since the NPV is a significant positive figure the machine should be acquired.

(b) Sensitivity analysis

(i) *Annual demand*

This requires setting NPV at zero, putting in all inputs except annual demand and solving for annual demand

i.e. $(D(4-1)2.673) - 15\,000 = 0$

$$D = \frac{15\,000}{3 \times 2.673} = \underline{\underline{1871}}\text{ units}$$

(ii) *Selling price per unit*

$2000(S-1)2.673 = 15\,000$

$$S = \frac{15\,000}{2000 \times 2.673} + 1 = \underline{\underline{£3.806}}$$

(iii) *Variable cost per unit*

$2000(4-v)2.673 = 15\,000$

$$v = \frac{-15\,000}{2000 \times 2.673} + 4 = \underline{\underline{£1.194}}$$

(iv) *Discount rate*

$2000(4-1)A_3^r = 15\,000$

$$A_3^r = \frac{15\,000}{6000} = \underline{\underline{2.500}}$$

Looking at the annuity table for the 3 years row, 2.5 lies between 9 per cent and 10 per cent, nearer to 10 per cent, so say $\underline{\underline{10\text{ per cent}}}$.

(v) *Years of the project*

$A_n^6 = 2.500$ (from (iv) above)

Looking down the 6 per cent column in the annuity table, 2.5 lies between 2 and 3 years, nearer to 3 years, so say 3 years.

(vi) *Initial investment*

$I = 2000(4-1)2.673$
$$= \underline{\underline{£16\,038}}$$

Table of Sensitivities

Factor	Original estimate	Breakeven point	Difference	Difference as % original
D	2000 units	1871 units	129 units	6%
S	£4	£3.806	£0.194	5%
V	£1	£1.194	£0.194	19%
r	6%	10%	4%	67%
n	3 years	3 years	0 years	0%
I	£15 000	£16 038	£1038	7%

Note that r and n could be found with considerably more accuracy (if this were thought to be useful) by linear interpolation.

3   Miles

Machine A

Annual operating cash flows:

Year	Sales units 000	Sales £000	Sales receipts £000	Air conditioning operating costs £000	Operating costs £000	Variable costs £000	Net £000
1	20	200	140	(10)	(40)	(100)	(10)
2	30	300	60 210	(10)	(40)	(180)	40
3	50	700	90 490	(10)	(40)	(300)	230
4	50	700	210 490	(10)	(40)	(300)	350
5			210				210

Tax on operating profit

Year	Sales £000	Variable Costs £000	Operating Costs £000	Air Conditioning £000	Net £000	Tax @ 50% £000
1	200	(100)	(40)	(10)	50	25
2	300	(180)	(40)	(10)	70	35
3	700	(300)	(40)	(10)	350	175
4	700	(300)	(40)	(10)	350	175

Each of the tax charges is payable one year after the year to which it relates.

Incremental cash flows for machine A

Year	0	1	2	3	4	5
	£000	*£000*	*£000*	*£000*	*£000*	*£000*
Purchase price and tax	(300)	150			60	(30)
Air conditioning and tax	(40)	20			10	(5)
Housing	(50)					
Operating cash flows		(10)	40	230	350	210
Tax			(25)	(35)	(175)	(175)
	(390)	160	15	195	245	—
Discount factor @14%	1.000	0.887	0.769	0.675	0.592	
PV	(390)	140	12	132	145	

NPV = £39 000

Machine B (no repairs case)

Annual operating cash flows

Year	Sales receipts £000	Operating costs £000	Variable costs £000	Net £000
1	140	(30)	(80)	30
2	270	(30)	(150)	90
3	580	(30)	(250)	300
4	700	(30)	(250)	420
5	210			210

Tax on operating profit

Year	Sales £000	Variable costs £000	Operating costs £000	Overhaul £000	Net £000	Tax @ 50% £000
1	200	(80)	(30)		90	45
2	300	(150)	(30)	(80)	40	20
3	700	(250)	(30)		420	210
4	700	(250)	(30)		420	210

Incremental cash flows for Machine B

Year	0	1	2	3	4	5
	£000	£000	£000	£000	£000	£000
Purchase price and tax	(400)	200			40	(20)
Housing	(30)					
Operating cash flows		30	90	300	420	210
Overhaul			(80)			
Tax			(45)	(20)	(210)	(210)
	(430)	230	(35)	280	250	(20)
Discount factor @ 14%	1.000	0.877	0.769	0.675	0.592	0.519
PV	(430)	202	(27)	189	148	(10)

NPV = £72 000

Machine B (minor repairs case)

This will give an identical NPV to the 'no repair' case except that it will be altered by the present value of £50 000 payable in year 2 and the tax relief thereon in year 3.

	£000
NPV in repairs case	72
Repairs 50 × 0.769	(38)
Tax relief 25 × 0.675	17
NPV in minor repairs case	51

Machine B (major repairs case)

Differences in incremental cash flows from Machine B (no repairs case).

Year	1	2	3	4	5
	£000	£000	£000	£000	£000
Repair and tax		(140)	70		
Salvage and tax				(20)	10
Variable costs			(50)	(50)	
Tax				25	25
	–	(140)	20	(45)	35
Discount factor @ 14%	0.877	0.769	0.675	0.592	0.519
	–	(108)	14	(27)	18

Difference in NPV (£103 000)

	£000
NPV in no repairs case	72
Difference	(103)
NPV in major repairs case	31

Expected NPV of Machine B

	£000
0.5×72	36
0.3×51	15
$0.2 \times (31)$	(6)
	45

On the basis of expected NPV, machine B would be preferred to machine A

(b) The worth of the credit consultant's fee is the present value increase which accelerated receipts will cause.

Year	1	2	3	4	5
Original receipts	140	270	580	700	210
Revised receipts	200	300	700	700	–
	60	30	120	–	(210)
Discount factor of 14%	0.877	0.769	0.675	0.592	0.519
	53	23	81	–	(109)
NPV	£48 000				

Therefore it would be worth paying up to £48 000 for the consultancy.

CHAPTER 7

1 Specific risk factors might include:

- The possible loss of business arising from the opening of the channel tunnel.
- Decline in trade between the UK and Western Europe.
- A loss of interest in UK residents taking holidays in Western Europe.
- Bad publicity arising from an accident involving one of the company's vessels.

Systematic risk factors might include:
- Levels of interest rates.
- Fuel prices.
- Levels of demand in the economy.

2 (a) Court plc

Year	r_m	$r_m - \bar{r}_m$	$(r_m - \bar{r}_m)^2$	r_i	$r_i - \bar{r}_i$	$(r_i - \bar{r}_m)(r_i - \bar{r}_i)$
1	.13	.07	.0049	.19	.12	.0096
2	(.07)	(.13)	.0169	(.08)	(.15)	.0195
3	(.13)	(.19)	.0361	(.12)	(.19)	.0361
4	.04	(.02)	.0004	.03	(.04)	.0008
5	.08	.02	.0004	.08	.01	.0002
6	.10	.04	.0016	.17	.10	.0040
7	.15	.09	.0081	.14	.07	.0063
8	.16	.10	.0100	.14	.07	.0070
9	.16	.10	.0100	.14	.07	.0070
10	(.02)	(.08)	.0064	.01	(.06)	.0048
$\sum r_m =$	.60	$\sum (r_m = \bar{r}_m)^2 =$ .0948		.70 =	$\sum r_i$	.0953 =

$$\bar{r}_m = \frac{.60}{.10} \qquad \bar{r} = \frac{.70}{.10} \qquad \sum (r_m - \bar{r}_m)(r_i - \bar{r}_i)$$

$$= .06 \qquad\qquad = .07$$

$$\text{Var}(r_m) = \frac{.0948}{10 - 1} = 0.0105$$

$$\text{Cov}(r_i r_m) = \sum \frac{(r_m - \bar{r}_m)(r_i - \bar{r}_i)}{10 - 1} = \frac{.0953}{9} = \underline{0.0106}$$

$$\beta = \frac{\text{Cov}(r_i r_m)}{\text{Var}(r_m)} = \frac{0.0106}{0.0105} = \underline{1.0}$$

(b) Since Court's β is 1.0, irrespective of the risk-free rate, if the expected return from equities generally is 12 per cent, then the expected return from Court will also be 12 per cent.

CHAPTER 8

1 Jackson plc

Since financial leasing is, in effect, loan financing to assess the desirability of leasing rather than buying the asset, we need to assess the NPV of the lease payments, against the NPV of the cost of buying the asset discounting in both cases at the debt financing cost.

NPV of lease:

Year	£000	Discount factor (12%)	PV £000
0	35.0	1.00	35.0
1	35.0	0.89	31.2
2	35.0	0.80	28.0
3	35.0	0.71	24.9
4	35.0	0.64	22.4
5	0.2	0.57	0.1
6	0.2	0.51	0.1
7	0.2	0.45	0.1
8	0.2	0.40	0.1
9	0.2	0.36	0.1
		NPV of lease	142.0

The NPV of buying the asset is £150 000 (presuming that payment would be made immediately).

Therefore the asset should be leased rather than purchased.

Note that this is purely a financing decision. The decision whether or not to acquire the asset at all has already been made. In making that decision the expected cash flows arising from the ownership and use of the asset were presumably discounted at a rate which reflected the risk inherent in these cash flows, perhaps the firm's weighted average cost of capital.

Note that tax has been ignored because the firm has 'substantial tax losses' which implies that tax relief on interest, lease payments and on the cost of the asset, were it to be bought, would not in effect be available.

2   Forward plc

(a) The market capitalisation after the announcement of the mineral deposit

Market capitalisation before the announcement (100p × 25 m)	£25m
NPV of deposits of minerals	8m
	£33m

(b) Shares to be issued to raise £4m (£4m divided by 80p)   5m shares

(c) The market capitalisation after the rights issue

Market capitalisation before the rights issue	£33m
Proceeds of the rights issue	4m
	£37m

(d) Likely trading price of the rights

Market capitalisation after the rights issue	£37m
Number of shares after the rights issue (25m + 5m)	30m
Ex-rights share price (£37m divided by 30m)	123.33p
Theoretical trading price of the rights (123.33p − 80p)	43.33p

(e) The reasons why rights issues are made at a discount on the current market price of the shares include:

- There is an inevitable delay between fixing the rights issue price and the actual rights issue. This period could see a fall in the shares' market price to one below the rights issue price. If the rights issue is not priced at a substantial discount, such a fall in price could cause the failure of the rights issue, an expensive matter.
- The discount puts pressure on shareholders either to take up the shares offered or to sell the rights to someone who will. This is because the discount means that shareholders will lose financially if they simply allow the rights to lapse. Again this should help to avoid an expensive failure of the issue.
- The discount does not represent a 'give away'. As was illustrated in Chapter 7 the rights issue price has no effect on the wealth of individual shareholders provided that they take up the shares offered to them.

(f) Evidence cited in Chapter 7 shows that a rights issue is much cheaper to make than is a similar sized issue to the public. This is because the legal requirements surrounding a rights issue to existing shareholders are much less stringent than those relating to an issue to the public.

CHAPTER 9

1 The statement implies that the person making it has superior knowledge than do those who by their actions, i.e. buying and selling, in the stock market influence share prices. Evidence on the efficiency of the capital market, cited in Chapter 9, suggests that this is only likely to be true if the person making the statement has 'inside' information. Otherwise the evidence shows that the market knows best on average.

2 CME does not imply that all investors know all that there is to know about all securities traded in the market. It does not even imply that any individual investor knows all that there is to know about any particular security. CME simply implies that the current market price of a security at any given moment reflects a consensus view of the security and therefore reflects all information which is known by investors.

CHAPTER 10

1 **Milnthorpe Engineering plc**

(a)

	£
Annual Pre-tax profit	3 840 000
Less: Corporation Tax @ 50%	1 920 000
	1 920 000
Less: Preference dividend 5% x £6m	300 000
Available to ordinary shareholders	£1 620 000

Cost of preference shares (K_p)

$$= \frac{\text{dividend}}{\text{market value } (V_p)} = \frac{300\,000}{6m \times 0.80} = 6.25\%$$

Cost of ordinary shares (K_e)

$$\frac{\text{Profit available to ordinary shareholders}}{\text{market value } (V_e)} = \frac{1\,620\,000}{3\text{m} \times 2 \times \pounds 2} = 13.5\%$$

$$\text{WACC} = \left(K_p \times \frac{V_p}{V_p + V_e} \right) + \left(K_e \times \frac{V_e}{V_p + V_e} \right)$$

$$= \left(0.0625 \times \frac{4.8\text{m}}{4.8\text{m} + 12\text{m}} \right) + \left(0.135 \times \frac{12\text{m}}{4.8\text{m} + 12\text{m}} \right)$$

$$= 0.018 + 0.096 = 11.4\%$$

(b)

	£
New pre-tax annual profit	= 4 080 000
(£3 840 000 + £240 000)	
Less: Debenture interest	=　120 000
	3 960 000
Less: Corporation tax @ 50%	= 1 980 000
	1 980 000
Less: Preference dividend	300 000
Available to ordinary shareholders	£1 680 000

Assuming that investors expect the same returns from ordinary shares this would value at :

$$\frac{\pounds 1\,680\,000}{0.135} = \pounds 12\,444\,444 \text{ or } \frac{\pounds 12\,444\,444}{6\text{m}} = \pounds 2.07 \text{ per share}$$

$$\text{WACC} = \left(0.135 \times \frac{12.44}{12.44 + 4.80 + 1.00} \right) +$$

$$\left(0.0625 \times \frac{4.80}{12.44 + 4.80 + 1.00} \right) +$$

$$\left(0.12 \times \frac{1.00}{12.44 + 4.80 + 1.00} \right)$$

$$= 0.092 + 0.016 + 0.007$$

$$= 0.115 \text{ or } 11.5\%$$

This solution presumes that the additional risk to ordinary shareholders engendered by the introduction of loan finance will not affect returns required by them.

It would be surprising in practice to find debentures generating greater expected returns than preference shares.

2 **(a)** The terms can be defined as follows:

D_1 = the dividend which will be paid in one year's time
P_0 = the current price of an equity share
g = the annual growth rate of the dividend
k_e = the cost of equity (i.e. the annual rate which if multiplied by 100 would give a percentage return)

Example
The current price of an ordinary share of XYZ plc is £2.00. Next year's dividend is expected to be 12p per share. The rate of growth of dividends is expected to be 10 per cent per annum for ever.

The cost of equity, according to Gordon's growth model is:

$$k_e = (£0.12/£2.00) + 0.1 = 0.16 \text{ or } 16\%$$

(b) The formula suggests that the cost of equity is the dividend return on the market price plus a loading for the fact that dividends are expected to grow. The formula can be used to deduce the cost of equity which can then be used in making financing and investment decisions. For example, in an all-equity financed firm it can be used as the discount rate to be applied to project cash flows to deduce the NPV of some project. In a geared firm it can be used to deduce a weighted average cost of capital used in an NPV analysis.

(c) The model is very simple to use once the variables have been identified. However, making a judgement on the perpetual rate of growth of dividends can be very difficult and the reliability of the resultant figure is open to serious doubt. No account is taken of risk. Thus applying the output of the model to the projected cash flows to deduce an NPV would ignore the riskiness of the particular project concerned.

(d) Two possible methods are:

- Historical return, both dividends and capital growth, based on actual data relating to the particular equity over a past period.
- Using the capital asset pricing model (CAPM) whose logic and use are discussed in Chapter 7.

3   **Spirax Holdings plc**

(a) Calculation of the weighted average cost of capital (assuming the use of the Gordon growth model)

Cost of equity = $[(0.12 \times 1.03)/1.20] + 0.03 = 0.0133$, i.e. 13.3%
Cost of debt = 8% less corporation tax at 35%, i.e. 5.2%
Weighted average cost of capital = $[(105/150) \times 13.3] + [(45/150) \times 5.2]$
$$= \underline{\underline{10.87\%}}$$

(b) Directors' comments:

- The borrowing rate is not the correct rate to use. The bank loan would almost certainly be secured on the company's assets and thus represents a very low risk loan. The rate charged by the bank reflects this fact. It would be illogical for the company to use this rate to assess its own investment since it is not necessarily a low risk investment. The illogicality of using the borrowing rate to discount the cash flow is emphasised in that what may appear to be a viable investment when the funds are being borrowed might not be viable if it were to be financed by equity. It would be the same investment project in either case and should, therefore, be assessed similarly in either case.

- The weighted average cost of capital is more logical than the cost of debt as the discount factor. However, it fails to take any account of the riskiness of the particular investment being assessed.
- The planning director's suggestion that the discount rate should take account of the riskiness of the proposed investment is valid and therefore his suggestion is probably the best one made. However, the risk assessment suggested is very informal. It might be better to assess the risk more formally through CAPM.

(c) Computation of the NPV using the planning director's suggestion (6 per cent discount rate)

	Year 0 £m	Year 1–50 £m	Year 50 £m
Cost	(4.5)	–	–
Net rentals	–	0.4	–
Residual value	–	–	1.0
Discount (annuity) factor	1.0	15.8	0.05
Present value	(4.5)	6.32	0.05
Net present value	1.87		

(d) The effect of inflation on the project.

If the rate of inflation of 10 per cent were to have the same effect on all of the factors in the analysis, including the discount rate, the same conclusion would be reached.

One of the problems with inflation in the present context is that it tends to have different effects on different factors e.g. the cost of capital may increase by 10 per cent per annum whilst the rental income only increases by 5 per cent per annum. In these circumstances the project would be less favourable, possibly not viable.

4. **Univo plc**

(a) Recent dividend growth rate

19X0	$(2557 - 2335)/2335 = 0.095$
19X1	$(2800 - 2557)/2557 = 0.095$

i.e. a steady 9.5% growth rate.

$$\text{Univo plc's asset } \beta = \text{equity } \beta \times \frac{S_G}{S_G + L_G(1-t)} + \text{ loan-stock } \beta \times \frac{L_G(1-t)}{S_G + L_G(1-t)}$$

Where S_G and L_G are the values of the firm's equity and loan stock, respectively and t is the Corporation tax rate.

$S_G = (£2.17 - 0.07) \times 40\text{m} = £84\text{m}.$

$L_G = £89.5 \times 15\text{m}/100 = £13.425\text{m}.$

Thus $0.763 =$ equity $\beta \times 84/[84 + 13.425(1 - 0.35)] + [0.2 \times 13.425(1 - 0.35)]$
$/[84 + 13.4259(1 - 0.35)]$

$0.763 = ($equity $\beta \times 0.906) + 0.019$

equity $\beta = (0.763 - 0.019)/0.906 = 0.82$

cost of equity $\quad = 12(1 - 0.35) + [17 - 12(1 - 0.35)] \times 0.82$

$\quad\quad\quad\quad = 7.8 + 7.5 = 15.3\%$

Current dividend per share $= 2800/(20\ 000 \times 2) = £0.07$

Value of a share in two years' time $= \dfrac{£0.07\ (1.25)^2 \times 1.095}{0.153 - 0.095} = £2.06$

i.e. 19X1 dividend plus two years' growth at 25% and one year's growth at 9.5%, divided by the equity rate of return less the growth rate.

Current value $= \dfrac{0.07\ (1.25)}{1 + 0.153} + \dfrac{0.07\ (1.25)^2}{(1 + 0.153)^2} + \dfrac{£2.06}{(1 + 0.153)^2}$

$\quad\quad\quad\quad = 0.08 + 0.08 + 1.55 = £1.71$ (ex-div) or £1.78 (cum-div).

(b) Value of the company's shares assuming a risk free rate of 10%, but that all other data are as used on part (a) (i). In fact a lower interest rate would affect the market price of the company's debentures.

cost of equity $\quad = 10(1 - 0.35) + [17 - 10(1 - 0.35)] \times 0.82$

$\quad\quad\quad\quad = 6.5 + 8.6 = 15.1\%$

Current dividend per share $= £0.07$

Value of a share in two years' time $= \dfrac{£0.07\ (1.25)^2 \times 1.095}{0.151 - 0.095} = £2.14$

i.e. 19X1 dividend plus two years' growth at 25% and one year's growth at 9.5%, divided by the equity rate of return less the growth rate.

Current value $= \dfrac{0.07\ (1.25)}{1 + 0.151} + \dfrac{0.07\ (1.25)^2}{(1 + 0.151)^2} + \dfrac{£2.14}{(1 + 0.151)^2}$

$\quad\quad\quad\quad = 0.08 + 0.08 + 1.62 = £1.78$ (ex-div) or £1.85 (cum-div).

CHAPTER 11   **1**   **Ashcroft plc**

(a) Earning per share

	Debt option	*Equity option*
	£m	*£m*
Profit before tax and debenture interest	1.80	1.80
Less: debenture interest	0.30	–
	1.50	1.80
Less: Corporation Tax @ 50%	0.75	0.90
	0.75	0.90
Earnings per share (after tax): (0.75m ÷ 4m) =	18.75p	
(0.90 ÷ 5.3) =		16.98p

(b) Let p = profit before debenture interest and tax where earnings per share are equal under each option.

$$\text{Then } \frac{(p - 0.30) \times 50/100}{4} = \frac{p \times 50/100}{5.3} \qquad p = £1.2\text{m}$$

(c) In deciding on which option to accept, the directors would need to try to identify an optimal level of gearing as their target ratio. In deciding this, the following points would need to be taken account of:

1. volatility of the firm's operating cash flows
2. rate and certainty of tax relief on loan interest payments
3. 'Bankruptcy costs', i.e. the reduction in the shareholders' wealth which would result from the firm being forced into liquidation
4. the attitude of the directors towards risk
5. current and expected future levels of interest rates
6. servicing costs of equities.

For a family controlled firm like Ashcroft, any loss of control which an equity issue would engender must also be carefully considered.

2   **Aspley Engineers plc**

(a) A term loan is one where the loan is repayable on some specified contracted date, or dates if it is repayable by instalments. The contract may contain clauses which seek to protect the lender by imposing specified conditions on the loan and/or obligations on the borrower. Such conditions are known as covenants.

Normally a breach of one of the covenants would have the effect of altering the loan's date of repayment to become more or less immediate following the breach.

Examples of covenants which are found in practice include:

- A requirement for a borrower firm to maintain a minimum current ratio (i.e. current assets/current liabilities).
- A requirement that the ratio of interest on the loan to profit (interest-covered ratio) is maintained at some minimum level.

(b)

		Debt	Equity option
(i) *Interest cover* (profit before interest and tax/loan interest)			
$100/(30 + (80 \times 12\%)) =$		2.53	
$100/30 =$			3.33
(ii) *Earnings per share* (profit after interest and tax/number of shares)			
$(100 - 39.6) \times (1 - 0.35)/100 =$		39.3 pence	
$(100 - 30) \times (1 - 0.35)/(100 + 20) =$			37.9 pence
(iii) *Debt equity ratio* (total long-term borrowings (share capital + reserves))			
$(260 + 80)/(360 + 19.3$ (i.e. 19X9 retained profit)) $=$		0.90:1	
$260/(360 + 80 + 21.5$ (i.e. 19X9 retained profit)) $=$			0.56:1

(c) The two issues are probably risk and taxation.

Taking on additional loan finance increases the shareholders' risk that the burdens of loan finance will force the company into 'bankruptcy'. Though this may not be seen as a very large risk, it will still be a greater one if loan finance is increased. The fact the interest cover is expected to be 2.53 while the covenant specifies a minimum of 2.00 does seem to make the company look vulnerable to the loan being called in should profit expectations not be met. Similarly the debt/equity ratio of 0.90:1 does not leave too much of a margin of safety relative to the covenant figure of 1:1. Unprofitable trading would reduce reserves, weakening this ratio.

Loan interest is tax deductible which makes it cheaper to have loan finance than to have additional share capital.

3 (a)

			£m
(i) Total issue value			
For investment in new contract			1.000
To redeem debentures			
$16\% \times £10m \times 6.247$ (i.e. 9 years annuity factor @ 8%)		9.995	
10×0.500		5.000	14.995
Total required			15.995

i.e. £16 million

A one-for-three rights issue involves 4 million shares. Therefore the issue price will need to be £4 per share.

(ii) Since the new contract and the value of the debentures are known to the capital market, the uses to which the cash is to be put will not have an effect on the value of the equity, beyond the value of the cash.

Before the issue, the equity is worth 12 million × £5 = £60 million.

After the issue the equity will be worth £60 million + £16 million = £76 million.

Value per share (theoretical ex-rights' price) = £76 million/16 million = £4.75 per share.

(iii) The value of the right to buy a share worth £4.75 for £4.00 is £0.75. Each old share has one-third of this value attaching to it (one-for-three issue), i.e. £0.25.

(b) Theoretically the size of the discount is irrelevant. Any size of discount should leave each shareholder as wealthy after the issue as before the issue. Only shareholders who allow the rights to lapse will be economically disadvantaged by the discount.

(c) The rights issue will substantially reduce the level of gearing. This should reduce the return required by equity holders since it will reduce the risk. According to Modigliani and Miller, the reduction in the cost of equity will exactly be balanced by the reduction in the amount of 'cheap' loan finance, to leave the weighted average cost of capital equal to that which applies before the rights issue.

(d) (i) The present value of the bank loan is the same as the debentures, i.e. £14.995m. If this can be redeemed at a cost of £10m the value of the firm will increase by £4.995m, say £5m. This cash saving can be invested in a project with an NPV of £1m, increasing the value of the firm by a total of £6m.

Before the issue and the announcements, the equity is worth 12 million x £5 = £60 million.

After the announcement the equity will be worth £60 million + £6 million = £66 million.

Value per share (cum-rights) = £66 million/12 million = £5.50.

(ii) After the issue the equity will be worth £60 million + £6 million + 16 million = £82 million.

Value per share (theoretical ex-rights' price) = £82 million/16 million = £5.125 per share.

The fact that the market reacts rationally to public information implies that it is semi-strong efficient. The fact that it does not react to unpublished information implies strong form efficiency.

CHAPTER 12 **1** **Feret Ltd**

(a) Since the current share price is £0.90 on the basis of expected dividends of £0.10 p.a. the implied return required by shareholders is:

$$\frac{0.10}{0.90} = 11\%$$

Presuming that they continue to expect this rate of return, the value per share, after the announcement of reduced dividends and of the new contract would be:

$$S = \frac{0.05}{(1+0.11)} + \frac{0.05}{(1+0.11)^2} + \left(\frac{0.135}{0.11} \times \frac{1}{(1+0.11)^2}\right)$$

$$= 0.045 + 0.041 + 0.996$$

$$= £1.082$$

Thus there will be an increase in the share price of £0.18.

Note In two years' time, the value of a share expected to produce dividends of £0.135 p.a. when the required return is 11 per cent p.a. is 0.135/0.11; its present value is that amount discounted.

(b) The annual dividends from the shareholdings have been $100 \times £0.10 = £10$. Say the shareholder wished slightly to increase his spending over the next two years. Since the dividends will drop to £5, he could in fact sell five shares in each of the next two years.

Value per share after one year will be:

$$\frac{0.05}{1+0.11} + \left(\frac{0.135}{0.11} \times \frac{1}{1+0.11} \right)$$

$$= 0.045 + 1.106 = £1.151$$

Value per share after two years will be:

$$\frac{0.135}{0.11} = £1.227$$

Thus selling five shares at the end of each of the next two years will give the investor, with dividends, the following spending potential:

Year 1
$(5 \times £1.151) + (100 \times £0.05) = £10.76$
Year 2
$(5 \times £1.227) + (95 \times £0.05) = £10.89$

This will leave him with 90 shares which from year 3 onward will produce:

$90 \times £0.135 = £12.15$ p.a.

Thus it will be possible for the investor to increase his spending potential from the present £10 p.a. for the foreseeable future.

2 (a) The factors which might influence the dividend decision include the following:

- Legal restriction that only realised profits may be paid.
- The company's liquidity position may make it commercially imprudent to pay a dividend.
- Signals are believed to be given by the level of dividend paid by a company. It seems to be believed that high and increasing dividends indicate the faith of the directors in the company's future. Thus a high level of dividends may have a favourable effect on the share price.
- Shareholders may hold the shares because of the level of dividends paid by the company. Thus the company may choose to keep dividend levels fairly static. The shareholders may have a particular preference for high or low dividends in accordance with their personal tax position. This is because there is an element of differential tax treatment of dividends as against capital gains.

(b) Miller and Modigliani argued that shareholders should be indifferent to the level of dividends paid since what they fail to receive in the form of current dividends they will have in enhanced share values. The MM analysis is based on a number of assumptions which may not be valid in reality. The analysis also fails to take account of the possible signalling factor, i.e. the level of dividends can be seen as some statement of the company's management's confidence in the future.

3 (a) With a purchase by the company of its own shares from some of its shareholders, the company simply buys shares in the capital market. Having bought them the company cancels the shares, thus reducing the total number of shares. The fact that the company might be inclined to consider such an action implies that there are funds for which the directors cannot find a profitable purpose. In these circumstances, a reduction in the number of shares might mean that the remaining equity finance will be used more efficiently in the future. Thus the fall in earnings is likely to be less than proportionate to the fall in the amount of book equity. This could lead to the remaining shares having a higher unit value after the share purchase. It seems unlikely that the shareholders, who decide to accept the purchase offer, will be advantaged since they always have the option of selling their shares through the capital market. It is only where the shares are not traded in an established market that the company will be able to offer shareholders, who are keen to sell their shares, a facility otherwise not open to them.

(b) The factors which will affect the level of dividends would normally include the following:
- The availability of legally distributable reserves.
- The availability of investment opportunities for the company and the need for investment finance.
- The company's liquidity position.
- Any covenants attaching to borrowings by the company which restrict the size of dividends.
- The tax position of the company. Can it set advanced corporation tax payments against a mainstream liability?
- The 'clientele effect'. Shareholders may have acquired their shares because of the dividend levels. The decision to acquire may have been caused by the tax position of the shareholders. It may have related to their needs for a cash income.
- The informational content of dividends. Will a particular level of dividend send signals to the market, which could affect the wealth of the shareholders.
- The volatility of earnings. Companies seem generally to avoid increasing dividends in years of high earnings if the directors feel that the higher dividend level cannot be sustained in future.

CHAPTER 13   **1**   **Arcadia Ltd**

Cash budget for six months to June

		January £	February £	March £	April £	May £	June £
Receipts from							
debtors		2 800	3 200	3 200	4 000	4 800	5 200
Receipts from cash							
sales		4 800	6 000	7 200	7 800	8 400	9 600
	(A)	7 600	9 200	10 400	11 800	13 200	14 800
Outflows							
Payments to							
creditors		4 000	4 800	4 800	5 600	6 000	6 000
Wages etc.		3 000	3 600	3 600	4 200	4 500	4 500
Advertising		1 000	–	–	1 500	–	–
Salaries etc. 80%		1 280	1 280	1 280	1 280	1 600	1 600
20%		280	320	320	320	320	400
Fixed assets							
acquired		–	–	2 000	2 000	2 000	–
Dividend		–	–	–	600	–	–
	(B)	9 560	10 000	12 000	15 500	14 420	12 500
Surplus/deficit for							
the month (A–B)		(1 960)	(800)	(1 600)	(3 700)	(1 220)	2 300
(Cumulative							
surplus/deficit)		5 540	4 740	3 140	(560)	(1 780)	520

2   **Dixon plc**

(a)

$$E = \sqrt{\frac{2AC}{H}}$$

Where E is the economic order quality
        A is the annual usage
        C is the cost of placing each order
and H is the annual holding cost of one unit

$$\text{i.e. } E = \sqrt{\frac{2 \times 23\,000 \times £50}{£1.50}}$$

$$= \sqrt{1\,533\,333} = 1238.3 \text{ units}$$

so orders should be placed of 1238 or 1239 units, but since the round figure of 1250 is not too far away, orders of that size would probably be placed.

(b) During the one week lead time $1/52 \times 23\,000 = 442$ units would be used, so the order must be placed when the stock is no lower than 442 units if 'stock outs' are to be avoided.

3   **Williams Wholesalers Ltd**

(a) *Trade discount.* This is a discount given to customers who are themselves in business. The objective of such a discount is to encourage business from customers who are likely to be bulk purchasers and/or likely to place repeat orders.

Cash discounts. These are given to customers, trade or otherwise, if settlement is made within a pre-specified period. The objective is to encourage prompt payment. The levels at which discounts are offered tends to make them a fairly expensive way of improving liquidity.

(b) Calculation of the approximate equivalent cost of a 2 per cent discount. 2 per cent for 40 days saving is roughly equivalent to $(365/40) \times 2$ per cent over a year = 18.25 per cent. (Strictly the rate is a little higher than this.)

(c) Effect of the new credit terms

		£000
Average level of debtors under the existing debtor policy		
	$((70/365) \times £4m)$	767
Average level of debtors under the proposed debtor policy		
	$(50\% \times (80/365) \times £4m)$	438
	$(50\% \times (30/365) \times £4m)$	164
		602
Potential reduction in debtors level		165
Potential financial cost saving	$(13\% \times £165\,000)$	21.45
Bad debt cost saving		10.00
Administrative cost saving		6.00
		37.45
Potential cost of discounts $(50\% \times 2\% \times £4m)$		40.00

Thus there is a potential cost of £2550 per annum of operating the proposed new debtor policy.

4 **(a)** The important components of working capital are:

- Stocks (raw materials, work in progress and finished goods)
- Debtors
- Creditors, which represent a source of finance for stock and debtors.

(b) The main principle in the management of the three working capital elements is to minimise stocks and debtors and maximise trade creditors, subject to the need to retain commercial effectiveness and the goodwill of those whose goodwill the firm needs to retain.

More specifically, management routines should include the following:

Stocks

- Establish routines for the management of stock movements, including authorised staff to place orders, withdraw stock from stores etc.
- Establish routines for the physical management of stock, including stock rotation and care of stock which is susceptible to physical deterioration.
- Establish reporting systems for monitoring stock levels, including the use of accounting and other ratios.

● Establish, using such mathematical techniques as are useful in the circumstances, minimum stock re-order levels and economic order quantities.

Debtors

● Establish routines for deciding on who is to be allowed credit and credit limits.
● Establish a policy on giving discounts for prompt payment.
● Establish routines for the management of debtors, including rapid invoicing, frequent statements and reminders and for dealing with bad debts.
● Establish reporting systems for monitoring debtor levels, including the use of accounting ratios and age analyses.

Creditors

● Establish a policy for creditors including credit periods and the claiming of discounts for prompt payment.
● Establish routines for dealing quickly with invoices so as to be able to take advantage of discounts for prompt payment.
● Establish reporting systems for monitoring creditor levels, including the use of accounting ratios.

5   **Torrance Ltd**

(a) Option

	1	2	3
	£	£	£
Amount of debtors:			
(600 000 + 30 000) × (30 + 10)/365	69 041		
(600 000 + 45 000) × (30 + 20)/365		88 356	
(600 000 + 50 000) × (30 + 30)/365			106 849
Less: Current debtors (600 000 × 30/365)	49 315	49 315	49 315
Net increase in debtors	19 726	39 041	57 534
Contributions from increase in sales			
30 000 × 18/36	15 000		
45 000 × 18/36		22 500	
50 000 × 18/36			25 000
Less: Financing cost of increase in			
debtors @ 15%	2 959	5 856	8 630
Annual increase in profit	12 041	16 644	16 370

This suggests that the optimum increase in sales is £45 000. The difference between the additional profit at this level and at the higher level of sales is so slight, however, that it seems unlikely to be significant.

(b) The obvious advantage of trade credit is that it is normally cost free, up to moderate levels, at least. It is a very popular and important source of finance for most businesses.

Other advantages include:

- Administrative convenience, it is normally impractical to pay at the point of supply. This tends also to be true from the supplier's point of view as well.
- Spontaneity. It arises naturally in the normal course of trading, special requests are normally required. It tends to expand and contract as the need for finance arises.

Disadvantages include:
- Loss of discounts for prompt payment (cash discounts).
- Loss of supplier goodwill and, therefore, possible loss of supplies if credit terms are not adhered to.

(c) At present, the company pays 97.5% of its purchases after 10 days. If it were to abandon this approach it would pay 100% after either 30 or 45 days. The implicit interest costs of abandoning the present policy are as follows:

30 days' credit	$2.5/97.5 \times 365/(30-10) = 46.8\%$ p.a.*
45 days' credit	$2.5/97.5 \times 365/(45-10) = 26.7\%$ p.a.*

[* These calculations are not strictly correct as a comparison with interest payable once a year since the 'pay-off' from trade credit occurs at 10 day intervals. Strictly the calculation of the annualised rate is $(1 + 2.5/97.5)^{365/(n-10)}$, where n is the number of days' credit.

30 days' credit	$(1 + 2.5/97.5)^{365/(30-10)} = 58.7\%$ p.a.
45 days' credit	$(1 + 2.5/97.5)^{365/(45-10)} = 30.2\%$ p.a.]

This shows the enormous benefit which the company currently derives from trade credit. Since the company normally raises finance at a cost of 15% p.a., it might be advised to look elsewhere for solutions to its liquidity problem.

The fact that 45 days is longer than that which suppliers willingly allow, action might be taken against the company for taking so much credit, e.g. discontinuing supply.

6 (a) The annualised rate of interest is $(1 + 5/95)^{365/(n-30)}$, where n is the number of days' credit.

(i)	30 days' credit	$(1 + 5/95)^{365/(60-30)} = 86.6\%$ p.a.
(ii)	45 days' credit	$(1 + 5/95)^{365/(90-30)} = 36.6\%$ p.a.

These figures can be approximated in the same way as done in the answer to Question 5 (above).

Since the company can raise overdraft finance at 12%, a cash discount would be a very expensive approach, were no other aspects involved.

(b) Net cost of the new credit terms in the 'Main' division.

Contributions from additional sales
$(120 - 100\%) \times (100 - 80\%) \times £100\,000$ .... (4 000)
Discounts $60\% \times 120\% \times £100\,000 \times 5\%$ 3 600
Increase in bad debts $(2\% \times 120\,000) - (1\% \times 100\,000)$ 1 400
Saving in interest
Original debtors £100 000 × 90/365 24657
New debtors .... £120 000 × 60% × 30/365 .... 5 918
.... £120 000 × 20% × 60/365 .... 3 945
.... £120 000 × 20% × 90/365 .... 5 918 ...... 15 781
Reduction in debtors 8 876
@ 12% .... (1 065)
Net cost of the new policy .... (65)

i.e. a new benefit from adopting the new policy. The small size of the difference means that no clear signal emerges from the analysis.

(c) (i) Profit from the order if Green does not default

Contribution (£50 000 – 40 000) £10 000
Cost of 2 months' credit £50 000 × 60/365 × 12% ...... (986)
.... £9 014
× 0.6 .... 5 408
Profit if Green defaults .... (£40 000)
× 0.4 .... (16 000)
Expected cost of taking the single order £10 592

(ii) Profit from the orders if Green does not default

Contribution (£50 000 – 40 000 × 8) £80 000
Cost of 2 months' credit
.... £50 000 × 8 × 60/365 × 12% .... (7 890)
.... £72 110
× 0.9 .... 64 899
Profit if Green defaults .... (£320 000)
× 0.1 .... (32 000)
Expected benefit of taking the further orders £32 899
Discounting at 15% for one year = £32 899 × 0.870 .... £28 622
Net benefit if Green does not default on present order and, as a result, the further orders are accepted = £9 014 (from above) + (0.7 × £28 622) = 29 049.
× 0.6 .... 17 430
Cost if Green defaults on the initial order .... (£40 000)
× 0.4 .... (16 000)
Expected value of taking the initial order, with
.... the prospect of further orders £1 430

The analysis suggests that the initial order should be undertaken, but the relatively small size of the expected value means that the signal is not a very strong one, given the uncertainties involved.

The main deficiencies of the analysis include:

- The difficulty of deducing the probabilities.
- The size and stability of Jerome plc. A default on a large adverse contract could fatally damage a small or vulnerable company.
- Expected value are averages and, therefore, potentially misleading.

CHAPTER 14   **1**   **Global Communications plc/Wessex Newspapers plc**

(a) Value of the proposed bid

Number of GC shares to be issued(100m/4)	25m
Earnings per share of GC (£31m/(90 × 2))	17.22 p
Value of a GC share (17.22p × 20)	£3.44
Value of the bid (25m × £3.44)	£86m

(b) Post-takeover EPS of GC

	£m
Earnings of GC	31
Earnings of WN	7
Administration cost savings	2
Projected post-takeover earnings	£40m
Total GC shares in issue post-takeover (180 + 25)	205m
EPS (£40m/205m)	19.51 p

(c) The investigation which GC would be expected to have carried out before the takeover attempt would include:

- Examination of the financial results of WN over recent times.
- An assessment of the future trading prospects of WN in the future.
- An assessment of the quality of the staff of WN.
- A valuation of the shares of WN to GC.
- An assessment of potential synergistic benefits of the takeover, including consideration of the extent to which the two companies' activities and personnel would fit together.

(d) Defensive tactics which WN might use to resist the takeover include:

- Actions to increase the WN share price, including the release of new information and promises of increased dividends.
- Persuading the WN shareholders that the bid price is too low in the light of the company's prospects.
- Making WN less attractive to GC by such means as giving senior staff new contracts which guarantee large compensation payments in the event of the takeover.

2   **Alpha plc/Beta plc**

(a) Bid consideration

Number of GC shares to be issued (125 000 × 4 × (17/20))	425 000
Bid consideration (425 000 × £200p)	£850 000

(b) Post-takeover EPS of Alpha

	£000
Projected earnings of Alpha	100
Projected earnings of Beta	65
Distribution cost savings	15
Projected post-takeover earnings	180
Total GC shares in issue post-takeover	
(1 000 000 + 425 000)	1 425 000
EPS (180 000/1 425 000)	12.63p

(c) Theoretical post-acquisition price

12.63×20 £2.53

(d) There is clearly an argument against using the pre-acquisition PE of Alpha to value the post-acquisition shares. This is that a substantial part of the new Alpha is the business of the less fast expanding Beta. It could be argued therefore that a weighted average PE of the two companies would be more appropriate. On the other hand investors (who determine share prices) may feel that with Beta's business now in the hands of the Alpha management a higher rating for that part of the business is justified.

(e) The point about the dividends is true. On the other hand, on the basis of recent history, the capital appreciation prospects have greatly improved for former Beta shareholders.

The balance sheet is not a list of current market values of the assets, nor is it intended to be. The market value of the assets shown on the balance sheet may well be greater than the value at which they are recorded. Also the balance sheet typically omits the asset of goodwill which could have a value in the case of Beta.

CHAPTER 15   1   **Small chemical company**

(a)   (*i*)   Gross dividend yield

$$= \frac{\text{dividend per share (gross)}}{\text{price per share}}$$

Price per share

$$= \frac{\text{dividend per share (gross)}}{\text{gross dividend yield}}$$

$$= \frac{(0.7\text{m} \div 4\text{m}) \times 10/7}{0.07}$$

$$= \underline{£3.57}$$

(*ii*) Price/earnings ratio

$$= \frac{\text{Price per share}}{\text{earnings per share}}$$

Price per share $= PE \times EPS$

$$= 8 \times (1.2m \div 4m)$$

$$= \underline{\underline{£2.40}}$$

(*iii*) Net assets (per balance sheet)　　= £6.4m

$$\text{Therefore, price per share} \quad = \frac{£6.4m}{4m}$$

$$= \underline{\underline{£1.60}}$$

(b) The first two of the methods seeks to relate the dividends or earnings of the company whose shares are to be valued to those of a similar quoted company. The third method assumes that balance sheet values represent something like the economic worth of the firm's assets.

Each approach has its flaws including the following:

Dividend yield
1　difficulty of finding a comparable firm
2　doubt on the relevance of dividend pattern to value
3　dividends paid do not necessarily relate to earnings

Price/earnings
1　difficulty of finding a comparable firm
2　differences in accounting practices and year end dates
3　earnings do not necessarily reflect cash generating potential and it is the latter which is more likely to bear on value than the former

Net assets
1　book values are unlikely to relate too closely to economic values of assets
2　even when book value and market value of individual assets are reasonably close, this would only be a relevant basis for the valuation of a share where liquidation of the firm is envisaged.

2　　　　　　　　　　　　　**Woodhall Engineers plc**

(a)　Calculation of the net asset value per share.

	£m
Net asset value of the total equity at 31 December 19X4	20
Goodwill	8
Undisclosed land value (£10m – 4m)	6
	34

Divided by the number of shares (4 × 16)　　　　= 53.125p per share

(b)　*(i)*　Calculation of the value per share on a PE basis.
19X4 Earnings per share (£1m divided by 64m)　　= 1.5625p per share
Multiplied by 8 (comparative PE) = value per share　　= 12.5p per share

(ii) Calculation of the value per share on a discounted cash flow basis.

Year	Cash flow	Discount factor	Present value
	£m		*£m*
19X5	(6.0)	0.89	(5.34)
19X6	9.6	0.80	7.68
19X7	9.6	0.71	6.82
19X8	9.6	0.64	6.14
19X9	9.6	0.57	5.47
19X0	13.6	0.51	6.94
			£27.71m

Divided by 64m = 43.40p per share

(c) Points relevant to the valuations include:

Net assets valuation

- The balance sheet is not intended to be a basis for valuation of the company because balance sheet values of individual assets are not market values.
- The sum of the values of the business component parts may not be the same as the value of the business as a going concern.

PE valuation

- There are difficulties in finding a quoted company sufficiently similar to the company whose shares are to be valued.
- It is necessary to take account of the fact that typically the shares of an unquoted company would be valued at a lower figure than the equivalent quoted one because of the lack of liquidity of the shares.
- Basing a shares valuation on the company's historic earnings is illogical when the value is really based on its future profitability.

Discounted cash flow basis

- This is probably the most logical basis of valuation in that it relates to future financial benefits.
- There are difficulties in predicting future cash flows.
- There are difficulties in deciding on a suitable discount rate to apply to the predicted cash flows.

INDEX